THIS COPY OF

THE MG STORY

IS SIGNED BY THE AUTHOR

MALCOLM GREEN

THE MG STORY

THE MG STORY
1923-1980

BY MALCOLM GREEN

Herridge & Sons

ACKNOWLEDGEMENTS

This book could not have been written or illustrated without help from a great many people. All the owners of the MGs I have photographed over the last thirty years have very generously given up their time whilst this amateur photographer tried to take pictures that would do justice to their superb cars. I have also gained enormously from details about their vehicles that they have been kind enough to impart. I have also benefited from knowledge gained from those who are involved professionally in MG restoration or parts supply and it is certainly true that without their enthusiasm and skill we would not see in running order many of the cars featured here. I would particularly like to mention the following, many sadly no longer with us. If due to memory fade I have missed out anyone, I can only apologise.

Colin Alderman, Mike Allison, Peter and Suzanne Arnell, Margaret and Richard Ashby, Christopher Balfour, Sheila and Colin Ballard, Christopher Banton, John Bates, Philip and Rosemary Bayne-Powell, Michael Bean, Jerry Birkbeck, Chris Blood, Fred Body, Bob Borchardt, Cliff Bray, Gerry Brown, Pam and John Butler, Paul Campfield, Michael and Andrea Card, Roger Chamberlain, Quentin Chases, Bob Clare, John Clark, Chris Collingham, Dave Cooksey, Jimmy Cox, Martin Curren, David Davies, Dr. John Davies, Bill Day, Les Deykin, Bryan Ditchman, Jim Edwards, Phil Edwards, Tim Edwards, Geoff Enoch, Richard Finch, Barry Foster, Ron Gammons, Patrick Gardner, Steven Gardner, Paul Garett, Albert Giddings, Jon Goddard, Peter Green, Bill Grudgings, Ted Hack, Keith Hall, Duncan Hallows, Peter Hemmings, Keith Herkes, Keith Hodder, Alan Hogg, Nicky and Terry Holden, David Hutchison, Dave Jarvis, Phil Jenkins, Adrian Jones, Rodney Kettel, Angie and Andy King, Rev. Richard Knudson, Richard Ladds, Stephen Law, Gary Lowsley, Geoff Mansfield, Ken McGowan, Richard Monk, Dixon Morris, Al Moss, Peter Neal, Malcolm Newman, Hiro Nishio, Rob Overington, Gerald Palmer, Chris Pamplin, Phil Parmenter, Laura Peaple, Stuart Penfound, Peter Pimm, Derek Porter, Peter Prosser, Geoff Radford, John Reid, Oliver Richardson, Alastair Ross, Christopher Rowe, John Rowe, Ray Shrubb, Barry Sidery-Smith, Clint Smith, Doug Smith, Malcolm Sockett, Gavin Steill, Jeremy Targett, John Taylor, Tony Taylor, Cyril Tebb, Roger Thomas, Peter Thornley, Jonathan Toulmin, Barry Walker, Dave Washbourne, David West, John Weston-Smith, Brian Wigg, Stephen Williams, Jack Wilms and Steve Wilson,

Last, but certainly not least, I must thank my wife, Andrea as without her help and encouragement, plus her skilled researching through the finer details of automotive history, it is unlikely that this or any of my previous books would have seen the light of day.

Malcolm Green
Shropshire 2020

Published in 2020 by Herridge & Sons Ltd
Lower Forda, Shebbear, Beaworthy, Devon EX21 5SY

Designed by Ray Leaning, MUSE Fine Art & Design

ISBN 978-1-906133-97-9
Printed in China

CONTENTS

WHICH WAS THE FIRST MG?

Some regard the six Cowley chassis fitted by Morris Garages with two-seater bodywork by Raworth as the first MGs, others disagree as the modifications were solely cosmetic and did nothing to improve performance.

A debate amongst enthusiasts unlikely ever to be fully resolved is that of the first car to qualify as an MG. One candidate for the honour is said to be the Morris Garages four-seater sports model built for Jack Gardiner on a 14/28hp Morris Oxford chassis. This car was first registered on 13 March 1924 and, despite his ordering it as a 21st birthday present, Jack was a salesman at Morris Garages. The question arises, however, is this car the first MG?

Morris Garages were agents for a number of different marques, not just Morris. Advertisements they ran in the early 1920s, whilst listing all the Morris, Humber, Dodge and Sunbeam models on offer, also say that they could supply any make of car. The Morris Garages special bodies they sold could likewise be fitted to any suitable chassis, not just those from Morris, and pictures exist to prove that this did occur. With the benefit of hindsight, we see that when Cecil Kimber started offering his customers special bodywork for their Morris cars he had sown the seeds of what was to become the MG marque. However, as a large dealership, there was nothing unusual about Morris Garages offering to supply cars fitted with bespoke coachwork; this was the accepted custom in the case of most vehicles sold by the manufacturers in chassis form. What was more unusual was the Morris Garages practice of making chassis alterations to improve road-holding and performance. It was from this aspect of their work that the MG marque really developed.

So, going back to Jack Gardiner's car, was that really the first MG? Kimber himself seems to have been somewhat ambivalent about the early cars and in fact later wrote a note in a book he gave to Wilfred Mathews to the effect that when he went with him on the 1925 Land's End Trial in the car we now call Old Number One he was his first passenger in his first MG. If we take that at face value then the first MG was built in 1925, not 1924. Old Number One can certainly lay claim to the title of being the first MG built specifically for competition, but perhaps not the first car sold as an MG.

The use of the MG octagon can be traced back to the December 5 1923 issue of the Oxford magazine *The Isis*. This contained a Morris Garages advertisement for The MG Super Sports Morris that gave customers "Real Speed, Real Comfort, Distinguished Appearance, Beautiful Proportions, Superlative Coachwork, 11.9hp, all at a cost of £350". What was on offer was the Morris Cowley chassis fitted with two-seater coachwork made by the local Oxford firm of Charles Raworth and Sons. Kimber had ordered a batch of six bodies and was trying to sell the cars he had devised as an improvement on the standard Morris Cowley, which sold for just £195. At the higher price he was asking for his six cars it took a while to shift them.

In their excellent book on the early MGs, *Oxford to Abingdon*, Phil Jennings and the late Robin Barraclough discuss what they feel is the first MG. Of the Raworth-bodied cars their research revealed that the first to be built was the one sold to Oliver Arkell and registered on 16 August 1923. However, they say that, despite being advertised alongside the MG octagon, those cars did not have the vital ingredients that made MGs stand apart from the

MF 8068 is considered by some experts to be the first MG. This picture was taken early in 1924, before it was used on the London to Edinburgh trial by Russell Chiesman.

Morris Garages salesman Jack Gardiner at the wheel of an early MG 14/28. This picture was taken on 26 June 1924 and, unlike the car he previously had ordered for himself as a 21st birthday present, was built with raked steering and other features to be come associated with the MG models.

standard product – better performance and road-holding. Of the Jack Gardiner car they raise the same point. It is apparent from photographs that his car did not have the raked steering column and other small chassis changes given to the later cars. His was really just a standard Morris with a different body. Their candidate as the first real MG is the car sold on 31 May 1924 to Billy Cooper and driven by Russell Chiesman in the London to Edinburgh Trial in June that year. MF 8068 had the modified steering box and the other features that made those early MGs so attractive and desirable.

There is actually another contender for the title, a car built some years later. Before a move to the purpose-built factory in Edmund Road, all the early MGs were really just Morris chassis assembled at the Cowley factory, modified by Morris Garages and then fitted with bodies by a coachbuilder, usually Carbodies of Coventry. These carried Morris chassis plates and registration records reveal that they were usually described at the time they were first licensed as Morris-Oxford 13.9hp Sports, not as MGs. Once MG had moved to the new factory the cars all carried Morris Garages chassis identification and guarantee plates. For the first time MG was seen as a marque in its own right and were thus able to have a stand at the 1927 Motor Show. The first car to carry the Morris Garages chassis plate was a 14/40 model, chassis number 2251 built 24 December 1927. Might that be a better candidate as the first true MG?

WILLIAM MORRIS, LORD NUFFIELD

William Richard Morris was born on 10 October 1877 in Worcester, although his family originally came from Oxfordshire and they returned to Oxford when he was three years old. His father had gone to Canada to seek his fortune, but returned home to marry a Headington farmer's daughter, Emily Ann Pether. Coming himself from farming stock, he first became a bailiff on his father-in-law's farm before frequent asthma attacks forced him to take indoor employment to support a growing family. Once his son William Morris became established in business he took an active part as shop manager and book-keeper.

As a boy, William liked using his hands and exhibited an aptitude for things mechanical. He had his first bicycle when he was 14, having taught himself to ride a borrowed penny-farthing. His savings purchased a safety cycle with solid tyres and this he constantly dismantled and re-assembled. This expertise was to stand him in good stead when he was forced, by his father's illness, to give up his ambition to study medicine in favour of employment in a local cycle repair shop. This job was to last but a short while. With a capital of just £4, ambition led him to start his own business trading as a bicycle repairer. He used a building behind his father's house, with the front room converted to use as shop premises and as a showroom. He gained a good reputation locally and built up a strong client base amongst the local cycling fraternity at a time when there was an ever-growing market for the machines. His reputation must have been enhanced by his success as a racing cyclist. By 1900 he was the holder of seven local championships and he applied himself to his training and racing with a dedication he also displayed in his business life.

Early portrait of William Morris.

It was not long before the energetic Morris started to produce his own bicycles, spurred on by an order for a special machine from a local rector, Mr Pilcher. As his reputation grew, he built bicycles to order and also acted as agent for other company's products. Having outgrown his parent's house, he rented shop premises at 48 High Street, Oxford, a much more convenient position to serve the customers in the town. He also took a workshop and storage area just around the corner at 1 Queen Street.

By 1902 William Morris had made his first moves towards motorised transport by constructing a motorcycle using an engine he had built himself from castings he purchased. This machine was successful and, drawing upon the experience he had gained building and developing it, Morris decided to go into partnership with a friend, Joseph Cooper, to assemble motorcycles for sale. Additional premises were acquired in Holywell Street and machines built up around 2.75hp de Dion engines were on offer. The venture was successful, although the partnership was short-lived because of a difference of opinion between the two men. The Holywell Street/Longwall premises were also useful for storing customers' cars and by 1903 he was offering "a repair service for motors".

Another partnership followed, trading as The

Oxford Automobile and Cycle Agency, this time together with W. Lancelot Creyke, a wealthy ex-undergraduate and an Oxford businessman. Unfortunately this venture was something of a disaster and after just over one year of trading the business was wound up. Morris had debts of £50 and little else to show for all his efforts. Lack of experience had led the two other partners to spend more on promotion than had been justified by sales, and this was a lesson that Morris was to remember in later years. He was determined to avoid partnerships in future. Back in business on his own account, Morris concentrated on servicing, repairing and selling various makes of cars, as well as operating a car hire and taxi business.

In 1910, increasing amounts of work necessitated the rebuilding of the Longwall premises. The business was now formally called The Morris Garage, a title later changed to The Morris Garages as additional premises were acquired. By 1912 he was ready to try his hand at producing his own motorcar and an announcement was made at the 1912 London Motor Show that the first Morris motorcar was to be produced the following year. Impressed by the detailed specification provided, Stewart & Arden placed an order for 400 cars and were later appointed main dealers for London. Morris was spurred in his efforts by the success achieved by imported American Model A Fords as he felt that Britain should have its own volume car production. Designed by Morris, the Morris Oxford had features that his considerable experience servicing customers' cars had taught him were practical. Although not the cheapest car on

In the days before there was a network of filling stations, petrol was sold in cans like the one being used here in the 1920s to fill the tank of a Bullnose Morris.

A Bullnose Morris two-seater drophead coupé.

Morris with the Abingdon staff during the celebration to mark the opening of the factory.

sale, the Morris Oxford was well built and well engineered, using components purchased from outside suppliers, and the orders he received justified acquiring new premises at a disused military training college at Cowley, just east of Oxford.

The first Morris Oxford was a two-seater 8.9hp car priced at £165, but by the time of the 1913 London show in the autumn the cars incorporated many improvements and the range now included a closed coupé. The cars soon established a reputation for strength and gained some successes in reliability trials. Each of the entrants driving Morris Oxford cars in the 1914 London-Edinburgh Trial was awarded a gold medal.

Other models followed, including a four-seater Cowley. The first Oxfords used a White & Poppe engine, but the Cowley shown to the press in 1915 used an 11.9hp American Continental power unit as well as American-made front and rear axles, gearbox and steering gear. The First World War saw production at the Cowley factory switching to munitions, with volume car production only returning with peace in 1918. Morris Motors was now a separate entity from Morris Garages, which under the ownership William Morris continued in business selling and repairing cars.

After the end of the war in 1918 there was an initial boom is sales, but by 1920 this had turned into a slump. The prices of the Morris models had risen considerably since the first cars were built and the Oxford two-seater cost a whopping £535. With sales falling, in February 1921 the price was reduced by £25 and at show time a further reduction brought the cost down to £415, while at the same time £110 was taken off the list price of the four-seater tourer. The dealers had to take a reduced commission as part of the deal, but benefited from increased turnover. A proportion of sales were of rolling chassis and some of these were given saloon coachwork by outside firms. It was not until 1924 that Morris listed their own four-seater saloon model, necessary in view of a growing preference by buyers for this type of car. The engines were still of Continental pattern, but were now produced in England at a factory built by Hotchkiss et Cie for military work, which had dried up at the end of the war.

Until 1935 Morris Garages and the MG offshoot were owned by Morris privately and were separate from the Morris car building business. In addition, Morris had considerably widened his interests by buying a number of other companies, some of which were already suppliers of components for his cars. So we see him buying Hotchkiss for engines, Hollick and Pratt coachbuilders and Osberton Radiators. From the outset, Morris had built light commercial versions of the Bullnose Morris, with first a 5cwt and later an 8cwt light van. He could see, however, that Ford were selling many imported 1-ton trucks and decided to enter this market. In 1923 he purchased E.G. Wrigley & Co. of Soho, Birmingham, from the liquidator to gain access to their large factory and production facilities. Under the name Morris Commercial Cars Limited, the factory built a 1-ton commercial vehicle and later extended the range so that by 1931 it could supply everything from a 10cwt van or a 7-ton truck to a taxi and a double-deck bus. The company also tried to develop an "Empire" car suited to conditions in countries like Australia, but lack of development saw this project fail. However, Morris was keen to export and by 1925 had established an overseas trade department in London.

One of his major acquisitions came in 1927 when, after a bidding war with Austin and an American prospective purchaser, he managed to get hold of Wolseley from the liquidators. That company had expanded after the war with a larger factory and lavish London premises, but had run into financial difficulties. On the plus side, they had a good reputation for quality and engineering expertise and had developed a range of power units that would be very useful for any new Morris products. For the MG Car Company the availability of Wolseley power units with considerable development potential proved to be the vital ingredient in the sales and competition success the cars later achieved. Another company acquired by Morris was the SU Carburettor Company, and for years their products were fitted to virtually all MG cars.

One result of William Morris holding all the shares in any particular company was that the Inland Revenue started to try to claim that any profits retained against future need could be liable to super tax at a high rate. He fought two court actions to argue that case against such tax and won both. However, it was the possibility of future difficulties with the Inland Revenue that led eventually to him disposing to the main organisation listed on the Stock Exchange some of the companies he owned privately, including the MG Car Company.

In 1929 William Morris was created a baronet, becoming a baron in 1934 and in 1938 given the title of Viscount Nuffield of Nuffield in the County of Oxford. In 1917 he was given an OBE and in 1941 a GBE. Morris cars may no longer be made and a Chinese company now own MG, but 50 years after he died Lord Nuffield's name lives on in institutions like Nuffield College, Oxford, and the Nuffield Foundation. His home, Nuffield Place near Henley-on-Thames, is now in the hands of the National Trust and is well worth a visit. Preserved almost exactly as it was when he and Lady Nuffield lived there, it is full of personal belongings and gives a real insight into their private life.

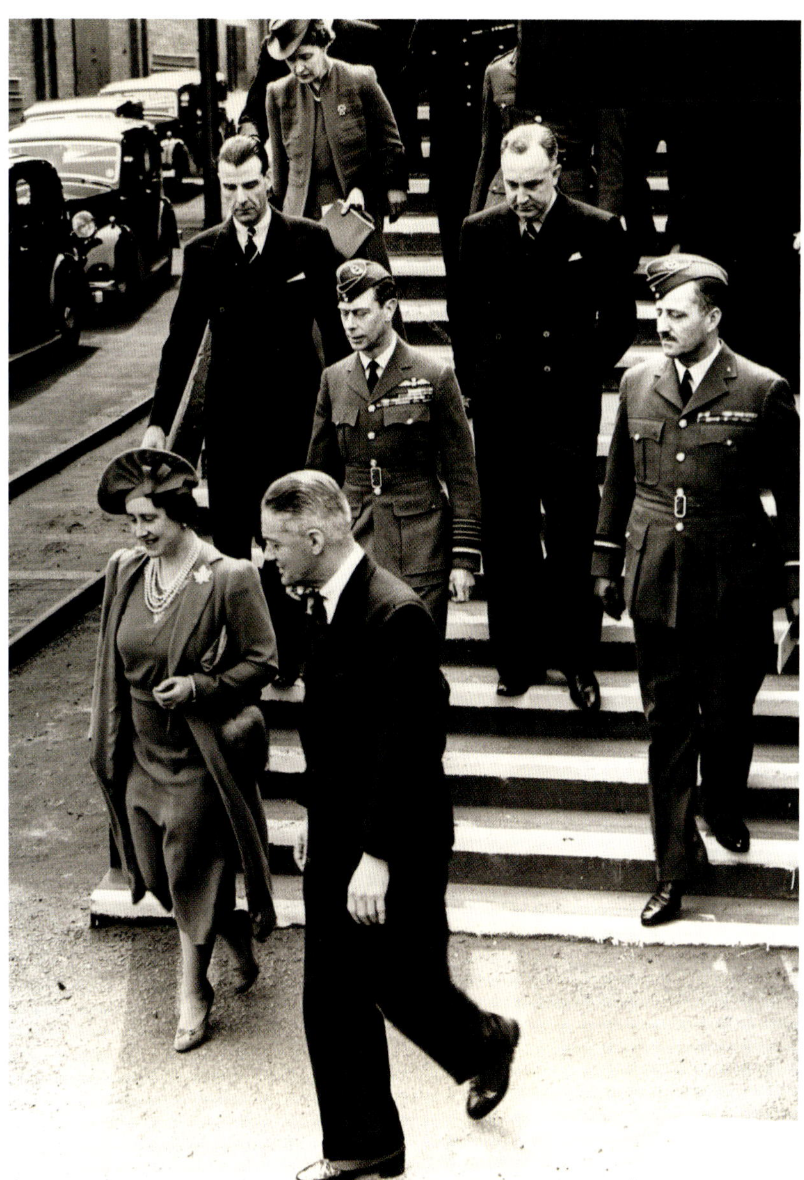

During the Second World War all of the Nuffield Group facilities were turned over to producing weapons, and here Lord Nuffield is showing King George VI and Queen Elizabeth around the Wolseley factory. Miles Thomas is seen just behind the King and the RAF officer.

CECIL KIMBER

The Cecil Kimber story begins with his birth in London in April 1888. His parents, Henry and Fanny Kimber, lived in West Dulwich, at the time a fashionable area to the south of London where some substantial family houses were being built. The family firm of Hughes and Kimber were innovators in the world of printing. They had exhibited their copper and steel printing plates at the 1855 Paris Exhibition, and the presses they made to produce fine art prints were considered to be amongst the finest available. This was obviously a family that enjoyed some of the advantages that money can bring, but for Cecil it was also one with its fair share of difficulties. Cecil's mother, whose maiden name was Matthewman, was an accomplished artist painting in watercolours and her work was regularly exhibited. She apparently had little real interest in her children, although Cecil was said to have adored her. Unfortunately she died from cancer at the early age of just 42 but, according to his daughter Jean, Cecil inherited some of her artistic talent. This may explain why when the factory was under his control there were no ugly MGs.

Cecil Kimber with his supercharged K1 Magnette fitted with a Corsica body.

MR. CECIL KIMBER'S IDEAL CAR

A standard M.G. Magnette touring chassis fitted with a supercharger and a special all-weather body. It has a maximum speed of 94 m.p.h. and yet is perfectly normal to drive slowly and in traffic without any trace of oiling up troubles, usually associated with a "blown" engine.
This car has been put into commission for the personal use of Mr. Cecil Kimber, of the M.G. Car Company, for experimental reasons, with the idea of developing the supercharged car for ordinary every-day use.

389

In 1896 Henry Kimber and his brother Walter opened a separate printing supplies business in Manchester and the family moved north. They first lived in Stockport and then in Heaton Moor. Cecil went to Stockport Grammar School and holidays were taken at Runswick Bay in North Yorkshire, where he developed a lifelong passion for the sea and sailing. After this Cecil went into his father's business, while also attending evening classes at Manchester Technical School. Like most of his peers at a time when motorised transport was developing rapidly, he took a keen interest in motorcycles and used to ride his pedal cycle long distances to see time trials and other competitive events. All this came to an abrupt end when, riding a motorcycle owned by his friend Billy Sutton, a car hit him. The accident was not his fault, but he was nevertheless seriously injured. His right leg was very badly smashed and resulted in him having a series of operations over the next three years. Although the leg was saved it ended up shorter than the other and left him with a limp for the rest of his life. Luckily he could still drive a car and with the compensation of around £700 he received he was able to buy a 10hp Singer.

Cecil continued to work for his father in a business that to all accounts was struggling to survive. He travelled around selling printing ink and other supplies, earning the princely sum of a pound a week. He met and courted Irene Hunt, always known as Rene, and when they decided to marry he asked his father for an increase in pay. This was refused and in addition his father was insisting he put the residue of his compensation money into the business. This Cecil refused to do, and the ensuing row meant that he left the family firm;

for the rest of his life his father refused to speak to him, or to even see him, despite overtures from his son in later years.

Obviously, given his injury, unlike most of his generation he was not called up for war service. With his now highly developed interest in the motor industry, Cecil took a post as personal assistant to the chief engineer at Sheffield-Simplex, who built 30hp cars, examples of which Cecil had many opportunities to drive. He married Rene in September 1915 and they took their honeymoon trip in an ex-Brooklands Singer fitted with open and rather uncomfortable bodywork. In 1916 the couple moved to Surrey as Cecil had obtained the post of buyer for AC Cars at Thames Ditton, with Rene as his secretary.

Obviously very ambitious, in 1918 his next move was to Birmingham, where he joined E.G. Wrigley Limited, who in 1913 had moved to new premises at Foundry Lane, Soho. For that year only they built their own car, but the main business was producing precision tools and parts for gearboxes and transmissions. The company had become one of a number involved in supplying components to a new factory established with the intention of mass-producing cars by Sir William Angus Sanderson and Company in vacated government wartime premises at Birtley, Tyne and Wear. Unfortunately, for a number of reasons, the new factory never achieved full production and the receiver was called in. The knock-on effect meant the E.G. Wrigley was in difficulties and eventually in 1923 went into receivership, with William Morris purchasing the assets.

It is said that Cecil Kimber may have had some of his own capital in the failed venture, but anyway in 1921 Morris offered him the post of sales manager at Morris Garages. The following year the general manager, Edward Armstead, committed suicide and Kimber took over his position. Kimber at the time must have had a fairly close relationship with William Morris. The Morris Garages business was separate from Morris Motors and Kimber seems to have been given a fairly free hand in running the retail sales and servicing activities spread over several premises around Oxford.

His years selling printing equipment, and later in various positions in the motor industry, must have given him the ability to persuade others of the merits of his ideas. It has been said, however, that he was often so convinced of the value of his plans that he would not tolerate opposition. That aside,

The Queen Street, Oxford, showroom of Morris Garages at the time Kimber was General Manager.

he must have been able to convince Morris, a man unwilling to spend time and money promoting or building sports cars, of the virtue of first modifying and selling as Morris Garages Specials products from the Morris range, and, later, cars designed and built specifically as MGs.

Kimber was always very keen to promote the competition role for his cars. He entered the Land's End Trial in a Morris in 1923 and in the Morris Special, Old Number One, in 1925. Whenever he could he went to any race meetings or record attempts where cars prepared at the factory were involved. Daughter Jean recalled going with him to races at Brooklands and attending MG Car Club events, like the Abingdon Trial, and this must have affected family life. They often entertained both business acquaintances and well-known drivers at The Boundary House, for some years the home in Abingdon the family rented. It is now a public house and restaurant.

The changes brought about in 1935, when The MG Car Company was transferred from William Morris's personal portfolio to the main Nuffield Group, were probably a considerable blow to his pride as a large measure of control over the development programme for future MG production was now transferred to Cowley. Entries by factory-supported cars in motor racing were no longer sanctioned, although a rearguard action saw participation in trials and in record breaking continue almost unabated. However, troubles at home at the time would have been making his life difficult.

From the early 1930s his marriage may not have been going that well. Rene had begun suffering badly with colitis and for someone who enjoyed company and good meals in restaurants this would have been quite a burden. Cecil was probably away from home quite a lot and by now they had two daughters, Betty and Jean. Medical and nursing home expenses for Rene's periods of illness mounted up and in that pre-NHS age would be a hardship, even for the moderately well paid. Jean recalled that by 1935 her mother was often hysterical and difficult, and with hindsight she feels that this may have been because she had cancer, something then rarely discussed, especially in front of the children. Rows between her parents occurred, with her mother blaming her father for everything.

It is perhaps unsurprising that Cecil Kimber should look elsewhere for congenial company, and in 1935 he met divorcee Muriel Dewar, who had a daughter by her first husband. They met frequently, but never alone, as any hint of scandal would have been a disaster at that time. As the marriage was obviously over, divorce was discussed, but bolstered by opposition from her family, Rene refused. The couple separated in 1937 with Rene and their eldest daughter going to live in a flat at Parkstone, Dorset, and Cecil to rooms in the Crown and Thistle in Abingdon. Jean went to a boarding school.

In the spring of 1938 Rene was persuaded to go into Poole Hospital for an operation to remove part of her colon, but a relapse saw her die on 21st April 1938. Now free to marry, but keen to keep the matter quiet so soon after the death, Cecil and Muriel were united in a very quiet ceremony on 25th June, with just a couple of close friends and the immediate family as witnesses. One of the reasons for the early ceremony was the prospect of war with Germany at the time of the Munich Crisis. By all accounts this second marriage was a happy one and Jean recalled that laughter was once again heard in the household.

Working with and for William Morris, Lord Nuffield could be difficult, particularly as he was much influenced by Lady Nuffield, who had some very puritanical views. It has been said that the couple were not much amused by Kimber's private life and that this may have been one of the reasons why his rule at MG came to an end. The outbreak of war in September 1939 changed everything. At Abingdon car production was curtailed and all the spares moved to premises acquired nearby in the town. Some of the workforce was immediately called up, but others remained and needed employment. The factory was to be converted to produce munitions, but contracts for this were very slow in coming through. Kimber, never one to sit on his hands, took the initiative and went out to secure work to keep the factory going, including a good contract for repairing tanks.

In a large organisation individualists do not always fit in, and one wonders if this was just the excuse some at the top of the group were waiting for. Sir Miles Thomas, who worked with Lord Nuffield for 23 years, said that Cecil Kimber had been able to persuade Lord Nuffield to carry on making small profits in the hope that the prestige earned by The MG Car Company in competition would result in sales. Miles went to see Kimber at Abingdon in November 1941 and told him that he had better look for another outlet for his energies because he did not fit into the wartime pattern of the Nuffield Organisation.

Kimber's friend John Howlett later wrote the following about the sacking: "I happened to see

Kimber when he brought the news home. He was white-faced and stunned. He just could not understand why he deserved the sack." He told Kimber that he should go and see Lord Nuffield. This he did but he came back from the interview even more bewildered, saying that Nuffield had him in the office for an hour but managed to avoid directly talking about the issue, so he left none the wiser.

Having led The MG Car Company from its inception to the prominent position it then held, being ousted from the job for the sin of trying to do his best for the workers and the business must have been an enormous blow. He had been well paid, his salary in 1934/35 amounting to £1259 and in 1939/40 £2750. However, he obviously spent most of his earnings, what with owning and running a yacht, having house servants, and all the costs of the entertaining required for his job, so he needed to find other work. His reputation meant that this was not difficult, but one has the feeling that anything he found would to him be a step backwards.

His first job was at Charlesworth coachbuilders, where he spent six months reorganising the factory, He then went as works director in the autumn of 1942 to Specialloid Piston Rings. This job did not work out quite as well as expected, but he remained on the board as the company were keen to capitalise on his experience. There then followed a period of ill health, and this seems to have been a very difficult time in Kimber's life. However, his reputation in the industry led to him being in demand as a speaker. In February 1945 Kimber boarded the 6pm Kings Cross to Bradford train to visit Perkins Engines at Peterborough the following morning. It was a heavy train, the track was wet, and in the tunnel outside the station the locomotive lost traction and started to run backwards. As it was dark, the crew failed to realise this and did not apply the brakes. The rear coach derailed at a set of points and overturned, killing two and injuring others. Kimber was one of the dead. Thus ended at just 56 the life of this talented man.

In the 1930s Cecil Kimber had an office in the administration block situated at the end of Cemetery Road, alongside one of the entrances to the factory.

OLD NUMBER ONE

Cecil Kimber at the wheel of his one-off MG following the 1925 Land's End Trial, where he was awarded a gold medal. He sold the car shortly after this for £300.

Prior to the accident that severely damaged his leg Cecil Kimber had entered a number of motorcycle trials, so it is not surprising that in 1923 he should enter a tuned Morris Cowley with a Morris Garages Chummy body in the Land's End Trial, winning a Gold Medal. His partner in the car was Russell Chiesman, who the following year was to earn the distinction of taking the first award in a car with an MG badge, his Raworth-bodied MG Sports earning a Gold Medal in the 1924 Land's End. It is known that William Morris, although not a huge fan of motor sport, realised the value of success in trials following his own Gold Medal in the 1913 event at the wheel of an early Morris Oxford. He was therefore likely to be sympathetic to an approach from Kimber to allow him to build on company premises a Morris special to enter in the 1925 event.

The organisers of the 1924 Land's End limited the entry to motorcycles and light cars with a capacity of under 1500cc, or an RAC rating of 12hp or less. For the 1925 event the capacity increased to 2000cc, but at the time when Kimber first considered entering the lower limit was in force. Consequently he chose a Hotchkiss power unit in preference one from the 14/28 Morris Oxford as that would not have been eligible under the old rules.

The Hotchkiss engine was a development of the 11.9hp Morris Cowley engine given overhead valve gear to improve its output. In this form it was supplied for use by the manufacturers of the short-lived Autocrat and Gilchrist cars. With a bore of 69.5mm and a stroke of 102mm the capacity was 1547cc. The camshaft was mounted low down in the cylinder block and drove the overhead valves through the usual arrangement of tappets, tubular push rods and rockers. A large-capacity pump powered by the camshaft fed oil under pressure to the main bearings, but the big ends relied on splash lubrication. Ignition was by magneto and the fuel system used air pressure to feed the SU carburettor; there was a hand pump and pressure gauge in the cockpit. Drive to the three-speed crash gearbox was via a cork-faced clutch plate running in oil and the gearbox was linked to the rear axle by a prop-shaft enclosed in a torque tube.

The overhead-valve Hotchkiss engine was stripped at the Morris Garages Longwall premises and carefully prepared for Kimber's special. An early MG employee, Charlie Martin, remembered this as one of his first jobs when he started work there in 1924. The chassis was a one-off and was built at Longwall by the machine shop foreman, Frank Stevens, using just a few hand tools. The front half was standard Morris, but the rear section was fabricated by hand and featured side members that were sharply curved above the rear axle. The front axle was of the type used on the 1925 model year 13.9hp Morris Oxford and had 12-inch brake drums. The one-off braking mechanism was constructed using many special parts made in the little machine shop at the Morris Garages premises.

Work seems to have been carried out on the car only as other jobs allowed, and it was finished just in time for the entry in the 1925 event. The completed chassis had been fitted with a workmanlike two-seater body and the purposeful competition machine was first registered in Kimber's name on 27 March 1925 as FC 7900, an Oxford number. When road tested by Cecil Kimber the car was reputed to have been capable of a top speed of 82mph, and great hopes were held of success in the trial.

Here we can turn to the account of the proceedings as related by Barré Lyndon in his book *Combat*, which we must remember was written some eight

Launches of new models often saw Old Number One pressed into service, as it was in 1947 for the display at Abingdon of the new Y-type saloon.

Old Number One must be the most publicised of MGs.(Photo Knudson Collection)

years after the trial, probably with Kimber's own recollection forming part of his source material. Lyndon says that with less than 48 hours to go before the start of the event, it was discovered that the carefully constructed special chassis frame had developed a crack. With time short, emergency repairs were needed, and these consisted of some hand-cut steel strengthening plates welded in place by Frank Stevens. The car was then ready for action and Cecil Kimber, accompanied by Oxford insurance broker Wilfred Mathews, drove to the start at Slough.

The trial incorporated most of the West Country hills feared by competitors, Porlock, Bluehills Mine, Lynton and Beggars' Roost, but the car coped with these with little difficulty. They had some carburettor trouble, and needed to change the plugs, but it was a puncture at the top of Beggars' Roost that nearly caused them to be late at the next control. However, some frantic driving saw them make up the deficit prior to the Launceston check, and they reached the finish at Land's End without losing any marks, earning them a Gold Medal and an enduring place in the history books for the MG special.

Soon after the trial Kimber sold the car for £300 to a friend, Stockport Morris agent Harry Turner, who was to keep it for a number of years. In November 1930 Turner sold the car for £50 to Ronald Davison, who wrote to Morris Garages in February the following year requesting more details about the car. His request was passed to Abingdon who, in a letter bearing Kimber's facsimile signature, replied that the car was a one-off but that some of the components were standard Morris Cowley and that the local agent would be able to help with spares for these.

In February 1932 Davidson wrote to the factory offering his services as a racing driver, which was declined, but in his reply Cecil Kimber said, "We have now confirmed the fact that the car you own, No. FC 7900 is virtually the first MG ever produced". The letter went on to ask if it still had the original body and if he wanted to sell it. Unfortunately, Davison had already disposed of the car for 11 guineas at auction and it is thought that it went to a Birmingham butcher. At one time the car was spotted towing a trailer of pig food, but luckily a later sighting by an MG employee of FC 7900 in a Manchester scrapyard led to it being purchased by the company.

By the mid 1930s FC 7900 was at Abingdon to take up the role of company mascot, a task it has ably fulfilled ever since. At some time it lost its original registration number and in the 1950s was re-registered FMO 842. Happily, and largely at the instigation of the historian, Wilson McComb, the original registration number was restored to the car in the 1960s. Old Number One is now usually on display at the Heritage Motor Centre at Gaydon.

CERAMIC OLD NUMBER ONE

One piece of MG memorabilia is the ceramic model of Old Number One. In the 1960s the British Motor Corporation commissioned from Carlton Ware a ceramic model of an early two-seater Bullnose Morris. These were finished in grey and distributed through Morris dealers for display and sale to interested customers. The same model was produced again in the 1970s for British Leyland, this time painted yellow. Carlton Ware also produced another model of the Bullnose Morris that was really a caricature and far less attractive than those made for BMC.

In 1974 British Leyland commissioned a model of Old Number One use as part of the celebration of fifty years of MG production. They sent 1000 of these to dealers in America and the remaining 1500 of the limited edition of 2500 to UK BL distributors and dealers for sale at £5 each. At the time not all went easily and some could be picked up for less than the asking price from stands at autojumbles and elsewhere.

Like the majority of pottery companies, the original Carlton Ware factory went out of business in the late 1980s, although the name was purchased from the receiver and has been used for items produced for the collectors' market

The ceramic model of Old Number One produced in 1974 by Carlton Ware for British Leyland under the pattern number 3132.

THE MG 14/28 AND 14/40

The 14/28 MG Super Sports tourer was an elegant car.

The familiar octagonal MG logo began appearing in advertisements late in 1923, and for the 1924 model Morris Oxford chassis Cecil Kimber decided to offer a range of exclusive Morris Garages coachwork. The Hotchkiss-based engine of the Morris Oxford had been enlarged from 11.9hp to 13.9hp in January 1923, the larger engine first being offered as an alternative at an extra £10, before being standardised for 1924. Additionally, prices of all the production Morris cars were reduced and a wider range of models listed as standard. With a rolling chassis then costing £195, Morris Motors now offered a two-seater with a folding dickey seat at £300. This was similar in appearance to the first Morris Garages special that had been on sale the previous year for £350. The 11.9hp Morris Cowley was even cheaper, with the two-seater costing £198 and a basic chassis just £160.

The revised Morris Oxford chassis was fitted with a Kimber-designed aluminium panelled saloon body that featured a V-shaped windscreen. This was advertised for sale early in 1924 at £460 as the MG Four-door Saloon Morris Oxford, "Just the car for the theatre". A subsequent advertisement carried in *The Morris Owner* of March 1924 placed emphasis on the fact that the special bodies were fitted to the famous Imshi chassis. Imshi (Arabic for "get a move on") was the name given in 1920 to a Morris driven by the *Daily Mail* motoring correspondent, John Prioleau, when he carried out a six-month journey through Europe and North Africa. There were similar journeys undertaken in Imshi II and Imshi III – also Morris Oxfords.

The advertisement announced that the coachwork fitted to the Morris 14/28 chassis was lavishly equipped and beautifully finished, and went on to point out that in addition to the saloon there were also a Landaulette, a coupé and two- or four-seater sports models in the range. In subsequent issues of

Spare wheels were a necessity at a time when many roads were not surfaced and tyres less robust. The Salonette carries two, one on each side.

The attractive design of the Salonette features a good area of glass, not always the case with cars of this age.

this Morris house magazine the other body styles were illustrated. Looking at the April 1924 advertisement for the four-seater, we see that the body was finished in polished aluminium with the wings either painted black or left as polished aluminium to match the body. The seats were upholstered in leather with a choice of colours. The windscreen was of unique design, having glazed side panels that both improved weather protection and served to brace the windscreen frame. The price of this four-seater was £395. In spite of the availability of the 14hp models, the May advertisement carried a picture of the MG Super Sports built on the 11.9hp chassis – presumably because there were still some 1923 models unsold. The price for this remained £350.

The most unusual body offered on the 14/28 chassis in 1924 was The MG De Luxe Landaulette. With this style of coachwork the driver had a fixed roof over his head, whilst the roof over the rear seat passengers could be lowered in fine weather. The virtues of this type of body were said in the advertisement to make it "Ideal for the professional man, for station work, for paying calls, for the theatre or the ball". It was, after all, a different world in 1924. Said to be the first-ever landaulette body offered on the Morris Oxford chassis, it was expensive at £395 and it must have had modest performance in view of the weight of such sophisticated coachwork.

The Morris Oxford was modified late in 1924, the changes including better brakes and a longer chassis. These improvements were incorporated in the 14/28 MG, which received further improvements to the steering, suspension and controls at Alfred Lane before being fitted with their special MG coachwork. The MG Super Sports range comprised an open four-seater, an open two-seater and a two-door Salonette at prices from £350 to £475, which could still be considered as being quite expensive in 1924. However, for those with smaller wallets, Morris Garages still produced cars that had special bodywork on unmodified Morris chassis,

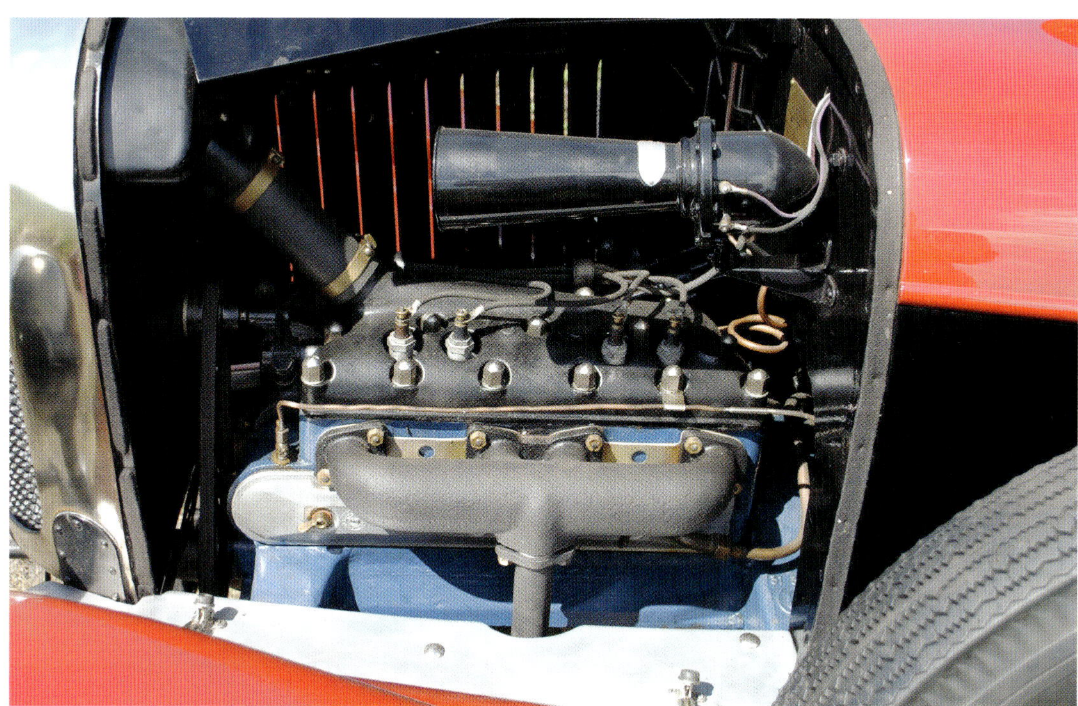

Morris Garages modified the 1802cc Morris engine for use in the MG Salonette.

and these were on sale at lower prices.

Morris Garages had a number of premises around Oxford town, but space was always at a premium. Chassis modifications and final finishing of the cars was usually carried out in the small mews garage at Alfred Lane, but by September 1925 it was proving incapable of accommodating the numbers needing to be built there. The solution was to lease a section of the newly completed Morris Radiators factory in Bainton Road, Oxford, for the MG production line. As there were now 25 employees working on car production, a works manager was appointed and he was installed in a separate, glass-sided office.

By the time the 1926 models were offered for sale the whole marketing of the MG marque was much improved. Initially sales catalogues had consisted of separate photographs pasted into card booklets, with the description of the cars typed on slips of paper and attached to the card alongside the pictures. This was obviously perfectly acceptable while volumes were small and most vehicles were sold directly from the Morris Garages showrooms. However a much more professional approach was needed as the numbers of cars built increased and sales from motor show stands, and through other distributors, became more common.

The catalogue of 1926 MG models was a much more professional affair than those previously issued by The Morris Garages. This booklet was either incorporated within the one for the other Morris products, or was issued separately. The front cover featured a head-on view of the attractive Salonette and just inside the booklet was the proud statement, "Such is the popularity of the various MG models that a special factory has been erected to cope with the ever-increasing demand". The Super Sports models were available as two- and four-seat tourers and also as a Salonette, a small two-door saloon. This model was fitted with steel disc wheels in place of the wire wheels now standardised for the other models. To keep the price down, the basic Morris chassis with solid artillery wheels was used for the four-door saloon and the Weymann Sedan, although the latter body could be fitted to the Super Sports chassis for an additional £30.

Weymann bodies were popular in the late 1920s as their flexible wooden framework construction and fabric covering was thought to give a quieter ride on poorly surfaced roads and fewer rattles. An advertisement for the Weymann saloon in the January 1925 *Morris Owner* extolled the virtues of the fabric covered body for those unable to spend the time cleaning painted coachwork as "mud and dust can be wiped off dry with no detriment to the surface". The light construction was also praised, the weight of the body being given as just 320lbs, and performance was said to be even livelier than the open tourer. At that time every new Morris car was sold with one year's free comprehensive insurance and this cover was also available for new MGs.

By 1925 the MG marque was certainly beginning to take on an identity separate from the parent Morris. In July that year *The Motor* gave a whole page over to the MG Salonette, describing it as an occasional four-seater designed to accommodate two children in the back seats, or adults for short distances. They detailed the comforts included as standard in this attractive little car, making particular note of the blinds at every window, the twin roof lights and useful door pockets. The dash lamps looked like plated knobs when not in use but operated immediately they were pulled out.

To gain some idea of the performance of the MG 14/28 we have to turn to the report of a road test of the four-seat tourer carried out for *Motor Sport* in October 1925. This testers noted that although no major structural changes were made to the chassis, a programme of careful polishing and assembly of the engine, and of minor alterations to the chassis, had improved the performance of the car out of all recognition. In fact, changes to the rake of the steering wheel, a flattening of the road springs, and the adoption of better dampers for the axles, produced a car far more suited to the needs of the sporting driver. The test car was fitted with an SU carburettor, a make to become familiar to generations of MG owners, and the testers noted that it suited the engine particularly well in all conditions. A maximum speed of 65mph was recorded and, whilst acceleration figures were not taken, the drivers expressed their surprise at just how quickly the car reached touring speeds.

The standard colour schemes for the open two- and four-seater tourers certainly added to the appeal of these cars. Initially all the bodywork was polished aluminium but later the cars were finished with the upper portion painted in either smoke blue or claret with the wings, valances and chassis painted to match. The body sides remained as burnished aluminium. The leather upholstery matched the chosen paint colour.

Although not quite as good looking as the earlier model, the 14/28 flat radiator tourer is still a handsome vintage car.

Towards the end of 1926 the Morris Oxford, on which the early 14/28 MGs had been based, was radically redesigned. It must have come as something of a shock to the thousands of Morris owners around the world to find that the most recognisable feature of their car, the Bullnose radiator, was to be consigned to history. The revised Morris Oxford and Morris Cowley, in line with then current practice, were called 1927 models from their launch in the autumn of 1926. The Oxford chassis was extensively redesigned and was wider, shorter and much heavier than its predecessor. The distinctive three-quarter-elliptic rear springs used on the earlier cars gave way to more conventional semi-elliptic springs, and the rear of the chassis was upswept to accommodate them. The strengthening work extended to providing a more substantial mounting for the scuttle and the seven-gallon petrol tank mounted there. A pressed-steel facia board was fitted, incorporating provision to adjust the rake of the steering column and four-spoke steering wheel.

The engine, gearbox and back axle came unchanged from the earlier model. The braking system was slightly redesigned for mounting on the new chassis; there was now a tubular cross-shaft to transfer the braking effort from the pedal to the rods operating the brake shoes which were duplicated for the rear drums, the second set being operated by the handbrake lever. Wing nuts on the ends of the rods provided adjustment. At the front, the new, wider flat radiator changed the appearance of the car, requiring that the bodywork be adapted to suit.

Modifying the 1927 chassis to improve performance, and designing new bodies to fit it, caused Kimber a number of problems and he resorted to asking for assistance from a young engineering graduate, H.N. Charles, whom he persuaded to join his team in the part of the Bainton Road radiator factory leased to Morris Garages for car production. Working largely in the evenings and at weekends, they tried to sort out what would be required in the way of modifications to the chassis, and to the styling of the bodywork, in order to get the MG range back into production as soon as possible. Long periods were spent working on

The Salonette body fitted to the 1927 MG 14/28 flat radiator chassis. The model was 21-year-old actress and film star Madeleine Carroll, who in 1938 was the highest paid actress and starred in Alfred Hitchcock's film The 39 Steps.

sketches trying to adapt the body styles to suit the flat radiator, with Kimber's wife helping with ideas.

With the important London Motor Show at Olympia a mere few weeks ahead, the pace of work at Bainton Road must have been hectic. By the time the show took place new cars had been developed, and an advertisement in *The Motor* magazine for 26th October 1926 invited those attending the show to visit the display of 1927 MG Super Sports Models staged at a nearby garage. MG representation within the exhibition was limited to a single salesman based on the Morris stand but wearing an MG badge.

The new 1927 MG models put into production featured a number of chassis and brake modifications in an effort to improve on the Morris chassis. As the cars were to carry lightweight sporting bodywork, in an endeavour to improve the handling the springs were flattened to reduce the ground clearance of the chassis. A Dewandre vacuum servo and a modified cross-shaft were fitted to the braking system, although the complex system of brake operating rods was retained for the time being. The Morris Oxford 13.9hp engines were stripped, balanced, polished and fitted with stronger valve springs to improve performance, and a modified dash panel and altered steering column rake helped make the driver feel more comfortable. A straight-through silencer aided performance and enhanced the sporting appeal of the car. The rear axle had a higher final drive ratio and five-stud hubs were fitted with bolt-on wire wheels carrying balloon tyres.

In spite of the difficulties faced by Kimber and his team, the 1927 MGs still possessed that element of style that set them apart from the standard Morris products. The range of bodies for the new Super Sports was essentially as previously available on the Bullnose cars, with some exceptions.

A 14/28 MG Super Sports flat radiator two-seater tourer.

A factory picture of a 14/28 retouched as a 14/40 or Mark lV by adding the cover to the front dumb irons.

The 14/40 Mark lV Drophead Coupé.

In truth, all the new models were heavier than the previous cars and did not look quite as good. Undoubtedly, many were sold on the strength of the reputation built up by the Bullnose cars but, with the open cars costing £340 and £350 for the two- and four-seater models respectively, they did not quite possess the advantages over other cheaper cars that the prices charged would suggest.

However, the road tests of the period convey little of this, the article in *Motor Sport* for May 1927 describing the two-seater they tried as "one of the most delightful little motor cars it has been our lot to try for many moons". They described also a visit to the showrooms to inspect the rest of the MG range, where they were favourably impressed by the colour schemes on offer for these cars. The testers reported favourably on the positioning of the toolbox. This was now carried between the rear dumb irons, fitted with a neat lid to keep the tools secure and dry. They liked the two-seater bodywork on the car they drove and said that the single dickey seat gave room for an extra passenger, or for a quantity of luggage when undertaking touring holidays.

Since the overall weight of the car as tested was

A 14/28 MG Super Sports tourer photographed with a First World War tank.

over 2200lbs, and the 1802cc side-valve engine produced only about 36bhp, it is hardly surprising that it took over 25secs to reach 50mph. Modest though this may seem, it was still a lot quicker than the majority of cars in use then, some of which would have struggled to reach that speed given all day to do it.

In view of some of the shortcomings of the 1927 model, development work continued to try to improve matters, resulting in various alterations being progressively incorporated into the car. The exact order of events is a little confusing but what is certain is that by autumn 1927 the car had received a number of modifications to the engine and braking system and that, at the time of the announcement of the 1928 cars in September 1927, the 14/28 model name had changed to 14/40 Mark IV.

The Autocar tested a two-seater 14/40 in harsh winter conditions during January 1928. They recorded acceleration to 50mph in just below 20secs, a 5secs improvement over the 14/28 tested the previous year, and reported that, with a maximum speed of over 65mph, high average speeds were possible. They said, "It speaks much for the excellence of the standard chassis from which the MG is developed, that it should give the results obtained in the matter of performance without any loss of reliability. At the same time it should be realised that the original chassis is so modified that it becomes an entirely different production in the end."

EDMUND ROAD – THE FIRST PURPOSE-BUILT MG FACTORY

A batch of Morris chassis awaiting attention. At this stage they still have a central handbrake and Morris steering wheel.

As a mains supply was not available, a 45kw Crompton generator supplied power for the MG factory.

We have seen that Morris Garages rented a section of a new factory in Bainton Road, Oxford, built for Morris Radiators, and that MG production had been transferred there. As demand for radiators for the Cowley factory grew in line with the increasing sales of Morris cars, the MG lines were moved early in 1927 to a new section of the works. It was becoming obvious that new premises would eventually be needed to accommodate the car assembly work, so Cecil Kimber approached William Morris for permission to have a separate factory built especially for MG production. The go-ahead was given, and work commenced on buildings in Edmund Road, Cowley, where they were close to the Morris works with easy access to the bulk of the required components.

Cylinder head ports were first polished and, after running in on coal gas, the heads were decarbonised.

The presence of power tools demonstrates progress made since the first cars were modified at Morris Garages premises, where only hand drills and a set of spanners were available.

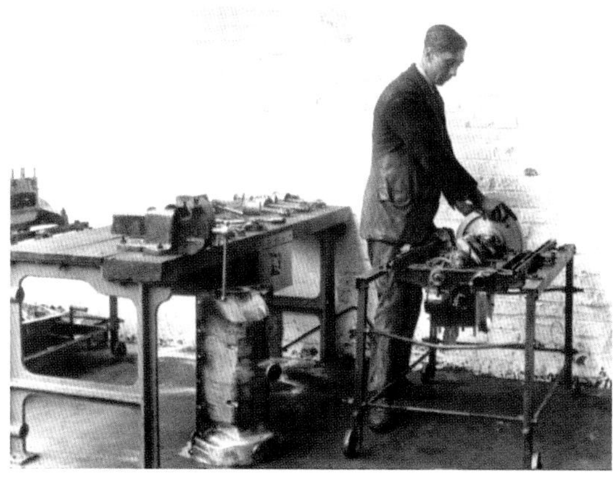

Careful engine assembly ensured the improved performance expected by MG customers.

14/40 chassis during the running in process were supplied with water for cooling. To simulate road conditions the rear wheels drove rotating drums.

The new factory had an eight-bay assembly area and the only real problem Kimber encountered during construction was with the electricity suppliers, who were proving unhelpful. Kimber told them he would install his own plant if necessary so, when a public supply was not forthcoming, he fitted a 45 kilowatt Crompton generator, belt driven by a Rushton engine, with lighting and power cables run into the assembly areas. The factory also had its own boiler house to provide steam heating. The entire job was carried out very quickly and production was moved from Bainton Road in September 1927.

The MG enterprise now had a proper factory in which to build cars. A production line was laid down for chassis assembly, stores were set up to serve the assembly lines and provide customer service, and a small part of the factory was set aside for the engine tuning work. A special running-in bay was installed where completed chassis had their engines connected to a supply of coal gas to provide fuel, and to a water supply for cooling, before being run for the equivalent of 750 miles. The chassis was then taken back to the main assembly area where

A completed chassis sits on the Comparator, an early form of rolling road designed by H.N. Charles.

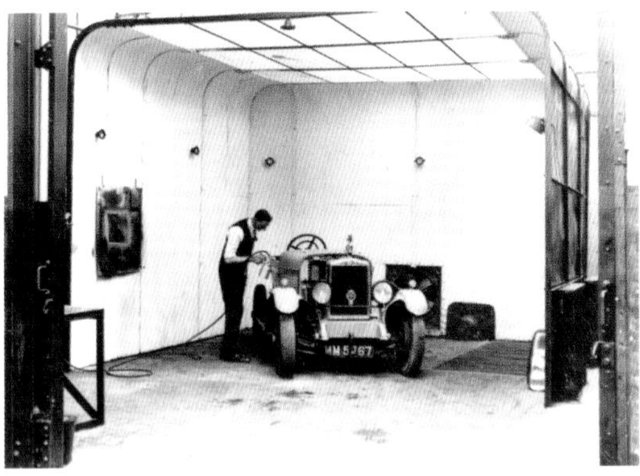

The spray booth, with a road registered 14/40 receiving attention. No mask for the operator, however.

Some completed MG 18/80 six-cylinder cars in the despatch area receive final attention prior to going to the customers.

A completed chassis leaves the factory for the journey to the coachbuilder.

the head was removed and decarbonised and the valves reground. The wings and valances, bulkhead, fuel tank, etc., were then attached to make the car roadworthy for a test drive. Brake and shock absorber settings were adjusted and the car returned to the works for running on a Comparator designed by Hubert Charles, which was the equivalent of a modern rolling road. A temporary seat was then installed for its journey by road to the coachbuilders where the body was fitted. Upon its return the final small fittings were added and the car readied for sale.

Much was made by the company, in a series of advertisements, of the facilities at this new factory.

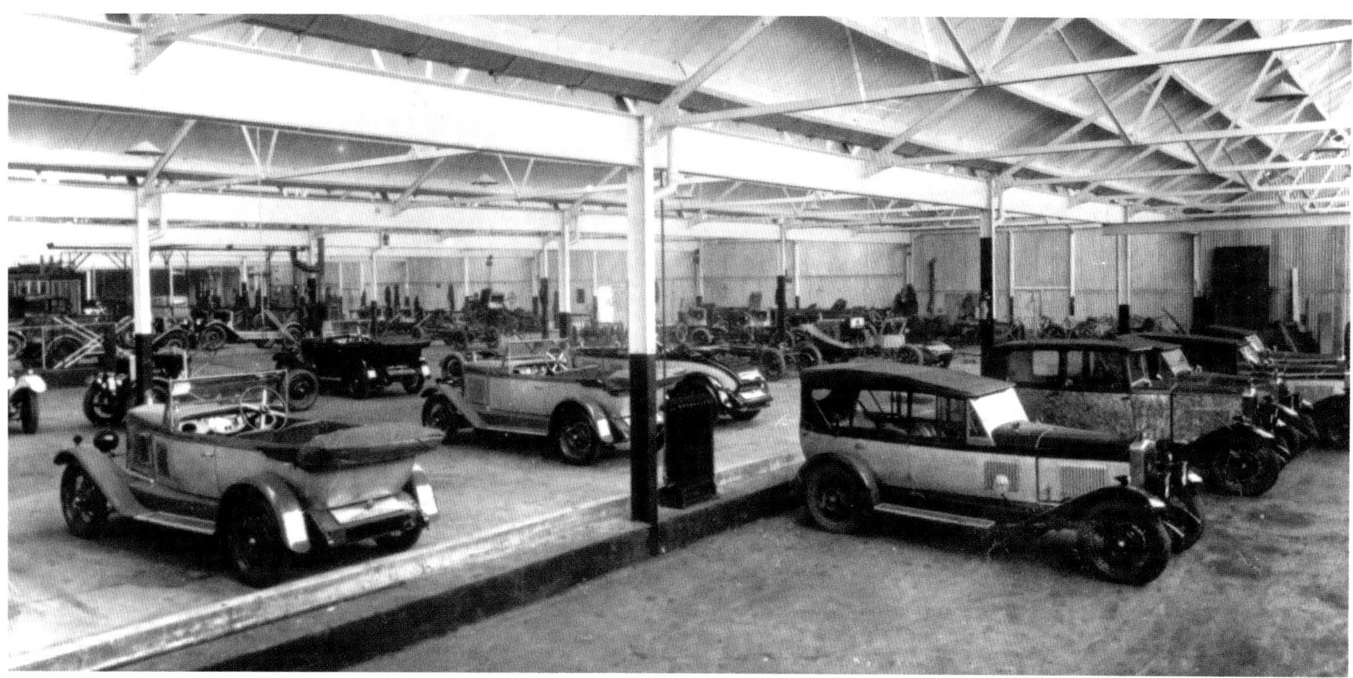

The Service Department at Edmund Road.

A series of advertisements in motoring magazines explained the assembly process at the new MG factory.

The Stores held stocks for the assembly lines and for the Service Department.

Cecil Kimber was justifiably proud of the achievements of this offshoot of The Morris Garages, which was fast becoming larger than its parent. To acknowledge this The MG Car Company (Proprietors: The Morris Garages Ltd.) was registered as a separate entity in March 1928. MG was slowly evolving into a builder of cars in its own right, rather than merely a modifier of Morris products.

An Unique Enterprise

The new  **Works.**

The Stores.

Whether you want a nut and bolt or a complete chassis frame for an M.G. car you will get it instantly from the Works Stores—here are stocked all the components of the chassis and the aim of this department is to feed the Assembly Line Service Section and Spare Parts Requisition with whatever they require.

Only by careful organisation and attention to detail in every way is it possible to turn out such a delightful car as the M.G. at such a low price—and equally important, to give adequate after Sales Service.

"It's the finishing touch that means so much."

The M.G. Car Company

Proprietors: The Morris Garages Ltd.)

Head Office & Showrooms — QUEEN STREET OXFORD.

'Phone 2241 — Wire: Auto.

THE 18/80 MARK I

In the 1920s, the rapid growth of the MG marque had seen a small operation established to supply modified Morris cars to a few well-off customers transformed into a full-scale production line for sporting cars, all assembled in a purpose-built factory. As a deliberate policy, Cecil Kimber had been trying all that time to establish the MG cars he produced as totally separate from the their Morris parentage, if only to be able to justify the higher prices he charged for them. Unfortunately, however charitably one looked at the 14/28 and 14/40 models, their origins were plain to see. What Kimber really needed was a car that could be seen to be entirely different from those built by the parent company, whilst having sufficient performance and handling advantages over the competition to fully justify the sporting pretensions of the marque. Salvation came in the form of a new engine of advanced design from Morris Engines built to power the Morris Light Six. That car was initially not a success as the chassis, basically an elongated Oxford frame retaining the same four-foot track, was simply not rigid enough for the task. Eleven cars were built and eight were subsequently dismantled; one of the remaining three going to Cecil Kimber for use as the basis for designing an entirely new MG.

The engine was of advanced design and was also to subsequently find use as the basis of a marine engine. It was also found a place in a Morris Six with a revised chassis, this time with an eight-inch wider track. With a capacity of 2468cc, the six-cylinder unit had a chain-driven overhead camshaft and in single carburettor guise for the Morris Six it produced 52bhp. With sporting performance in mind, twin carburettors were used for the MG production cars and these were mounted on the nearside, below the exhaust manifold. In twin-carburettor form power output was around 60bhp at 3800rpm.

An 18/80 Mark I show chassis for the 1928 London Motor Show.

The MG Sports
The M.G. Car Company
Pavlova Works
Abingdon-on-Thames
'Phone: 251 (3 lines)
Wire: "Emgee," Abingdon

Given one of the prototype Morris Light Six cars with which to experiment, the team at MG had discarded most of it and set about designing a chassis more suited to their needs. A frame with deep side rails and substantial cross-members ensured the necessary rigidity, whilst the novel design of the dumb-irons provided a substantial forward mounting for the wide front leaf springs. These springs carried a new front axle and were mounted so that they sloped downwards towards the rear. The car retained the four-foot Morris track and the modified Morris Cowley rear axle was mounted on half-elliptic springs. Damping was by single-arm Hartford Duplex friction shock absorbers. The braking system was built up using some Morris components and some MG-designed items. The prototype cars retained bolt-on wheels, Rudge-Whitworth knock-on hubs and wire wheels appearing once production was fully under way.

The whole philosophy behind the concept of the 18/80 seems to have been to build a car that would appeal to a different market from the one catered for by the earlier cars. A great deal of attention was paid to the appearance of every part of the car, the engine received a number of polished aluminium components, there were scuttle-mounted tanks for reserve supplies of petrol and engine oil, a magnificent array of dashboard instruments was installed, and the driver enjoyed the benefit of a fly-off handbrake for the complicated braking system. A three-speed gearbox was retained, however.

The crowning glory of the new car, which was called the "Quick Six" within the factory, had to be

A publicity picture of the 18/80 Mark I saloon taken at Letcombe Regis. The building survives as a village shop and café for the nearby retirement properties.

The 18/80 M.G. Six Sportsman's Salonette

Built for the sporting motorist who will put up with the occasional inconvenience of only two doors for the sake of a more shapely body and the advantage of carrying all the weight *between* the axles.

Thanks to the deep footwells there is the same amount of leg room as in the four-door model. This close coupled saloon combines, with its terrific performance, magnificent coachwork with graceful exterior lines.

The 18/80 M.G. Six Sportsman's Salonette Mk. I . . . . { Fabric £550 0 0 / Coach-built £555 0 0 }

The 18/80 M.G. Six Sportsman's Salonette Mk. II (with Chromium Plating and Triplex Glass) . . . . { Fabric £655 0 0 / Coach-built £660 0 0 }

The 18/80 M.G. Six Sports Tourer

The introduction of the four-speed gearbox with its silent third to the M.G. Six Sports Mk. II chassis has greatly improved what was already a marvellous performance. With a cool sixty on third, there are few cars that can hold their own against this wonderful production on a give-and-take road, and the brakes match the speed.

The 18/80 M.G. Six Tourer Mk. I . £515 0 0

The 18/80 M.G. Six Tourer Mk. II . £630 0 0 (with Chromium Plating and Triplex Glass)

The 18/80 M.G. Six Sports Four-door Saloon

Neither the beauty of exterior line nor its splendid engine performance is sacrificed in producing this charming saloon with its four doors which give the maximum ease of entry or exit. When one sinks luxuriously into the leather-covered pneumatic seats, and the throttle is opened just slightly, then one realises what effortless mile-a-minute cruising can mean.

The 18/80 M.G. Six Sports Four-door Saloon Mk. I . . . . { Fabric £560 0 0 / Coach-built £570 0 0 }

The 18/80 M.G. Six Sports Four-door Saloon Mk. II (with Chromium Plating and Triplex Glass) . . . . { Fabric £660 0 0 / Coach-built £670 0 0 }

The 18/80 M.G. Six Sports Two-Seater

Dainty lines and perfect finish are second only to the uncanny acceleration in all M.G. Six Sports Models. The Two-Seater, favourite of the open car sportsman, offers all that is best in comfort and ease of control. Making use of the four-speed gearbox on the Mk. II model, one reaches the pinnacle of perfect performance. The magnificent M.G. Six engine, though, makes the Mk. I model with its three-speed box equally fascinating to drive.

The 18/80 M.G. Six Sports Two-Seater Mk. I . . £510 0 0

The 18/80 M.G. Six Sports Two-Seater Mk. II . . £625 0 0 (with Chromium Plating and Triplex Glass)

For its time the 18/80 Mark I saloon had good performance and was capable of carrying four people in comfort over long distances.

the radiator. This was designed by Cecil Kimber and was to become the trademark of every subsequent MG until the arrival of the TF and the Z-Magnette in the 1950s. Even after that, the design influenced the grilles fitted to the MGA, MGB and Midget prior the British Leyland take-over.

When the early announcements were made it was envisaged that a four-seater tourer would cost £425; reasonable in view of the £350 charged for the 14/40 tourer. However, by the time the London Motor Show arrived, the accountants had added up the cost of all the refinements incorporated in the new car, and the brochures gave the price of the running chassis alone as £420. Complete cars were to cost £480 for the two-seater, £545 for the two-door Sportsman's Salonette, £485 for the four-door, four-seater tourer and £555 for the four-door saloon.

18/80s were built to a high standard and were well equipped. For the driver, the Bluemel steering wheel and Marles Weller steering box gave good control whilst the hand throttle, ignition and horn levers were conveniently located around the steering wheel boss. The crackle-black painted instrument panel carried a Jaeger speedometer and tachometer,

The 18/80 Mark I two-seater tourer.

The 2½-litre six-cylinder engine in the 18/80 gave the heavy car reasonable performance.

clock, ammeter, oil pressure gauge, petrol gauge, water temperature gauge, ignition warning lamp and Lucas head/sidelight switch. There was a full range of colour schemes. With so much at stake, and with a car carrying a price tag that placed it well above previous MG products in a market already full of expensive sporting cars – Bentley, Lagonda, Alvis, Riley, etc. – it must have been with some trepidation that the salesmen on the MG stand at Olympia awaited the verdict of the buying public. Whilst there was not quite the rush to buy the new car he would have liked, Kimber was happy to take a few orders. However, the limelight was rather stolen by another new model on the MG stand, the 8/33 Midget, a car that was to prove far more important for the long-term survival of the marque.

One of the most elegant and desirable versions of the Mark I was the Speed Model.

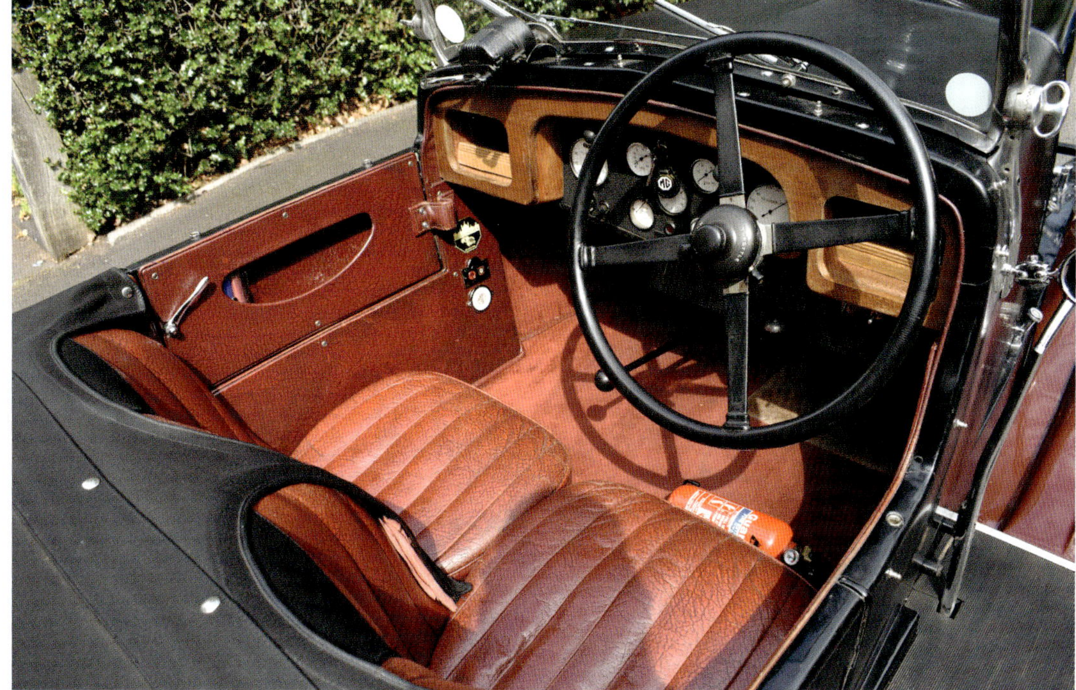

Despite the narrower body fitted to the Speed Model, the cockpit is still comfortable.

The Speed Model is an elegant touring car.

Delivery of production versions of the MG 18/80 did not really start until early 1929, some of the first cars going to favoured customers, to the press, or to drivers taking part in competitions where they would be expected to gain publicity for the marque. Some dealers took cars as demonstrators, hoping to eventually sell them. The 18/80 was never going to be a runaway success, but with figures of only about 280 sold in their first full year of production, it must have been something of a disappointment to the company.

The 18/80 Mk I was a superb touring car. The engine was powerful and, whilst not quite as simple or robust as its predecessors, was capable of achieving high mileages without problems. The chassis was strong and provided the occupants with a comfortable ride. In September 1930 the Mark I Speed Model was announced and was to prove a popular choice for sporting motorists at the time, while the body style is highly favoured by current enthusiasts for the vintage MGs.

The back seats in the Speed Model are comfortable and, unlike this car, some were built with a door to make getting into the rear easier.

THE 18/100 MK III TIGRESS

Prominent features of the sports/racing Tigress models were the metal valances fitted to cover the chassis sides.

Cecil Kimber was keen to prove that MG could build cars to challenge the larger British sporting cars like Bentley and Lagonda. The reputation Bentley had earned was due in no small part to the competition successes at Le Mans and elsewhere. Perhaps if the MG 18/80 enjoyed similar sporting success then it too would reap rewards in the form of improved sales. Of course, with the benefit of hindsight, we all know that the days of the large vintage sporting cars were numbered. The dramatic fall in sales following the Wall Street crash of 1929 did not help the already shaky finances of the Bentley concern, which was to fail in 1931 to become absorbed by Rolls-Royce, who took over the assets of the company.

The amount of worldwide coverage given to the Le Mans race and the interest it aroused amongst both enthusiasts and the general public was not lost on British race organisers. Attendances at race meetings tailed off in 1928, possibly as many found that the diet of a succession of short handicap races seen at the average Brooklands meeting lacked sufficient drama to interest them. Even the usually popular Junior Car Club 200-mile race did not attract the anticipated crowd. One of the difficulties facing British motor racing at the time was the shortage of suitable venues. Unlike the position on the Continent, racing on public roads was banned. Road races, like the Tourist Trophy Race, had to be held in Northern Ireland, on the Isle of Man where such restrictions did not apply, or at Brooklands where an artificial road circuit would be created by using straw bales and wattle fencing to lay out a tortuous route on the wide expanses of concrete.

Much of the appeal of the French sports car race lay in the endurance aspect. Running continuously in near-standard production cars for 24 hours

The outside exhaust system and Brooklands silencer dominate this view. Someone seems to have left on the pipes a mug and probably their lunch.

This Tigress was delivered new to Victor Rothschild in July 1930 and survives today in superb condition.

appealed to the public and made good copy for the daily newspapers' sports reporters. In an attempt to gain more publicity and encourage larger attendances, the Junior Car Club decided to stage a race run on similar lines in Britain. The only possible venue was Brooklands, but night racing was banned here following earlier complaints from local residents when endurance runs had been undertaken during speed record attempts.

Their solution was to run the race in two sections, each of twelve hours duration, with the cars incarcerated in a parc fermé overnight so that no repairs could be made. The 1929 Double-Twelve-Hour race ran from 8am to 8pm on the Friday and Saturday and the club staged Le Mans-like entertainments, such as an amusement park with dodgem cars and the like, dancing, and even the RAF band. A good entry was received and 52 cars started the race, the two-man crews having to erect hoods after the flag fell, travelling the first ten laps with them in place. All this was meant to demonstrate that the race was designed for ordinary, road-going sports cars.

After applying a strange marking system that saw each entrant's distance covered being divided by their target distance to produce an index of merit, the winner was declared to be Ramponi in the Alfa-Romeo by a margin of 0.003 marks. His car had covered 1824 miles in the race, whilst the second-placed Bentley had actually covered a greater distance, 1953 miles. The event had obviously been enough of a success for the club to decide to repeat the race the following year.

It may have been the possibility of having an MG win outright against the likes of Bentley, Alfa-Romeo and Talbot that tempted Kimber, or it may just have been because some customer showed an interest in entering an 18/80 in the race. Anyway, for whatever reason, Kimber decided that MG would build a special car for the 1930 event. The 18/80 most suitable was the revised Mark II version developed around the same time.

It was Kimber's intention that an initial batch of 25 cars be built; he obviously felt that at a price of £895, ready to race, he would have no trouble finding that many willing buyers. Enough modified engines, differing considerably from standard 18/80 units, were ordered from Morris Engines Branch for the initial production run. Although the capacity remained the same, the crankshaft

The Brooklands race car at the MG factory.

The Rothschild Tigress is carefully maintained by the current owner, Geoff Radford. The body made by Carbodies for the 18/100 is narrow and the handbrake sits outside.

Twin spare wheels mounted on a substantial carrier bolted to the rear of the chassis were specified by the first owner.

was machined to reduce mass, the con-rods were machined all over and fitted to different pistons, and the whole assembly was carefully balanced. The cylinder head was modified so that the mixture from the twin SUs was fed via a pair of curved pipes directly into two inlet ports machined in the side of the head, each serving three combustion chambers.

On the standard 18/80 the carburettors sat beneath the exhaust manifold and fed the combustion chambers in the cylinder head through inlet ports in the block. The special engines were far more efficient, with the mixture fed to one side of the head and the exhaust gases exiting from the other side into three downpipes. Compression ratio

The layout of the dashboard differs from that used for the standard 18/80s and for competition use features a large black-faced speedometer and matching tachometer.

was raised to 6.9:1. A neat feature was the incorporation of a pair of breather pipes that fed the carburettors so that ingested oil vapour provided some upper cylinder lubrication.

Also special was the dual-plug ignition. Each of the six combustion chambers was fitted with two spark plugs. Twin coils were used, and a special distributor ensured that both plugs in each cylinder fired at the same time. Engine oiling followed racing-car practice, employing dry-sump lubrication with oil from the tank mounted between the front chassis dumb-irons being pumped round the engine before being returned to be cooled by the stream of air flowing over the tank. The starting handle passed through the centre of the oil tank.

The fuel tank was not at the rear of the car, where one would expect to see it, but in the centre of the chassis to assist weight distribution. The tank was shaped to fit round the prop-shaft and had two fillers – one to take the petrol and the other to let the air out. Twin electric fuel pumps, with separate pipes and switches, fed the petrol to an under-dash two-way tap, thus allowing either pump to be used to feed the carburettors.

The chassis itself was exceptionally sturdy. Behind the engine and gearbox there were two deep cross-members, linked by a tube that carried the prop-shaft through its centre, and these cross-members also supported the battery mountings. Large double Hartford shock absorbers were fitted to the front axle and two pairs of double Hartfords to the rear axle. Those at the back were set at right angles to each other and the spare wheel mounting could be released and swung outwards to gain access to the inner pair for adjustment. As the car was supplied ready to race, all the nuts and bolts on the chassis were drilled and wired to stop them working loose on a bumpy track and the steering arms, track rods, etc., were filed and polished to relieve stress and to ensure there were no defects.

Carbodies constructed a batch of bodies for the racing cars that conformed to the then current international racing regulations. These were built so as to be just wide enough to take the driver and mandatory driving mechanic, the brake lever having to go outside the bodywork. Valances were fitted below the sides of the body, covering the chassis. The full-width windscreen could be folded flat and if required the glass could be replaced with gauze mesh to protect the occupants from flying debris during a race. The elegant tubes that supported the headlamps, and provided a mounting point for the front wings, were of streamlined section.

The first car built seems to have been chassis B0251. It was painted grey and was fitted with cycle wings, the front pair of which were not semi-circular but had a straight section at the back. This car was used at Brooklands as a practice car for

The second set of spark plugs sit beneath the free-flow exhaust pipes.

the 1930 Double Twelve-hour Race. One imagines that the cream and brown car for the race, chassis B0252, was probably not quite ready to run. Leslie Callingham and Harold D. Parker, who both worked for Shell, were entered to drive the 18/100 in the race. Also entered were a whole gaggle of modified 850cc M-type Midgets. The factory must have been under a lot of pressure with such a large number of cars to prepare and this may have some bearing on subsequent events.

Following the success of the previous year's race, the Junior Car Club had made a number of changes. The Friday start saw the cars lined up by the pits with the crews standing alongside. Once the flag fell they had to get in the cars, start them and begin racing. The weather was less than kind, with dry conditions at the start being replaced by a succession of squally showers. The race took place in early May and it was none too warm either, so the drivers, riding mechanics and the pit crews must have wished for a bit of sun. In the MG camp there were problems. Initially the 18/100 had run well, although with a smaller engine it lacked the outright speed of the Bentleys. However, it seems that one of the carburettor butterfly valves came loose, jamming the throttle, and this allowed the engine to over-rev. Leslie Callingham brought the Tigress into the pits for lengthy repairs. He later rejoined the race but soon retired, the official explanation being that piston damage had resulted from ingestion of a screw that held the butterfly valve to its spindle. However, the story goes that actually the engine had well and truly cooked its big-ends, perhaps as a result of over-revving; anyway the one and only works entry of the 18/100 in a competition ended in failure. Geoff Radford, the owner of the remarkably original ex-Rothschild car, GH 3501 illustrated here, discovered a possible explanation for this when he ran it at the banked Montlhéry track. The oil pick-up was from one side of the tank and when the car was turning continuously in one direction the oil surged to the opposite side, resulting in the pipe no longer sitting in the oil. Apparently, in practice for the Brooklands race, cars had run the opposite way round the track and this problem did not materialise.

Further disappointment was to follow for the Tigress as Cecil Kimber had totally misread the possible demand for the racing car. The M-type Midgets gained honours in the race and this led to the production of a batch of replicas for public sale, but the lack of similar publicity for the 18/100 certainly could not have helped him promote that model. In the event only five cars were built and these took some while to sell. The existence of more components than cars built led the factory to fit the unused Tigress bodies on 18/80 Mark I chassis to create the successful Speed Model.

THE 18/80 MARK II

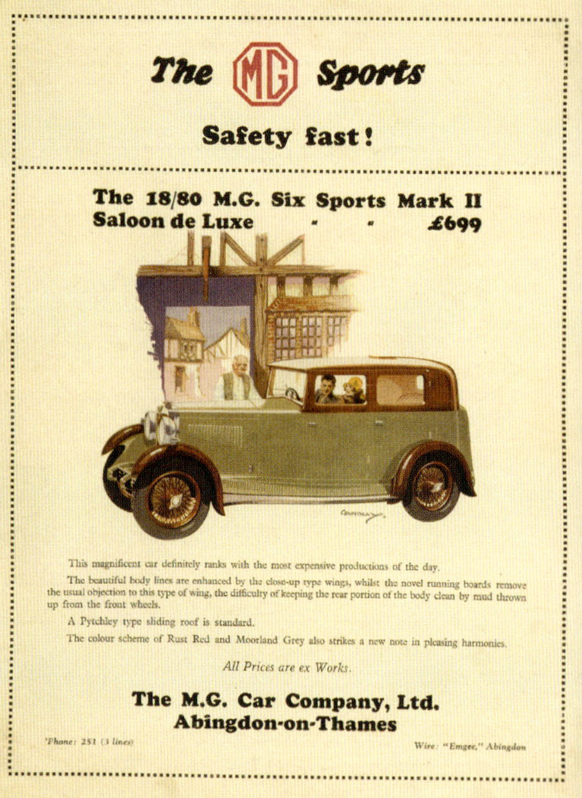

An advertisement for a Mark II De Luxe Saloon.

Although the 18/80 had been well received by the motoring press and the buying public alike, it was not by any means perfect. As one of the necessary compromises to get the car into production quickly at a reasonable price, some Morris-derived components had been used in place of the specially built items the designers would probably have preferred to employ. The four-foot-wide track, for example, compromised both stability and the width of the bodies the car was capable of carrying. Although comfort was not high on the list of priorities of the more sporting drivers, to appeal to the luxury end of the market the car really needed to be capable of carrying wider bodies.

The three-speed gearbox was also something of a disadvantage. Given the torque produced by the 2468cc six-cylinder engine, the deficiencies of the gearbox were not too apparent in the lighter two-seaters and tourers, but drivers of heavily laden saloons must have found the widely spaced ratios something of a handicap. Also, the braking system was over-complicated and the Morris-based rear axle a trifle frail. To remedy all these shortcomings a revised model was introduced in September 1929. Called the 18/80 Mark II, it was catalogued as an addition to the range, rather than as a replacement for the earlier car. The braking improvements were, however, eventually to find their way into the Mark I, although that car retained the smaller brake drums.

A standard 18/80 Mark II two-seater tourer.

Close examination of a Mark II 18/80 reveals that the car incorporated a long list of modifications and refinements. The chassis frame, for example, was massively constructed. Deep side members were linked by a central box-section cross-member that doubled as a mounting for a pair of six-volt batteries. At the front there was a tie-rod between the dumb irons and a cross-member beneath the radiator, whilst at the back yet another cross-member and a rear tie-rod braced the frame. The prop-shaft was carried in a large-diameter tube.

New front and rear axles gave the car a four-inch wider track. The back axle was mounted on wider half-elliptic springs that were carried outside the

A Drophead coupé by Carbodies on the 18/80 Mark II chassis.

chassis frame, with the front mountings bolted to the side of the chassis rails. Chassis lubrication was by an ingenious Tecalemit system that fed oil to all the points, springs, steering joints, etc., as the car was in motion, leaving only the task of maintaining the oil supply to the owner.

The complicated braking system of the Mark I was completely redesigned. Fourteen-inch brake drums replaced the previous twelve-inch ones and Bowden cables from a central cross-shaft operated the brakes. In what was to become a standard layout for MGs, the fly-off handbrake was linked to the cross-shaft and thus worked on all four wheels. The engine was basically unchanged, apart from minor alterations to breathing and carburettors. A four-speed gearbox with a neat remote control replaced the three-speed unit.

Announcement to the buying public of the new car came in a preliminary leaflet issued by the company in September 1929, incidentally around the time they were moving to new premises in Abingdon. Both the Mark I and II models were covered, with the prices for the newer version over £100 more than the Mark I. There were now a bewildering number of body styles available from the factory.

In the hands of the motoring press the revised 18/80 fared well. The report carried by *The Motor* in June 1930 praised the black two-seater they borrowed. This achieved a top speed of 78mph at

The 18/80 De Luxe Saloon is an imposing car that the period colour scheme shows off to best advantage.

Carbodies of Coventry built the coachwork for the 18/80 De Luxe Saloon.

Brooklands when not fully run-in and accelerated in third gear from 10mph to 60mph in less than 30 seconds. Run in the Land's End Trial the car performed well, climbing all the difficult hills with ease. The handling, performance and braking came in for praise and, in conclusion, the report said that they felt that the Mark II was a car that they would be happy to drive under any conditions.

With both versions of the 18/80 available in chassis form, the Mark I for £445 and the Mark II for £550, many were fitted with bodies by outside coachbuilders. The list of concerns willing to carry out this work was extensive, giving potential customers a wide variety of body styles from which to choose. However, the number of cars sold in chassis form was relatively small, 12 Mark I and 23 Mark II being the generally accepted totals. In all honesty, the standard range of cars offered by the MG Car Company would have satisfied most, with only those seeking drophead coupé coachwork needing to look elsewhere.

In the factory when it was new, the 18/80 Saloon built for artist Gordon Crosby with special running boards.

Carbodies of Coventry were the major contract suppliers of MG bodies at that time, their products being used for the standard 18/80s. However they also produced the body for the Mark II Folding Head Coupé De Luxe. This luxurious car was priced at £695 and records show that a few chassis were fitted with this coachwork. Hoyal coachbuilders of Weybridge were in deep financial trouble at the time when they built a couple of drophead foursome bodies for 18/80 Mark II chassis. A special body that survives to this day is the unique Carbodies two-seater fitted to a prototype chassis for the 1929 London Motor Show. This was removed after the show and subsequently placed on another chassis and exhibited at the Scottish Motor Show in 1930. Sold off the stand, the car spent the next forty years in Scotland and today remains in superb order.

London MG agents, University Motors, bought

The Mark II 18/80 built for Gordon Crosby looks particularly attractive in this colour scheme.

There is a reasonable amount of room in the luggage compartment and extra cases can be stowed on the opened lid.

a number of 18/80s in chassis form and most of these were fitted with drophead coupé coachwork. One, however, seemed to have received a saloon body of Weymann construction although it is not clear which coachbuilder was involved. It was probably similar to the close-coupled coupé offered by Jarvis of Wimbledon, a firm that by this time was contracting out some of the actual building work to Abbey Coachworks. Jarvis did supply bodies for at least two Mark IIs, with one of these listed as a coupé and the other a drophead coupé. 1930 advertisements give the price of the closed coupé as £695.

The Carlton Carriage Company of Waldo Road, Willesden, was involved in building bodies for

18/80 MGs do not just look good. The large six-cylinder engine gives them sufficient performance to enable them to cope well with modern traffic.

All the 18/80 saloons have comfortable and well-trimmed cabins.

many different models of MG. For the 18/80 they made an attractive drophead coupé body and at least one Mark I and two Mark IIs were fitted with these. Similar in conception to the Carbodies drophead coupé, it was rather more elegant. Some of the specially built one-offs were less attractive. Particularly odd was the Brainsby-built, two-door coupé fitted to AO 260. Registered FL 8943, the car was built for a Mrs Gough but its top-heavy appearance did the car no favours. Rather more attractive was the metal-panelled Mark II De luxe saloon fitted with special streamlined running boards for artist Gordon Crosby.

The Mark II was a splendid car and a ride in one today is an enjoyable experience. However,

The wider front axle and larger brake drums fitted to the Mark II versions of the 18/80, like this Carlton drophead coupé, give them a more purposeful appearance.

On the drophead coupé body built by Carlton Carriage Company it is easy to undo the top section of the hood, fold back the side rails above each door and stow the rolled fabric, to provide fresh air but also some protection from the elements.

This 18/80 Mark II carries a one-off body built by Carbodies and exhibited by them initially on a Mark I chassis. It was later fitted to this chassis for a Scottish Motor Show, where it was sold. It has survived in remarkably original condition.

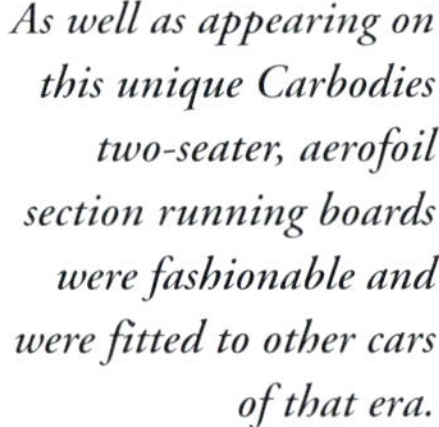

As well as appearing on this unique Carbodies two-seater, aerofoil section running boards were fashionable and were fitted to other cars of that era.

even as it arrived on the market cars of its type were rapidly going out of favour, with the combination of a depressed economic climate and the arrival of much cheaper MG models doing little to help sales. Although the cars remained in the price lists until as late as 1933, they sold in very small numbers, with some new cars still in dealers' showrooms as late as 1935. With the most expensive standard model in the range, the Mark II Saloon De Luxe, costing £699, this was hardly surprising.

Comfortable seating and a roomy cockpit make longer journeys pleasurable in the Carbodies 18/80 Mark II.

As with all 18/80s the interior of the Carlton Coupé is well appointed.

THE M-TYPE MIDGET

The despatch bay at Morris Garages' Leopold Street premises in Oxford, where some of the very earliest M-types await collection by owners or selling agents.

H.S. Linfield of The Autocar *used RX 6795 to take a Gold Medal in the 1930 MCC London-Edinburgh Trial.*

Much has been written about the importance of the M-type Midget in MG history. It is rightly said that the decision taken in 1928 by Cecil Kimber to build a small sports car based on the just-conceived Morris Minor was the first step in ensuring the survival of the marque. That decision may not have been taken by Kimber alone as at that time William Morris owned Morris Garages privately and played an active part in the running of the company. He had seen the huge impact on the market created by the Austin Seven and was probably keen to have a product from his specialist car company to rival the sporting versions of the successful Austin product.

Expensive sporting cars were, by and large, the playthings of the wealthy, and in the world depression that followed the Wall Street crash there were few willing to be seen spending a large sums on such a vehicle. Whoever it was who had the foresight to design and build a miniature sports car based on the chassis of the just-announced

At a very early meeting of the MG Car Club the preponderance of M-types is evident.

Morris Minor read the market well, as there is little doubt that had a more affordable alternative to the relatively expensive contemporary MG 18/80 not been available, then the marque would have faded into obscurity within a very few years.

Promoted by the slogan "a full-size car in miniature", the Austin Seven had been launched in 1923, and its design had virtually wiped out the opposition from the quirky and unreliable cyclecars that had previously provided budget motoring. Sports models had been available from 1924 and these were successful; the Brooklands Super Sports at £265 came with a certificated top speed of 75mph. Several outside firms also offered sporting coachwork for the lightweight chassis with its quarter-elliptic rear springing.

Morris, on the other hand, relied for most of the 1920s on variations of his successful Bullnose design, the smallest capacity engine of which was rated at 11.9hp. In an era when the road tax was calculated by bore size under the RAC system, the lack of a 7hp car to rival the Austin Seven was a disadvantage. When the acquisition in 1927 of the bankrupt Wolseley Motors by Morris gave him access to sufficient talent and capacity to design and build a small OHC power unit, this was the opportunity to produce a much-needed small car for the Morris range.

The Morris Minor appeared at the 1928 Motor Show in two forms: a fabric-covered, two-door four-seater saloon of lightweight construction, and a four-seater tourer. The saloon cost £135 and the open car £125. The idea of building an MG version was obviously there from early on and one of the two prototypes built shared the limelight with the Minor at that 1928 Motor Show, albeit without an engine installed. The second car was running and served as a demonstrator. The work on the chassis to convert it from a Morris to an MG followed a pattern established by Kimber for previous models. The springs were flattened, the steering column set at a lower angle, the gear lever re-shaped and the foot pedals altered. To set the whole car off, a smaller version of the MG radiator designed for the 18/80 headed a fabric-covered, two-seater body. Although an entirely new concept in small sporting cars, the Midget attracted a lot of attention at Olympia.

Most sports car owners in the early 1930s expected to have to do their own maintenance – indeed it was considered part of the fun.

This metal panelled M-type is on the late chassis number CM 2981, completed in June 1931 just before production ceased.

A publicity picture of the interior of the coupé. The rear seat does not provide much space for adults, but could be useful for a child or extra luggage.

In the event, it was not until March 1929 that a production line was established at the new MG factory at Edmund Road, Oxford. Even at that time, so popular was the new MG that there was insufficient room there for cars to be fully finished and the Leopold Street premises of Morris Garages were pressed into service for completing the work on the cars. At this stage the rolling chassis were towed from the Morris works at Cowley to Edmund Road for conversion to MG specification. Later, once production had moved to Abingdon, the entire assembly process was carried out within the MG works.

The earliest sales brochures produced to help sell the M-type described the new model as "The MG Midget Sports Mark I" and emphasised the virtues of the small engine, tax at only £8 per annum, petrol consumption of 40 to 50 miles per gallon, and proportionately low running costs. This leaflet listed the colours available as red or light blue fabric, with the bonnet, valances and wheels cellulosed to match and the wings painted black.

In the first season over 300 cars were built and sold, well up to expectations and about as many as could be assembled in the cramped conditions of the current premises. It must have been fairly time-consuming to collect Morris Minor chassis from the Cowley factory, bring them to Edmund Road to convert them to MG specification and fit

Many early owners of the M-type used their cars in competition and here one is taking part in the 1932 MCC Land's End Trial.

A factory publicity picture of an early coupé built on chassis CM 1116. This car was completed in March 1930 and finished in black, with green wheels and trim.

the bodies, and then take them to Leopold Street for finishing before returning them to Edmund Road for inspection and despatch to dealers. Things had to change.

Salvation arrived in the form of the move to Abingdon. This was accomplished early enough for the production of cars for the 1930 season to commence at the new factory. With the move came the opportunity to completely assemble the cars there and to make a number of alterations to the design of the Minor chassis and running gear. The standard MG system of Bowden cables, operating from a cross-shaft in conjunction with the hand-brake, replaced the Morris rod-and-cable brakes and transmission handbrake.

To take full advantage of their increased production facilities MG needed to sell as many cars as they could. More imaginative marketing included colour brochures illustrated with attractive paintings, and support for owners wishing to use their cars in motor sport. The first such event for the M-type came in the 1929 Land's End Trial, when four brand-new Midgets were amongst the 14 MGs entered. The Midgets did well, their drivers taking two Gold and two Silver Medals. A long association between MG Midgets and sporting trials had begun.

The 8/33 MG Midget Mark I Sportsman's Coupe.

Introduced for those who prefer closed car comfort allied to the wonderful liveliness and ease of control for which this car has already won fame. The coachwork (fitted with sunshine roof) is of the very highest procurable quality and, except for size, is definitely produced to rank with the most expensive cars built.

The 8/33 Midget Sportsman's Coupe . . . . £245.

The first outing for the Midgets on the track came with the Junior Car Club event at Brooklands in June 1929, where the drivers of all three Midgets entered achieved Gold Medals. Brooklands was also to be the scene for another notable M-type competition success the following year. Cecil Kimber had been approached by two enthusiasts

Like all the later Midgets, this attractive car has the helmet-shaped wings that provided more protection from road spray than the earlier cycle type.

of the M-type Midget who felt that the cars, given some modification, were capable of winning the team prize in the 1930 Double-Twelve-Hour Race at Brooklands. Modifications consisted of improving the power output of the 850cc engines by raising the compression ratio, polishing the cylinder

The MG Car Company often used the road outside the Barley Mow pub in publicity pictures, as it was not far from the factory. This is the Sportsman's Coupé.

As an Abingdon-built car this M-type has cable brakes all round and thus nothing protrudes through the louvres in the side valances.

The 850cc M-type engine has a single SU carburettor.

It is not surprising that the M-type was an immediate success, selling for the very reasonable price of £185. (Photo Dr Rachel Bolton-King).

heads, and fitting a camshaft with improved valve timing. Additionally, the bodies were modified by giving them cut-down doors, an undershield to reduce drag, and staggered bucket seats for driver and riding mechanic. Larger fuel tanks were fitted, the headlamps were re-positioned closer to the radiator, the exhaust systems were modified, and fold-down gauze racing windscreens replaced the standard V-screen. In the race the Midgets driven by Cecil Randall and F.M. "Freddie" Montgomery, W. Townend and R.R. Jackson, and G.J. Roberts and A.A. Pollard, took the Team Prize. Replicas of these were catalogued for sale to the general public at £245 and a total of 21 examples were built.

These competition cars were not the sole M-type variant produced by the factory as a closed coupé was also listed to satisfy those looking for a small sporting saloon car. MG had already built a number of saloons for their larger chassis and it was logical to produce a scaled-down version for their small sports car. The Midget Sportsman's Coupé was described in the sales literature as an occasional four, but really was no more than a two-seater with a minuscule rear bench seat. To lighten the interior of this attractive little car, a large sunshine roof with inset roof-lights was fitted. Well appointed and attractively trimmed, the diminutive coupé was popular, despite being considerably more expensive than the mechanically similar offerings from the parent Morris works.

In addition to the factory-built cars, some M-types were sold in chassis form to coachbuilders for fitting with bodies of differing designs. The most numerous of these were the Jarvis-bodied M-types; 36 were reputed to have been built. The Jarvis M-type initially had a fabric-covered body, and later a metal-panelled one, but both were attractive cars and in many ways more practical than the standard M-type. The body was roomier and the full-width windscreen offered more weather protection. MG main dealers University Motors offered a two-plus-two drophead coupé on the M-type chassis and this was built for them by Carlton Carriage Company.

The 8 33 MG Midget 2-Seater Sports Car.
The car that won the coveted Team Prize in the Brooklands Double-Twelve race. Speeds well in excess of 60 . . . . terrific acceleration. Holds the road in the most amazing manner. "The finest little 'big' car ever produced."
2-Seater Sports Car . . . . £185.

A new Double-Twelve M-type posed in the factory for a publicity picture.

A line of M-types prior to their success in the 1930 Double-Twelve-Hour Race at Brooklands.

The 8/33 M.G. Midget Sports Mark I

Chassis Specification

CHASSIS DIMENSIONS.

Number of cylinders—4.
Bore and stroke—57 mm. by 83 mm.
C.c. of cylinders—847.
Treasury rating—8.05 (tax £8).
Size of tyres—27 in. by 4 in.
Track—3 ft. 6 in.
Turning circle—34 ft.

Wheelbase—6 ft. 6 in.
Overall width—4 ft. 2 in.
Overall length—9 ft. 2¼ in.
Capacity of petrol tank—5 gals.
Ground clearance under rear axle—8½ in
Weight (2-seater)—10 cwt.

Engine.—8.05 h.p. Treasury rating (tax £8 per annum), 57 mm. by 83 mm. 847 c.c. Four cylinders cast *en bloc*. Exceptionally sturdy two-bearing crankshaft. Overhead valves operated through fingers by overhead camshaft carried on detachable cylinder head. Three-ring aluminium pistons with steel connecting rods.

Carburetter.—S.U. automatic piston type with hand mixture control on dash.

Lubrication.—ENGINE. Pressure throughout, by gear type pump. Oil is carried in a large aluminium sump with cooling fins having a capacity of one gallon.

CHASSIS. Tecalemit grease gun and the necessary connections at all chassis points. A semi-grouped system is used on Coupé models.

Cooling.—By thermo-syphon, chromium plated solid brass radiator.

Transmission.—Single dry-plate clutch and gearbox unit with engine. Three speeds forward and reverse gears, direct drive on top—central control: Top, 4.89—1; Second, 8.96—1; Bottom, 17—1; Reverse, 13.83—1.

At 1,000 r.p.m. speeds on the forward gears are approximately: Bottom, 4.7 m.p.h.; Second, 9.0 m.p.h; Top, 16.5 m.p.h. Engine is capable of over 4,000 r.p.m.

Drive taken to three-quarter floating spiral bevel rear axle by open propeller shaft which has a Hardy disc universal joint at each end.

Chassis Frame.—Exceptionally sturdy; tapered and upswept fore and aft with sturdy cross members which ensure rigidity.

Springs.—Long flat semi-elliptic springs fore and aft provide very low centre of gravity and excellent road holding. Hartford shock absorbers.

Steering.—Worm and wheel type, column adjustable for rake. 16 in. Bluemel celluloid-covered spring-spoked steering wheel.

Electrical.—Ignition by Lucas 6-volt coil and battery—starter motor of gear type—electric horn, large headlamps, side- and tail-lamps.

Brakes.—Foot brakes operate on all four wheels, single point adjustment for all brakes, also individual adjustment for each wheel. Hand brake (central lever) coupled independently to all four wheels.

Petrol.—Five-gallon tank carried in dash.

Instruments.—80 m.p.h. speedometer, oil gauge, ammeter and switches. Open model with rim lit instruments. Coupé model has a clock in addition to above and two neat dash lamps in place of concealed lighting.

Wheels.—Five wire wheels with 27 in. by 4 in. Dunlop balloon tyres.

Finish.—All bright parts are chromium plated.

The right is reserved to vary this specification without notice.

THE MOVE TO ABINGDON

The engine test area in the early 1930s.

The party held to mark the opening of the Abingdon factory.

The quest in 1929 to find a new site for MG production was a consequence of the launch at the 1928 London Motor Show of the first MG Midget, the Morris Minor based M-type. The earlier MGs had been built in comparatively small numbers and when, just two years previously, the company had moved to a new purpose-built factory at Edmund Road, Oxford, it had been designed with every modern convenience in the firm belief that it would serve them for many years. Had they continued to build the low-volume 14/40 and 18/80 models this would have been the case. Those cars were sent to outside coachbuilders for body fitting and, bearing in mind that in 1927 just 341 MGs were built and sold, the space at Edmund Road would have been adequate.

The immediate appeal of the new Midget meant that a large number of orders were taken, both at

One of the first Abingdon assembled M-type Midgets with part of the stores in the background. The sign top left reads Goods Inwards.

the motor show and as a result of later promotion in newspapers and magazines. A permanent solution to the shortage of space had to be found and the only answer was yet another move of premises. An intensive search of the locality led Kimber to the nearby market town of Abingdon. The leather industry had been established there since the early years of the 19th century and flourished and expanded, reaching a peak in the 1914-1918 war when the Pavlova Leather Company increased production to accommodate the huge demand for military coats, boots, belts, harnesses, etc. To cope they had enlarged the premises and built a new administration block. The declaration of peace in 1918 led to an inevitable fall-off in work and in consequence there was redundant factory space. The area alongside the Marcham Road remained unused for many years and in 1929 this site, together with the administration block in Cemetery Road, appealed to Cecil Kimber, who could see that there was sufficient space there to cope with any increases in production. Having approached

The main stores for the factory.

For its time, despite the lack of a moving assembly line, the factory was well equipped, and here brakes are being adjusted on an electric-powered rig.

Following a road test and rectification of any faults the cars were cleaned prior to going to owners or dealers.

Sir William Morris for permission, it was leased by Morris Garages for MG assembly.

The move to a new site was announced in the press in July 1929 when the local paper printed an article under the heading "New Industry for Abingdon". However, considerable work was needed before the new factory could be brought fully into use. There were a large number of brick-built vats that had been used in the leather tanning process and these had to be demolished, and large areas of concrete floor re-laid. It was also necessary to construct partitions for the stores, offices, etc., and it was September before all the car assembly work could be transferred from Oxford to Abingdon.

Although it took some time to set up the new production lines and transfer the necessary tools, equipment and spares to the renovated factory buildings, by January 1930 the company was sufficiently established for an inaugural luncheon to be held. The guest list included Sir William Morris, representatives of the motoring and motor sport world, plus the press. There were many speeches, including one from Sir William, who was fulsome in his praise of Cecil Kimber. In reply Cecil Kimber said that those who had toured the factory would appreciate the work involved in equipping the

Once full production was under way at the new factory, adjacent lines assembled 18/80 rolling chassis and complete M-type Midgets.

The dispatch bay at Abingdon must have looked an impressive sight.

production lines and went on to pay tribute to the wonderful support he had received from Sir William Morris.

With a larger factory and the degree of autonomy afforded by the separation from The Morris Garages, the business set out on what was to be the most exciting and innovative period of MG history. Production of the M-type Midget and the 18/80 took just part of the new premises and there was room for the competition shop, stores and other departments. For the Midget, assembly methods had been adapted to suit the new situation and a production line was established that saw the cars being put together in much the same way as was to be the case for all the cars built there over the next 50 years.

JARVIS OF WIMBLEDON

One of the longest established MG dealers in the Greater London area was Jarvis and Sons of Wimbledon, who are remembered now for the prominent part the company played in the MG story during the early 1930s. Like many others in the motor industry, the origins of the business were in the late 19th-century bicycle trade. By the early 1920s Jarvis had established a coachbuilding business operating from premises in the Wimbledon area and also a car dealership.

As coachbuilders Jarvis built up a reputation for making racing car bodies and also for the boat-tail designs fitted to a number of different chassis, like Aston Martin, Bentley, Darracq and Rolls-Royce. They were established in March 1921, and in 1926 and 1927 exhibited at the London Motor Show at Olympia. The business was involved in making bodywork for a number of notable racing cars, including the prototype 3-litre Bentley raced by Woolf Barnato at Brooklands and the Chrysler-Bluebird driven at that track by Sir Malcolm Campbell. At the lower end of the market, along with other coachbuilders, Jarvis offered sporting bodywork for the Austin Seven chassis. The company also tried marketing, without much success, a racing car powered by a JAP motorcycle engine that they proclaimed was the world's smallest racer. The first connection between the MG marque and the coachbuilding side of the Jarvis business seems to have been in 1927 when a flat-radiator 14/28 Super Sports chassis was fitted with one of their boat-tail bodies.

When in early 1929 Cecil Kimber was trying to establish a comprehensive dealer network he appointed Jarvis of Wimbledon as agents for the marque in the South-West London, North Surrey and Berkshire areas. Previously all the cars MG sold were supplied through Morris main agents, Stuart and Arden. As dealers for Morris and Wolseley production models, in addition to MG, the majority of their new car sales would have been for these less expensive vehicles. However, surviving records and a look through contemporary classified advertisements reveal that they managed to sell a few of the 18/80 and 18/80 Mark II MGs. Of these it is recorded that Mark I chassis 6606 was fitted with a Jarvis Sportsman's Coupé body and sold for £585. Mark II chassis AO439 had Jarvis drophead coupé coachwork and was sold in February 1931, registered PL6382. The standard range

DECEMBER, 1930 — MOTOR SPORT — 71

THE NEW JARVIS

MIDGET

Produced with the approval of the M.G. Car Co. to meet the demand for a "de luxe" body on this outstanding chassis. Specification includes leather upholstery, adjustable bucket seats, 3-piece screen and "One Man" hood with side screens.

Price ... £225 Complete

In 3 colour schemes.

Prompt delivery. Demonstration car available.

GET PARTICULARS TO-DAY FROM

OF WIMBLEDON

WHOLESALE AND RETAIL DISTRIBUTORS OF

For S.W. London, Northern Surrey and Berks.

Main Showrooms:
Victoria Crescent
Wimbledon
(opposite Wimbledon Station)
'Phone: Wim. 2526 (3 lines)
Telegrams: "Jarvis, Wimbledon."

Service Depot:
Grove Works
South Wimbledon
(opposite South Wimbledon Station)
'Phone: Wim. 4366 (2 lines)

Please mention MOTOR SPORT when corresponding with advertisers

An early Jarvis M-type with a fabric covered body.

of models on the 18/80 chassis in the MG Car Company catalogue did not include a drophead coupé, and a number of coachbuilders stepped in to plug this gap.

Jarvis as Morris agents had been selling the Cowley and Oxford models in reasonable numbers, but could not compete with Austin Seven dealers in the cheaper price range. However, when the Morris Minor and related M-type Midget appeared at the 1928 Motor Show, dealers like Jarvis must have sensed an opportunity to exploit a new market. After The MG Car Company moved from Oxford to Abingdon and there started to assemble Midget rolling chassis these were made available to coachbuilders. This presented Jarvis of Wimbledon with the opportunity to build and sell a much-improved version in time for the 1930 Olympia Motor Show. Press releases stated that The MG Car Company approved the Jarvis Midget to meet a demand for improved bodywork. The Jarvis specification included leather upholstery for the bucket seats, a three-piece windscreen and a hood that could be easily raised and lowered.

The same style of Jarvis bodywork used on the Midget was also fitted to some Morris Minor chassis, at lower cost. Once the MG Car Company introduced their new chassis for the four-cylinder D-type Midget and the F-type Magna, Jarvis versions of these were on offer. Two D-type Midgets are known to have received the Jarvis treatment and more than 20 F-types. Examples of both models survive.

The part that Jarvis played in the MG story spreads beyond selling cars and building special versions. Managing Director James Palmes was keen on motor sport and was thinking about trying to take the 750cc speed records from Austin in an MG Midget. At Cambridge he had shared rooms with George Eyston, who to tackle the same records was proposing fitting a reduced-capacity Riley engine in a racing car he already owned. They decided to combine their efforts and Eyston realised they would have a better chance of success if they could involve the MG Car Company in their venture.

Palmes, Eyston and Ernest Eldridge, who had worked with Eyston on previous record attempts, went to see Cecil Kimber at Abingdon to discuss the project. There they discovered that the MG design team were already working on a completely new chassis better suited for a record car than the standard M-type, and they were offered this for their car. As the ordinary Midget engine had a capacity of 847cc it was necessary to reduce this to no more than 750cc. At the instigation of Palmes, a special crankshaft was made to shorten the stroke from 83 to 81mm, while the cylinder bores were fitted with liners and reduced from 57 to 54mm. The volume of the modified engine was 743cc.

The Jarvis M-type had a more conventional windscreen than the standard model.

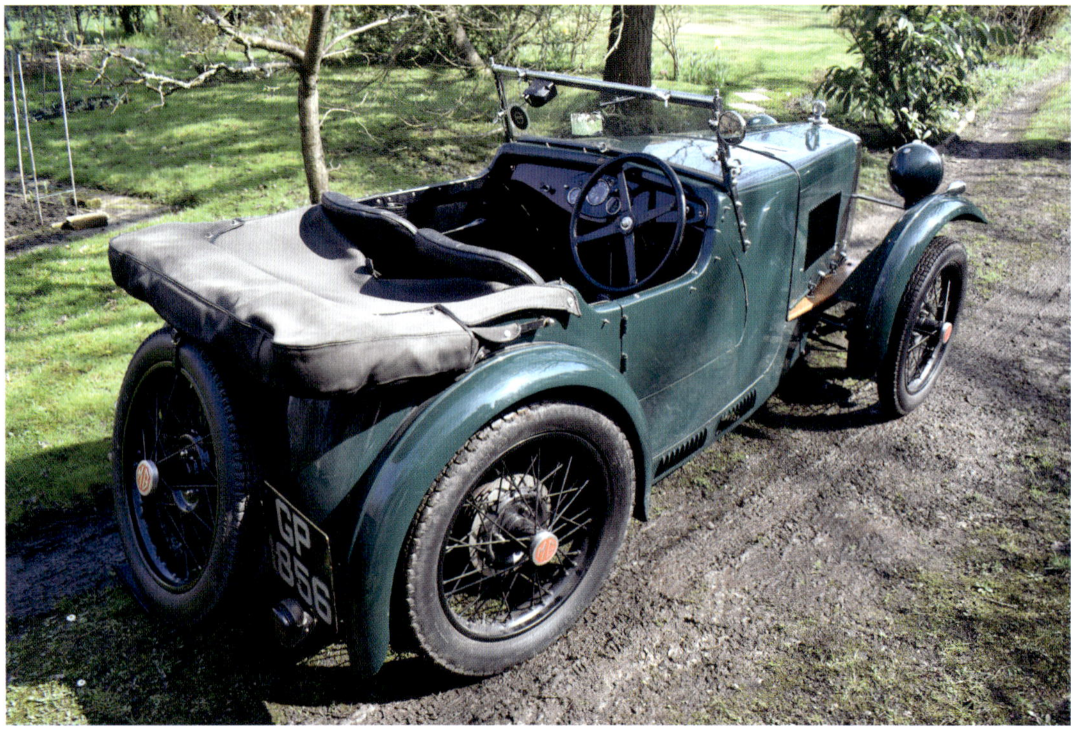

A more spacious cockpit and a better hood were some of the features of the Jarvis M-type.

MG had already produced and tested the rolling chassis fitted with the modified engine, and the Jarvis coachworks built a neat two-seater body with the passenger seat removed and a faired headrest behind the driver's seat. A road test with Eyston at the wheel saw the car managing to reach an estimated 87mph, just about enough to take the record from the supercharged Austin. After this the engine was stripped, and to increase the compression ratio offset little-end bushes were fitted to raise the pistons in the bores. At Montlhéry on December 30th 1930 new records for the 50 and 100 kilometres flying start and 50 miles flying start were set at speeds of around 87mph. It was obvious that this was the limit for the unsupercharged unit so the engine went back to the factory for attention.

On 9th February 1930, the now supercharged EX120 took the five kilometres and 10-mile flying start records at speeds of 97.07mph and 96.91mph, just short of the target of 100mph. After this, Cecil Cousins and Gordon Phillips were despatched from Abingdon to assist. They fashioned a makeshift cowl for the radiator and ensured that to prevent icing in the cold conditions only air warmed by the radiator was fed to the carburettor. On February 16th 1931 records for the five and 10 kilometres and five- and 10-mile distances were all raised to over 100mph. Both the MG Car Company and Jarvis of Wimbledon could celebrate. At the end of 1933 George Eyston became a director of Jarvis and he often featured in their advertisements.

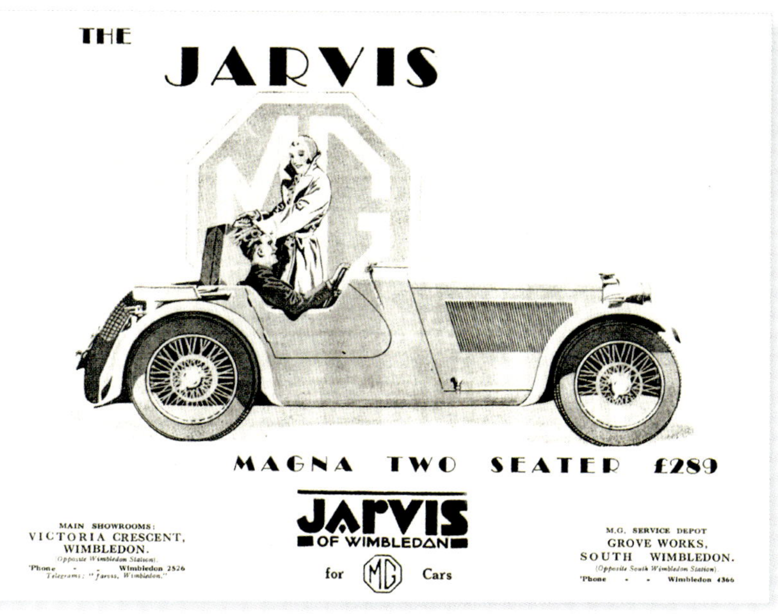

Advert for the F-type Magna with Jarvis body.

EX120 at rest on the track at Brooklands in March 1931 during mile and kilometre record attempts. Cecil Cousins in hat stands alongside, with Reg Jackson working the plug spanner and George Eyston at the wheel.

EX120 in its original form before a cowl was fitted to the radiator and prior to the car being supercharged.

GEORGE EYSTON OBE, MC, LEGION D'HONNEUR

George Eyston OBE, MC, Légion d'Honneur.

If anyone is deserving of a place in this account then it must be George Edward Thomas Eyston. By 1930, when he first became associated with the MG marque, he was already a well-known racing driver, but his part in both the racing and record-breaking efforts of The MG Car Company were crucial to the success later achieved. He was to be actively involved with MG from 1930 until his death in 1979, in the latter years supporting in every way the MG Car Club as its president.

A direct descendant of Sir Thomas More, George was born into a prominent Roman Catholic family at Bampton, Oxfordshire, on 28 June 1897 and was the elder of two sons. He was educated at Stonyhurst College and read engineering at Trinity College, Cambridge, but like many of his generation the First World War interrupted this process. Joining up, he was commissioned as second lieutenant in the 3rd Battalion, Dorset regiment, but in view of his mathematical and engineering skills was transferred to the Royal Artillery, where these talents were of more use. Throughout the war he was to serve on the front line in France and was wounded in April 1917 at the battle of Arras. He was promoted to the rank of staff captain, his bravery earned him the Military Medal and he was twice mentioned in dispatches.

When the armistice was declared in 1918 he returned to Cambridge to resume his engineering studies. The competitive side of his nature that later made him a formidable racing driver was channelled into his sport of rowing, in which he became captain of the Trinity boat club and was the reserve to the Cambridge rowing crew that won the 1919 international eights in Paris. After leaving University in 1921 George decided to return to France to study the language. He stayed with a French family at a château near Le Mans. He describes in his book *Flat Out*, published in 1933, how he toured the area in his GN light car visiting the ancient châteaux and suffering numerous punctures on the unsurfaced roads.

One day, with two passengers aboard, he was travelling along a quiet road when suddenly the roar of a low-slung racing car speeding past shattered the peace. American driver Ralph de Palma was testing a French Ballot racing car up and down that stretch of road prior to the French Grand Prix at Le Mans, as George discovered when he spoke to him and his mechanics. Enthralled by the sight and sound of the car travelling at speeds of up to 100mph, George read what he could in the local papers of the forthcoming race. He went on to watch both the practice session and the actual race, won by a Duesenberg, and was so taken by the experience that he decided that he must become involved.

Returning home, he saw an old Sunbeam grand prix car for sale at a local dealer's and bought it. Although outdated and not in the best of health, this car nevertheless was capable of reaching 80-90mph on a good day, even if its open exhaust attracted the unwelcome attention of the local police. At the end of 1922, to gain more experience of racing cars, he bought and stripped down to recondition a 4½-litre Vauxhall said to be capable of 110mph. Once restored, the car was taken to Brooklands, but George was unable to beat the handicap allotted to him.

Although he didn't win anything with his Vauxhall, he was gaining experience and also made contact with Lionel Martin, who had built the 1½-litre Aston Martin that raced in the 1922 200-mile race at Brooklands. Martin sold George the car entered in that race, plus another that was set up for road racing. At the 1923 Brooklands Whitsun meeting George won two races and was placed second in two others. With these two cars he went on to compete in a variety of events, sprints, hill-climbs, road racing, races on sand and at Brooklands, gaining experience all the time. He was to continue for the rest of the 1920s to drive many marques of racing car, including Bugatti (in which he won the 1926 Boulogne Grand Prix), Monza Alfa Romeo, Maserati, Bentley and Riley. He also briefly took up racing a speedboat fitted with the Aston Martin engine from his car before returning to his first love, cars. But we are concerned here with the link to MG that began when he became the first to pass the 100mph mark in a 750cc car.

His efforts with EX120 have been previously mentioned. However, during a final slowing down lap after setting records at over 100mph, EX120 caught fire and George was seriously burned and the car destroyed. Even while the old car had been enjoying success, work had been proceeding on a new one built with the object of having the minimum amount of wind resistance. To achieve this George Eyston needed to be seated as low down as possible, so the chassis for EX127 received a rear axle that placed the differential unit tight up against the left-hand rear wheel, with the engine, gearbox and prop-shaft at a seven-degree angle, allowing the driver to sit alongside the transmission.

The new car was taken to Montlhéry at the time of the last run of EX120 and tested after that car was damaged. However, it was found that EX127 overheated badly. Any serious running was out of the question and the car went back to Abingdon. For its first proper outing Ernest Eldridge took the wheel as George was still recovering from his burns. The five kilometres record was raised to 110mph before radiator damage caused the session to be abandoned. Back at the factory a new radiator and revised supercharger drive were installed, and by the end of December George Eyston had recovered enough to be able to take the wheel during a session at Montlhéry when the shorter distance records were raised to over 114mph.

George Eyston with EX120, the first MG record car, and the first 750cc car to exceed 100mph.

Kimber was keen for an MG to be the first 750cc car to reach 120mph. For this to count as an international record it could not be undertaken at the Paris track as it did not have the necessary approval. It was therefore decided to make an attempt at Pendine Sands, a site that had been used by other record breakers. The car performed well and hand timing showed it had reached 126mph. However, the official timing equipment ran out of ink and the speed was not recorded. By the time they were ready to make a further attempt conditions had worsened and puddles were appearing on the sand causing extra drag that slowed the car appreciably. Nevertheless, the records for the flying start kilometre and mile were raised to just over 118mph, but not the 120mph they needed.

After the disappointment over the attempt to reach 120mph on British soil the car had received

MG CIGARETTE LIGHTERS

Although no longer fashionable, in the 1930s when smoking was the usual practice both at home and at work, cigarette lighters and cigarette cases were produced in vast numbers and in many forms. Most interesting to MG memorabilia collectors are those produced for sale to MG dealers and customers. The lighters produced as models of EX127, the Magic Midget record-breaking car that set a number of new class speed records in the hands of George Eyston, Bert Denly and Bobby Kohlrausch, are gems. Made by Sanders & Mackenzie of Birmingham, they were available in silver and chrome on brass. There was also a version in chromium plate without the lighter and one made in Enturn Pewter by the same company. The lighter fuel was stored in a tank in the tail with the filler underneath, and lifting the flap in the cockpit area gave access to the flame, which was ignited by pressing a button on the side of the car. At least one example of the pewter version was mounted on a plinth and used as a trophy in motoring competitions. In a picture of Cecil Kimber in his office at the Abingdon factory one of the lighters can be seen on the desk in front of him. Probably produced in larger numbers was the charming lighter modelled on the first MG Midget, the M-type. Made and marketed by E. Deguingand and Son of 48 London Wall, London EC3, the lighter cost 45 shillings, £2.25 in new money. Made mainly of brass and chrome plated, there were two different styles of lighter mechanisms. With the first, pressing the steering wheel opened the bonnet to reveal the lit flame. With the later and more common version illustrated here, pulling back a lever in the cockpit operated the flint mechanism and ignited the flame. Fuel was again stored in a tank under the tail section. In addition to the plated models, at least one was finished in red paint with black wings.

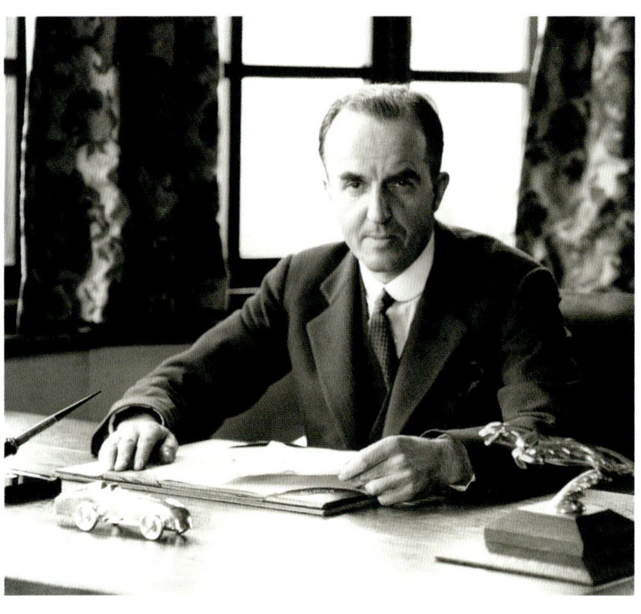

Cecil Kimber with a silver Magic Midget lighter on the desk in front of him in his Abingdon office.

The advertisement for the lighters was carried in the MG house magazine sent out to owners, club members and dealers.

The chrome on brass version of the Magic Midget cigarette lighter. The flame was housed under a flap on top of the car and ignited by pressing a button on the side.

The lighter mechanism on this version is housed in the cockpit and was operated by pulling back the "gear lever".

a thorough overhaul. The engine was rebuilt using a cross-flow cylinder head and the cockpit was altered so as to totally enclose the driver beneath an aircraft-style canopy. These alterations proved a step too far and George Eyston found driving the car very claustrophobic, so part of the canopy was cut away to improve the air circulation. The result of these efforts was a list of records for EX127 that included, on the first day, three at speeds in excess of 120mph. Long-distance runs the following day saw EX127 take the three-hour record at 94.60mph, the six-hour record at 92.80mph and the twelve-hour at 86.67mph. Bert Denly and George Eyston shared the driving and they also took a number of other distance records. There followed further records with the car before Cecil Kimber sold it in 1934 to the German driver Bobbie Kohlrausch, an act that upset George.

In addition to the MG record attempts, George had also been closely involved driving various MG racing cars – C-types, K3s, NEs and R-types – and managing teams of these cars, even one composed of six ladies who were entered in the 1935 Le Mans driving P-type Midgets. He enjoyed a lot of success, including in the 1933 Mille Miglia when the K3s took the team prize and led their class in the final results.

Following his triumph with the MGs in establishing 750cc records for long and short distances, George realized that world records were also within his grasp, and in 1932 he decided to attack the world hour record using an 8-litre Panhard et Levassor. This old car was by no means the ideal vehicle for the purpose but even after a tyre burst Eyston succeeded in averaging 130.73mph for the hour; tyres of the day were an ever-present hazard in record attempts. In another run in 1934 at the wheel of the Panhard he managed to set the hour record at 133.21mph. He achieved many other records in a great variety of marques, including Riley, Hotchkiss and Delage, and in diesel-powered cars that he designed and built himself. In fact he held more records than any driver before him. One car was Speed of the Wind, powered by a V-12 Rolls-Royce Kestrel aero-engine. In July 1936 Eyston drove it at 162mph to take the world hour record. This success led to him building Thunderbolt, with two Rolls aero-engines totalling 56-litres. In 1937 he set a new world land speed record at 312mph, later raised in 1938 to 345.5mph and again later the same year to 357.5mph.

There is no doubt the George was an accomplished engineer and his own company, Powerplus Limited, designed and manufactured the Powerplus vane-type supercharger. He was also a director of a number of other engineering companies. During the Second World War he was appointed a regional controller for the Ministry of Production. After the war he became a director of Castrol and in 1950 even found the time to return to Cambridge to read geology. He was also a qualified pilot and used an aircraft for both business and pleasure. He continued to fly when he was in his seventies. After the war and the death of Kimber, George resumed his association with the marque and assisted with the record-breaking efforts in America.

The cockpit of the second MG record car EX127 was a tight squeeze for someone of the stature of George Eyston.

EX135 was built around a modified K3 chassis and supplied to George Eyston with two bodies, one for track work and one for record attempts.

THE C-TYPE MIDGET

This superb overhead view of a newly built C-type in the factory exhibits the high standard of preparation achieved with all racing cars constructed at Abingdon. This was possibly the red-painted car built for Ron Horton.

Although the first Midget, the M-type, proved a hit with the buying public and a popular choice for those looking for a car to use in inexpensive club competition, in major track events its chassis design and engine power output were not up to the task of beating the opposition in their class. However, as we have seen, a measure of success came in the 1930 Double-Twelve-Hour Race at Brooklands where some suitably modified Midgets took the team prize. In spite of this class victory, it was realised that a new chassis was really required if the MG Midget was to be developed into a better car for both road and track. It was also important to address the situation that placed the 847cc MG in a different racing class from its natural rival, the 750cc sports model Austin Seven. The MG had inherited from the parent Morris Minor a short wheelbase and high centre of gravity and to address this a new chassis frame was designed that was to form the basis of all MG sports cars until the TD was announced in 1949.

Kimber used the publicity achieved by the record attempts with EX120 to announce in March 1931 that a new 750cc racing car was to be made available to the public, the MG Midget Mk II Montlhéry Model that is now better known as the C-type. For a time the M-type continued in production and was joined in September 1931 by another Midget, the D-type. This used the new chassis but was only available as a four-seater open tourer or a Salonette. The C-type was given a wheelbase of 6ft 9ins, just three inches more than the M-type, but crucially the chassis sat closer to the road, with the side rails running under the rear axle. The engine used was a short-stroke version of the M-type unit with a considerable number of modifications, and this was mated to a new four-speed gearbox. The initial cars were unsupercharged and their power output was

Two of the Earl of March team cars in the pits at Brooklands during practice for the 1931 Double-Twelve race. Car 60 was to take first place overall.

about 37bhp. Given supercharging at moderate boost this was raised to 45bhp and, when the factory produced a revised cylinder head with the inlet and exhaust ports on opposite sides, the improved gas flow raised power to 44bhp unsupercharged and 53bhp in blown form.

The production C-type had an ash-framed body incorporating a pointed tail that concealing the spare wheel, much like the arrangement on the M-type. However, the C-type also had a fuel tank fitted within the tail section rather than on the scuttle, as was the case with the earlier model. Ahead of the driver and passenger prominent twin humps in the scuttle introduced a style that was to be carried over in MG sports car design until the introduction of the MGA in 1955. Copying a feature found to have improved the aerodynamics of EX120, a shaped cowl enclosed the radiator. Most

The Hon. Mrs Chetwynd at the wheel of Ronnie Horton's brand new C-type. The red-painted car did not keep the standard body for long.

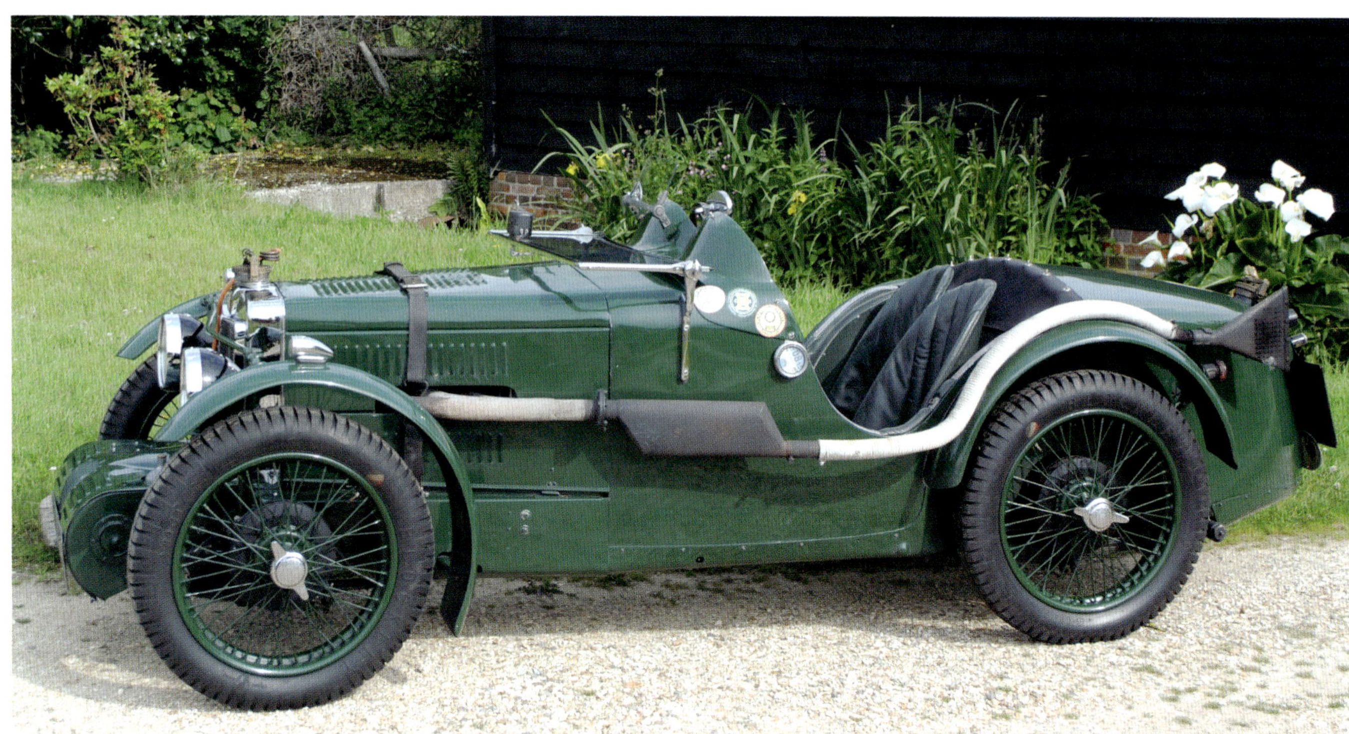

Although some C-types were purchased primarily for use on the road, rather than the track, there were few creature comforts, such as doors. The outside exhaust pipe conforms to then current regulations to race at Brooklands.

competitors later discarded these as they found that in warmer weather they caused overheating. Because of its competition pedigree, the C-type could be fitted with either the mesh screen for racing, or a glazed screen for touring. The company brochure for the model lists a number of extras, including a speedometer for use on the road, but ordering the car in anything other than the standard British Racing Green incurred an additional charge. However, the overall appearance of the C-type in

The C-type is beautifully proportioned and the prominent scuttle humps were designed to deflect the airflow over the cockpit The fuel tank is in the tail section of the body. Under the lid there is also space for the spare wheel and a small amount of luggage.

The 750cc power unit fitted to C0272 retains a cylinder head with the inlet from the supercharger and the exhaust on the same side, as the car was equipped from new. The bulkhead between the engine and cockpit is the one fitted to the car when built and carries the oil tank.

The dashboard is the 1931 original and has an impressive array of instruments. The PUSH OFF sign is needed to comply with current competition regulations.

C0272 today looks as it would have done in late 1931, after the supercharger was fitted. Almost all the bodywork, including the wings, is original. The bonnet panels have been replaced, but the damaged originals are retained in storage.

any colour was particularly pleasing; a real racing car in miniature.

Following the success of the M-type team in the 1930 Double-Twelve, the MG Car Company wanted a repeat the following year, so the debut for the initial batch of cars was to be the 1931 Brooklands race. To meet the deadline the Abingdon factory had to work at full stretch to ready the cars. Fourteen C-types were entered and all were immaculately turned out. The result was a triumph for the Abingdon cars, witnessed by almost all the employees at the factory, who had travelled by bus as a group to Surrey to cheer for their team. The car driven by The Earl of March and C.S. Staniland was placed first overall and the MGs took the team prize and the first five places in the race. The cars didn't have an entirely untroubled run as a number suffered failed valve springs, thought to be caused by faulty manufacture, and other troubles inevitable when a new model is subjected to such a severe test.

In the Double-Twelve the cars ran unsupercharged but the factory offered the option of having a Number 7 Powerplus supercharger fitted once the car had been purchased. All the cars were initially fitted with cylinder heads to the original Wolseley design that placed the inlet and exhaust manifolds on the same side, but when the more efficient cross-flow heads arrived in 1932 to improve power output the majority of cars being actively campaigned were converted. Another alteration adopted for some cars early in their racing career was to fit a lighter body. The enclosed tail section was replaced with a slab petrol tank and spare wheel mounting, a style adopted for the production sports cars with the arrival in 1932 of the J2 model.

With a total production run of 44cars, the C-type was the most numerous of the purpose-built MG racing models and in terms of race results was probably the most successful. The list of owners and drivers reads like a *Who's Who* of the racing world involving many of the most successful British competitors of the early 1930s.

MG AND THE ARDS TOURIST TROPHY RACES

In the 1931 Tourist Trophy Race the cars were started in groups and here the 750cc Austins and MGs Montlhéry Midgets leave the line.

A triumphant Norman Black after his victory in the 1931 TT. MGs had won in their first outing at the Ards circuit. Pushing the car are Cecil Kimber and on the right Cecil Cousins.

The series of Tourist Trophy Races that were to become associated with MG started when the event was run on the Ards circuit, near Belfast in Northern Island. The circuit was situated largely in the open countryside that lay outside the boundaries of the towns of Belfast, Newtownards and Comber. The start of the 13.6-mile course was on the then narrow road between Dundonald and Newtownards, and here there was a grandstand for those spectators prepared to pay to watch a spectacle that could be viewed free from other vantage points around the long course.

Soon after leaving the start line, cars had to negotiate the acute left-hand Quarry Corner before starting the climb, rounding a series of bends, to the summit of Bradshaw's Brae. The course entered the town of Newtownards by passing under a railway bridge and down the main Regent Street. Drivers were then faced with a sharp right-hand turn in

At the Abingdon factory prior to the 1932 race, Cyril Paul is in the car, with "Goldie" Gardner and Eddie Hall.

the town centre, opposite the imposing Town Hall building. After crossing the market square, competitors took the Comber Road and raced the four miles to the small town on a highway that would now be seen as little more than a good B road. They entered the town after negotiating a level crossing over the railway track where the nearby station area afforded a good view of the proceedings.

In Comber, with its narrow streets and unyielding walls of buildings for the drivers to avoid, there was another tight right-hand bend where the spectators crowded to get a good view of the cars as they slowed for the corner. The road to Dundonald had many twists and turns to trap the unwary and once the town centre was reached there was an acute hairpin bend on the approach to the wider road taken by the course on its way back to the start/finish line.

With road racing banned on the British mainland by that time, the Ards Tourist Trophy was popular with visitors from home and also Europe. Crowds were estimated to exceed half-a-million and steamers were specially chartered to transport people to the island from ports in England and Scotland. Many spent the night before the race out in the open, the better-prepared having equipped themselves with camping gear. The excitement of those road races is now a thing of the past, although some of the same sort of atmosphere can be found at the Isle of Man TT races for motorcycles.

The first year of MG involvement in the TT was 1931 and was to prove a triumph for the fast-

The start of the 1932 race for the 750cc cars. 29 is driven by Donald Barnes, 30 by Stanley Barnes, 31 by Cyril Paul, 34 by Eddie Hall, 33 by Stanley Hailwood, 27 by Norman Black, and 28 by Stanley Crabtree.

developing racing cars produced at Abingdon. No less than 13 C-type Midgets appeared in the entry list, all but two running supercharged. However, one of these failed to start. Ranged against them in the 501-750cc class were the experienced Austin team, who fielded four supercharged cars in the continuing battle with MG for honours. The handicap system in use that year saw the smaller-capacity cars starting with credit laps and, in some cases, also a time advantage. In the case of the MGs the supercharged cars had four laps less to cover than the cars on scratch and the unblown cars five laps. The system was seen to favour the smaller cars and only one 7-litre Mercedes entered.

The race started at 10.30 but the handicap system saw none of the excitement of a massed start as cars left the grid at predetermined intervals. However, the 750cc cars left together, and for them at least their position was fairly clear to spectators, who had only to remember the few unsupercharged cars with a lap advantage when working out their overall running order. The Midgets made a good start and by the end of an hour's racing had already established their superiority on handicap. Eddie Hall was in first place, Stan Crabtree in second and Hugh "Hammy" Hamilton in fourth. Only the hard-charging Sir Henry Birkin, running third in his Alfa-Romeo, was spoiling the total domination of the event by the small MGs.

Crabtree's C-type then broke the class lap record at a speed of 69.29mph and led Hall for overall honours. Bearing in mind the twisty nature of the circuit the record speed was remarkable for a 750cc car and shows just how hard-driven were the cars during this long race. Bearing this in mind, it is hardly surprising that some of the MGs ran into difficulties – Dan Higgin's car broke a valve spring and retired, Hall had engine failure – and this allowed Birkin to take second spot on handicap. By the end of the second hour of racing the MGs appeared to be losing out to the larger-capacity cars and first and third places were now in the hands of the Alfa-Romeo team.

Racing, however, is a fickle sport and an excursion into a sandbank saw Birkin lose a lot of time. Following three hours of hard racing MGs were again in the first three places, the running order being Crabtree, Hamilton and Norman Black. In the excitement Crabtree then overdid things at the right-angle turn in Comber and hit the sand, damaging a wing and necessitating a call at the pits for running repairs. The lead now passed to Norman Black and he was just able to hold off a late challenge from Borzacchini's 1750cc Alfa-Romeo to take first place in the race. Having lost time in the pits, Crabtree had to settle for third place. MGs also took seventh, 10th and 16th places and Norman Black was also awarded first place in class. The MG contingent was happy to celebrate their win in this high-profile event and there was little doubt that they would return in force the following year to try for a repeat performance.

The regulations for the TT were revised for 1932 and seemed to favour the 750cc MGs rather less than had been the case the previous year. Nevertheless, ten MGs were entered, including cars for the 1931 winner Norman Black, "Goldie" Gardner, Eddie Hall, Cyril Paul and "Hammy" Hamilton.

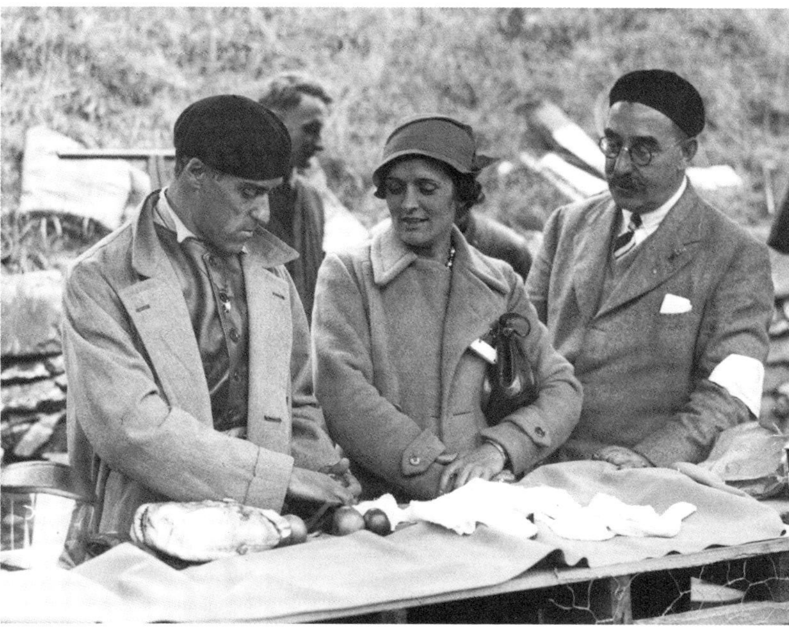

Tazio Nuvolari at the pit counter prior to the 1933 race that he won so convincingly.

Nuvolari's winning K3 at speed.

For much of the race the J4 driven by Hamilton was leading the Nuvolari K3. A seven-minute pit stop spoiled his chances of a win.

Once again C-type Montlhéry Midgets were the order of the day. That year things did not go well for MGs right from the first practice session. Although Eddie Hall and Cyril Paul posted good times, it was Hamilton who was fastest, perhaps too fast. He lost control of his car on a fast, bumpy corner and crashed into the garden of a house. Both Hamilton and his passenger, the Marquis de Belleroche, were badly hurt and had to be taken to a local hospital.

With Hamilton and his MG firmly out of the running, Stanley Barnes was nominated to take over his position in the team for the race, but driving another car. However, he too was fated not to finish the event, having to retire following a collision with the Talbot driven by Brian Lewis. One of the other stars of the MG team, "Goldie" Gardner, fared even worse. Whilst trying to overtake on a difficult part of this twisting circuit, he lost control of his car, which overturned, throwing him and his mechanic into the road. He sustained a very serious leg injury, broken ribs and much bruising. The damage to his leg was to cause him pain for the rest of his life.

Mechanical problems also took their toll. Cyril Paul's MG suffered big-end failure, Norman Black's car lost the oil in the rear axle, Stan Crabtree's had a punctured fuel float and Stan Hailwood's a burnt-out valve. Given all the troubles, MGs were lucky to figure at all in the results. However, Eddie Hall, an experienced and consistently fast driver, took third place at an average speed of 69.93mph. A privately entered unsupercharged MG, driven non-stop by John Low, was placed 10th. Battling with the handicappers, competitors and misfortune had meant no repetition of the previous year's victory. But there was always next year.

The 1933 race was to see one of the finest ever drives in an MG, and also a race lost in the pits by the driver most likely to have taken the chequered flag. Rule changes again played their part and the newly introduced six-cylinder K3 Magnettes looked to have less of a chance of overall victory than a car from the 750cc class. Under the 1933 rules the K3 was given a target average speed of 77.93mph, which was actually faster than the then current class lap record. However, neither the team nor the handicappers had made sufficient allowance for the extraordinary qualities of the driver chosen to lead the K3 challenge.

Tazio Nuvolari, the winner of the Mille Miglia a few months earlier, was probably the best racing driver of his era. From the start of the race he drove like a man possessed, breaking the lap record time and again at speeds over four miles an hour faster than similarly-sized cars had done the previous year. He beat his handicap by 0.72mph and won the race. His main rival for honours was the Irishman, Hammy Hamilton, in one of the more favourably handicapped 750cc Midgets. However, a mandatory pit stop, where one wheel was replaced by the spare taken off the rear of the car that then had to be replaced by another from the pit counter, plus trouble with jacks and a small fuel fire, wasted too much time. Nevertheless, it was mainly the brilliant drive by Nuvolari that sealed the fate of the local driver in the Midget.

The Royal Automobile Club, who still ran

Tazio Nuvolari and Alec Hounslow celebrate their victory.

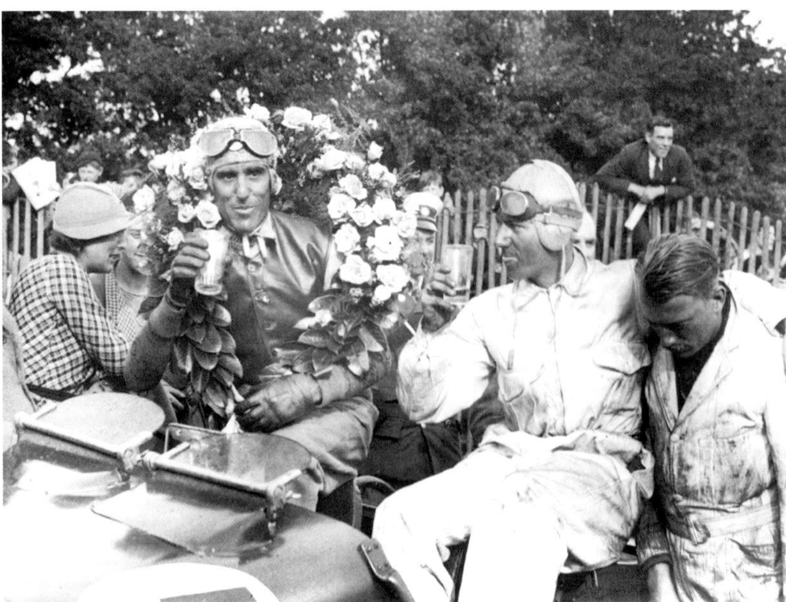

the Tourist Trophy Race, decided for the 1934 race that they would ban superchargers. They were concerned that the cars being entered were getting to be out-and-out racers, rather than the tourers previously envisaged. This meant that the factory could no longer rely on the supercharged K3 Magnette that had won the 1933 race so convincingly. Cecil Kimber was anxious to enter competitive cars and an unsupercharged K3 was considered unsuitable. The then current six-cylinder model was the N-type Magnette and it was decided to develop a new competition car based on this chassis. Lightweight aluminium-clad two-seater bodies designed to comply with the regulations were fitted to the N chassis, and the 1271cc engine was tuned to increase the power output to 74bhp. The extra power was transmitted by a two-plate clutch through a standard gearbox with different ratios.

If the change in the regulations had been designed to rob MGs of the chance of another TT victory then it failed. After a splendid drive, the NE Magnette in the hands of ex-motorcycle racer Charlie Dodson won the event. Four of the NE Magnettes went out with various mechanical problems and the sixth car finished in a lowly 14th place. Not, perhaps, the triumph the team had hoped for, but at least MG had won yet again and would be likely to return to Ards the following year.

1935 was the year when the disposal by Lord Nuffield of his personal ownership of The MG Car Company saw factory participation in motor racing come to an end. However, there were still four MGs entered in the Tourist Trophy: three of the NE Magnettes had gone to the Evans family and were racing under the Bellevue Garage banner, wearing their blue colour scheme. The drivers were Kenneth and Denis Evans and Dick Seaman. The fourth NE Magnette, painted red, was in the hands of Belfast driver W.R. "Bobby" Baird. The Bellevue Garage cars experimented in practice with a radio communication system between the pits and cars, but this was less than successful and was not used during the race itself.

Although the NE Magnette had won the previous year, the gear ratios chosen for the cars were less than ideal and for the 1935 race a lower axle ratio was used. Nevertheless, with the average speed set by the organisers for the 1200cc to 1300cc cars increased from 74.62mph to 75.19mph, plus increased competition from the Riley camp, things were never going to be easy for the MG drivers. It was to be Riley's year and the race fell to the experienced hands of Freddie Dixon in his long-tailed 1496cc car. The MGs did not fare well. Dick Seaman drove his car into tenth place; local driver Bobby Baird was twelfth and Kenneth Evans thirteenth. Denis Evans retired after six laps.

1936 was to see the last Tourist Trophy Race run on the Ards circuit, but MGs were not amongst the field of thirty-one cars entered, and Rileys again dominated the entry list.

George Eyston with one of the team of NE Magnettes entered in the 1934 Tourist Trophy Race.

Champagne for Dodson after his 1934 victory.

THE D-TYPE MIDGET AND F-TYPE MAGNA

The prototype for the long-chassis Midget D-type tourer, fitted with M-type axles and bolt-on wire wheels.

The process of developing the entirely new chassis first used in EX120 and the C-type Montlhéry Midgets illustrates just how few resources Cecil Kimber had at his disposal and how the small team at Abingdon had to look elsewhere for inspiration. There survives in the archives an interesting set of MG factory pictures taken in 1930 of a stripped-down little-known French sports car, the 1100cc Rally. The chassis for this used channel-section side frames that curved over the front axle but were otherwise straight and ran under the rear axle. This allowed the frame to be set low, increasing stability. A combination of square-section and tubular cross-members was used to complete the frame. The MG design followed this general arrangement, but used only tubular cross-members, these being fitted into cast and machined brackets bolted to the sides. An innovation for the MG was the use of sliding trunnions to secure the rear ends of the springs: the front pair were carried in housings bolted to the frame and at the back the springs ran in bronze bearings carried within the rear cross-tube.

The company, and particularly those at Abingdon involved with developing new models, would have had their minds focused on having cars ready to announce prior to the annual London Motor Show. This event was then the main shop window for the British motor industry, vital for obtaining newspaper and magazine publicity and for assessing the likely demand for cars to be built during the following year. Car sales were very seasonal and this meant that often assembly line workers would be laid off in the slack months. Factory wages were, however, higher than for other manual jobs in the Abingdon area, such as in agriculture, so these layoffs were tolerated.

Not all customers came to the factory by the regular route and a report in *The Autocar* for 10 October 1930 recounts how the works boiler had to be fired up so that the smoke from the chimney stack indicated the wind direction to enable a lady to land her light aircraft at the nearby airfield. She visited the factory, chose the car she wanted to buy, and flew off again. Kimber said in the report that he was thinking of having the company name painted on the roof to aid any other pilots interested in buying an MG.

The work expended on developing the C-type chassis would obviously not have been worthwhile for use merely in a small batch of competition cars. It thus would have come as no surprise to see a press announcement in September 1931 that for the 1932 season there were to be open and closed four-seater models produced using versions of the new chassis, and that these would be powered by either four-cylinder or six-cylinder engines. The four-cylinder cars were described in catalogues as the 8/33 Midget (long chassis) to distinguish them from the earlier model with a shorter chassis described in the same publication as just the 8/33 Midget. The new cars are now just known as D-types, and they were available alongside the existing two-seater M-type Midget, the last examples of these leaving the production line as late as June 1932. The D-type was built on a slightly longer version of the C-type chassis, but with the cross-tube mounting plates riveted, rather than bolted, to the chassis side rails. The 847cc engine, transmission and brakes were taken straight out of the earlier Midget, but the three-speed gearbox was fitted with a remote 'change and fairly soon after launch a four-speed gearbox was made available at an extra cost of £30. Unlike the M-type with its Morris Minor bolt-on wheels, the D-type chassis followed the C-type in having the Rudge-Whitworth type hubs with eared locking nuts. The spare wheel was mounted vertically at the back of the body.

All the first 100 cars built were equipped with an attractive open four-seater body. This had two front-hinged cut-away doors and, unlike the M-type, the petrol tank, which held six gallons, was safely located in the rear of the chassis with fuel delivered to the engine by the earliest form of SU electric pump, the Petrolift. Another improvement was the upgrading of the electrics from 6 to 12 volt. The cycle wings were of a similar design to those fitted to the last of the M-type two-seaters, having a deeper section than those on the earlier Midgets and with the front ones provided with fairings between the wings and body sides to give improved protection from spray. The front bucket seats and the small pair of seats at the back were trimmed in leather, with a choice of green, brown, blue, red or grey finish. The coachwork as standard was black, with the wheels sprayed to match the colour chosen for the upholstery. At extra cost a range of two-tone colour schemes was on offer.

Experience with the first batch of cars showed the chassis to be too flexible and after 100 D-types had been built the side rail section was strengthened and the wheelbase increased by two inches. The range of models was widened by the inclusion of a neat four-seater Salonette. Both this and the open car were fitted with bodies to all intents and purposes identical to the contemporary six-cylinder F-types. The closed coachwork fitted to both models was designed to appeal to those looking for a sporting saloon capable of transporting a couple of small children in the rear seats. Nice touches were the sliding sunshine roof with its inset glazed panels, and an opening windscreen. There were also armrests for all occupants and ample areas of polished woodwork.

The F-type six-cylinder 1271cc OHC Wolseley

September 1931 advertisement listing the new D- and F-type models.

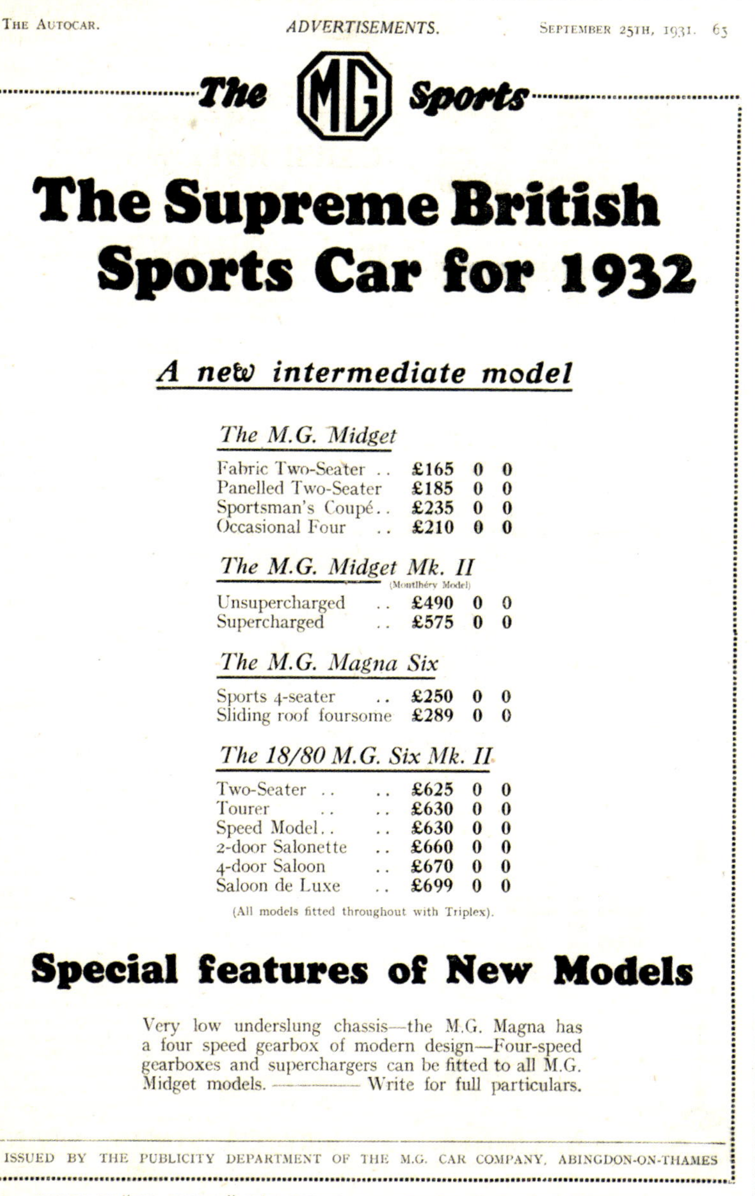

THE AUTOCAR. ADVERTISEMENTS. SEPTEMBER 25TH, 1931. 63

The MG Sports

The Supreme British Sports Car for 1932

A new intermediate model

The M.G. Midget

Fabric Two-Seater ..	£165	0	0
Panelled Two-Seater	£185	0	0
Sportsman's Coupé..	£235	0	0
Occasional Four ..	£210	0	0

The M.G. Midget Mk. II (Montlhéry Model)

Unsupercharged ..	£490	0	0
Supercharged ..	£575	0	0

The M.G. Magna Six

Sports 4-seater ..	£250	0	0
Sliding roof foursome	£289	0	0

The 18/80 M.G. Six Mk. II

Two-Seater	£625	0	0
Tourer	£630	0	0
Speed Model.. ..	£630	0	0
2-door Salonette ..	£660	0	0
4-door Saloon ..	£670	0	0
Saloon de Luxe ..	£699	0	0

(All models fitted throughout with Triplex).

Special features of New Models

Very low underslung chassis—the M.G. Magna has a four speed gearbox of modern design—Four-speed gearboxes and superchargers can be fitted to all M.G. Midget models. ———— Write for full particulars.

ISSUED BY THE PUBLICITY DEPARTMENT OF THE M.G. CAR COMPANY, ABINGDON-ON-THAMES

F7 MENTION OF "THE AUTOCAR," WHEN WRITING TO ADVERTISERS, WILL ENSURE PROMPT ATTENTION.

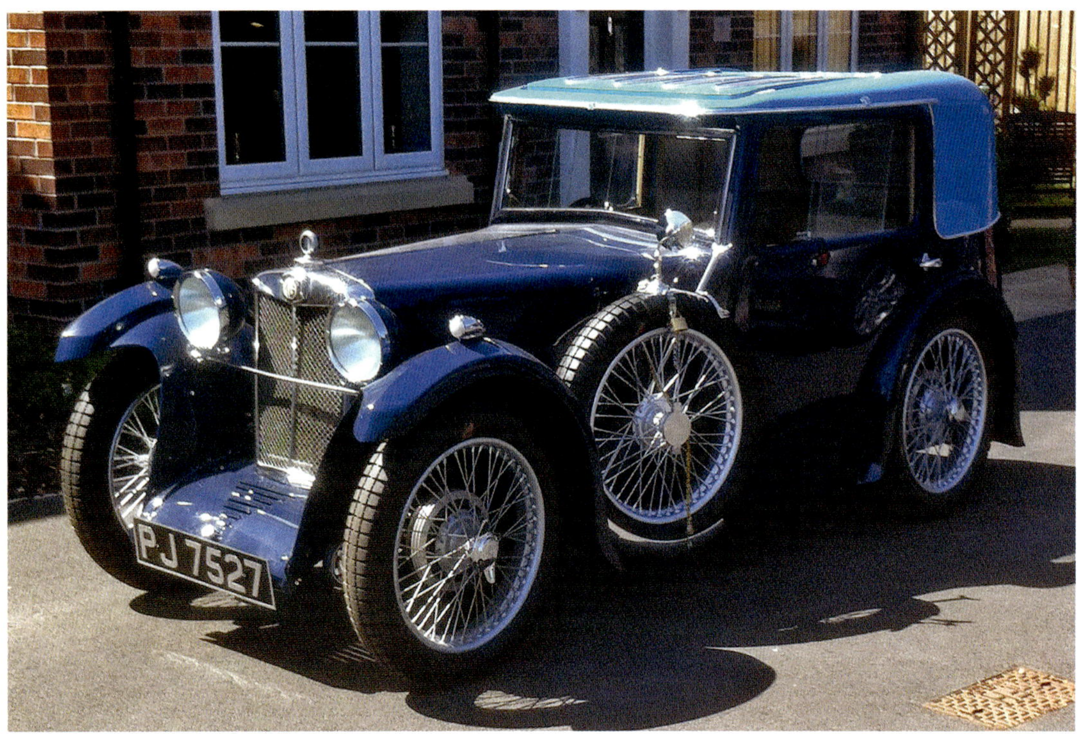

A newly-restored example of the now very rare D-type Salonette. (Photo Chris Blood)

MG
MIDGET
MARK ONE
SAFETY
FAST
INTRODUCTION
It is no idle boast to say that this little car is Britain's most popular Sports car, for it has more than adequately earned this title in the competition world. Innumerable awards for the best performance of the day stand to its credit. In all the classic reliability trials the greatest number of awards go to M.G. Midget owners.
In the 1930 Double Twelve Hour Race at Brooklands the M.G. Midgets walked off with the coveted team prize. In the 1931 Double Twelve event M.G. Midgets were placed first, second, third, fourth and fifth in the general classification, the same places for the class awards, and won the team prize. Under R.A.C. observation an M.G. Midget has made one hundred consecutive ascents of the noted Beggars Roost Hill, near Lynton, N. Devon. The M.G. Midget was the first car of 750 c.c. to exceed 100 miles per hour; also the first to cover over 100 miles in one hour.
The 1931 Irish Grand Prix was won by a Midget, and the team prize; also the Ulster T.T.
Ask your nearest Agent to let you try one and enjoy a new thrill in motoring.
8/33 M.G. MIDGET
FOURSOME COUPÉ
(Long Chassis)
£250 - - ex Works

The small MG Salonettes provided sporting motoring for those who preferred closed cars.

Hornet power unit supplied drive to a rather fragile rear axle through an ENV four-speed gearbox. The axles and eight-inch brakes were the same as fitted to the D-type, although, when the F-Magna was later revised, 12-inch drums were adopted to improve the rather marginal braking effort. Kimber obviously saw the F-Magna as appealing to those customers looking for a sporting family car and initially it was available only as a four-seater, with the option of either a saloon or open tourer body. As we have said, these closely resembled those for the four-cylinder D-type launched at the same time. Additionally, in an attempt to create a wider demand for the new model, the Magna was available in rolling chassis form and 188 of the six-cylinder MGs found their way to outside coachbuilders.

The MG Car Company was always effective when it came to getting publicity for new cars and the F-Magna was no exception. Press reports in all the major motoring magazines announced the arrival of the 12/70hp MG Magna, as it was called, and much was made of the sporting pretensions of a chassis based on the one used for the successful C-type Montlhéry Midget racing cars. The low build of the car, with floorboards set nearly five inches lower than the M-type Midget's, and the underslung rear chassis frame attracted favourable comment. By January 1932 *The Autocar* had subjected an F-Magna to a road test and reported that the car could cruise at over 70mph and could accelerate in second gear from 10mph to 30mph in six seconds. They praised the gearbox for its well-chosen ratios and for a third gear that was good for over 60mph.

Although the six-cylinder F-type engine was related to the four-cylinder unit in the M- and D-types, it did feature a number of significant differences. Firstly, the crankshaft ran in four main bearings, rather than just two, and secondly the F-type had duralumin connecting rods and the white-metal big-end bearings had bronze liners. During 1932 the factory replaced the connecting rods with stronger J-type ones, also modifying the cooling system and bearing housings to improve reliability. The majority of rebuilt cars today successfully use revised camshaft timing to improve power output.

Alongside the engine changes came the introduction of the twelve-inch brake drums brakes mentioned earlier, and to emphasise the improvements the official model designation changed from F1 to F3 for the four-seater cars. Alongside the F3 a new two-seater F2 was brought into the range, which outwardly looked similar to the recently introduced four-cylinder J2 Midget, but with a longer bonnet and a sloping radiator shell. This attractive sports car had lightweight motorcycle-style mudguards, rather than the heavier ones fitted to the four-seater cars. It also gained a J2 dashboard layout with a full range of instruments. Unfortunately the model had a short production life and only 40 of these appealing cars were built, although in recent years quite a number F1 and F3 chassis have been rebuilt as F2s.

The closed Salonettes in F1 and F3 form were popular and 390 were built. They were beautifully equipped and possessed considerably more appeal and performance than the average small family car of the period. The rear seats were rather too small to accommodate two adults for long periods, but they were certainly large enough for one adult, or two children, to travel for a reasonable distance in some comfort. Early cars had a rear-mounted spare wheel but this was soon re-located at the side, just ahead of the passenger door, freeing up space for a hinged luggage compartment lid. This pivoted at the bottom, opening outwards to be supported by two chromed stays. In this position extra luggage could be strapped in place.

There were leather facings for the seats and polished woodwork for the dashboard and around the windows. The windscreen could be wound out at the bottom to increase ventilation and a sliding sunshine roof was provided for hot weather. The latter had small windows inset to light the cabin when it was closed. The large doors initially had sliding windows and full-length armrests but these were later changed for an ingenious system incorporating wind-down windows. Unfortunately very few of the closed Magnas have survived. It was easier to rebuild them as open cars when the bodywork deteriorated.

The open four-seater tourers were the most

Black paintwork with red upholstery and wheels was one of the standard options for the D-type. This is an early car with the shorter chassis.

Like all the small OHC MGs, the D-type vertical dynamo also provided the drive to the camshaft and this often became soaked with oil in the days before modern seals were available. Applying an oil gun to the grouped nipples mounted alongside the firewall provided chassis lubrication.

The 8/33 MG Midget Occasional Four.
This new model, providing greater accommodation than the Two-seater, is mounted on a longer and lower Chassis. Upholstered in Leather. Rear Petrol Tank. Remote Gear Control. Rudge Racing Wire Wheels.
Occasional Four - £210

popular version of the Magna and 632 were sold. The rear seats may not have been generously proportioned but for children, or those small in stature, they provided a reasonable level of comfort. The hood folded down behind the rear of the body and there was a set of four side curtains that provided some protection from the elements even when the top was lowered. When used as a two-seater for touring the rear of the cockpit provided sufficient space to stow luggage and a full tonneau cover was available to hide this from unwelcome attention.

An overhead view of the cockpit of D0311 reveals the seating for four and that this car has a later four-speed J2 gearbox.

In this view of a later car on show are the longer doors that made access easier.

As with all the MG Salonettes of the time, the Magna has an opening roof with small inset windows to let more light into the cabin.

The comfortable cabin in the F-type Salonette was a major selling point.

An F-Magna four-seater tourer.

The Wolseley Hornet 1271cc six-cylinder power unit fitted to the F-Magna

Constructed in recent years on an F1 chassis, this F2 has been fitted with the later N-type engine, enhancing the performance considerably.

FOLDER No. 2 SEE OTHER FOLDERS FOR THE M.G. MIDGET MODELS AND THE M.G. SIX MARK II.
MG
MAGNA
MG
SAFETY
FAST
12/70 M.G. MAGNA
SPORTS FOUR-SEATER
£250 - - ex Works
INTRODUCTION
THE M.G. Magna is an entirely new addition to the M.G. range. With its two carburetters, overhead valve and camshaft, six cylinder engine, low underslung frame and dainty coachwork, it represents the small luxury car *in excelsis* withal its modest price. There are two body styles, both panelled, both of the close coupled four-seater variety, one open and one closed, obtainable in a range of pleasing colour schemes. Nothing has been left undone to make this the most perfect miniature Six Cylinder car obtainable with a decidedly sporting performance.
A car that will make its mark in the 1932 competition world, as well as appealing to those who appreciate a thoroughbred mount.
The M.G. Car Company Ltd. Abingdon-on-Thames

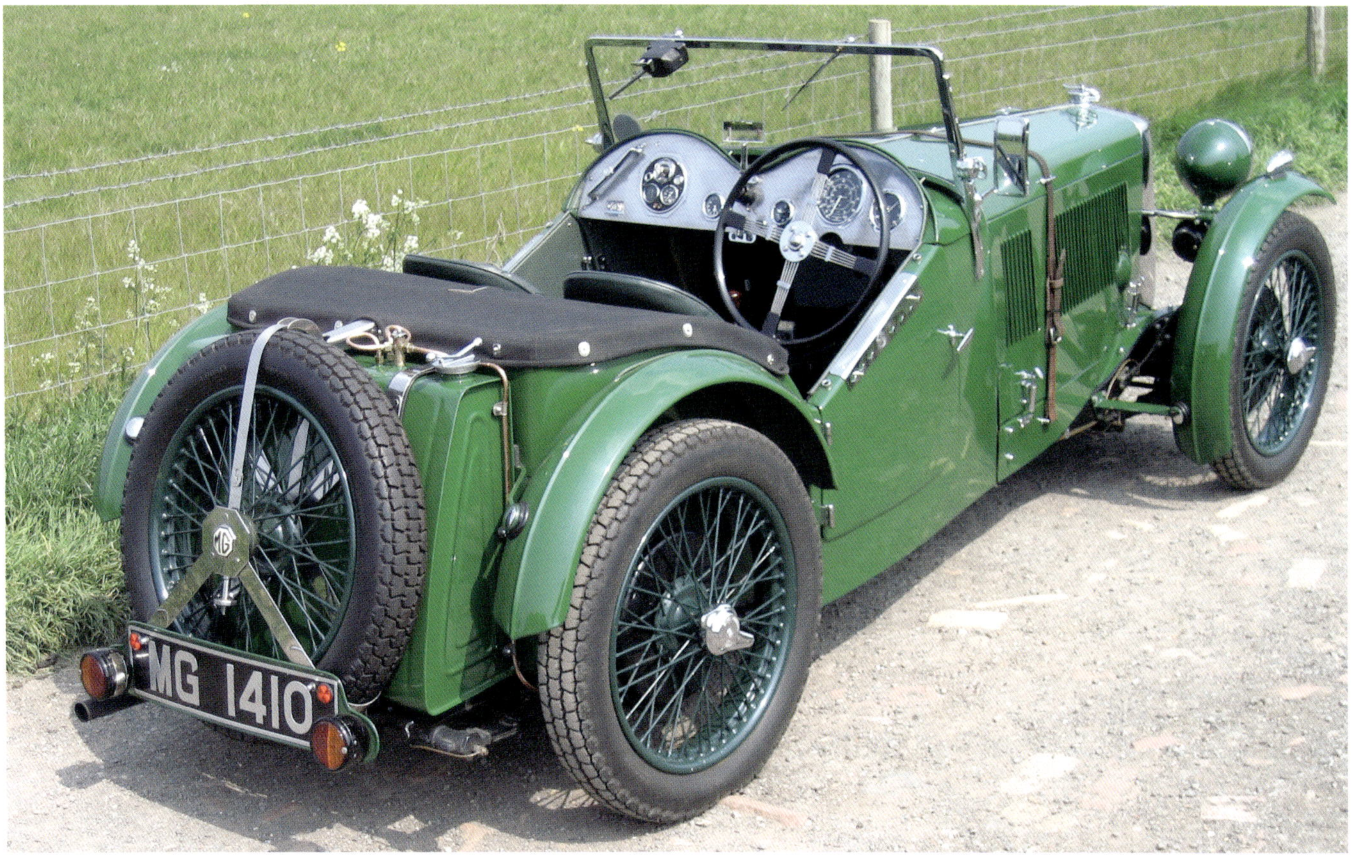

The F2 Magna is an extremely elegant car

The grey and red colour scheme looks very attractive. Unlike the four-seater F-Magnas, the F2 was equipped with lightweight cycle wings

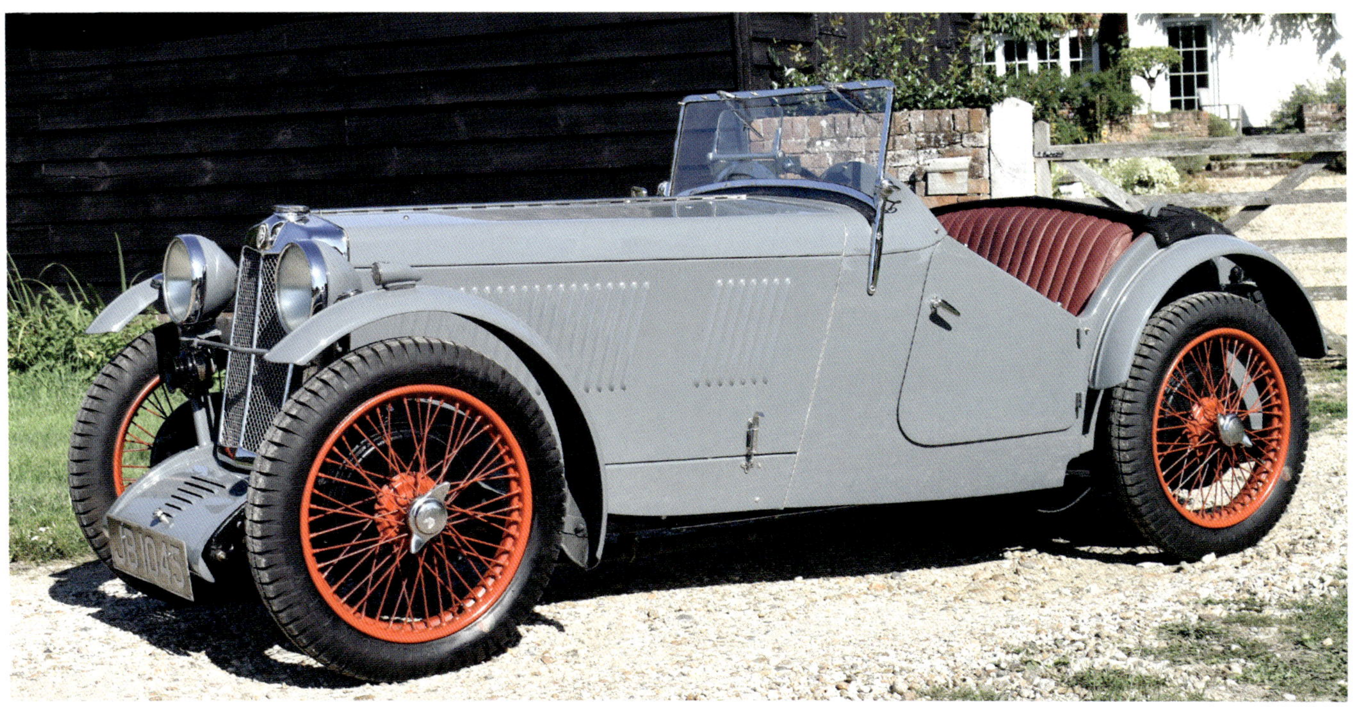

The seats in the F2 feature a one-piece, adjustable backrest. There is a small amount of space for luggage under the tonneau cover behind the seat.

Some of the F2s, including the one sold to racing driver "B Bira", had the top of the door on the driver's side cut down a bit more, like this one, to give greater elbow room.

Although the engine-turned aluminium faced dashboard is as standard for the J2/F2, this one has the normal combined speedometer/ tachometer on the left, a clock, an ammeter, water temperature and oil pressure gauges and a racing-style tachometer ahead of the driver.

This F-Magna engine has larger carburettors than standard, to improve power output. The firewall is the one fitted to the chassis when it left Abingdon in 1932. As an F2/F3 specification engine, water is carried through additional pipes attached to the cylinder head.

The spare wheel is carried behind the fuel tank. The two upper lights are period but not original: when built the only rear illumination was the tiny lamp alongside the number plate, an arrangement now illegal.

SPECIAL BODIED F-MAGNAS

From this view the many differences between the standard factory tourer and the more expensive Abbey version are apparent. The rear of the body has a more rounded look and the fuel tank and filler are placed below the spare wheel, rather than within the body. The wings were made by the coachbuilder and have a different profile from the standard items.

The F-type rolling chassis went to a number of coachbuilders, many of whom were in dire straits at that time of economic depression and the collapse of the market for expensive, hand-built cars. Some of the coachbuilders who took on the job of designing and constructing their own individual versions of the new MG did so on a speculative basis in order to try to generate new business, others were working for car dealers who wanted to offer something different to their customers.

Abbey Coachworks was a new firm set up by Mr Compton, an ex-employee of Jarvis Ltd. As newcomers they produced quite a number of different styles of bodywork, probably in an effort to test the market, and offered a stylish fixed-head two-seater coupé for £345, which was £50 more than the factory Salonette. This car was very low built and boasted wind-up windows, an opening windscreen and had space behind the forward tipping, adjustable bucket seats capable of taking large suitcases. Abbey also produced a two-door, four-seater saloon with a steeply raked windscreen and a two-door coupé with a protruding rear luggage compartment and rear-mounted spare wheel. Dummy pram hood irons were fitted to the sides of the fixed roof. In all, the company would appear to have completed 29 F-Magnas, but few survive.

New to MGs was Abbotts of Farnham, who in post-war years were known first for building their

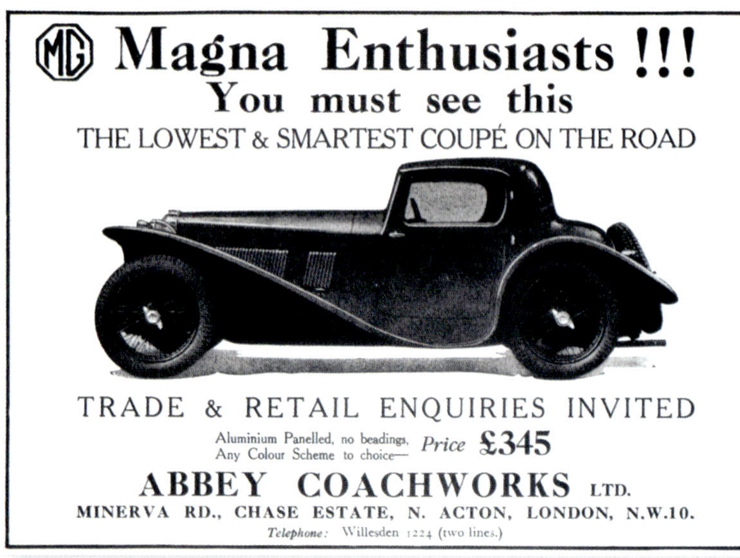

The Abbey Coupé advertisement reveals just how striking this model must have been; it is a pity none survive.

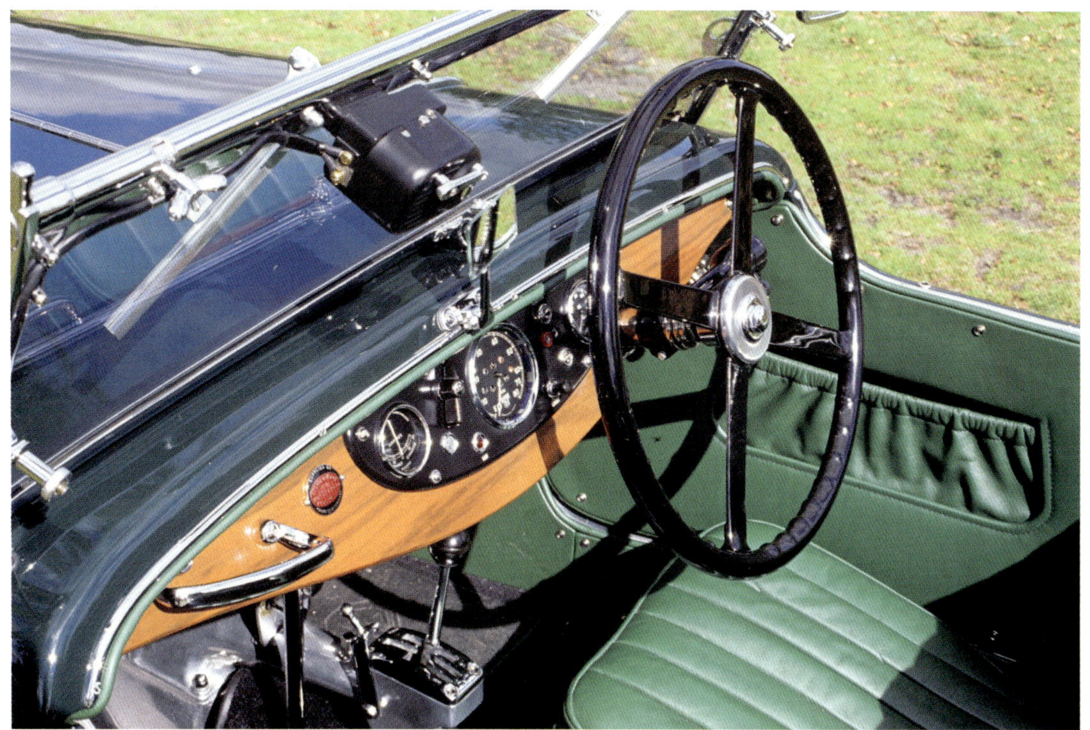

The Abbey F1 was given the same type of Rotax instrument panel as the standard cars, but the wooden dashboard was unique to that model. The interior trim was bespoke.

FARNHAM DROP HEAD COUPÉ ON M.G. MAGNA CHASSIS £325.

The Farnham Coupé built by the long-established firm of E.D. Abbott, who were based at Farnham in Surrey and survived post-war by building estate versions of Ford cars.

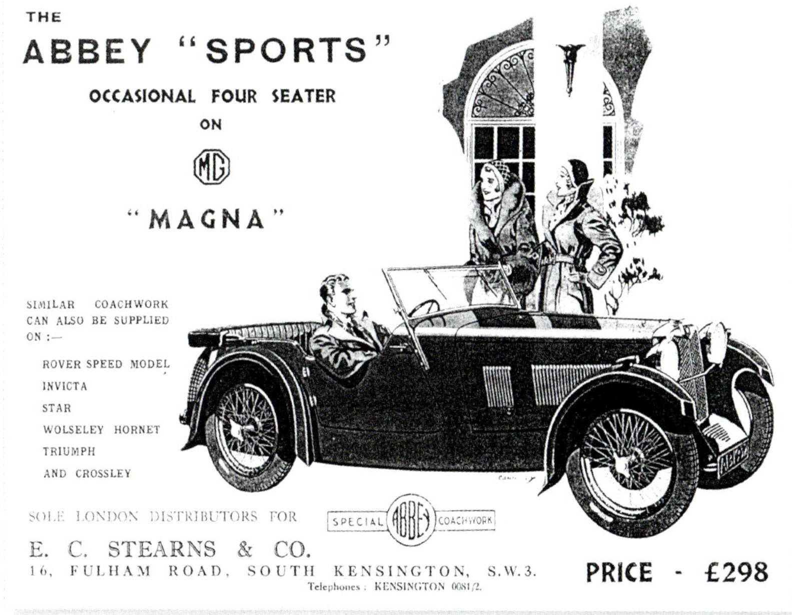

THE
ABBEY "SPORTS"
OCCASIONAL FOUR SEATER
ON
MG
"MAGNA"
SIMILAR COACHWORK CAN ALSO BE SUPPLIED ON :—
ROVER SPEED MODEL
INVICTA
STAR
WOLSELEY HORNET
TRIUMPH
AND CROSSLEY
SOLE LONDON DISTRIBUTORS FOR
SPECIAL ABBEY COACHWORK
E. C. STEARNS & CO.
16, FULHAM ROAD, SOUTH KENSINGTON, S.W.3.
Telephones: KENSINGTON 0081/2.
PRICE - £298

An advert for the Abbey F-type. Note the differences between the drawing here and the colour pictures. It is likely that in these hand-built examples the design changed in detail from car to car.

version of the 2.4-litre Healey and later for the estate car variants of the larger Ford models. They went out of business in the early 1970s. The Abbott MG Magna was a drophead coupé with the spare wheel mounted at the rear. Their car was priced at £325, but only four were built, of which none seem to have survived.

Carbodies of Coventry were the suppliers of the standard bodies fitted to the catalogued models. These were built down to a price and the quality of the closed model can be judged from the fact that after a couple of years owners of some cars with rapidly deteriorating bodies were offered replacement open coachwork by the factory for an all-in price of £125. Carbodies also built a coupé as a special order for a Canadian who asked Cecil

A contemporary picture of the Stiles Magna taken to illustrate a sales brochure.

Kimber to provide him with a drophead version of the standard F-type Salonette. This car differed in many respects from the standard cars as it had swept wings, a slatted radiator grille, different doors and one-off interior trim.

Carlton Carriage Company produced a drophead coupé body that was marketed by MG main agents, University Motors Ltd. The high-sided doors had wind-up windows with an integral sliding section that closed off the rear of the window opening. A token rear seat was provided, although few would have considered spending much time squeezed into the very small space available. The spare wheel was mounted on the nearside, ahead of the passenger door, and this kept the rear compartment lid free so it could act as a luggage platform when lowered. The car could be used with the front half of the roof rolled back but the rear seats under cover.

Jarvis & Sons Ltd., of Wimbledon, mentioned earlier for their version of the M-type also offered similar coachwork for the D-type and F-type chassis.

Stiles Ltd. of 3, Baker Street, Portman Square, London W1, were primarily Alfa Romeo agents and had sold examples of that marque fitted with coachwork to their own design. F.W. Stiles had been with the coachbuilding firm Arthur Mulliner (London) Limited and thus was probably well qualified to commission bodies for the cars sold by his own company. Perhaps endeavouring to widen what for them must have been a small market at the time, when the D-type and F-type MGs appeared Stiles produced and extensively advertised a very attractive three-seater body for these chassis. This was obviously intended to be a serious venture carried out in full consultation with MG as they printed a four-page catalogue, much in the style of those issued by the factory for the standard cars, and this even had an illustration of the car by the usual MG artist, Harold Connolly on the front cover.

The Stiles body was unusual as it combined the appearance of a two-seater with the virtue of having an extra seat for occasional emergency use. The backrest for the extra seat was attached to the luggage compartment lid and the seat cushion sat directly on the floor. Designed for access by the fit

Magazine advertisement for the Stiles Magna.

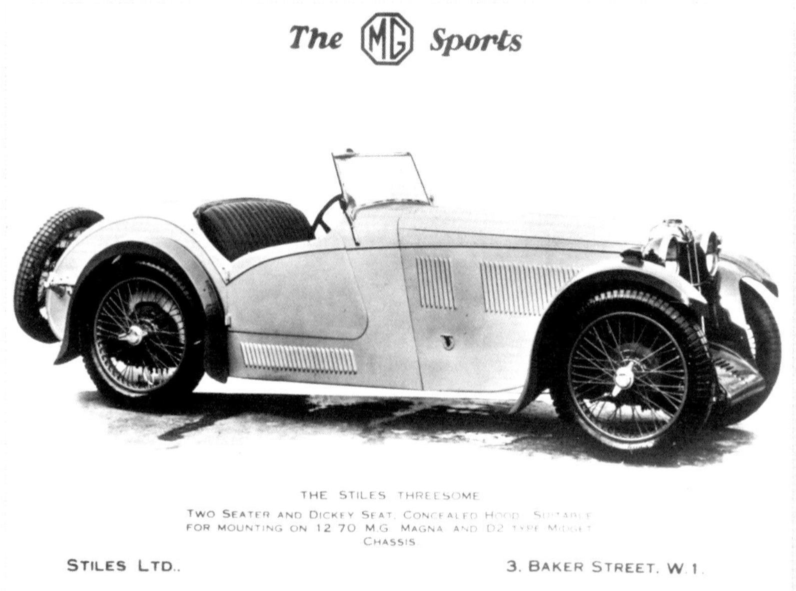

The MG Sports
THE STILES THREESOME
TWO SEATER AND DICKEY SEAT. CONCEALED HOOD.
FOR MOUNTING ON 12/70 M.G. MAGNA AND D2
CHASSIS
STILES LTD.,
3, BAKER STREET, W.1.

The Stiles Magna was fitted with standard factory helmet wings, but the louvred side valances were made specially for this model.

Among the many different types of MG made over the years, the Stiles Magna must be the most unusual and recognisable. The rounded shape of the body, which mirrors those fitted by the same company to Alfa Romeos, gives the rear view of the car a distinctive appearance.

and agile, it required the occupant to climb over the side of the body aided by footplates. Legroom was very limited and as the hood only covered the front two seats there was no protection from the weather. An adult using the seat actually looked over the top of windscreen; this being a special Stiles item that narrowed towards the top. The deluxe version of the windscreen frame could be

The Stiles Magna's lid for the luggage compartment doubled as the backrest for the rear seat. The unfortunate occupant was not provided with weather protection as the hood only covered the front seats.

either folded down flat or opened outwards from the bottom to provide ventilation with the hood up and extra visibility in the foggy weather then a common feature of British winters.

Despite having a special body, much was standard F-type. The wings were the usual, separate helmet variety fitted by the factory, but the louvred valances on the lower part of the body were specially made. Instruments, controls, lighting, etc., came from the standard car, but the seats and interior trim were made solely for this body style. The hood frame was a complicated affair that folded away behind the seats, along with the hood, and the sales brochure for the car makes much of the fact that the top could be raised or lowered without the passenger or driver leaving their seats; given the limited space in the cockpit this manoeuvre would have been worth watching. To keep out the bad weather there also was a pair of side-screens that when not in use must have been stowed in the luggage/rear seat compartment.

The one-off Vanden Plas F-type constructed especially for the racing driver Eddie Hall. It was not the prettiest car around.

Windovers of Oxford Street, London, produced an attractive closed two-seater coupé for £360. This was described at the time as being a high grade, quality car, with good accommodation and plenty of luggage space behind the front seats. The design and construction were under the supervision of Lord Portington, who used his name and influence to try to promote the car. The body was of aluminium on an ash frame and looked quite elegant, although it was probably fairly heavy. Despite receiving much publicity in the motoring press only three examples were constructed.

Of the other coachbuilders, who each took just a single chassis, we know that in March 1932 a Vanden Plas body was put on F-Magna chassis number F0280 for the racing driver Eddie Hall. This car was lightly constructed and looked very sporting but Hall could not have been all that keen on the result as a few months later it was offered for sale by Thomson and Taylor at £215. The following year it was again offered for sale secondhand for £175. Martin Walter of Folkestone, Kent, and Maltby Motor Works are also said to have each produced one body for the F-type, but details and pictures of these do not appear to have survived.

Windovers of Oxford Street marketed this elaborate drophead coupé version of the F-Magna. It was expensive and not financially successful.

THE J-TYPE MIDGETS

The low-slung chassis designed by H.N. Charles that appeared first in the EX120 record car and C-type Montlhéry Midget for the time gave the new car excellent handling and roadholding.

By 1932 the First World War had been over for 14 years and, for those young enough not to have been directly involved, memory of that dreadful conflict was starting to fade. The colourful excesses of the 1920s may have been over, and the economic depression caused in the aftermath of the 1929 Wall Street crash had cast its shadow, but at least the rise to power of the European fascists had yet to occur and talk of another war was still in the future. For those in work, or with sufficient private income, they were not bad times. Many roads had yet to be properly surfaced, but at least there were fewer cars and those running them were still a privileged minority. Motoring was, however, starting to become more regulated. 1931 had seen the printing of the first Highway Code and the same year third party insurance became compulsory. It may not, as some have said, have been the golden age of motoring, but it was certainly not a bad time to enjoy driving an MG.

The first MG Midget created its own sector in the market and was a commercial success. There were other small sporting cars, including up-market versions of the Austin Seven, and some of the continental cycle-cars appealed to a similar type of buyer, but none of these was anywhere near as successful in terms of overall sales. It is true to say that the Midget gave a new generation of budding sports car drivers the chance to buy a car that was cheap to run, that outperformed most family saloons with engines of twice the capacity, and that looked the part in terms of styling and sporting appeal. It was the popularity of the Midget amongst its younger owners that led to the formation of the MG Car Club and to the growing participation by the marque in sporting events such as trials and club racing.

If the M-type had been crucial to the survival and expansion of The MG Car Company, the model that succeeded it was to be just as important. The J-type Midget range came to public notice with the press announcement of the new cars in August 1932 and, although the basic components

The J1 four-seater tourer was mechanically identical to the J2, but the heavier coachwork affected the performance.

The design of the J2 had a stark simplicity achieved by few subsequent MGs. Every part seemed well proportioned, and with an appearance similar to the sports racing cars of the period it must have been the car to be seen driving in 1932.

SAFETY FAST!
THE CAR WITH THE RACING PEDIGREE

MIDGET

Entirely new head design

Two carburetters

Ten miles an hour faster

More commodious coachwork

Twelve volt lighting and starting

Brakes better than ever

Racing type wheels on all models

of the new model had all been seen before, it was the overall package that made such an impact on the buying public.

Now, when almost every family car can easily top 100mph and we all think nothing of driving hour after hour on motorways at (or above) the legal speed limit, it is difficult to realise just how slow was the average 1930s family car. Drivers of most of the underpowered Austin and Morris small saloons in use were happy to cruise at around 45mph; 60mph, downhill, would be a hair-raising adventure. Then comes an announcement of an 850cc sports car with a top speed of 80mph for just £199 10s 0d, according to a magazine report. It is now part of MG lore that the car tested was, shall we say, well prepared before being handed to the journalists. A more representative speed for the average J2 was probably a few miles-per-hour less than that. Nevertheless, the potential was there and anyway a new J2 was still a quick car for its time.

To add to the undoubted appeal of all that performance was the stunning appearance of the new cars. One can suppose that the overall design of the two-seater J2 came about as much from

The later J2s with swept wings have a more solid and grown-up appearance and closely resemble the Midget models that followed.

Lift the bonnet for routine maintenance and the overhead-camshaft power unit is easily accessible.

evolution as from deliberate policy. After all, the M-type started out with the then-fashionable boat-tailed look and similar styling was used for the C-type competition car. The latter had adopted a twin-hump scuttle as, in theory, this gave some lift to the airflow over the cockpit and a measure of protection to driver and passenger when travelling without a full windscreen. Competitors quickly discovered that the best way to gain extra performance from the C-type was to lighten the bodywork, and they started to chop off the pointed tail section. They also found that a larger fuel tank could be accommodated if it was placed across the back of the car behind the shortened body. Thus, for purely practical reasons, was evolved the archetypal MG shape: the traditional radiator ahead of a long bonnet, a curvaceous, double-humped scuttle housing a dashboard containing business-like instrumentation, a skimpy body with just enough room to accommodate driver and passenger, and a large rear-mounted fuel tank with the spare wheel neatly placed behind it. A 1930s design classic that in essence served MG until the 1955 MGA brought streamlining to MG owners.

The J2 was an efficient small sports car and its eager-sounding engine, developed from the 850cc M-type unit, encouraged free use of the available performance. During the production life of the 750cc C-type, the factory had produced a far more efficient cylinder head of cross-flow design that liberated a lot more power. Where the valve timing had been set correctly – critical with these units – an 80mph top speed was just about possible without any further modification

The downside of the availability of extra power from the improved cylinder head was that it

EXPORT
SAFETY FAST!
THE M.G. MIDGET
J.2 TWO - SEATER
The M.G. MIDGET
FIRST 750 c.c. CAR TO EXCEED 100 m.p.h.
FIRST 750 c.c. CAR TO COVER OVER 100 MILES IN ONE HOUR
HOLDER OF ALL THE EXISTING INTERNATIONAL CLASS "H" RECORDS AT 18th SEPTEMBER, 1933
FIRST 750 c.c. CAR TO EXCEED TWO MILES A MINUTE
MG
TRIPLEX GLASS
DUNLOP TYRES
THE CAR WITH THE RACING PEDIGREE

A bench seat was standard in the J2 but like many others this swept-wing car has been fitted with a pair of bucket seats.

revealed a certain frailty in the bottom end of the engine. The Morris Minor power unit produced just 20bhp and its two-bearing crankshaft coped quite adequately. However, when asked to perform wonders for budding J2 boy racers, the poor thing was stressed beyond its design limits and broke. In an effort to remedy this, an extra out-rigger bearing at the front of the crankshaft was introduced and this was partly successful. A real cure came when the successor to the J-type, the PA, was given a three-bearing crankshaft and a power unit of altogether stronger construction. The disadvantage was that the engine was a lot heavier and the car did not perform nearly as well as the early J2s.

The J-type was made in a number of guises. The J2 was the two-seater for the young bloods, but there was also a four-seater version, the J1, which took over the mantle of the D-type in providing sporting family tourers and saloons. In addition, for the out-and-out motor sport enthusiasts, there was a supercharged version of the J2 called the J3, and a racing model, the J4.

The J3 is commonly regarded merely as a J2 with a supercharger bolted on the front, or sometimes as a road-going version of the J4 racing model. A close examination reveals neither view to be true. Because so few were built – just 22 examples – they were so outnumbered by standard cars as to make little impact on most enthusiasts. The J3 was priced at £299.10s, a 50% increase over the cost of a J2. For this not inconsiderable sum, the buyer would have expected something rather special, and the J3s were built at Abingdon on a separate production line used solely for special orders.

From a study of the specification of a typical J3, bearing in mind that it is likely that no two were exactly the same, one can see why they had to be assembled on a separate line. Starting from a bare chassis, they were built up with the different piping needed to supply the Autopulse pump mounted on the bulkhead, stronger front road springs to counteract the extra weight of the supercharger, and a more substantial front axle. The rear axle was also different as higher-ratio gears giving 16.4mph per 1000rpm were fitted in place of those used in a standard J2. There was also a stronger clutch and an additional support bracket for the gearbox to

Unusually, this J3, chassis J3765, left the factory with 12-inch brakes in place of the eight-inch ones that were standard for all J2s and J3s. The J4 racing model included 12-inch brakes as part of the standard specification.

counteract the greater torque produced by the supercharged engine.

The body was the same as that used on the ordinary cars, but the fuel tank had a wider neck to take a racing filler cap. Inside the cockpit the upholstery and trim was as the cheaper model, but the dashboard layout incorporated a boost pressure gauge; this was probably in addition to the extra instruments found on de luxe J2s. However, with most of J3 production being built to special order, it is likely that the instrument layout varied from car to car.

The heart of the J3 was the engine/supercharger installation. The factory designed a new, stronger crankshaft with larger diameter big-end bearings. This was not the fully counterbalanced shaft used in the J4, but was a lot stronger than the one fitted to the J2. This special crankshaft had a reduced throw to take the engine capacity to 746cc, comfortably within the 750cc international racing class. The cylinder head was 3/32in. thicker to increase the volume of the combustion chamber and thus reduce the compression ratio from 6.2:1 to 5.2:1. This was necessary with a supercharged engine. The connecting rods were stronger and different pistons were used. Fitted with a Powerplus blower the output was rather optimistically quoted in contemporary sources as 72bhp at 6000rpm, the 850cc engine in the standard car producing 36bhp at 5500rpm. However, even if the power was slightly less than that given above, the J3 was certainly a quick car.

In their road test published in May 1933, *Motor Sport* recorded a top speed well in excess of 80mph and acceleration to 60mph in about 17 seconds; this may not sound fast now but in 1933 would have seen off almost all other small-capacity production sports cars. They remarked on how quietly the engine and blower ran, although the exhaust note was strident above 3000rpm. Perhaps because of its high cost, sales of the J3 were slow and records show that the 22 cars were built and delivered over an 11-month period. All had cycle wings, except for the final car, which was fitted with swept wings from new.

The J4, the racing version of the J-type Midget, is now highly regarded and original examples are

Over the 1933/34 winter the first owner modified his nearly new J3765 to near J4 specification. The doors were removed and apertures closed, an external exhaust system and duplex shock absorbers were fitted, and the springs were bound with tape to stiffen the suspension. In June 1934 Edward and Ian Gillett drove the car in the JCC Brooklands High Speed Trial.

A publicity picture of one of the nine J4 sports/racing cars.

A LITTLE BIT OF BLING – MAKING YOUR PRE-WAR MG LOOK DIFFERENT

Purchasers of MGs by definition are probably more enthusiastic about their cars than the average motorist. They may just wish to stand out from the crowd by driving a distinctive vehicle; or perhaps they are attracted to the extra performance available from such cars. In either case the accessory industry has from the earliest days of motoring been around to sell items to enhance the cars owned by those wanting to improve their appearance, performance or comfort. The MG Car Company was also keen to improve profits and help owners personalise their cars by offering a range of extras to be fitted either at point of manufacture or by the dealer. In the 1920s and early 1930s the extent to which buyers could make their cars different were almost limitless.

During the 1930s the accessory adverts concentrated on items for the sports cars, often products aimed at those wanting to update older models. For example, in 1932 M.A. McEvoy of Notting Hill and West Bromwich were selling twin carburettor sets and remote gear-change controls to owners of old M-types, who probably wished they could afford a new J2 that boasted such features.

One of the main suppliers, right up to the early 1970s, was V.W. Derrington of 159 London Road, Kingston-on-Thames. His full-page advertisements listed a number of useful accessories for those who wanted to update their M-type. For 59s 6d you could buy a smart remote change lever with a proper gate for your three-speed gearbox or even upgrade to a four-speed unit with remote change for £18 10s. For the same model there were larger-capacity sumps, stronger road springs, a camshaft giving the engine the improved timing developed for the Double-Twelve-Hour Race at Brooklands. The company also marketed stone guards for radiators and lights as well as the sprung Brooklands steering wheel, all of which were produced by Frank Ashby and Sons of Stirchley, Birmingham.

Another major retailer of bits and bobs to MG owners was The Central Motor Institute of Finchley Road, Hampstead, London NW3. Their advertisement featured many items, ranging from tonneau covers for all models to luggage racks. They sold a twin spare-wheel adaptor for the Midgets, Magnas and Magnettes with strap-type carrier, and felt-lined tool trays for some models. Badge bars for club insignia were another popular item, as were protectors for the rear wings of cycle-wing cars.

Sold widely and still available to current owners of the pre-war MGs was the passenger grab handle. Fixed to the left-hand side of the dashboard, these often had the MG octagon cast into the chromed brass and served a useful function when the driver indulged in over-enthusiastic cornering. Water temperature gauges for the radiator cap were popular and a number of different versions were available, the Calorometer being the most popular. Despite their usefulness, however, many owners preferred to fit mascots to their radiator caps and one of the most sought after for an MG is the Midge mascot produced from around 1933 by H.J. Randall of 177 Balden Road, Harborne, Birmingham. Made in two sizes, these were sold directly by the manufacturers and through MG agents and dealers.

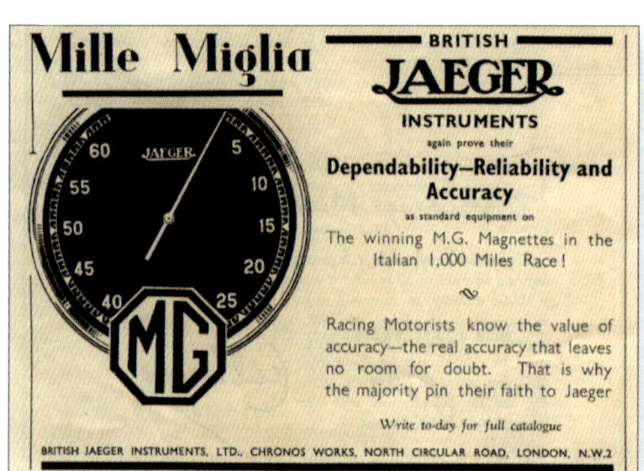

The attractive lines of this J2 rebuilt to J4 specification are enhanced by the chosen colour scheme.

thin on the ground. However, quite a number of J2s have been rebuilt to approximate J4 specification and make exciting road cars. Engine development was proceeding apace and by early 1933 all the six-cylinder engines built were of the much stronger, large-cam configuration. Obviously for racing it would have been desirable to have a three-bearing crankshaft and stronger valve gear for the four-cylinder J4, but development of the four-cylinder power unit was not that advanced and it was the ordinary J2 block that formed the basis of the J4 power unit.

There are a considerable number of differences between the J2 and J4 models and as a result very few parts are interchangeable. The J4s were assembled using standard J2 chassis frames that had been modified as required to accept the different components. Stiffer road springs were used, bound with cord in line with usual racing practice. Hartford 306M dampers were fitted. The steering had a Bishop Cam unit in place of the usual J2 Marles Weller box and there was a divided track rod and special drop and steering arms fitted to a different front axle. The braking system had 12-inch drums and could be adjusted from the driving seat. The 750cc engine had a counterbalanced crankshaft, special con-rods and pistons and a pumped cooling system. A Powerplus number 7 supercharger was fed by a single 1 5/8-inch SU carburettor and there were special inlet and exhaust manifolds and a side-mounted exhaust pipe with a Brooklands silencer. A scuttle-mounted reserve oil tank was fitted.

The considerable power produced by the 750cc engine was transmitted to the rear wheels through a twin-plate clutch, a cross-tube mounted ENV gearbox, a stronger prop-shaft and straight-cut final drive gears. Unlike the standard J2, the J4 body had no doors, and twin bucket seats replaced the usual one with a one-piece backrest. The fuel tank had a quick-release filler cap and there were twin SU petrol pumps and a Hobson fuel level transmitter. The dashboard was deeper than the one on the road car and a row of seven Rotax toggle switches replaced the ordinary ignition/lighting switch. In addition to the usual tachometer, ammeter and clock, there were gauges for fuel and oil tank levels,

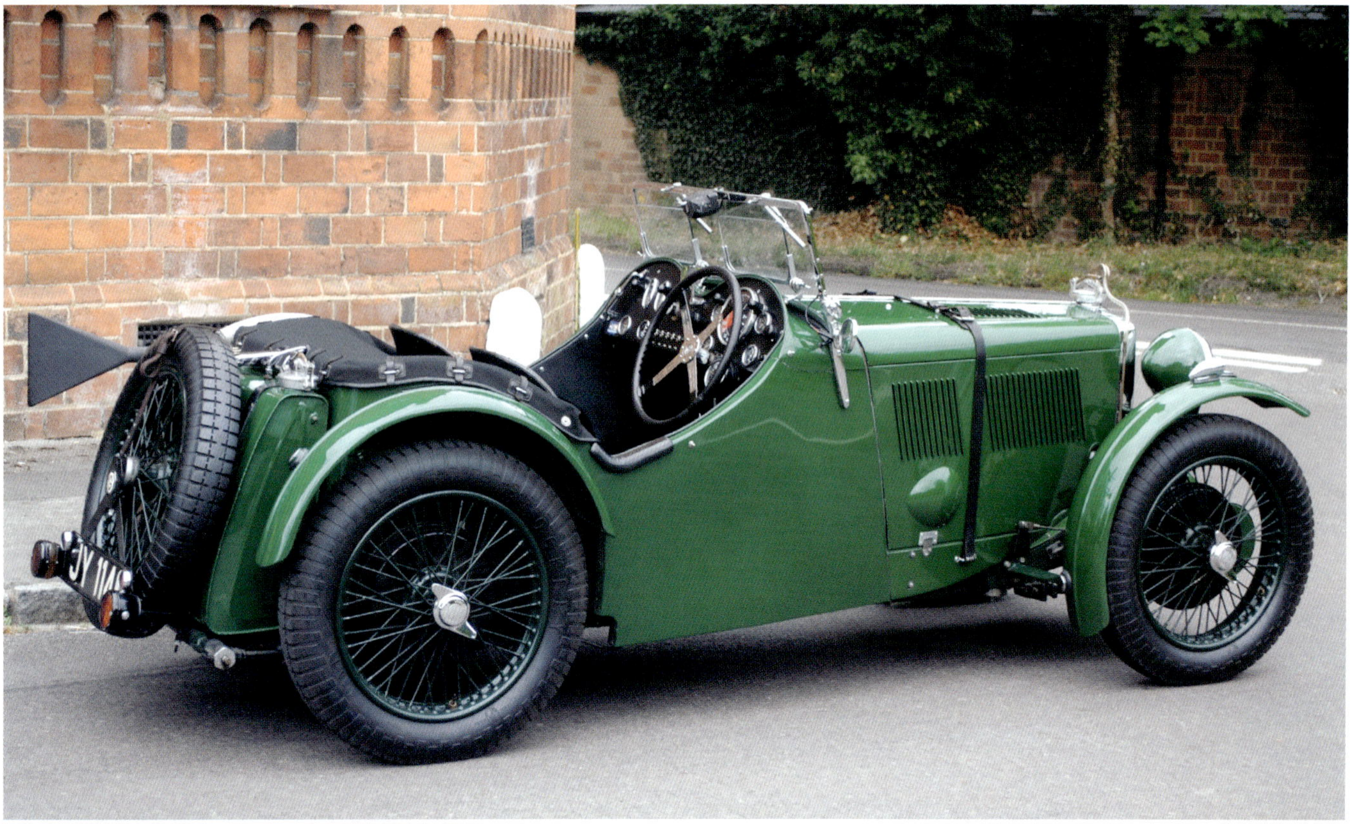

The J-type Midgets are small cars, a mere 10ft 4in long.

supercharger boost and oil temperature and pressure. This was a proper racing car that had been carefully designed for the job in hand; even the tonneau cover was securely located by straps, rather than with the usual lift-a-dot fastenings. Bearing in mind the time it would have taken to build a J4, even at the final catalogued price of £495 one cannot see how they made much profit.

The range of instruments and equipment provided as standard was impressive, but nevertheless there were a few extras available, at a price. The October 1933 brochure covering both the K3 and J4 racing models lists a chronograph clock, 120mph speedometer on a special bracket for road use, wire gauze racing windscreen and a streamlined detachable tail section. One could also order the car finished in a non-standard colour, should the available wide selection not be to your liking. There were also optional rear axle ratios and supercharger sizes on offer.

The J-type Midgets can now be seen as an important milestone in the development of the MG sports car. That the Company managed to produce such an influential car so few years after it had been formed is a tribute to the calibre of the men in charge. It certainly was not perfect: generations of subsequent owners have struggled with weak crankshafts, oiled dynamos, cracked windscreens, and other failings, but its overall virtues far outweigh any drawbacks and even a basic J2 is still one of the best sports cars of that era.

OCTOBER, 1933

A Detailed Specification of the M.G. Midget J.4 and the M.G. Magnette K.3 Racing Models

THE MOST CONSISTENTLY SUCCESSFUL BRITISH SPORTS CAR

THE K-TYPE MAGNETTES

The first MG to use a small-capacity six-cylinder engine was the F-Magna, and its relative success prompted the development of new models to the same formula. The F-type 1271cc engine came from the Wolseley Hornet and was not highly tuned but nevertheless gave the MG a reasonable performance for the time. However, buyers must have been aware that in 1932 the new J2 Midget provided, at a lower cost, as much outright speed as the six-cylinder model. During 1931 MG's Chief Designer, H. N. Charles, had visited what had been the Wolseley factory that built the engines to discuss improving the performance of the small six-cylinder unit. The design of Wolseley OHC engines for their cars and those supplied to MG was already beginning to diverge, Wolseley having already gone over to chain drive for the overhead camshaft in the Hornet engine, while Charles preferred the original arrangement where the vertical dynamo shaft drove the camshaft.

Modifications to the design agreed for the six-cylinder engine retained the basic layout but dispensed with the front ball-race used on the F-type, replacing this with a plain bearing with thrust pads to locate the crankshaft. The rest of the main bearing carriers were now made of steel. The designers increased the size of the crankshaft journals and reduced the stroke to 71mm, giving the engine a capacity of 1086cc. A larger oil pump was fitted and the oil system incorporated for the first time full-flow filtration. A magneto mounted on the offside of the engine block provided ignition. The major improvement was to the cylinder head, which followed the route already established with the four-cylinder unit used in the J-type with a

A good hood and set of side-screens made the four-seater tourers practical for all-year-round use.

This K1 tourer is a rare survivor in original condition. (Photo Barry Walker)

The K1 tourer sold in relatively small numbers, with just 97 built. (Photo Barry Walker)

cross-flow design and separate ports for each inlet and exhaust valve. The six-cylinder engine was now given three SU carburettors. It was designated K-series and shared virtually no parts with the old F-Magna unit. These small capacity, six-cylinder engines were probably designed with an eye to the 1100cc International class for racing and record breaking, and the new range of chassis intended for the engine were called Magnettes.

The frame was of similar basic design to the F-type's, but of much stronger construction with deeper channel sections for the side rails and, to stiffen the chassis, a substantial cross-brace in the centre. The track was increased from 3ft 6in to 4ft and the rear axle was of altogether of heavier construction, similar to the one fitted to the contemporary Wolseley 14. A system of divided track rods was used for the steering. One of the options was an ENV pre-selector gearbox; the engines for these had modified valve timing to improve slow running at tick-over and so reduce creep. These engines were designated KA. The KB engine, using standard MG valve timing, was coupled to a newly introduced Wolseley-designed four-speed gearbox via a twin-plate clutch.

The KA carried a new pillarless saloon on a long-wheelbase chassis, while the KB came as a four-seat tourer with the same long wheelbase, and there was a two-seater sports car built on a short-wheelbase version of the new chassis. The long-wheelbase cars, both tourers and saloons, were known as K1s, while the short wheelbase version was known as K2. A third variant was also produced on the short-wheelbase chassis, and this was the K3 competition car, which was given another engine specification also known as K3. These cars were principally designed for long-distance racing and record breaking, although several were bought as fast touring cars. The K3 was designed to be supercharged and both the factory and private competitors subsequently carried out a great deal of development to increase the cars' performance. It would be true to say that the K3 remains the most well known of any of the pre-war MG competition models.

The K1 Magnette saloon with the pillarless body weighed well over a ton and, with less than 40bhp available from the unsupercharged six-cylinder engine, obtaining good performance required frequent gear changes to keep engine speed high. However, the handling and roadholding were good and for a saloon car of the period it was capable of respectable journey times. Although the K1 received good press reports, most customers were less happy and the Service Department had to deal with complaints from them, often routed through dealers. The factory early on must have been aware of the complaints of lack of power and during 1933 started installing a larger-capacity version of the engine. Even on the open cars this engine, known as the KD, was usually fitted with the pre-selector gearbox. By October 1933, when the company issued a new brochure for the Motor Show, only the 1271cc engine (wrongly quoted as

The K1 body provided sufficient room to carry four adults. The trim in this example is as it left the factory. (Photo Barry Walker)

The K1 saloon initially was powered by the 1100cc KA engine fitted with an ENV pre-selector gearbox. Many complaints from customers led to later cars having the 1271cc KD engine as standard.

1286cc by adding a millimetre to the stroke) and the pre-selector gearbox were on offer.

Troubles reported with the ENV gearbox were either those of selecting neutral and difficulty in starting the car because of drag from the gearbox, or of noise or slipping in lower ratios. It was certainly difficult to maintain a low enough idle speed to avoid the car creeping in neutral, even with the modified valve timing of the KA engine. To overcome this a single-plate clutch was introduced between the engine and gearbox, and this operated when the car was in neutral, thus avoiding creep. An additional benefit was a reduction in snatch when pulling away from rest.

Most of the early saloons had major body repairs early in their lives. In particular, these were carried out to counter complaints about fumes from the engine entering the car. Four vents were cut in the roof panels and additional sealing was introduced between the engine compartment and the cabin. This was a major job and cars were usually at the works for two to three weeks. The poor performance of the K-types was the subject of many complaints from owners and can fairly be laid at the door of excessive weight. The six-cylinder cars lost out badly to the successful four-cylinder J-type in terms of performance, and the improved engine power of the K-type over the previous Magna was more than offset by the increased weight. Even the two-seater sports model, the K2, compared unfavourably to the four-cylinder J2, being much more expensive and no faster, and it is hardly surprising that only a few were built.

The changes in specification for the 1934 model year cars that included the larger-capacity engine prompted most owners of the earlier K-types to be anxious to have their cars similarly modified. Whether or not the factory carried out this work seemed to have depended largely on how much pressure the owner or his dealer was able to exert. With the gearbox, in most cases at first the company referred complainants to ENV and then, usually reluctantly, would only replace the gearbox themselves as a last resort. However, by late 1933 the Service Department had agreed to

THE M.G. MAGNETTE
FOUR-SEATER - - £399
ex Works

The open sports tourer on the M.G. Magnette chassis is outstandingly smart even in these days of attractive coachwork. The patent M.G. luggage carrier, similar to that on the saloon, is employed, the same lavish dashboard equipment and sensible sidescreens provide saloon comfort when the hood is erected. The cut-away doors and the flared scuttles give just that touch of smartness and practicability that is appreciated when the windscreen is folded flat and the speedometer needle soars up to eighty.

Pre-selector gearbox.

. . .

Racing type o.h.v. 6-cylinder engine.

. . .

Dunlop Fort tyres 4.75 in.—19 in.

Safety  **fast!**

The two-seater in the range was this K2 model. Powered again by the 1100cc engine, it proved more a comfortable touring car than out-and-out sports car and only 20 examples were built.

The cockpit of the K2 was well equipped. It is a pity that so few cars were built, although some of the bodies ordered in anticipation of greater sales found their way onto N-type chassis to produce the un-catalogued ND model.

SAFETY FAST!
MG
"UNIVERSITY" FOURSOME
FOLDING HEAD
COUPÉ
A Folding Head Foursome Coupé
specially designed for the connoisseur who appreciates the best.
Beauty of Line and luxurious appointments are but two of the many outstanding features. This body, as the sketches show, can be used either completely closed, as a coupé-de-ville or an open tourer, winding windows giving ample protection in any position.
Chassis Prices
Midget J2 - £160
Magna L - - £245
Magnette K2 £340
Body Prices
£135
£140
£150
Including Wings, Bonnet, Tank, Prop. Shaft Shroud and Foot Wells, which are not included in chassis equipment.

A brochure from University Motors offering their drophead coupé coachwork for the J2, L1 and K2 chassis.

do more such KD conversions – that is, a change to the later gearbox with a clutch and the fitting of the larger engine – than there were spare engines and gearboxes available and Service Manager, John Thornley kept a list of cars still awaiting completion of the work. However, even once converted to 1934 specification, which also included the body modifications, cars still gave trouble, as many letters in the correspondence files confirm.

To some extent the reputation of the K-saloon

A K1 chassis fitted with an Abbey Coachworks drophead coupé body that has been given a Gallay patent steel trunk.

was redeemed with the later KN model, produced using remaining stocks of saloon bodies mounted on K-type chassis, but fitted with the N-type power unit and four-speed manual gearbox. University Motors marketed as its Speed Model Magnette the leftover tourer bodies and K-type chassis, utilising N-type engine and gearbox. As with previous models, The K-type was available as a rolling chassis so that customers could commission from a coachbuilder something that was not like the standard catalogued models. In all 35 cars were sold in this form to be completed by outside coachbuilders, including a long-wheelbase K1 chassis with a supercharged engine and Corsica DHC body built for Kimber's personal use.

Another K1 chassis was given an Abbey body, and at least two went to University Motors to have their design of drophead coupé bodywork fitted, possibly also by Abbey Coachworks. In addition to a later batch of KNs fitted with K1 bodies by University Motors, at least three other chassis went through their hands and were given drophead coupé bodies. Whittingham and Mitchel produced an attractive K1 with a straight waistline and a flat rear panel on to which the spare wheel was mounted. The Carlton Carriage Works offered to fit their sliding roof coupé and drophead foursome on K1 chassis. Jensen constructed a striking road body for W.E.C. Watkinson's K3, later fitted on a K2 chassis when the original K3 body was re-installed, and Tickford built a special drophead coupé body on a K1 fitted with a KD engine.

Although originally built by Jensen to fit on K3 chassis K3025, this attractive body was later transferred to a K2 chassis.

THE MG K3 AND THE MILLE MIGLIA

If there is a pecking order for all the various MG models produced since the marque came into existence, few would dispute that at the at the top of the list are the 33 K3 Magnettes sports/racing cars built by the factory in 1933 and 1934. Exciting to drive, successful in competition and a delight to the eye, they attract attention wherever they appear. With so few leaving Abingdon at the time, it is not surprising that there has been a healthy trade in replicas. Many of these have been built to a very high standard using modified K1 or KN chassis and are all but indistinguishable from the real thing.

Because the K3s were the supercars of their day, they attracted a special kind of buyer. Wealthy young sportsmen and women drawn to the glamour of racing at Brooklands were obviously one market. Another consisted of those looking for something out of the ordinary who could afford to buy a car costing more than twice as much as the standard road model – which was probably a more practical proposition for everyday use anyway. At 1087cc, the version of the new K-series, six-cylinder engine fitted to the K3 fell conveniently within the 1100cc competition class and when supercharged produced around 120bhp at 6500rpm. The shorter K-series chassis used for the model provided a suitably rugged basis for a sports/racing car likely to see service on relatively rough surfaces. Here then was just the car for tackling an arduous event like the Mille Miglia.

Although the last time that race was staged was in 1957, the notion of covering 1000 miles on ordinary roads at racing speeds still has the power to capture the imagination of motor sport fans. Indeed, the retrospective events held over part of the route in recent years are extremely popular with both competitors and spectators, even though they lack the drama and danger associated with the original races.

The idea of running a race over such a long distance emerged during a discussion between four friends who thought it would present an interesting challenge. One can only marvel at their audacity, especially since this was at the time when many parts of Italy itself were very poor, with a largely rural economy where the strange practice of driving on the left-hand side of the road in towns and on the right in country areas had only just been abandoned. There were also, of course, a great many Italian skilled craftsmen, artists and engineers, and the motor industry produced many world-beating cars.

The friends had sketched out a rough route that totalled some 1600 kilometres, and as that equated to around 1000 miles they came up with the title Coppa della Mille Miglia, which they thought had the right sort of ring to it. The justification for not using the kilometre distance was that the mile was originally a Roman measurement and the Italian ruler, Mussolini, was keen on recreating the past glories of the Roman Empire. Anyway, the idea received approval and the government detailed 25,000 soldiers to organise and police the route.

The first event was staged on 26/27 March 1927

The prototype K3, K3752, was taken to Italy for a trial run early in 1933. Here during a visit to Scuderia Ferrari are Siena, winner of the Spa 24-hour race, Earl Howe, Tazio Nuvolari, Enzo Ferrari, "Johnny" Lurani and George Eyston.

Plug problems plagued the K3s in the 1933 race and here George Eyston examines one from the engine in his car.

and resulted in Italian cars taking the first 10 places. A total of 78 cars took part and 51 completed the course. The winner averaged 47.9mph over the 1000-mile course on open roads which, considering the state of some of these and the type of mountainous terrain that comprised part of the route, was a creditable performance. Over the following few years the event grew in stature and attracted more and more foreign interest and competitors, while still remaining largely an Italian occasion. In 1932 the entry list included an MG Midget C-type, CO252, driven by Lord de Clifford and V.G. Selby. Although they had to retire with engine trouble just before the end of the race the speed they had shown during the mountainous section placed them second in the 1100cc class at that point and inspired British racing enthusiast Earl Howe to consider entering a team of MGs in the 1933 race.

Howe decided that the new K3 would be ideally suited to compete in the 1100cc class in the 1933 race. Count "Johnny" Lurani, who had driven an Alfa-Romeo in the 1932 race and was fuelling Earl Howe's enthusiasm for the event, came over to England to try one of the prototypes and pronounced himself satisfied that it would be competitive in the 1100cc class. Howe then went to see Sir William Morris and managed to transfer to him some of his enthusiasm for the race. In consequence Morris agreed to place three of the new K3s at his disposal, while Earl Howe said he would personally bear the cost of organising and running the team.

The K3 Magnette first shown at the 1932 London Motor Show at Olympia was far from being fully developed. The prototype on display was fitted with a body based on that used for the C-type Midget, and the car had yet to be proven on the track. Once the decision had been taken to run the cars in international events, there followed a busy period for the small Development Department at Abingdon. Early in 1933 Lord Howe, Count Lurani and George Eyston took one of the two prototypes, K3752, in convoy with other cars to Italy for testing over part of the route. The object of the trip was to learn about the strengths and weaknesses of the K3. In the light of the experience of running the car in the sorts of conditions they would face a couple of months later, some modifications were incorporated into

The three team cars with Tim Birkin at the wheel of JB 1474.

the team cars being built back at Abingdon. The test car returned to the factory towards the end of February, leaving just three weeks to go before the race cars had to be sent to Italy. Modifications to the gearbox and wheels had been deemed necessary and the cars only just made the cargo boat SS Florentine before it left Fowey in Cornwall for the small port at Genoa in Italy.

Once there and with the team based at the Continental Hotel in Milan, testing and practice runs in the warmer weather revealed that the electron brake drums were cracking, spark plugs kept oiling up, and that the steering was erratic. The latter fault was traced to wrongly positioned torque reaction cables but to cure the braking problems new drums were made and sent to Italy. The spark plugs gave continuing trouble as oil fed to lubricate the supercharger found its way onto them. Frequent stops to clean or change plugs proved necessary.

The three K3s that ran in the race were K3001 driven by Earl Howe and Hugh Hamilton, K3002 in the hands of Tim Birkin and Bernard Rubin, and K3003 for George Eyston and "Johnny" Lurani. Birkin and Rubin were allocated the task of driving their car as quickly as they could in order to try to break the opposition. This they did in grand style, smashing the class record to the first control, which was 220 miles after the start, but then the engine succumbed to a burnt exhaust valve. The two remaining K3s were left to battle with the main opposition in their class, the supercharged Maseratis and the Fiat team. The former had run into trouble trying to match the pace of the flying Birkin and were effectively out of the running, so to

The Lurani/Eyston Magnette at Parma. Despite having to stop to change plugs on numerous occasions these drivers managed to maintain an average speed of 56.89mph over ordinary roads that at times were steep, winding mountain passes, often poorly surfaced.

Count Lurani cornering at speed on the Futa Pass.

The Birkin and Eyston K3s enter Bologna together, where officials wait to stamp the control discs.

The three 1934 team cars at the factory: JB 3182/ K3017, JB3181/K3016 and JB 3180/K3015. All three cars survive.

take class honours it was merely a matter of beating the four Fiats. By the time they reached Rome, Eyston and Lurani had taken 25 minutes off the existing class record, with Howe and Hamilton in the third car some 20 minutes behind them. Both of the K3s finished the 1000-mile race ahead of their rivals and the MG team took first and second places in their class, winning the team prize for the first time by a foreign team.

The victory by the MG team played well in the British press, especially in the motoring magazines. Beating the Italian cars in their home event was seen as quite a coup. The publicity given to the K3 by this and other successes helped sell the rest of the K3s to other racing drivers. They were priced at £795 as production racing cars fitted with Tourist Trophy regulation coachwork and pre-selector gearboxes. The 1933 cars mainly left the works fitted with this body; a detachable streamlined tail costing £35 was an option and it was also possible to order a special lightweight body. For the 1934 model year a lightweight body was standard, made of aluminium and with a new larger-capacity fuel tank forming the pointed tail section.

In 1934 Earl Howe wanted to repeat the success his team had enjoyed in the Mille Miglia the previous year. Three new K3s were readied at Abingdon, K3015, K3016 and K3017. All were fitted with 1933 two-seater bodies and slab fuel tanks. Following the troubles with spark plugs experienced the previous year, Roots blowers replaced the single-rotor Powerplus superchargers and the compression ratio was lowered. This reduced the available power and put the cars at a disadvantage in comparison to the improved Maseratis. K3015 was driven in the race by Count Lurani and C. Penn-Hughes and, after a race-long tussle with the Maserati driven by Taruffi, was placed 10th overall and second in class to the Italian driver. K3017 was Earl Howe's car but he

A pit stop in the 1934 race. In search of greater reliability the superchargers were changed and compression ratio lowered that year. However, the performance of the 1934 cars was not as good as those used in 1933 and the team were unable to repeat the success earned then.

Earl Howe sitting in K3017. Unfortunately, after leading the 1100cc class for a time he slid off the road and hit a telegraph pole, suffering a minor arm injury.

One K3 with a very interesting history is K3008. This car was purchased new by Enid Riddell and delivered to her at the smart London hotel where she lived. After a brief track career, when Hugh Hamilton drove it in the Mannin Beg race, Enid used the K3 to tour Europe and also to enter some rallies. She had e xtra storage space created in boxes fixed to each side of the body. Enid is seen here by a travel stained K3008 cleaning yet another spark plug during a stop in the 1935 Paris/St Raphael Rally.

crashed when descending the Futa Pass in driving rain, putting him out of the race. The experienced driver Eddie Hall entered K3016, partnered for the event by his wife. Unfortunately, the engine chose to shed a core plug and lose its water whilst Eddie was pushing the car to its limit in pursuit of Taruffi's Maserati. Their race was run and all hopes of a team prize vanished.

K3008 survives today in remarkably original condition, even to retaining the marks on the sides of the car where Enid Riddell fixed her storage boxes.

K3016 was one of the three 1934 Mille Miglia team cars that had been entered for the experienced driver Eddie Hall and his wife. Unfortunately, the engine shed a core plug and lost its water whilst Eddie was in hot pursuit of Taruffi's Maserati. Their race was run and all hopes of a team prize vanished. After having spent many years in Australia, the car returned to Britain in 1999 and remains today in largely original condition, still having the body and all the major components carried when it was new.

K3014 was built as a standard slab-tank car and the guarantee plate was issued on 6th September 1933. It was imported into Switzerland by Sportcar AG of Zurich for Dr Hans Aichele who, whilst studying in England, had decided to buy the car for road use after seeing a K3 in a London showroom. Having subsequently passed through a few hands, and spent a long period in hibernation, the car found its way back to Britain in 2002. This K3 is almost totally original, although now carrying a UK registration number.

MGS IN THE 1933 AND 1934 MANNIN BEG RACES

By the end of the 1920s almost every form of motor sport had been tried somewhere in the world. In Britain events had been staged over open roads (until this was banned), on purpose-built closed circuits like Brooklands, up hills and even on flat stretches of sand. Abroad, use had been made of mountain passes and stretches of new public highways, while races were staged on the beds of dry lakes and rivers, and sometimes in winter even on frozen lakes.

Maintaining public interest and involvement was vital for the sport, and organisers were always looking for new venues. Although many of the earliest races had used street circuits, and from 1905 in the British Isles the Tourist Trophy race had been run for a time on the Isle of Man, it was the establishment in 1929 of the Monaco circuit that attracted a lot of attention. The under-two-mile track, comprising public roads that wound through the city, promised much excitement for the spectators. So it proved, and every house and hotel overlooking the course was crammed with people watching from windows or balconies.

The staging of the Mannin Beg and Mannin Moar were important events on the Isle of Man and here we see the governor meeting Hammy Hamilton prior to the start of the race.

The close proximity of the cars to the spectators, and the way the buildings contained and amplified the sound of exhausts and tortured tyres, obviously added to the appeal, as did the chance to see the action for free, and many other Continental towns decided that they too could run similar events. In Britain the emergence of these new meetings did not go unnoticed and the authorities on the Isle of Man, where the last Tourist Trophy race was run in 1922, tried to persuade the Royal Automobile Club to return to the island. Since 1928 the Ards circuit in Belfast had staged the race and were obviously reluctant to lose their place in the motor sport calendar.

In 1933 the Manx authorities initially proposed a race similar to the Tourist Trophy, but run over a shorter course or, alternatively, an event for cars of under 1500cc on the circuit originally used for the Tourist Trophy. Failing the adoption of either of these proposals, they suggested that a race after the style of the Grand Prix de Monaco should be run through the streets of Douglas. The Royal Automobile Club decided that this would attract British drivers and a course was approved. It was decided that two scratch races should be held, The Mannin Beg for supercharged cars up to 1100cc, to include also unblown models up to 1500cc, and the Mannin Moar for cars of any capacity.

As the circuit devised was over four miles long, in the 50-lap race competitors would cover some 230 miles. Start and finish was on the promenade, with the grandstand facing the sea and the pits on the opposite side of the road backing onto the wide bay. The course was excellent and the race regulations stipulated that cars had to carry mechanics, thus excluding single-seater racing cars. Prize money totalled £500 for each race, the winner receiving £200. The event had certainly been very well organized. There were 500 volunteer marshals, three first-aid posts were established to every mile, and temporary hospitals had been placed at a dozen

On the first lap of the 1933 race Hammy Hamilton enters Balla Quayle Road from Woodbourne Road.

points. There were 35 marshalling posts, plus six mobile fire stations and a telephone network. Unfortunately, despite all these preparations, the entry list for the smaller-capacity race was not as good as expected.

MGs dominated the entry list for the Mannin Beg, and following the good result by the team of K3s in the Mille Miglia much was expected of them. However, the race was to prove to be extremely disappointing for supporters of the marque. George Eyston entered K3003, the machine that he had driven so successfully in Italy. Eddie Hall was down to drive K3006; R. A. Yallop used one of the prototype K3s, K3752, and Robin Mere K3009. Bernard Rubin entered the K3 which he and Sir Henry Birkin had driven in the Mille Miglia, but nominated Kaye Don as driver, Hugh Hamilton was down to drive K3008, and Earl Howe had K3001, but injury sustained earlier precluded him starting the race. Ludovic Ford and Maurice Baumer entered a C-type Midget they had driven at Le Mans and Denis K. Mansell was down to drive his nearly-new J4. Ernest L. Gardner entered his C-type, doing all the preparation work on the car himself, and Stan Crabtree was to pilot another C-type.

The Ludovic Ford/ Maurice Baumer C-type rounds Onchan hairpin bend during the 1933 race. Despite finishing just out of time, they were classified third overall, the last car to actually complete the race.

Race day dawned with the sky overcast. Starting order was decided by ballot, rather than by practice times, and the cars were drawn up across the tramlines at the end of the promenade. At the last moment before the flag fell the sun broke through the clouds to brightly illuminate the scene for the many holidaymakers and enthusiasts cramming every available spare space. Despite the length of the race, all the drivers were anxious to get around the first corner as near the front of the field as possible and there was a scramble for places as the cars accelerated away from the start. After the first corner the leading cars were the Magnettes of Don and Hamilton, the Midget driven by Crabtree and Freddie Dixon's Riley. Holidaymakers for whom this was their first motor race were certainly experiencing some of the excitement of such events as the cars battled for position on the opening lap.

Hamilton, always a fast driver, was soon challenging Crabtree's Midget for second place, with Don's Magnette just ahead of them. There was little to choose in performance between the 750cc

Crabtree drove his C-type hard and at one time was in second position. Here he is just entering St. Ninians Road with Freddie Dixon, the eventual winner, following behind.

Midget and 1100cc Magnette. What the larger machine made up on the only fast section it lost to the more agile Midget on the corners. However, by means of some on the limit driving Hamilton overtook the smaller car just as they reached the promenade at the end of the first lap. Crabtree clung close to Hamilton as he chased the leading K3 driven by Kaye Don, and a short distance behind them was Dixon's Riley. Hamilton snatched the lead during the second lap and by the time the leading cars reached the promenade for the second time he was ahead by some 50 yards,

Meanwhile Eddie Hall made a brief stop at the pits to change an oiled plug and then had the misfortune to have a front tyre burst. In the resulting slide the offending wheel hit the kerb, bending the axle and taking the car out of the race. There then followed a string of misfortunes. Both Victor Gillow and Robin Mere visited the pits to change plugs, the former soon retiring with valve trouble. George Eyston then suffered a broken camshaft drive and although the race was only six laps old the field was slowly being depleted.

Hamilton continued to increase his average speed for the race and Don was nearly half a mile behind, with Crabtree in the Midget still following the Magnette. Mere was the next MG casualty when his back axle developed the same fault as had previously occurred in practice with Don's K3. This was worrying for those in the pits, but the drivers pressed on regardless. The next casualty amongst the MGs was Kaye Don. His camshaft drive broke in exactly the same way as the one on George Eyston's car. Hamilton was still leading the race, despite a stop for fuel, and was averaging a creditable 58mph on the twisting circuit. Gardner ran a bearing and joined the retirements.

At the 25-lap mark, just half race distance, of the 14 entrants only five machines were running. Hamilton was still in the lead with Yallop running behind him, followed by Dixon's Riley, Baumer, and in fifth position Denis Mansell's Midget. Six laps later Ronnie Yallop's car was out with another broken axle and then there were just four cars left. The next casualty was Hamilton when on his 37th lap rear axle trouble forced his retirement, and only three cars were still in the race.

Dixon now took the lead and was travelling at

Robin Mere passing the stricken K3 entered and driven by George Eyston. The car is stopped in Woodbourne Road, just by the corner with York Road.

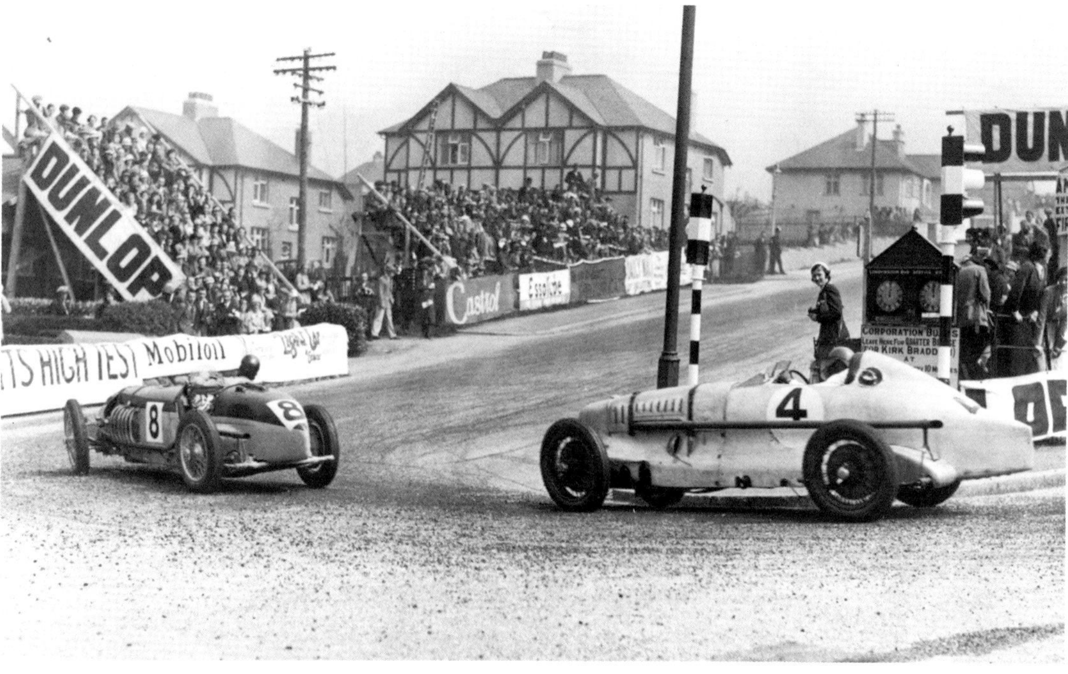

In the 1934 race the cars did not have to carry mechanics. Rounding Bray Hill Corner on to what is now the A2, Eyston in EX 135 leads Hamilton in the single-seater K3009.

such a pace that it seemed likely he would finish so far ahead of the remaining cars as to rule them out of gaining an award, because to earn one they had to cross the line within 15 minutes of the winner. Baumer was 10 minutes behind, while Mansell, who held third place, had fallen 12 minutes behind the leader. Baumer's engine then cut out because the wires from the ignition switch had broken away. He and his mechanic frantically tried to effect a repair but this took time and cost him a complete lap, with Mansell taking over his second place.

Dixon's car was almost out of oil and he slowed to a crawl on the last lap, only just making it to the finishing line. Mansell managed to take second place with a minute to spare. Baumer failed to reach the line in time and he was flagged off the course. Only two cars therefore actually finished the race, but as Baumer had been still running it was decided to award him the third prize.

Roy Eccles with his mechanic in the pits.

The majority of spectators, for whom motor racing was of only passing interest, must have found the latter stages of the race pretty boring. Fortunately, the Mannin Moar race saw far fewer retirements and, although the cars were fairly spread out, by the time the flag fell, the crowd had witnessed some exciting racing. Despite the organisers losing money on the races it was decided that the event would be repeated the following year, but some weeks earlier in the season so as not to inconvenience so many holidaymakers.

In 1934 the Mannin Beg was staged on Wednesday 30 May and again tempted many of the regular MG competitors to make the trip to the island. The entry list included 13 K3s, plus a couple of Midgets, six Rileys, an 1100cc ERA, a Singer and the Jameson Special. The sole unsupercharged entry was the 1454cc McEvoy Special. One of the Magnettes, K3004, was a non-starter, as was J4004. The only Midget left in the running was QA0251, driven by W.G. "Bill" Everitt.

Drawing on experience gained the previous year,

the organisers had devised a shorter, three-and-a-half mile long course that now had fewer bends and, with a couple of straight sections, favoured the faster cars. Even prior to the race proper the MG contingent suffered a terrible loss. K3021, which was to be driven in the race by Kaye Don, was not quite on song during practice and was worked on well into the evening by Abingdon mechanic Frankie Tayler. Once the car was running properly Don decided to take it out for an unofficial trial run after, it was alleged, having quite a lot to drink. He lost control of the car, hit a Buick taxi containing six passengers, and careered along a bank before coming to rest back on the road. Don was injured, but the popular Frankie Tayler was killed. Don was later convicted of reckless driving and jailed.

Nineteen cars started the race from the promenade and as soon as the flag dropped Wal Handley in his cream and brown K3 shot into the lead. George Eyston, driving the single-seater modified K3, EX 135, Freddie Dixon in a Riley and Charlie Dodson at the wheel of K3020, took the next three places. Handley's moment of glory at the head of the pack did not last long. After just one lap he misjudged his speed approaching the tight bend at the end of the promenade and ran into the sandbagged lamp standard. He was unhurt, but the car was too damaged to continue.

By the end of the seventh lap Eyston had a lead of five seconds over Eddie Hall, who had passed Dixon a few laps earlier. Hugh Hamilton and Norman Black were scrapping over fourth position. The road surface was very uneven and the competitors also had to contend with tramlines on part of the circuit. The bumpy circuit took its toll and Hall had to retire his K3 when the petrol tank broke loose; Cyril Paul in a Riley suffered the same fate. Dixon managed to take over the lead from George Eyston on lap 10, but with three fast-driven Magnettes in hot pursuit the race was far from over. Eyston was one of the few drivers who planned to stop for fuel. Doing this he lost nearly a minute in the pits and was passed by some of the other faster cars. Hamilton, now in second place, experienced a locking front brake and slid into a telegraph pole. Although unhurt, his race was over. Now at half distance, Norman Black in second place was being chased by Eyston as he recovered from his stop.

With the sun beating down on the tiring cars and drivers, P.L. Donkin lost concentration and slid his K3 wide at the end of the promenade, damaged a wheel and retired. Five laps from the end Dixon in the lead found that his engine was starting to misfire, a symptom of fuel starvation, and a few corners later it stopped altogether. He was out of petrol. Norman Black swept past the stationary Riley and into the lead. There he stayed to the fall of the flag, leading home in second place Charlie Dodson, with George Eyston just behind him. Eyston had set the fastest lap of the race and Magnettes also finished in fourth, fifth and seventh places. Overall the race was a triumph for MG, even if only by virtue of the leading Riley running out of petrol.

The Isle of Man is still much associated with motor sport and a magnet for enthusiasts, staging not only a number of motorcycle race meetings, but also rallies for current and historic cars.

In the 1934 race Hammy Hamilton is turning off the promenade into Broadway. The sandbags in the foreground were the undoing of Wal Handley when he skidded his K3 into them at the start of the second lap.

The pits were placed on the promenade facing the grandstands and with ocean behind them.

THE L-TYPE MAGNA

The L-type chassis. This was the same for all versions, although for the L2 the side rail extensions and rear cross-tube set behind the rear mountings for the back springs were removed.

Although the MG Car Company had introduced the six-cylinder Magnette models at the 1932 Motor Show they were all relatively expensive in comparison to the F-Magna and, in standard tourer and saloon guise, not that quick. However, even unsupercharged, the revised engine was a big improvement on the unit fitted to the F-type and, given a lighter chassis, had sporting potential. In 1933 MG launched a new six-cylinder Magna range, the L-type. This directly replaced the previous Magna, which had been in production since October 1931. The chassis retained the dimensions of the earlier car, having the same 3ft 6in track as the Midgets, but the larger-diameter 12-inch brakes used on the later F-types were fitted. The engine in the new cars was identical in design to that fitted to the 1100cc K-types, although for the Magna it had different valve timing, twin carburettors, and coil ignition in place of a magneto. Although the engine was of smaller capacity than the unit fitted to the F-type the power output of 41bhp at 5500rpm compared well with the 37bhp at 4100rpm available from the previous unit. The L-type had a manual four-speed gearbox fitted with a remote gear change, and the bell housing was mounted on the chassis via a cross-tube. To cope with the power of the six-cylinder engine, a twin-plate clutch was fitted.

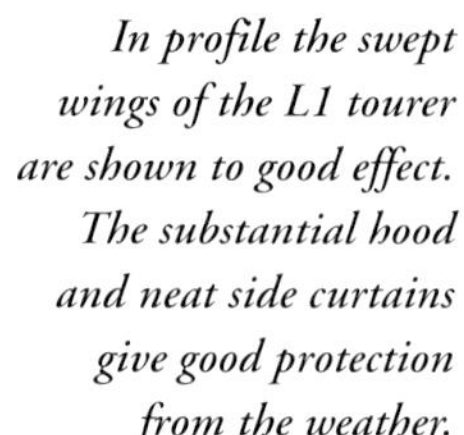

In profile the swept wings of the L1 tourer are shown to good effect. The substantial hood and neat side curtains give good protection from the weather.

The L2 two-seater is an attractive car and the close affinity with the later J2 Midgets with swept wings is evident in this picture. However, the longer bonnet and sloping radiator shell make the Magna the more attractive of the two.

The L1 Salonette. Unlike the closed version of the previous Magna, the rear seat passengers in the L-type had their own side windows. These were attractive cars and it is a pity that so very few survive.

MG
THE M.G. MAGNA
'L' Type Salonette
£345. ex Works
This delightful Salonette on the M.G. Magna chassis combines luxurious coachwork with the well-known M.G. sporting performance. The sliding roof with its dainty windowlets gives a well-lighted effect to the interior. The leather-covered pneumatic upholstery, the deep pile carpets, the Purdah glass rear window, and the generously-equipped facia board, all combine to make this little Saloon the finest value obtainable in present-day sports cars. Luggage accommodation has not been overlooked, and the rear panel of the car folds outwards, making a neat luggage platform. The bodywork is obtainable in any of the M.G. two-tone colour finishes without additional charge. Triplex glass is fitted throughout, and Dunlop Fort tyres are standard.
THE M.G. CAR COMPANY LIMITED, ABINGDON-ON-THAMES

The L-type retained an attractive, sloping radiator shell that had been introduced with the F-type to distinguish the six-cylinder car from the cheaper Midget models. However, the L-type had elegant swept wings in place of those that had enclosed each wheel separately on the previous model. Fitting the new-style wings both improved protection for the occupants against spray and vastly enhanced the appearance of the car. The L-type was available not only in two- and four-seater open form, but also as a saloon or, as it was called by MG possibly because of the limited space in the cabin, a Salonette. There was also another closed version of the model, the two-seater Continental Coupé.

Like the F2, the attractive L2 was fitted with the same style of body as that used for the Midget, which gave the two occupants the bare minimum of space required for the bench-style seating and rear luggage area. The dashboard fittings and instruments of the L2 mirrored those on de luxe versions of the J2 Midget. The tachometer, which

The two-tone colour scheme mimicked one used by Bugatti for their models and gave the Continental Coupé a distinctive appearance. The rear trunk contained the petrol tank and spare wheel. In common with the Salonette, the lid could be used to carry extra luggage.

had road speeds in each gear marked on its face, sat in front of the driver, and the oil pressure gauge, ammeter and switches were installed in a matching panel ahead of the passenger. Both of these had attractive octagonal surrounds. In the centre of the engine-turned aluminium-faced dashboard were the horn button and dip-switch, flanked by a clock and oil thermometer, also with octagonal bezels. A pair of helmet lamps provided dashboard illumination. A neat petrol gauge was fitted to the top of the fuel tank.

In spite of its relatively high price, the L2 seems to have been popular and sold well. All 90 cars were built in an eight-month period from March to November 1933, and the last to be sold was delivered to its owner by January 1934, a quick turnover for the time. The closed L-type had a different style of body from the one fitted to the superseded F-type Salonette. It had a larger area of glass, with rear side windows replacing the solid quarter panels of the earlier cars. The sliding roof was again fitted with a number of glazed panels to increase the amount of light entering the cabin. As previously, the small luggage locker had a drop-down lid that could be used to carry additional suitcases. With the car fully laden the 1100cc engine struggled a bit on gradients and there is no doubt the handling would have suffered. Like many cars of its time, the coachwork deteriorated rapidly, and cracked door pillars and flaking paintwork often featured in claims under guarantee.

The tourer provided similar cockpit space to the closed car and the hood and the four detachable side curtains gave adequate weather protection. The curtains could be stored behind the rear seat back. When lowered the hood remained attached to the rear of the body and sat on a pair of brackets that doubled as number plate supports. Although similar in some respects to the open F1/F3 tourer, the L-type had cut-away tops to the front doors and, of course, swept wings. It was overall a handsome car

THE NEW M.G. MAGNA

THE M.G. MAGNA
'L' Type
Continental Coupé
£350 *ex Works*

The new M.G. Magna Continental Coupé strikes an entirely new note. The illustration hardly does justice to its pleasing and dainty lines, all of which have been achieved without in any way detracting from its really sporting performance. A glance at the interior of the car reveals that it has received as much attention as the exterior, for the upholstery, with delightfully soft pneumatic cushions, is covered in real leather. The colour scheme illustrated is standard in the case of the Continental Coupé model, as well as the other M.G. colour finishes. The instrument board carries everything the most exacting motorist could demand, and the luggage problem is solved by means of the container mounted behind the body, as well as the space behind the seats. Needless to say, Dunlop tyres and Triplex glass are included in the standard equipment.

The long bonnet and narrow track of the L-type tourer combine to make the car appear bigger than it is. Surprisingly, the total length is just 12 feet, a foot shorter than an MGA.

It is in the rear view that the tourer differs from the two-seater sports model. The chassis is longer as it extends beyond the cross-tube that carries the rear spring mountings. The fuel tank sits lower, under rather behind the spare wheel. The lowered hood rests neatly on a bracket that also supports the number plate.

and quite a number survive in good running order. The only place to carry luggage when the rear seats were occupied, however, was on an optional rear luggage rack.

The oddball in the range was the Continental Coupé. This was fitted with two-seater closed coachwork inspired by offerings of European car builders like Bugatti. Behind the twin front seats the rear shelf was designed to carry luggage and lifted up to provide access to the rear axle and battery. The two doors had substantial upholstered armrests and the recessed areas above these were trimmed with upholstery stitched to represent the then-popular art deco rising sun pattern. A radio aerial

This smart L2 wears the understated grey colour scheme offered by the factory in period and this suits the car's 1930s styling.

It is easy to see why the L2 is prized as one of the most attractive of the pre-war MGs.

was built into the body and a receiver was available as an extra at £21. The 12-gallon fuel tank and spare wheel were mounted within a rear trunk, the lid of which also doubled as a carrier of additional luggage. Given a striking two-tone paint finish this was the stylish model in the range, if not the commercial success the company had anticipated. Only 100 of these bodies were made and records show that just 96 were sold, the final few unsold cars still languishing in dealers' showrooms as late as 1935.

With its long bonnet and swept wings, attractive radiator shell and that strong and potentially powerful engine, the L-type has remained a firm favourite over the years.

The two-tone colour scheme suits the lines of the L2, although originally the top of the bonnet, and the scuttle, would have been painted to match the rest of the body.

THE L-TYPE IN MOTOR SPORT

Promotion is important when any new model is launched and publicity is obviously helped by competition appearances. The debut on track for the L2 was the Light Car Club Relay Race at Brooklands in July 1933. Three cars were entered under the banner of the MG Car Club with G.W.J.H. Wright, Charles E.C. Martin and Alan C. Hess nominated as drivers. As their first major outing, the event could not have gone better as all the cars ran the full race distance, taking the team award at an average speed of 88.62mph. A more light-hearted publicity event at Brooklands in August saw 10 brand-new L2s being lent to former Brooklands drivers for them to use in a veterans' race. Nine of the ten cars actually started and Sydney Cummings won the race.

An L2 was also used for record breaking, and at Montlhéry, running with the front wings removed, it took six International Class G Speed Records. In the capable hands of George Eyston, Bert Denly, Ronnie Yallop and Tommy Wisdom, the L2 ran for 12 hours at 81.23mph, 1000 miles at 81.25mph, 2000 kilometres at 80.75mph, 3000 kilometres at 80.57mph, 2000 miles at 80.49mph and for 24 hours at 80.56mph. Not bad for what was still, basically, an ordinary production car.

In normal trim the average L2 was good for well over 70mph. In a road test *The Autocar* staff drove one with the windscreen raised and recorded a top speed of 75mph, rising to 77.6mph when it was lowered. The car took just under 25 seconds to reach 60mph from rest. *Daily Herald* journalist Tommy Wisdom, no mean driver himself, said that the standard car had a maximum speed of just over 80mph but that in stripped form, and with a modified induction pipe, he had lapped Brooklands at 96mph.

The Alpine Trial was one of the more arduous events in the calendar and one in which the British regularly competed; 1931 was the first year with MGs in the entry list. The Trial was organised by the national clubs of Austria, France, Italy and Germany and was staged over six days. There were twelve British starters, including the M-type coupé driven by Lord de Clifford and an open M-type in the hands of R.V.D. Sullivan. The latter failed to finish, but de Clifford earned a Glacier Plaque and a Souvenir Medal. Of the British drivers, Donald Healey in an Invicta and Humphrey E. Symons, driving a Talbot, also gained Glacier Cups for not losing any marks.

For the 1932 Trial, organised by the clubs in Austria, France, Germany and Switzerland, no less than 40 British cars were classified as starters. There was by now considerable interest in the event from the London-based motoring press, no doubt prompting support from manufacturers keen to see their products gain kudos for success. Both Talbot and Riley entered teams. That year, amongst the British contingent, four entrants were driving MGs: W.E.C. Watkinson, R.J.B. "Dick" Seaman and Walter E. Belgrave in F-type Magnas and T.A.W. Thorpe in a Midget. On the second day the latter missed the closing time at the final control, losing a total of 138 points. This trial must have been one

The first outing for the three new L2 Magnas was in the 1933 Light Car Club Relay Race at Brooklands in July. Here the drivers seated in one of the cars pose for the camera. Left to right, G.W.J. Wright, Alan Hess and Charlie Martin.

When the L-type two seater sports models were announced 10 brand new cars were lent to drivers who had competed at Brooklands in the early days of the track. One wonders if the subsequent new owners were aware that their new cars had a racing history.

of the first competitive events for the young Dick Seaman, who was later to drive for the Mercedes Benz Silver Arrows team. He was tragically killed when in the wet he lost control of his car at Spa during the 1939 Belgium Grand Prix. In the final results the British drivers fared very well, taking home two Alpine Cups and 17 Glacier Cups. Watkinson had a clean run in his Magna, finishing first in class and gaining a Glacier Cup. Belgrave earned a silver-gilt plaque for his second place in

In the Veterans' Race nine of the 10 L2s actually took part and the event was good publicity for the new model.

W.E.C. Watkinson in one of the L2s entered in the 1933 Alpine Trial. The team of three L-types won an Alpine Cup.

class and both Thorpe and Seaman were classified as finishers.

In 1933 the British entries included a team of three of the new L2 Magnas, driven by W.E.C. Watkinson, Lewis A. Welch and Tommy Wisdom. Those three cars were the ones used previously for the LCC Relay Race at Brooklands and, in addition, R.J. Nash entered a Magna and S. Sanders a Magna Drophead Coupé. Walter Belgrave participated again, this time at the wheel of a supercharged J3 Midget. In a trial with a time schedule that saw so many penalised, the British team of three L-type Magnas made good progress and by the time they reached the finish at Nice had taken first place in class and the team award, and with this a coveted Alpine Cup. Nash in a Magna was classified as a finisher, but Sanders retired his coupé. The star in the MG camp was, however, Walter Belgrave had taken his standard J3 and driven it so well as to have reached the finish with just 2 points lost, placing him overall just behind three competitors who had not lost a point and one who had been penalised just a single one. This was a tremendous effort for the driver of one of the smallest-capacity cars in the event, running against cars of up to 1100cc.

In 1934, although 46 British entrants started, just two were using MGs. As in previous years, there were also a small number of MGs entered by Continental drivers. There was no factory team this time, although Humphrey Symons had borrowed from Abingdon an NA two-seater, a car he was to use again for the 1935 Monte Carlo Rally. The only other British MG driver was Leslie Seyd in his C-type Montlhéry Midget. When it came to the final awards, Symons was given a Glacier Cup for his individual performance.

Aubrey Ashton-Rigby ordered a new L2 Magna from Caffyns Limited in Brighton with serious competition work in mind. He specified triple carburettors and magneto ignition, as fitted to some of the K-type Magnettes. The car was painted blue, with blue leather trim and blue wheels, and was collected by him from the factory on 19th June 1933. His running-in schedule consisted of an entry the following weekend in the Brighton/ Beer trial. Following this the car was first returned

Welch in an Alpine village passing a queue of other competitors during the 1933 Trial.

This surviving L2 Alpine Trial car is now shorn of the standard swept wings it carried in that event.

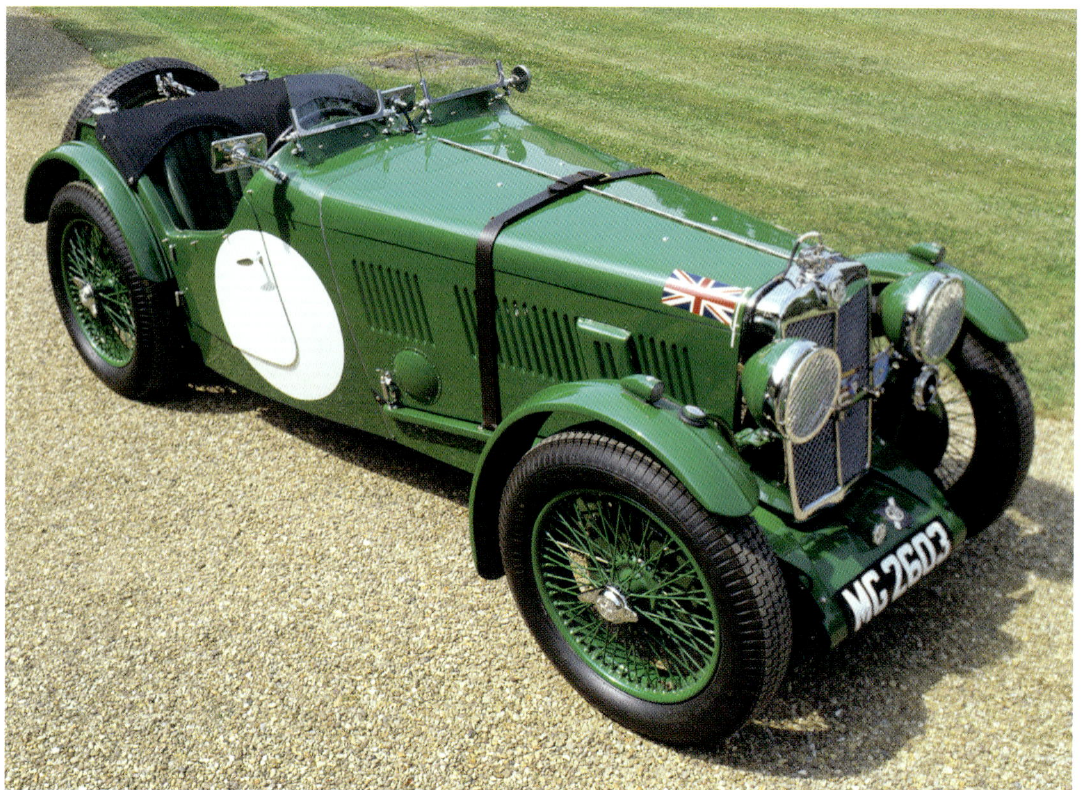

Unlike the standard L2, this car is fitted with bucket seats that hold driver and passenger more firmly during high-speed cornering. The dashboard has a full range of instruments and incorporates changes made by its 1934 owner.

to Abingdon for performance testing, and for work to rectify a flooding carburettor, and was then entrusted to Robin Jackson at Brooklands to prepare it for entry in the Brooklands Automobile Racing Club Inter-club meeting on 8 July.

In its first race the Magna performed well. Aubrey was placed first in the Junior Short Handicap, averaging 78.18mph and running a fastest lap of 80.89mph on the bumpy track. Thus encouraged, the car was entered for the August Bank Holiday meeting at Brooklands, where he ran in the first Byfleet Junior Short Handicap, taking third place. On 2 September Aubrey entered his car in the third Light Car Club Relay Race as one of a team of three cars entered by the Brighton and Hove Motor Club. This was the event where the factory-supported team of three L2s were entered, taking the Team Award. The Brighton and Hove Motor Club team were not disgraced and finished in eighth place, with the Ashton-Rigby lapping at 92.96mph.

Aubrey Ashton-Rigby (right) turning the headlamps round prior to making his timed runs at the 1934 Brighton Speed Trials. Note that he is wearing glasses – poor eyesight was to limit his competition career at the wheel and he later transferred his attention to playing golf, at which he excelled.

For 1934 Aubrey decided to undertake an ambitious programme of events, including the classic 24-hour race at Le Mans and the Ulster Tourist Trophy. The car was prepared with these in mind and the chassis was partly boxed and cross-braced to improve stiffness. Aubrey suffered from poor eyesight, not the best thing for a racing driver, and a recurrence of eye problems spoiled the earlier part of the 1934 season. He failed to make Le Mans and his first race meeting that year seems to have been the International Relay Race at Brooklands on 21 July, where he spun during a storm and retired the damaged L2. The car was back to full health by the time of the August Brooklands meeting, where he won the Esher Junior Short Handicap. He took the car to Ulster for the 1934 Tourist Trophy race and lapped at 70.25mph, but had to retire when his camshaft bearings seized because of oil starvation.

The car was sold in 1935 and passed through various owners, and a change of registration number, before being restored.

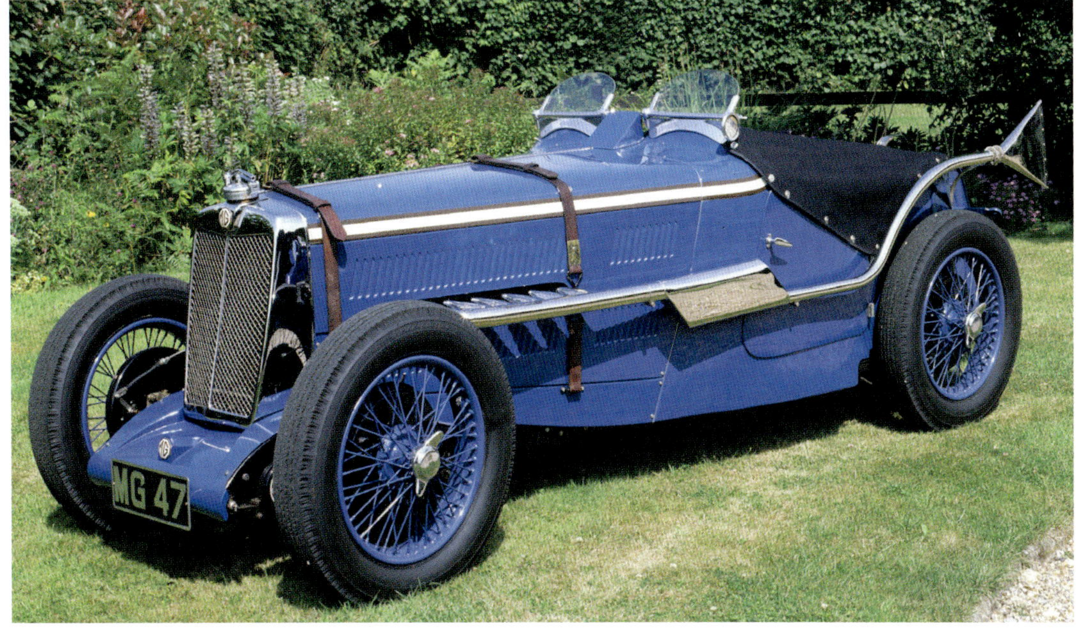

The sloped Magna radiator grille is particularly noticeable when the car is stripped for competition work. Aubrey chose the colour scheme when he raced the car in the 1930s, and during restoration it was matched from surviving areas of paint on the body tub.

THE N-TYPE MAGNETTE

An official picture of the N-Magnette four-seater tourer. On the NA the two-tone paintwork had the darker colour on the upper panels.

This illustration from the N-type sales brochure shows the rolling chassis that had been developed from the successful design introduced originally to the MG range for the C-type Midget.

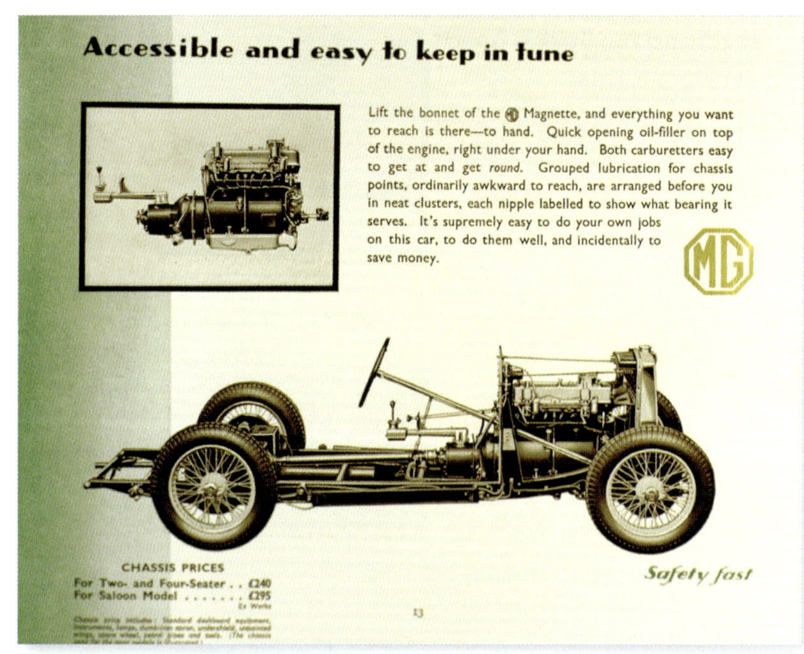

Accessible and easy to keep in tune
Lift the bonnet of the MG Magnette, and everything you want to reach is there—to hand. Quick opening oil-filler on top of the engine, right under your hand. Both carburetters easy to get at and get *round*. Grouped lubrication for chassis points, ordinarily awkward to reach, are arranged before you in neat clusters, each nipple labelled to show what bearing it serves. It's supremely easy to do your own jobs on this car, to do them well, and incidentally to save money.
MG
CHASSIS PRICES
For Two- and Four-Seater . . £240
For Saloon Model £295
Ex Works
Safety fast
13

The N-Magnette announced in early 1934 was designed to replace both the K-type and L-type as the six-cylinder car in the MG range. The enlarged 1271cc engine fitted to later K-type road cars was further improved and in twin-carburettor form produced 56bhp, which was usefully more than the 48bhp available from the earlier engine. The chassis for the new model generally followed established MG practice and the wheelbase remained at 7ft 10in, like the L and K2/K3 models. However, 3ft 9in wide axles gave the N-type chassis a three-inch wider track than the F- and L-Magna, but three inches narrower than the K-type. The problem with the K-type axles had been that they were both too heavy and also used parts that were not common to any other car in the MG/Morris/Wolseley range. If the complicated K-type divided-track steering had been an improvement over a conventional transverse drag link, this obviously was not considered of sufficient benefit to merit the extra cost.

The N-type's steering gear was by Bishop Cam, which had been used on the racing models since 1932 and was far superior to the Marles-Weller box in the previous MG road cars. Thus the directional stability of the new model should be at least as good as the K-type, and far better than the F- and

The standard two-seater NA lacked some of the appeal of the earlier sports models, but the roomier coachwork improved comfort and made it popular with owners.

L-Magnas. The brakes had 12-inch drums that had been developed for the 1932 racing season and used originally on the later F-type Magnas. Supplied by Alford and Alder, these drums and the MG brake system had proved very successful and trouble free, and by the standards of the time gave good performance. MG persisted with the mechanically operated cable system, which was considered was the best available for the car. This view contrasted with the thinking behind the design of the contemporary Wolseley and Morris models, which by then featured hydraulic brakes. Reliability of the hydraulic system was at the time thought to be an issue, and experience eventually proved the mechanical system to be outdated. In an effort to insulate the body from the chassis, sub-frames were provided for the ash-framed coachwork and were mounted on the chassis using bushes with rubber inserts.

Abingdon were keen to target as many potential customers as possible and thus offered the new model in various guises. The press announcement gave details of the two models initially available, a substantial two-seater sports car and a four-seater tourer. The latter provided just sufficient space for the average family to travel in reasonable comfort. However, there was mention in press releases of a closed two-seater coupé and an open two/four-seater that were be available shortly after the standard cars went into production. These two models were unusual in that their inspiration came not from the MG Car Company, but from an outside source, Henry W. Allingham, who was an entrepreneur and independent designer but not a coachbuilder. Carbodies made the coupé bodies and those for the open car came from Whittingham and Mitchel. Although the open car was only available on the six-cylinder chassis, the Airline Coupé was also fitted to some four-cylinder P-type Midget chassis. Known at the time as the Airline convertible, the Allingham N-type could be used either as a pure two-seater, with the rear seat concealed by closing the rear decking, or as a four-seater when the rear

The KN saloon was a hybrid model that used a K-type chassis with the improved N-type engine.

Safety fast
MG
The M.G. Magnette
"KN" Type
Pillarless Four-Door
Saloon £399
Ex Works
Race bred reliability

The long bonnet and short rear overhang on the KN follow the pattern set for the small MG saloons with the F- and D-type Salonettes.

panel was open. Unlike other occasional rear seat designs, all the occupants sat within the cockpit area and when it rained benefited from the weather protection offered by the soft top. The styling was attractive, enhanced by two-tone paintwork, and the spare wheel was mounted on a front wing, leaving the attractive back of the body uncluttered.

The Airline Coupé was a beautiful streamlined two-seater with a roof line that swept down to the back of the car and with the spare wheel recessed into the rear panel with its own metal cover. As with other closed MGs, a sliding sunroof had inset small windows that introduced light into the cockpit. The doors had one fixed and one sliding glass window, allowing the door panels to be recessed to provide elbowroom. The luggage area behind the seats was carpeted and a hinged panel behind this gave access to a small storage compartment. To keep the weight down, Carbodies built light timber frames, strengthened where necessary with steel straps or plates.

As had been common practice up to that time, in addition to the catalogued complete cars the new Magnette was available in chassis form with items like wings, bonnet, etc. also offered separately, so that a customer or dealer could either have a coachbuilder fit these to a different style of body or have special ones made if required. With many of the volume manufacturers moving over to all-steel bodies, and even unitary construction, the age of bespoke cars was coming to its end. Nevertheless in 1934 a number of coachbuilders were still in business and 48 N-types were sold in chassis form.

The N-type two-seaters were good cars and

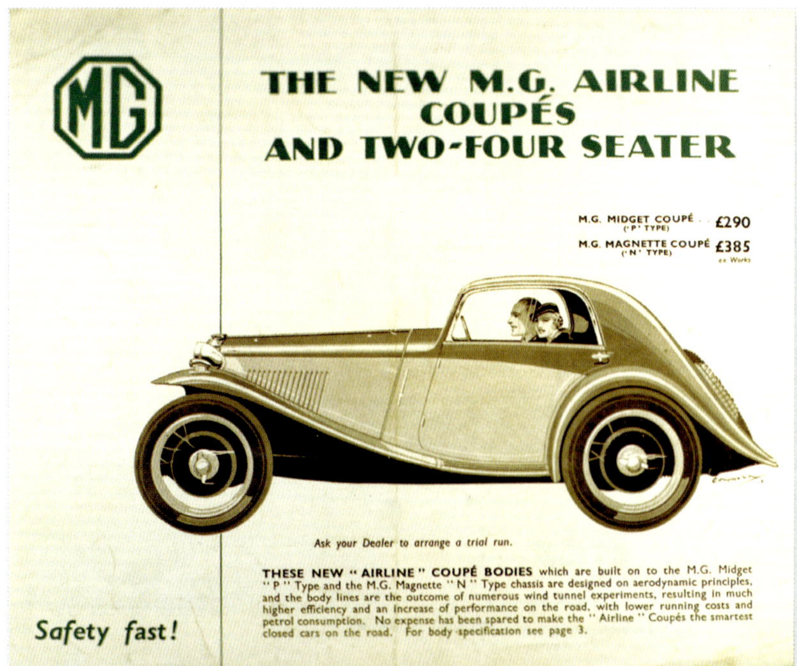

MG
THE NEW M.G. AIRLINE COUPÉS AND TWO-FOUR SEATER
M.G. MIDGET COUPÉ ('P' TYPE) £290
M.G. MAGNETTE COUPÉ ('N' TYPE) £385
ex Works
Ask your Dealer to arrange a trial run.
THESE NEW "AIRLINE" COUPÉ BODIES which are built on to the M.G. Midget "P" Type and the M.G. Magnette "N" Type chassis are designed on aerodynamic principles, and the body lines are the outcome of numerous wind tunnel experiments, resulting in much higher efficiency and an increase of performance on the road, with lower running costs and petrol consumption. No expense has been spared to make the "Airline" Coupés the smartest closed cars on the road. For body specification see page 3.
Safety fast!

The N-type Airline Coupé was built in very small numbers, probably no more than six, the majority of these bodies going on to P-type chassis.

The elegant shape of the sweeping front wings gives the impression that the car is longer than it actually is.

The front-mounted supercharger fitted to this KN is concealed beneath an attractive cover.

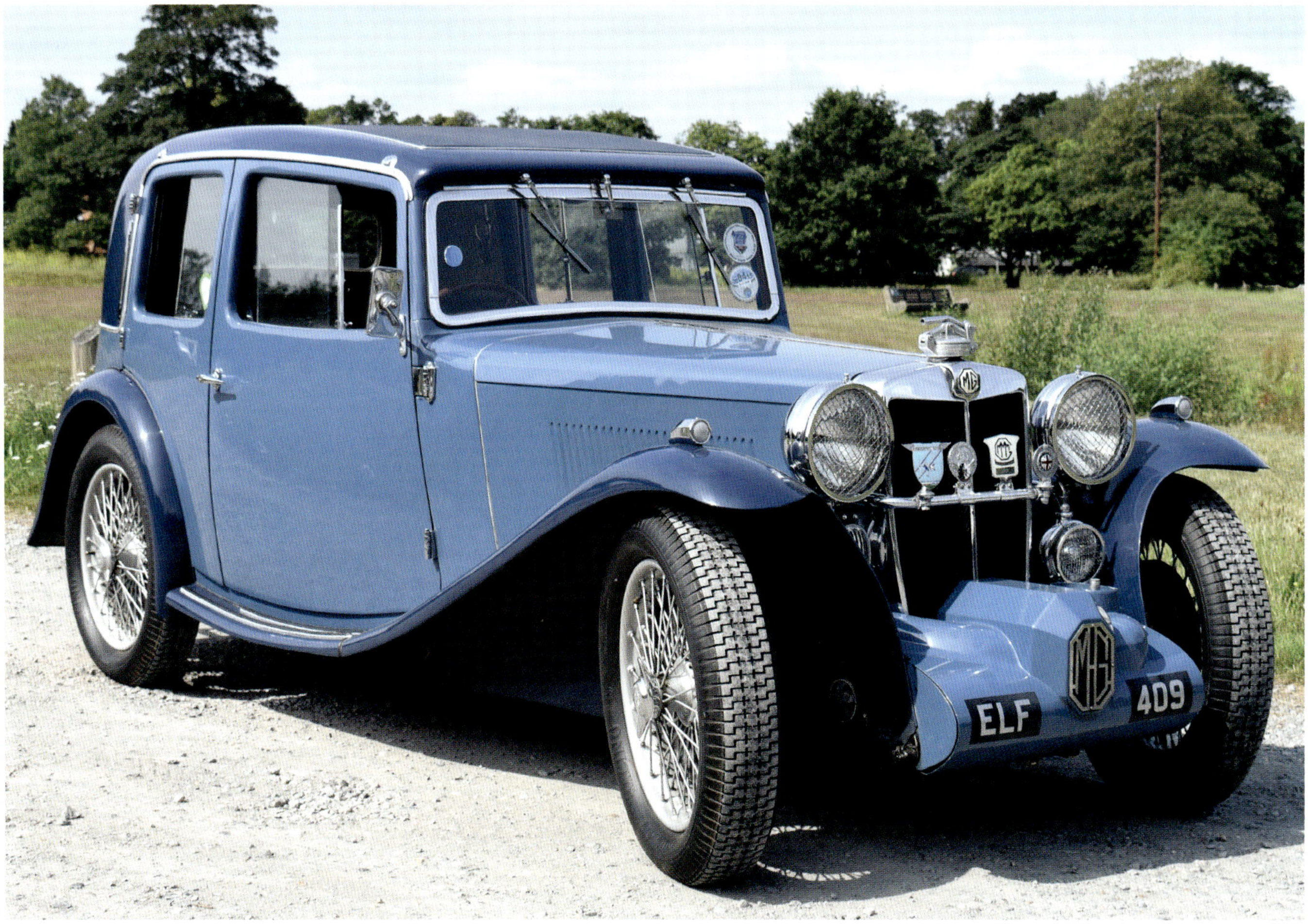

Opening both doors allows easy access to rear seats. The K1 and KN saloons were the only standard MGs to use this feature.

many were used for sporting events. However, there were still those who looked for something slightly better suited to competition work and for them the ND, with its slab tank and shorter rear overhang, suited the bill. This model is an oddity as it never appeared in the price lists or brochures, but it seems to have been a way of both satisfying a demand for a suitable car for competition and of using parts remaining in stock. The process of building the ND from standard NA and surplus K2 components was relatively simple. The NA chassis and running gear were used, largely unaltered. The sub-frame system of mounting was discarded and the K2 body was fitted to four fabricated brackets bolted to the side

The rear seats in the tourer were deeply bucketed and provided comfortable accommodation, so long as passengers were not too tall or broad in the beam.

Luggage capacity of the KN saloon could be increased by stowing cases on the lowered boot lid.

The rare ND model used a standard N-type rolling chassis and the body, fuel tank, wings, etc., from the discontinued K2.

rails and, at the rear, by irons bolted directly to the frame. The K2 inner rear wheel-arches were moved inwards to accommodate the three-inch narrower track of the NA chassis. This, in turn, meant that the standard K2 rear wings were set further in. The front wings were the same as those on the K2 and the peaks at their front edge no longer aligned with the centre of the tyre tread. Ideally, the wings would have been re-shaped, but this would have increased costs.

The neat solution adopted to align the front and rear wings was to shape the outside edges of the running boards, which now tapered in at the back to meet the inset rear wings. To complete the

An NB four-seater displays the front-hinged doors and revised colour scheme introduced for the 1936 model year cars.

The genius of the Allingham design is that with the rear panel closed it looks like a two-seater sports model.

The rear deck, when opened up, forms the backrest of the rear seat. Legroom is fairly restricted, however.

The Abbey NA appealed to buyers looking for a sports car in traditional style with a rear-mounted slab fuel tank.

Like all NA Magnettes, the Allingham does not have the slatted radiator grille used on the NB and later models.

sporting appearance of the car, a K2 slab tank and a rear spare wheel mounting fabricated from tubing, as on the P-type, were fitted. The scuttle/bulkhead area also received some modification, with the footwell enclosed, as it was on the standard NA. The windscreen came from the pile of K2 parts. A number of these interesting cars survive and are today much prized by their owners.

One of the most prolific of the 1930s coachbuilders was Abbey Coachworks, who produced an attractive two-seater sports car using the NA chassis. This featured a slab tank on the back, which maintained the classic MG body style while the factory had brought the N-type's petrol

A publicity picture of the Abbey NA two-seater.

From the rear the Cresta NA differs considerably from the standard cars. The panel carrying the spare wheel opens to reveal the luggage compartment.

tank inside a sloping tail. Abbey also produced a drophead coupé body for the N-type chassis, very similar to the coachwork they had offered for the K-type.

A newcomer to the special-bodied MG trade was the Cresta Motor Company of Broadwater Road, Worthing, Sussex. This garage had as directors A.N.L. Maclachlan, J. C. and R. C. Elwes and C.E.C. Martin, all of whom used to race in cars of various makes. J.C. Elwes had been one of Aston-Martin's official drivers at Le Mans and got to know the company's head designer, Gus Bertelli, extremely well. Elwes asked him whether Aston-Martin would be prepared to build an attractive and comfortable body for the MG chassis. Gus Bertelli ran Aston-Martin and his brother was responsible for the bodies through a separate coachbuilding company, E. Bertelli Limited, founded in 1930. A study of a Cresta body reveals that it is almost identical to those fitted by these coachbuilders to the contemporary Aston-Martin International, the main body support members being altered to suit the different layout of the MG chassis. The windscreen, seats and other details are the same as those used for the Feltham-built cars.

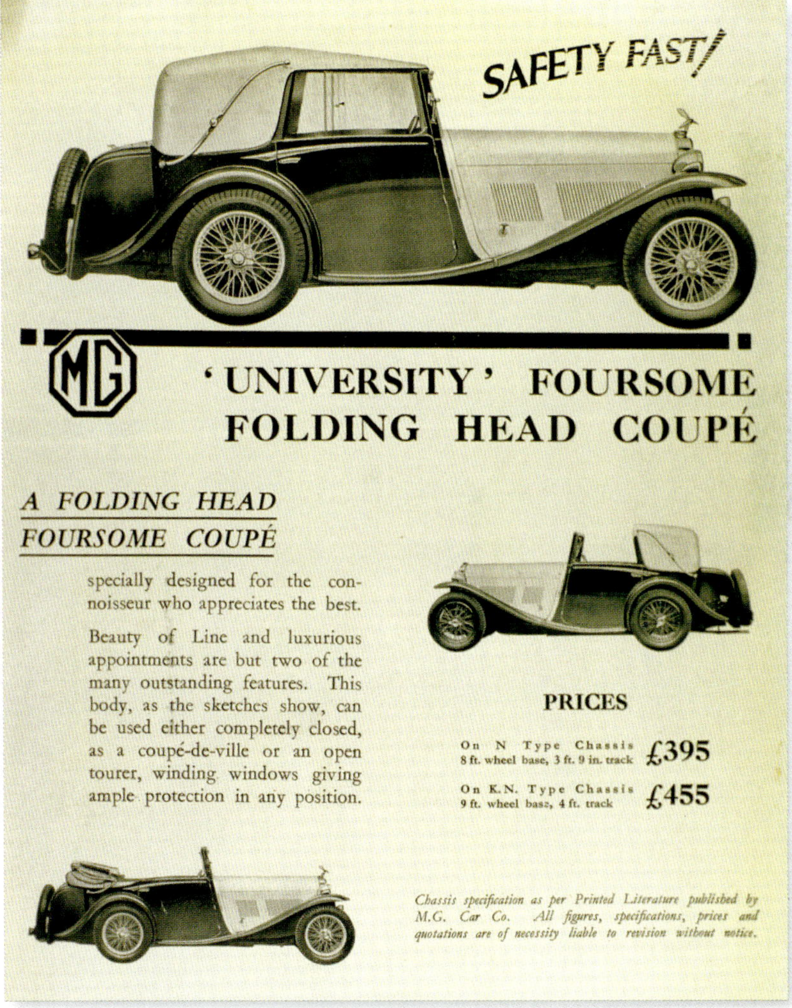

SAFETY FAST!
MG
'UNIVERSITY' FOURSOME FOLDING HEAD COUPÉ
A FOLDING HEAD FOURSOME COUPÉ
specially designed for the connoisseur who appreciates the best.
Beauty of Line and luxurious appointments are but two of the many outstanding features. This body, as the sketches show, can be used either completely closed, as a coupé-de-ville or an open tourer, winding windows giving ample protection in any position.
PRICES
On N Type Chassis 8 ft. wheel base, 3 ft. 9 in. track £395
On K.N. Type Chassis 9 ft. wheel base, 4 ft. track £455
Chassis specification as per Printed Literature published by M.G. Car Co. All figures, specifications, prices and quotations are of necessity liable to revision without notice.

The brochure showing the University Motors drophead coupé body available on the N-type chassis.

A superb example of the University Motors KN Tourer.

Another interesting car was the Maltby Drop Head Coupé. The Maltby Motor Works of Folkestone, Kent, had been in existence since 1902 and its activities over the years had included car manufacture and building commercial vehicles. Following a change of ownership in 1926 the emphasis switched to selling cars of various makes and building special bodies for customers wanting something different. They developed their drophead coupés and were the first British coachbuilder to automate raising and lowering the hood. The Maltby NA had an attractive, tail-heavy, body with the spare wheel set into a rear panel that folded down to give access to the boot and to reach the spare wheel.

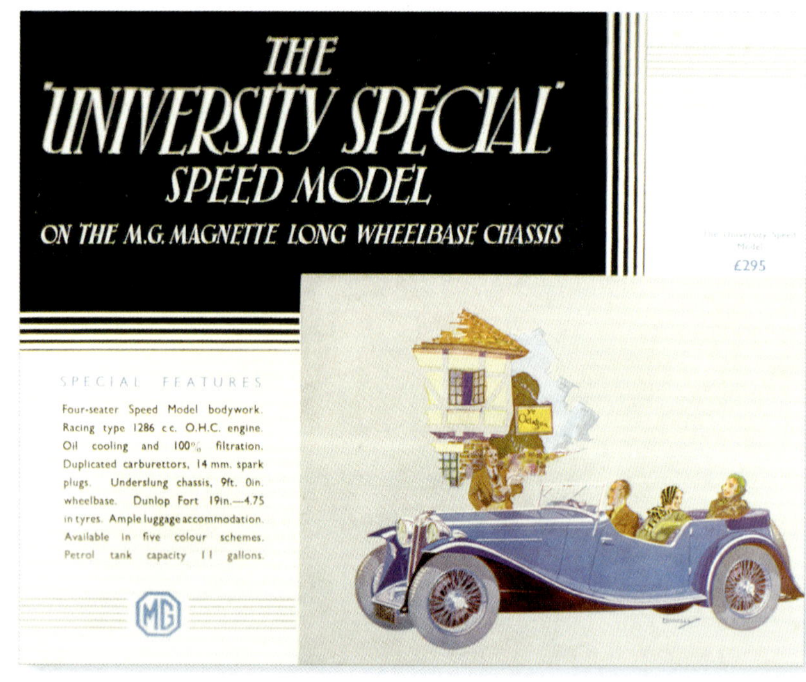

THE
'UNIVERSITY SPECIAL'
SPEED MODEL
ON THE M.G. MAGNETTE LONG WHEELBASE CHASSIS
£295
SPECIAL FEATURES
Four-seater Speed Model bodywork. Racing type 1286 c.c. O.H.C. engine. Oil cooling and 100% filtration. Duplicated carburettors, 14 mm. spark plugs. Underslung chassis, 9ft. 0in. wheelbase. Dunlop Fort 19in.—4.75 in tyres. Ample luggage accommodation. Available in five colour schemes. Petrol tank capacity 11 gallons.
MG

The special brochure produced for the University Motors Speed Model.

There had been a number of unsold K1 tourer bodies sitting around at the factory when the model was replaced, and a deal with the London main agents saw these being fitted to KN chassis and sold by them as "The University Motors Speed Model". Both the KN saloon marketed by the factory and the Speed Model proved to be much better cars than the original K1 versions. University Motors also advertised other models based on the N-type chassis. For some years the company had offered drophead coupé coachwork for MGs and a number had been built based on Magna or Magnette chassis. When the N-type arrived they advertised that they could supply this model on the standard chassis at £395 or on the KN chassis at £455. However, very few were produced.

Some other N-types were bodied abroad. Fritz Ramseier of coachbuilders Worblaufen put on a drophead coupé body, very similar to the Abbey K-type but with twin spare wheels and four horizontal bonnet louvres. In Switzerland, Sportcar AG of Zurich, the MG importers, also had a drophead coupé built. This had external pram irons and a large overhanging boot at the rear with spare wheel mounted behind that, making it somewhat tail-heavy. Also from Sportcar AG came a two-seater having a high rounded tail with twin spare wheels mounted behind. The bonnet sides had two rows of short, vertical louvres.

THE NE MAGNETTE

The TT-winning NE Magnette is now fitted with a modified P-type body similar to the one it would have carried in 1935 when it was one of the Musketeer trials team cars. Unlike the Cream Cracker cars, where the top of the bonnet was also painted brown, the colour scheme for the Musketeer cars was predominately cream, with only the wings and names being painted the darker colour.

When the N-Magnettes were introduced as the six-cylinder cars in the MG range there was no competition version on offer. In 1934 the factory were still disposing of the last few K3s they built. Racing cars date quickly, especially so when, partly because of the success enjoyed by models like the supercharged K3s, the authorities tended to adjust the handicapping or alter the regulations to give other entries a chance. Following a win in 1933 by the K3 driven by Tazio Nuvolari, one such change banned superchargers for the 1934 Tourist Trophy race and meant that the factory could not enter the K3. Keen to try to repeat their 1933 performance, thoughts turned to the N-type as an unsupercharged contender. In standard two-seater form it was neither quick enough nor light enough, so MG set about building a batch of cars tailored to meet the regulations.

Lightweight aluminium two-seater bodies designed to exactly conform to the rules were built and fitted to the N chassis, while the 1271cc engines were tuned to increase the power output to 74bhp. This was transmitted to the wheels via a two-plate clutch and a standard gearbox fitted with different ratios. To track-test the new cars, a team of three were run in the LCC Relay Race at Brooklands on 21 July. With drivers Miss Irene Schwedler, Miss Margaret Allen and Miss Doreen Evans, the team was placed third overall. After this debut for the new machines, the factory entered six cars for the TT. Three ran under the Eyston banner, one for George Eyston to drive himself and the others for Wal Handley and Charlie Dodson. Norman Black, A.P. Hamilton and W.G. "Bill" Everitt drove the other three cars. The three Eyston team cars' known as the Cream Crackers, were painted in cream with brown wings and brown stripes down the sides. Two of the other cars were

Charlie Dodson, who was also a skilled motorcycle racer, at the wheel of the NE Magnette in the 1934 Tourist Trophy Race.

painted dark green and the third, JB 4607 driven by Everitt, was painted Italian Racing Red as this was originally intended for Tazio Nuvolari to drive. One of the Eyston team cars, car 27 driven by Charlie Dodson, won the event.

As they were built specially for the 1934 race, all the cars returned to the factory once the event was over. Having some race cars on hand that were really surplus to requirements, it is not surprising that the Competition Department should try to see if they could fulfil another function. At that time a lot of effort was directed towards production car trials. Although the cars used in these events were nominally the property of their drivers, they were also usually returned to the factory afterwards for maintenance and modification.

In March 1935 the TT-winning NE, still wearing its competition number 27, was fitted with some deeply treaded tyres and taken, along with an ordinary two-seater N-type, to the Welsh mountains for a practice run for the Wye Cup Trial. Margaret Allen tried the NE on the hills and must have thought it sufficiently well suited to the task for the factory to convert three of the cars to trials specification. The changes made included fitting altered P-type bodies and standard full-width windscreens. The cars, called the Musketeers, with team drivers Lewis Welch, Freddy Kindell and Sam Nash, were painted the usual cream and brown and given the names Athos, Porthos and Aramis.

The trials NEs were driven in the Land's End and Edinburgh Trials, winning First Class awards, and were also used for the Abingdon/Abingdon and Rushmere events. The first Welsh Rally was a rather different type of competition but it seems to have been decided that an MG success in this would do

Three of the NEs raced under the leadership of George Eyston, here sitting on the side of his car. All his cars were painted cream, with brown wings and side stripes. Note the mesh windscreen, folded forward here, used to protect the driver against stones thrown up by other cars.

Charlie Dodson won the 1934 Tourist Trophy Race in the NE, thus thwarting attempts by the handicappers to stop MG being victorious for the second year in succession.

no harm. The three Musketeer NEs in the hands of the usual drivers set out from London, one of seven starting points, and the 1000-mile route took them via Bath, Leamington, Shrewsbury, Tenby, Llandudno, Llandrindod Wells and Chester to the Cardiff finish. Given their experience, it is not surprising that the MG team won their class, and Sam Nash in Aramis was placed first overall. It was another significant competition success to add to a growing list.

For the 1935 Tourist Trophy, in August the three NE Magnettes were stripped of their trials bodies and the special TT coachwork was refitted. By then the MG Car Company had withdrawn from participation in circuit racing and the cars had been sold to Bellevue Garage. There they were repainted blue and entered in the race under the name of the garage, but without repeating the success earned the previous year.

The 1935 Welsh Rally was a new event in the calendar and rather different from the trials usually tacked by the Musketeer cars. The three NEs converted for trials use started from London and at the end of the 1000-mile route had won their class, with Sam Nash in Aramis, JB 4750, placed first overall.

BELLEVUE GARAGE AND THE EVANS FAMILY

Kenneth, Doreen and Denis with the three J2s they ran as a team in a number of trials.

Any study of pre-war MG competition history is bound to make reference to Bellevue Garage and the Evans family. From the early 1930s up until the outbreak of war in 1939, cars prepared by the garage under the direction of their chief mechanic, Wilkie Wilkinson, were entered in numerous events. The Evans brothers, Denis and Kenneth, with their sister, Doreen, and the family-owned business, Bellevue Garage, certainly played a pivotal role in building the sporting reputation of the Abingdon cars in those exciting early years of the marque and in taking up the baton in 1935 once the factory ceased official participation in racing. Although it is not rare to find two members of the same family racing at the same time, having three siblings competing in events, often as a team, is rather more unusual. Also notable were the skill and bravery at the wheel they all displayed at a time when there were few measures to protect drivers in an accident and motor racing fatalities were all too common.

Interest in cars ran in the family. Their parents were early converts with their father, Bertrand Graham Evans, buying a Sunbeam in 1903, and their mother starting her motoring a couple of years later in a Renault. The family spent much of their spare time at Brooklands and so the children were raised with motor racing in their blood. They were comparatively affluent, the family owning Edwin Evans and Sons, Chartered Surveyors, and all the children had access to cars as soon as they were able to drive. Denis, the eldest, became so keen to be involved that he decided not to follow his father into the family firm but to make the motor trade his profession.

With the help of his father, in the early 1930s Denis established Bellevue Garage and Service Station in Bellevue Road, Wandsworth. At first they were general repairers and sold petrol, but the garage did provide a very useful base for maintaining the growing numbers of cars owned by the family. Bellevue also obtained a sub-agency from Jarvis of Wimbledon for selling MGs and Austins. The business would have probably stayed much like the majority of others at the time had it not been for the stroke of luck that led to Denis employing Wilkie Wilkinson. Based solely on his brilliance as a constructor and tuner of successful racing cars, the name of Bellevue Garage was to become almost as well known as those of the prominent drivers of the day who used their services.

Initially Wilkie was taken on as a fitter, but he quickly established himself as the most able man on the shop floor. Very soon he was given the job of running the workshop, and even the whole business when his boss was away racing. Denis had some success racing cars like the ex-Howe Bugatti, but it was the purchase of a C-type Midget that started his racing association with the MG marque and led to his garage gaining such a good reputation for preparing MG competition cars. In 1932 the C-type was used in a number of events, driven by either Denis or Kenneth, and on at least one occasion by Wilkie, who was also a very able racing driver.

At Brooklands in 1932 Denis entered the MG in the last event of the season, the BRDC 500-mile

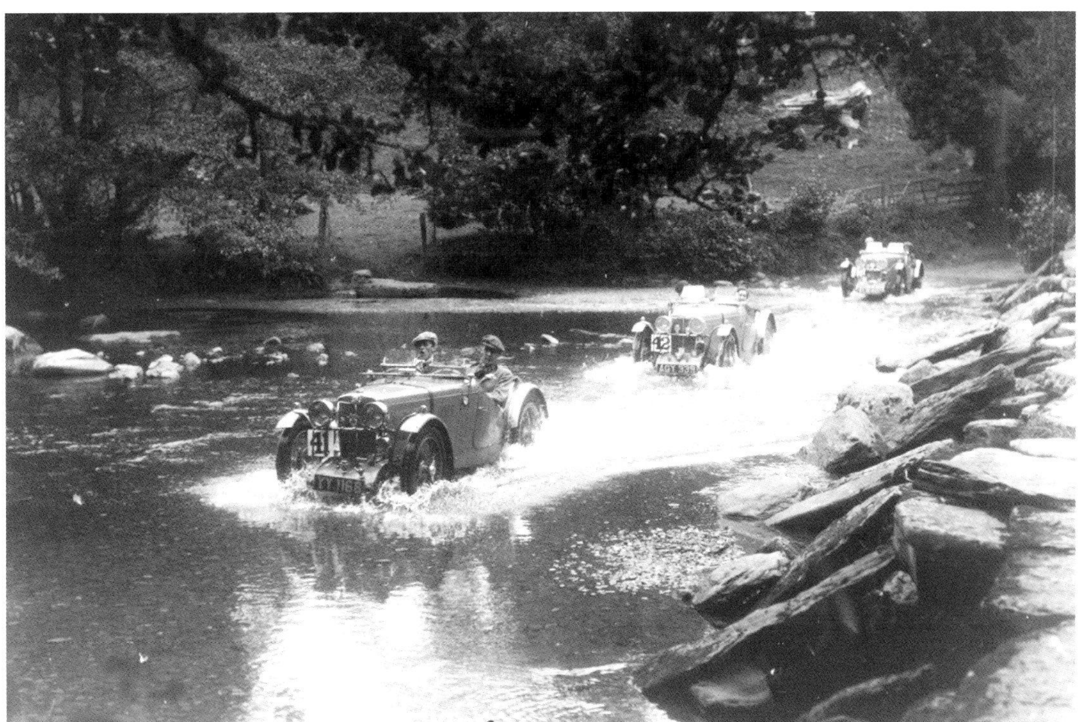

The Evans J2s at Tarr Steps on the Barnstaple Trial.

race. Sharing the car with Kenneth, who was still at university at the time, they were running in third place and putting in 100mph lap times when a piston failed. Kenneth had better luck with his MG at the opening Brooklands meeting in 1933 where he won a three-lap handicap on the mountain circuit. In the BRDC Empire Trophy Meeting that year Kenneth was placed second in the India Trophy race, with the MG prepared by Wilkie averaging 98.70mph.

The family purchased three J2 Midgets. The first to arrive was a brand new, green-painted example delivered to Kenneth Evans in October 1932. Doreen Evans reached her 17th birthday in June 1933 and her presents included a smart black cycle-wing J2. There was obviously every intention for this to be used in competition because before delivery the factory were asked to fit all competition modifications. The third J2 was not brand new, but sold originally in May 1933 to a Mr Clark of Bromley. However, he must have kept this black J2 for only a short while and within a few months it was in the hands of Denis Evans.

Although her car had been competition prepared at Abingdon, Doreen persuaded Wilkie to work his magic on the engine and to take her to Brooklands to see how well it went. However, the first real competition outing for her in the J2 appears to have been the W.A.S.A. Trial held in October 1933. Following a start at Virginia Water in Surrey, the route took in many of the hills used by the better-known Exeter Trial before reaching the finish at Shaftesbury. Wearing her finishing school hat and scarf in green with yellow bands, she did well enough in this ladies-only event to take a first class award and earn a mention in press reports. All three J2s were soon repainted in the Bellevue house colour of mid-blue, the exact shade being selected by Mrs Evans.

Doreen Evans driving her J2, AGY339, in Gypsy Lane on the 1934 Colmore Cup Trial. This car survives and is still occasionally used for such events.

Doreen Evans tackling a special test in a Bellevue Garage N-type special during the Eastbourne Rally.

BELLEVUE GARAGE & SERVICE STATIONS L^TD

Manager
DENIS G. EVANS
Phone ; Battersea 0479.
agents for the
MG
sports

Any make of car supplied.
Hire purchase terms arranged.
Cars taken in part exchange.
Cars specially tuned for racing and reliability events.

BELLEVUE GARAGE

18-19, BELLEVUE ROAD, WANDSWORTH COMMON, S.W.17.

1933 advert for Bellevue Garage.

1934 saw a full and successful season of events for the Evans family. The J2s often ran as a team, with Neville Lloyd taking the driver's seat in Doreen's car for those trials where in the days before political correctness ladies were not permitted to compete. Despite her youth and relative lack of experience, it quickly became apparent that Doreen possessed the skills of a natural racing driver. Quick reactions, sympathy with the machinery she drove, and no lack of courage when conditions were difficult, were some of the virtues mentioned in contemporary reports.

Things were really warming up at Bellevue Garage and they were being asked to prepare more and more cars for other drivers. Having outgrown their J2s, at the end of 1934 three N-type chassis were purchased. They were fitted with lightweight bodies and the minimum of equipment needed to make them road legal. All were finished in Bellevue Garage blue and then used for a wide variety of trials, sprints and hill-climbs. Earlier that year they had acquired a Q-type for serious circuit racing. In this car Kenneth had some success, including third place in a wet Nuffield Trophy Race at Donington Park and second place in a race at the last Brooklands event of 1934.

Over the 1934/35 winter, the Q-type was stripped of its two-seater road/racing body and fitted with single-seater coachwork designed by Wilkie Wilkinson and built by Alert Motor Works of Kentish Town. As part of the modifications, the springs were flattened to lower the car and the steering column was moved to suit a central driving position. Transformed in appearance and looking very like the newly announced R-type MGs, during the 1935 season the car was driven by both Doreen and Kenneth. Now a lot lighter and quicker, the Q-type won a handicap race at the first Brooklands meeting in 1935. Doreen was the driver.

Bellevue Garage was also an early customer for one of the all-independent suspension R-types, and the 1935 International Trophy Race at Brooklands was the first outing for the new model. The Bellevue team for the event consisted of Doreen in the R-type, Kenneth in the single-seater Q, and Donald Letts in the ex-George Eyston Magic Magnette. All the cars were immaculately turned

The 1935 BRDC Empire Trophy Race at Brooklands. Car 6, Denis Evans in the Q-type, finished in 14th place, but Kenneth (7) had to retire when his R-type developed mechanical problems.

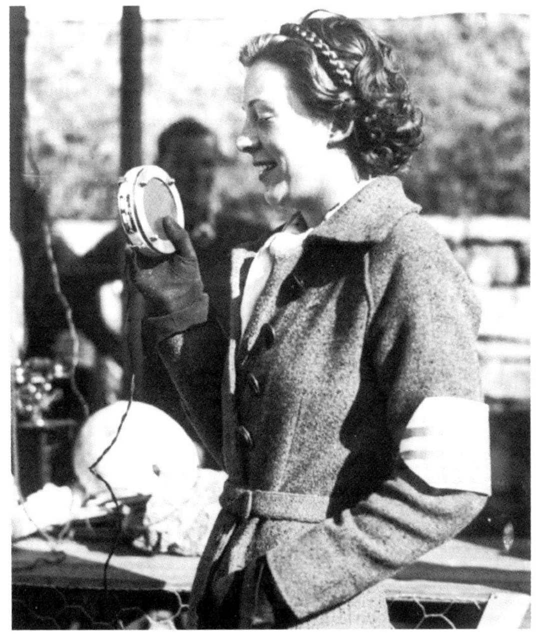

Doreen Evans using a microphone at the 1935 Ards Tourist Trophy Race.

During practice for the 1936 JCC International Race, Doreen Evans at the wheel of Kenneth's R-type talks to Wilkie, who is alongside the car.

out in their usual blue paintwork. There were in all five of the new R-types entered. In addition to the Bellevue car, three ran as George Eyston's team and were driven in the race by Norman Black, George Eyston, and Wal Handley. Bill Everitt and Sir Malcolm Campbell shared another R-type. The new racers ran well on the bumpy track but exhibited an alarming amount of roll on the corners. Various problems eliminated all but two of them, but these took first and second places in their class. Doreen was second in class and seventh overall, the Magnette of Letts was 11th and Kenneth qualified as a finisher. They were awarded the team prize.

Doreen was getting the lion's share of the publicity. This was hardly surprising seeing that she was still a teenager, very attractive, and competing on equal terms with men in a male-dominated world. The popular press had dubbed her a Speed Queen and her reputation for daring was enhanced

The premises of Bellevue Garage racing department in Althorp Road taken at the start of the war.

The Doreen Evans J2 survives in superb condition.

by exploits like the one when the R-type fitted with the experimental twin-cam head driven by her in the 1936 JCC International Trophy Race caught fire at speed. She had to leap from the car whilst it was still moving and suffered burns to her legs. This did not, however, stop her attending a dance that evening.

MG withdrew official factory support from racing in the middle of the 1935 season and this was bound eventually to have an effect on the activities of the Evans family. However, right up to the war Bellevue-prepared MGs were successful, although Kenneth increasingly turned his attention to competing in other makes of car. After leaving university he joined the family business and cars remained purely a hobby for him. Doreen was one of the team of ladies chosen by George Eyston to drive three P-types entered for Le Mans in 1935. She shared a car with Barbara Skinner, from whom that year she took the crown of ladies champion at Shelsley Walsh. Doreen on her first visit to the hill broke the record driving an R-type. That earlier incident with the fiery R-type was almost her last motor race for many years. She had become engaged to Alan Phipps of Colorado and the couple were wed on 29 July 1936.

In 1937 the racing car preparation part of Bellevue Garage was moved into separate premises in nearby Althorp Road. There some houses owned by the Evans family were demolished to make way for a purpose-built workshop, complete with their own dynamometer. Conditions were palatial compared to the old premises; it even had central heating and wood block floors. Wilkie was director and manager and his place at the garage part of the business was taken by his brother, Frank, who was a qualified engineer and well suited to the task. The pity was that all the expertise built up by the Bellevue team was lost a couple of years later when the war came. Racing cars were no longer a priority and the staff had to move to other jobs.

When the Doreen Evans J2 was restored it was repainted in the shade of blue used pre-war for the Bellevue Garages competition cars.

THE P-TYPE MIDGET

By 1934 the MG Midget was an established part of the motoring scene. Since they had first appeared six years earlier, hardly a race or production car trial in the country had been held without a gaggle of them appearing in the programme. The MG marque was now widely admired, and the fame they gained during those few years sustained many an advertising campaign for the cars that followed. The Midget, however, was starting to grow up and the new P-type model announced in March 1934 was a bit larger, heavier, and better equipped than its starkly simple forerunners.

The reputation for fragility gained by the eager little engine in the J-type was obviously not desirable and work carried out on the related six-cylinder engines had shown that a substantial re-design would be necessary. A heavier crankshaft running in three main bearings was the solution, whilst at the top end the diameter of the camshaft and bearings were increased, and other components strengthened. The revised engine had a similar power output to the J-type, approximately 36bhp, but was both smoother and more robust than the earlier unit.

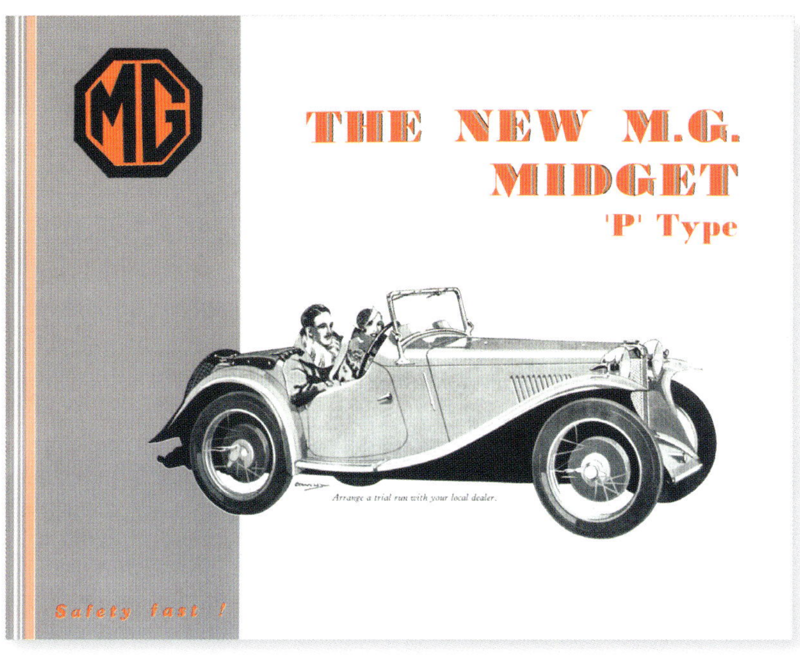

The lavish brochure produced when the PA was announced in September 1934.

There was nothing radically wrong with the J-type chassis, so with some minor revisions it was used for the P-type. The spare wheel mounting had proved to be easily damaged, so the main side members of the chassis were extended rearward to allow a rigid bracket for the spare to be bolted

As can be seen in this view of a P-type rolling chassis, the side rails were fairly slender and the cross-tubes also served as mounting points for the rear springs. The long rear-mounted 12v battery was a feature of most of the OHC models.

Prices and colour schemes from the 1934 brochure.

DE LUXE EXTRA EQUIPMENT

	£	s.	d.
Bluemel "Malcolm Campbell" or "Ashby" Steering Wheel	1	1	0
Eight-day Clock - - - -	1	17	6
Dash type Radiator Thermometer - -	1	8	6
Dash type Oil Thermometer -	1	8	6
Bonnet Strap and Fittings - -	1	5	0
Quick Filler Cap for Radiator - -		15	6
Quick Filler Cap for Petrol Tank - -		15	6
Head Lamp Stone Guards - - -	2	3	0

The de luxe equipment (listed above) ordered with the car is available at the inclusive figure of £10 : 0 : 0, including fitting. Individual items may be had at the figures quoted, including fitting.

	£	s.	d.
D.W.S. Four Wheel Jacking System - -	5	5	0

Complete list of extras may be had on application.

COLOUR FINISHES

Exterior	*Body*	*Wings*	*Upholstery*
Black/Green	Black	Black	Apple Green
Black/Blue	Black	Black	Cerulean Blue
Black Red	Black	Black	Deep Red
* Ulster Green Dublin Green	Dublin Green	Ulster Green	Apple Green
Oxford Blue Cambridge Blue	Cambridge Blue	Oxford Blue	Cerulean Blue
Carmine Red Saratoga Red	Saratoga Red	Carmine Red	Deep Red

* In the case of duotone colours the darker shade is listed first. Carpets and hoods are black on all models.

Every precaution has been taken to ensure accuracy of this specification, the right however is reserved to vary it without notice. March, 1934.

in place. The chassis extension also provided a convenient mounting for the rear number plate and lights, as well as for the optional luggage rack offered by some accessory manufacturers.

Track was unchanged, but the axles now carried 12-inch brakes, which considerably improved the stopping power of the now heavier car. As with the J-type, two- and four-seater open coachwork was available. In addition, there was the Airline Coupé, also available on the NA chassis. The body fitted to both open cars followed the general lines established with the J-type, although the addition of over an inch to the wheelbase, and the extension at the rear of the frame, allowed the designers to make the bodies slightly bigger. As with later J2s, swept wings were the order of the day, improving both the appearance and comfort of the cars.

The sturdy spare wheel mounting fixed to chassis side rail extensions was an improvement and on the two-seater these rails also supported the number plate. A single rear stop/tail lamp was all that was required at the time.

Cockpit changes included revised instruments with a panel placed centrally incorporating an odometer. Set ahead of the driver, the tachometer with octagonal surround doubled as a speedometer, with the speeds in each gear indicated on the dial markings. In front of the passenger a matching panel contained the ammeter, oil pressure gauge and ignition/light switches. The dashboard itself had a veneered wood surface, with chromed edging, and the instrument faces and dash lamps were painted brown. Additional instruments, like a clock and a water temperature gauge, were optional extras.

A range of single and duo-tone colour schemes was offered and an attractive 12-page brochure was produced to promote sales. For ordinary road use, despite the additional weight of the chassis and coachwork, the much smoother engine gave the car similar performance to the earlier model. The new Midget was well received by the motoring press and in their road test of a factory demonstrator *Motor Sport* recorded a top speed of 72mph, whilst commenting that 80mph was easily within reach given a favourable slope. However, many sporting motorists were by then starting to look for something more in the way of performance from their MGs.

The answer to providing more power was either to improve the breathing by supercharging, or to increase the capacity of the engine. Some owners chose the supercharging route, and for a total cost of £27 M. A. McEvoy Limited offered a works-approved Zoller supercharger kit that was claimed to increase top speed to over 80mph and to knock a few seconds off the time taken to reach 60mph.

A nicely restored PA Midget exhibits the appeal of the model.

PA Midgets remain popular cars with MG club members and are seen at many meetings.

A Marshall supercharger kit was also available at a similar price; this had a front-mounted blower driven from the crankshaft while the Zoller kit used a side-mounted unit and belt drive.

The MG Car Company, however, looked to increasing the capacity of the engine as a cheaper and more reliable alternative. The block casting was modified to allow it to be bored out to 60mm, increasing the capacity to 939cc and power output to 43bhp. Improvement was not confined merely to enlarging engine size. For the revised model, now called the PB, the superseded Midget being referred to as the PA, the gear ratios were changed and the steering box and prop-shaft modified. In

When the PB model was introduced a major visual change was the introduction of radiator grille slats, setting a style that was to last until the end of T-type production in 1955. When fitted, the hood and side-screens provide good protection from the weather.

Unlike some earlier models, all the P-type Midgets had silver painted wire wheels.

the cockpit, the driver was provided with a separate, centrally mounted speedometer and the tachometer was no longer marked with the road speeds in each gear. Externally, the PB had a slatted radiator grille to identify it from the earlier model.

In their January 1936 test of the PB, *The Autocar* road test confirmed the improved performance, recording a reduction of nearly five seconds in the time it took to reach 60mph, and a maximum speed of over 75mph. The revised model was priced

The PB is one of the most attractive of the pre-war Midgets.

The enlarged PB engine is externally identical to the PA unit and both are capable of being tuned or supercharged to produce more power.

at £222, with unsold stocks of PAs being offered at £199.10s. However, this was not altogether successful and the company resorted to converting 27 PAs to PB specification. Some PA owners even wrote to the factory requesting that their second-hand cars be converted to PBs but, unsurprisingly, this was refused and it was suggested they buy a new PB.

The PA and PB MGs are amongst the most appealing of pre-war small sports cars and a

With the ability to carry two children in the rear seat, a four-seater PB is ideal for family visits to club events.

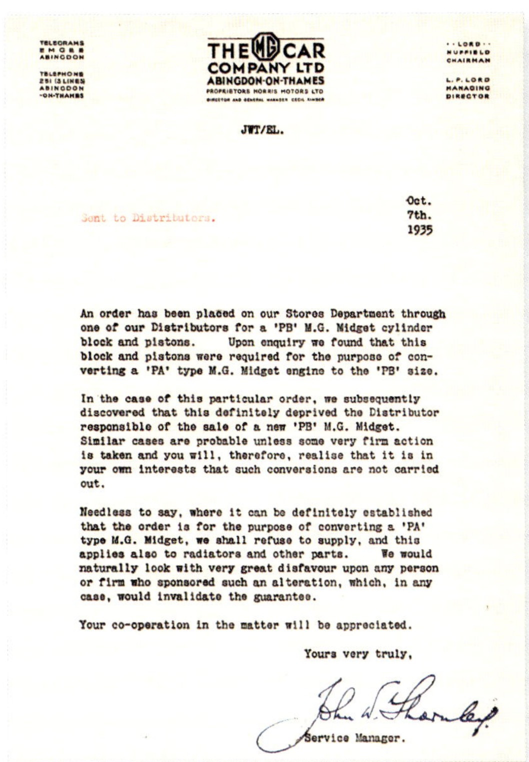

TELEGRAMS EMGEE ABINGDON
TELEPHONE 251 (3 LINES) ABINGDON-ON-THAMES

THE MG CAR COMPANY LTD
ABINGDON-ON-THAMES
PROPRIETORS MORRIS MOTORS LTD
DIRECTOR AND GENERAL MANAGER CECIL KIMBER

LORD NUFFIELD CHAIRMAN
L. P. LORD MANAGING DIRECTOR

JWT/EL.

Sent to Distributors.

Oct. 7th. 1935

An order has been placed on our Stores Department through one of our Distributors for a 'PB' M.G. Midget cylinder block and pistons. Upon enquiry we found that this block and pistons were required for the purpose of converting a 'PA' type M.G. Midget engine to the 'PB' size.

In the case of this particular order, we subsequently discovered that this definitely deprived the Distributor responsible of the sale of a new 'PB' M.G. Midget. Similar cases are probable unless some very firm action is taken and you will, therefore, realise that it is in your own interests that such conversions are not carried out.

Needless to say, where it can be definitely established that the order is for the purpose of converting a 'PA' type M.G. Midget, we shall refuse to supply, and this applies also to radiators and other parts. We would naturally look with very great disfavour upon any person or firm who sponsored such an alteration, which, in any case, would invalidate the guarantee.

Your co-operation in the matter will be appreciated.

Yours very truly,

John W. Thornley

Service Manager.

A letter to dealers regarding PA to PB conversions.

remarkable proportion of the original production run of 2500 survives. Hood up, the two-seater is no less attractive, but the four-seater looks rather heavy around the rear quarters. The rare P-type Airline Coupé is a gem. The body is little heavier than those of the open cars and thus performance is still good. These are one of the nicest closed cars of the period one could wish to find.

Streamlined cars were fashionable in the mid-1930s and the P-type Airline Coupé was a comfortable and attractive alternative to larger saloon cars.

The P-type Airline Coupé is a rare beast as only 28 PAs and 14 PB models were built.

GEORGE EYSTON AND HIS DANCING DAUGHTERS

Before receiving registration plates the MG cars and their drivers for the 1935 Le Mans Race are posed by the Abingdon factory for a picture.

An enduring debate in the world of Formula One concerns the lack of women drivers at the top end of the sport. When smaller stature and lighter weight are so advantageous for modern grand prix drivers it seems strange that so few women are even considered for a seat in one of the top teams. It certainly cannot be because women lack the courage or determination to succeed, as those who compete in many other sports have proved time and time again. Strangely, pre-war, when motor racing was arguably more dangerous and many top drivers lost their lives, there were a number of women who competed on equal terms with men and often beat them.

A major reason for any motor manufacturer to spend money supporting a racing team was to gain publicity for their products, and having women drivers is a sure way to attract attention. One of the most important events in the calendar was the

Under the direction of George Eyston, the cars and drivers were given a trial run at Brooklands before going to France.

24-hour race run on closed public roads near the French town of Le Mans. The first event was staged there in 1923 and the popularity of this endurance race grew year by year; by the early 1930s it enjoyed considerable coverage in the British daily press and weekly motoring magazines. One obvious reason for this was the consecutive outright victories achieved by the Bentley team.

Although the MG Car Company did not produce a road-going vehicle capable of outright victory in the race, there were other prizes for which they could compete. MG's involvement started in 1930 when the factory prepared two privately entered M-type Midgets, one for F.H.B. Samuelson and Freddie Kindell, the other for R.C. Murton-Neale and Jack Hicks. Neither completed the full 24 hours. In 1931 there were again two MGs entered, but this time it was the new Montlhéry Midgets that were used. One was driven by the 1930 team of Samuelson and Kindell, the other by the Hon. Mrs Chetwynd and H.H. Stisted. Once again neither featured in the results.

There were MGs at Le Mans in the following years and this must have prompted Cecil Kimber to enter a factory team for the 1935 event. That year there was a larger entry and the British dominated the programme with 37 out of the 58 that started. There were no less than nine Singers, seven Aston-Martins and seven MGs competing. The MG entry by George Eyston attracted a lot of attention, not least because an all-female team were driving three P-types. Three Magnettes joined the three P-types and another Midget in the race and many British spectators made the journey to France to support their countrymen.

Captain George Eyston was chosen to lead the MG factory entry for the 1935 race. His experiences in the army and in business had honed his organisational skills and his ability to get on with people of every class and type. A kindly man, he earned great respect from all who met or worked for him and he was the ideal leader of any team. The Dancing Daughters name given to his team was certainly not his choice and is said to have come from a song popular at the time.

In contemporary reports of the race the three P-types were described as being to standard specification except for having twin fuel pumps. However, a glance at the factory records for the cars reveals that they actually received quite a lot of additional attention before being shipped to France. A note in January 1935 from the Competition Department to the Works Manager gives an estimate that 205 hours work would be necessary to prepare each car to Le Mans trim. Taking a look at the job sheet reveals that in addition to those double fuel pumps many other items received attention. The engines, for example, were completely stripped: con-rods, crankshaft and pistons, were balanced, ports and combustion chambers in the cylinder head polished, and manifolds carefully matched. The engines were then assembled using racing valves and springs and mated to standard P-type gearboxes that had been rebuilt incorporating J-type gear ratios. A scoop was fitted to direct cool air on to the sump during the race.

The MG team on the dockside at Rouen after the cars had been lifted off the ship.

The basic chassis and springs were not altered, but Q-type brakes were fitted and the front axles had NE shock absorbers. Stronger 42-spoke racing wire wheels were specified, along with sets of 19 x 4.00 racing tyres. The standard bodies were carefully checked to see they complied with the regulations and the rear compartments had clips fitted to hold spares as at Le Mans only parts actually carried in the car could be used in the race. Special locks were used to make sure that chassis flex on the bumpy circuit could not cause a door to fly open at an inconvenient moment. The normal windscreen glass was removed and substituted with a mesh screen, which could be raised to protect the drivers if stones thrown up by other cars became a problem, and the drivers were also provided with aero screens.

To save weight and reduce drag, the swept wings were removed and K3 cycle wings fitted, using a pairs of J2 wing stays at the front. The

Posed for a picture on the Le Mans circuit before official practice began.

front valances had cooling holes cut in them and the radiators and headlamps were fitted with stone guards. Aluminium bonnets with additional louvres replaced the steel PA items and all the cars received a new coat of British Racing Green paint and Union Jack transfers. The bodies of all the lamps were given a dull finish to avoid reflections.

The weather for the 1935 race was poor right from the start. Immaculately prepared cars lined up in front of the pit counter were drenched by a heavy downpour, as were the drivers standing on the opposite side of the track awaiting the starting flag. The rain eased off moments before the start, but heavy showers dogged most of the race. Despite the weather, or perhaps because of it, British cars dominated the proceedings and of the 28 cars that finished, 22 were British, a Lagonda taking overall honours.

Prepared to the high standard that had become the trademark of the Abingdon Competition Department, the three MG P-types ran faultlessly in the race and finished in eighth, ninth and 10th places in the 1-litre class. The cars circulated steadily as the aim was to get all cars to the finish, partly in order to qualify to run a team in the 1936 race. The attention of the race reporters concentrated on the fact that all the drivers were female, even mentioning that one of the drivers took time to tidy her hair whilst rounding a slow corner. However, they were not the only women to compete and the Riley shared by Kay Petre and Mrs Elsie Wisdom put up a fine performance before a big-end failure put them out of the race.

Other MGs in the race had mixed fortunes. A K3 Magnette driven by Maillard Brune and Druck ran in the two-litre class because its 1100cc engine was supercharged. They finished the race at an average speed of 70.79mph and were placed first in class,

The team with their leader, George Eyston in front of the pits prior to the race.

The P-types were set a steady race pace in order to ensure the best chance of finishing. The weather that year was miserable and the wet track must have made things difficult, especially in the dark.

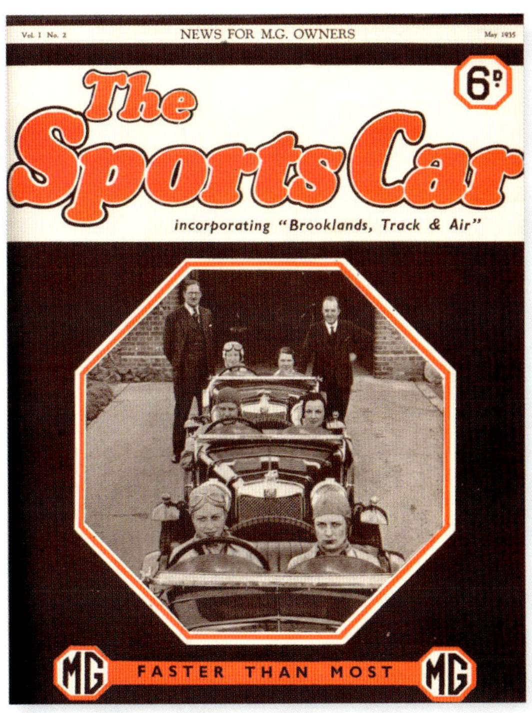

As part of the publicity, the team were featured on the cover of the MG Car Company supported magazine, **The Sports Car**.

This advertisement was placed in a number of magazines.

a great result. Magnettes piloted by Hertzberger and Ford retired during the hours of darkness, one through failure of the supercharger and the other after a piston expired. A Midget driven by Debille and Viale went out with supercharger problems.

All the efforts made to get the MG team to the finish intact in order to qualify for the 1936 race were to no avail. Not only had the factory withdrawn its official support of racing by then, but the race itself was cancelled just a week before it was due to run. France at that time was in a period of civil unrest and the effect of the communist-led strikes was to paralyse much of industry, including the car factories. Bugatti himself could not get into his own factory and not all of the many French cars entered that year were likely to be ready to race.

THE Q-TYPE MIDGET

As standard, the Q-type was fitted with a Brooklands silencer that did little to reduce the considerable volume of sound produced by the 750cc supercharged power unit.

Although the two-seater racing body seen here as fitted by the factory was quite light and produced very little drag, owners in search of even more speed later fitted single-seater bodies to almost all of the cars.

The J4 Midget had been introduced to provide a sports/racing car in the 750cc class, which MG considered their preserve following the success of the C-type Montlhéry Midget. However, as power output of the four-cylinder engine increased it was obvious that the chassis was unable to cope, and as a result a number of drivers found the car tricky to handle. Early in 1934 The Company announced a new four-cylinder racing car, the Q-type. Having had a season of successes with the K3 Magnette they provided the new QA Midget with a chassis of the same wheelbase as the K3 and utilising the four-inch chassis side members of the K-series cars. The track at 3ft 9in was the same as used on the NA model. N-type axles, steering and brake gear were fitted, but with uprated brake drums.

The four-cylinder, three main bearing P-type engine formed the basis of the power unit. Fitting a short-stroke 73mm crank produced a capacity of 746cc whilst a specially designed Zoller Q4 supercharger driven from the front of the crankshaft delivered a boost of just under 30psi. The claimed power output was 113bhp at 7200rpm. The gearbox was an ENV pre-selector unit and the flywheel incorporated a two-plate clutch without external actuating mechanism, designed to protect the gearbox and final drive by slipping when a specific torque level was reached. The Q-type was fitted

The Q-type cockpit. Dials include a tachometer, radiator and oil thermometers, plus inlet manifold pressure and oil pressure gauges.

Twin six-volt batteries were stowed beneath the detachable tail section.

with a lightweight two-seater body with pointed tail and to the casual observer it looked very similar to the 1934 K3 Magnette. The engine produced only slightly less power than the six-cylinder K3 so the overall package was extremely quick.

At the Brooklands Whitsun Meeting on 21 May 1934 the first Q-type was entered by Bill Everitt and on his first outing with the car he won the Fourth Merrow Mountain Handicap and in so doing broke the Brooklands Class H Mountain Lap Record with a speed of 69.97mph. Despite this success, the handling of the Q-type was not as much of an improvement over the J4 as had been hoped. However, for a car with a reputation of being a brute it is surprising that it seems to have reacted well to a delicate touch, as in their Q-types Doreen Evans and Dorothy Stanley-Turner, both petite young women, achieved several notable well-driven victories over their male counterparts.

The shortcomings of the chassis led directly to the introduction of the all independently sprung R-type the following year and no further development of the car took place at the MG factory, apart from improvements to the lubrication of the supercharger and alterations to the cooling system to prevent the overheating and cylinder head cracking which plagued the standard engine. However, private tuners did a lot of work on the model with Wilkie Wilkinson at Bellevue Garages modifying QA0254 to single-seater form for the Evans family and Robin Jackson at Brooklands rebuilding a crashed QA0258 into the single-seater in which George Harvey-Noble in August 1937 broke the Brooklands Class H Outer Circuit Lap record with a speed of 122.4mph, an all-time record for that capacity.

The Zoller supercharger developed by M.A. McEvoy was driven from the front of the crankshaft and produced nearly 30lbs of boost. The quoted output from the 746cc engine was 113bhp at 7200rpm.

THE R-TYPE MIDGET

In this picture of the nearside of the car one can see the way the engine and gearbox are mounted between the two legs that form the front of the R-type chassis.

Despite their success, both on the track and with the customers, the MGs built up to 1934 were based on exploiting conventional automotive practice, rather than being truly innovative. However, for a short few months the MG Car Company looked set to lead the industry in the search for new and better ways to build racing and sports cars. In 1935 they announced to the press a racing car that had a really advanced chassis and a suspension system promising new standards of roadholding and handling. Furthermore, this technology was already earmarked for use in a forthcoming MG luxury saloon. That both projects were to be axed within weeks was a tragedy, both for MG and for the British motor industry as a whole.

In the early years of the marque, under the leadership of founder Cecil Kimber the man most responsible for shaping the way the cars developed was Hubert Noel Charles. This talented designer held a BSc in Engineering from London University and Kimber met him after Charles went to Morris Motors at Cowley as a technical assistant on production. When the MG Car Company moved to Abingdon in 1930 Charles was engaged to run the drawing office and, as we have seen, it was under his direction that the effective and long-lived

A close-up view of the rear of the chassis shows the differential mounting and short driveshafts to each rear wheel.

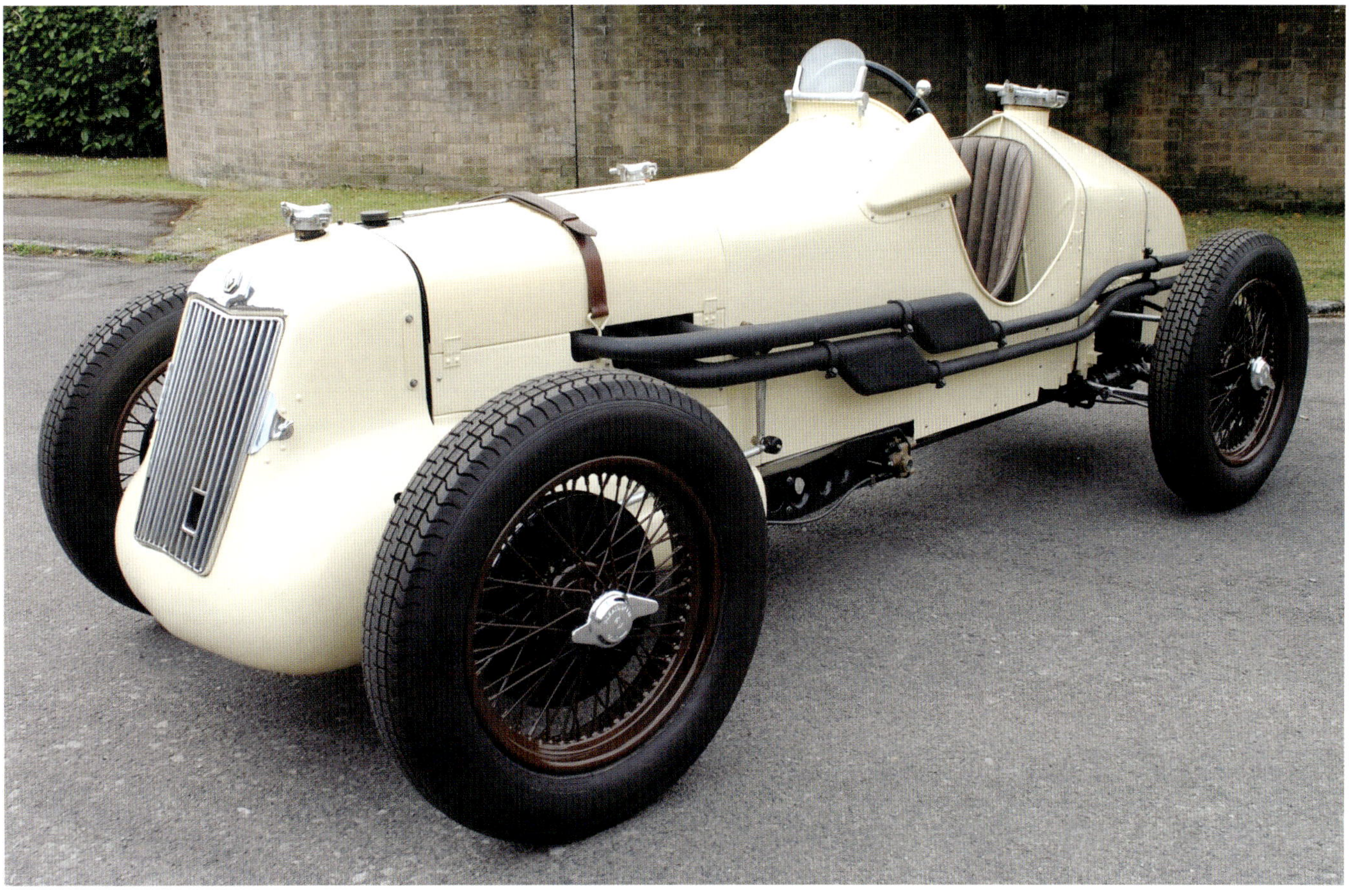

This superb, totally accurate replica of an R-type was built from scratch by Geoff Enoch.

MG chassis first used for EX 120 and the C-type was developed for subsequent models. By 1934 the Q-type engine was producing a greater power output per litre than any other of its time. This made the car a winner but also highlighted the relative lack of traction and roadholding available from the standard MG leaf-sprung chassis and its solid front and rear axles.

Current thinking was that stiff tape-bound leaf springs restrained by friction dampers were the best arrangement for reducing roll and controlling the movement of rigid front and rear axles. Often axle deflection was so restricted that over bumps only the flexing of the chassis kept all four wheels on the ground. This worked efficiently on well-surfaced circuits and gave the cars excellent handing. However, show the car a bump mid-corner and things went wrong very quickly, as many drivers found to their cost.

To better use the considerable power produced by the racing engines it was going to be necessary to devise a way of keeping all four wheels on the ground for as long as possible whilst coping with the indifferent surfaces found at many race venues,

Programme for the 1935 International Trophy Race, the first event with R-types in the entry list.

The R-type engine is a tight fit beneath the bonnet of this replica R-type single-seater racing car.

for example the notorious bumps in the Brooklands concrete. Elsewhere, particularly in Europe, designers were turning to forms of independent suspension. It was obvious that using solid axles imposed an inherent disadvantage, as the vertical movement of any one wheel would automatically affect the other mounted on the same axle, no matter how firm the suspension. It was relatively easy to fit separate axles for the front wheels, but less so for those at the rear where they also had to do the job of transmitting power to the road surface.

Charles quickly realised that there was little use in merely fitting a form of independent suspension to the existing design of MG chassis. To take full advantage of fitting softer springs to keep the wheels on the road, and in order to provide a rigid mounting for the suspension arms and springs, the chassis had to be far stiffer. This is where he was to take a totally different approach, producing a radical departure from previous practice.

Working under the direction of Charles, the design team of Cecil Cousins, Syd Enever and Bill Renwick devised a light and rigid chassis for the new MG racing car, the R-type. This consisted of a central backbone that ran from just behind the driver's seat to the back of the gearbox, where it divided into two separate arms, each running to the front on either side of the power unit. A box section united the front legs of the chassis and the differential was attached to the rear of the structure. The immensely strong chassis was electrically welded from 16-gauge steel, but was light enough to be carried by one man.

Double wishbones independently suspended by torsion bars replaced the beam axles and leaf springs fitted previously. These bars provided the springing medium by resisting twisting loads imposed as the wishbones were deflected. The bars were mounted parallel to the frame, and were adjustable to vary the ride height. Damping was provided by hydraulic shock absorbers; these were later to prove a weak link in the design. Power from the engine was transmitted to the rear by a short prop-shaft via a pre-selector gearbox fitted with the same slip clutch arrangement as the Q-type. A quadrant lever alongside the steering wheel operated the gear selection for the Wilson pre-selector unit with a foot pedal controlling the actual operation of the change. The chassis-mounted differential transferred power to the rear wheels via two short driveshafts that incorporated sliding splines and universal joints.

Power was provided by a slightly modified version of the already-successful Q-type engine. Efforts to improve reliability were made, necessary with the front-mounted Zoller blower giving induction pressures of around 28lb and an output of 113bhp. The central driver's seat was mounted over the transmission tunnel, placing the pedal operating the pre-selector gearbox on the left and throttle and brake pedals on the right. The fuel tank mounted behind the driving seat was shaped to match the external panels. The steering box was specially constructed for the car and featured twin drop arms, one to operate each front wheel. Despite the modernity of the rest of the design, the car retained a cable-operated system for the brakes, with the external handbrake working on all four wheels, as was usual MG practice. The instrument panel was carried on a steel framework fixed to the chassis so that it remained in place when the aluminium panels providing the bodywork were removed. A neat, sloping version of the MG grille was mounted ahead of the radiator and overall the car looked every inch a racer, as well as quite unlike anything else previously built by the company.

The plan was to assemble an initial batch of 10 cars and these were completed between April and June 1935. There was every hope that more would be needed, and that the advanced chassis technology would soon appear in the big MG saloon, a prototype of which was already at an advanced stage of development. However, this was not to be, and further development of the new racing car was halted soon after the car was launched by the announcement of a radical reorganisation of the company. The changes that followed from this were to alter the future direction of the MG marque and terminate their participation at the leading edge of technology, occasional record-breaking attempts and competition participation apart.

As for the R-types that were built, how successful were they? The revolutionary design was certainly not without its defects: the cars proved to have too high a roll centre and their torsion bars did not have exactly the right stiffness. As a result the lean on corners was rather disconcerting and the rear end tended to have more of a tendency to break away than should have been the case. Additionally, the shock absorber technology of the time was not well adapted to coping with relatively long-travel suspensions and the units overheated and became less effective as races progressed. None of those shortcomings would have hampered progress for long, given the full attention of the development department, but that was no longer an option now that it had been transferred to Cowley. So, without any improvements forthcoming from the factory, the future of the R-type rested with the private owners.

Programme for the 1935 British Empire Trophy Race.

Doreen Evans continued to campaign her car and at Shelsley Walsh on 18 May set a new ladies' record for the hill. As we have seen, George Eyston had entered a team of three cars for the first meeting, where their results had been rather disappointing, and on 20 May the team fared little better when they all had to retire from the Mannin Beg Race on the Isle of Man. However, Bobby Baird upheld R-type honours by taking fourth place in his car. For the British Empire Trophy race at Brooklands on 6 July Eyston again entered three R-types, driven by himself, Wal Handley and Norman Black. Handley was unclassified, Black finished in fifth place and Eyston was placed 14th after a troubled run. Following the withdrawal of factory support, Eyston must have decided not to

RA0257 in 1999 following a complete rebuild by Gerhard Maier.

continue running the R-types and his three cars were put up for sale. One of them was eventually owned and run by Kenneth Evans.

Despite its revolutionary design, the R-type was destined for a comparatively short career at the top level of motor sport. The reasons for this are not hard to find. In the 1500cc class for international events a 750cc car was at a severe disadvantage and in the 750cc class at national meetings MG's dominance was in serious jeopardy once the Murray Jamieson-designed Austin twin-cam racing cars arrived in 1936. These were lighter than the R-types and their Roots-blown engines would safely run to 9000rpm, giving the cars 125mph performance. Although the chassis lacked the sophistication of the R-type's – it had solid axles with a transverse leaf spring at the front and quarter-elliptic rear springs – the low build and light weight gave it superior road-holding on relatively smooth tracks. Although the factory team cars in the hands of Charlie Dodson and H.L. Hadley only raced in British events, they were very successful.

The McEnvoy/Pomeroy twin-cam head fitted to some of the R-types in an effort to increase the power output of the 750cc engine.

Perhaps the most interesting development carried out in an effort to improve the performance of the R-type for the 1936 season was the fitting of twin overhead camshaft cylinder heads to three of the cars. These heads were developed by Laurence Pomeroy and Michael McEvoy and were installed in the ex-Eyston car run by Bellevue Garage for Kenneth Evans, and to the cars raced by Ian Connell and Douglas Briault. The first race for the twin-cam cars was the British Empire Trophy Race at Donington on 4 April 1936. Disappointingly, all three cars failed to finish and whilst running did not exhibit quite the expected improvement in performance. Future races did reveal some of the potential of the special cylinder heads, but there were also a number of reliability problems.

With hindsight it is easy to see that with the R-type and the proposed new saloon the company were taking the first tentative steps towards building cars that possessed the handling, ride and roadholding characteristics we now have come to expect. However, there was still a way to go and at a time when sales, and thus profits, were not strong one can quite easily see why it was decided to curtail the pioneering efforts in order to concentrate on making conventional vehicles, which would be more profitable.

THE TA AND TB MIDGET

Following the changed ownership of the MG Car Company, all new models produced at Abingdon used as many standard Nuffield Group components as possible. The first MG Midget to appear under the new regime was the TA. This still had the basic design of MG chassis that had first appeared back in 1931, but it was both bigger and stronger than the one underpinning the outgoing PB Midget. The track was increased to 3ft 9in, the same as the NA Magnette, and the wheelbase to 7ft 10in. The brakes for the beam front and rear axles were now hydraulically operated; they were beginning to become universally adopted for new cars. Drivers at the time must have welcomed the change although, aesthetically, the smaller drums car didn't look as impressive as the 12-inch ones used previously. The handbrake design was similar to that fitted to the earlier cars but now only worked the rear wheels instead of all four.

The brochure issued when the TA Midget was announced to the public.

MG had developed the OHC engines to the point where they were producing higher power outputs per litre than almost any other engines in production. However, they were not then fitted to any other Nuffield products and this situation couldn't continue. For the T Series the design team at Cowley turned to the OHV engine destined for the Wolseley 10/40 and Morris Ten. This unit was given camshaft and manifold changes, and twin SU carburettors, to increase the power to 50bhp. The final version of the four-cylinder OHC engine, used for the PB, produced 43bhp at 5500rpm from its 939cc, whereas the 1292cc TA engine produced maximum power at only 4,200rpm. This was the essential difference between the two engines. One was a high-revving and very sporting unit capable of producing a good power output for its capacity whereas the other was rather less highly developed, but was nevertheless capable of reasonable

The TA chassis was similar to that used for the earlier Midgets, although slightly larger and stronger.

A restored TA Midget which retains its original 1292cc power unit. The majority of modern owners opt for a later XPAG engine.

performance and gave improved torque at lower engine speeds. The TA engine was, however, both larger and much heavier than the earlier OHC unit.

To improve refinement, the new engine was provided with rubber mountings to mate it to the chassis, dispensing with the previous three-point cross-tube mounting. The radiator was now fixed directly to the chassis, rather than hung off the front of the engine as was previous practice. The four-speed gearbox gained synchromesh on the two upper ratios and was driven from the engine via a cork-faced clutch running in oil. This system was very popular at the time as it was thought to give a smooth feel to the clutch.

The body followed the style that had been established for MG two-seaters when the J2 arrived in 1932. The ash-framed body now provided more generous room for both driver and passenger than had been available to owners of the earlier cars. In particular there was now considerably more room behind the bench-style seat for a reasonable amount of luggage. The sports car was becoming a much more serious form of everyday transport.

With an engine capacity larger than even the N Magnette, and really now the only proper sporting car available from Abingdon, the T Series Midget had to be good enough to appeal to both the owners of the earlier MG Midgets and to those who would have previously bought the rather more expensive two-seater Magnas and Magnettes. Judged by contemporary press reports, the average buyer welcomed the new car and was happy with the rather fewer demands made upon their skills to extract a similar performance from it than had been required with earlier models. Those using the cars competitively were, perhaps, rather less sure that the new cars were an improvement.

The first road tests to appear in the motoring press stressed that, although there had been a great many differences, the essential character of the car had remained unchanged. They said that it had exceptionally good performance for a car of that engine capacity and that its handling was vastly better than that offered by the average touring car of the period. They remarked upon the appearance of greater solidity given by the longer wheelbase, wider track, bigger body and longer bonnet. On the road they said that the car had a different feel, altogether softer, quieter and with the engine far more flexible at low engine speeds.

The performance figures they recorded, 23.1secs to 60mph and maximum of 77mph, compared well with the figures for the previous model, the PB, which were 27secs to 60mph and a maximum of 71mph. Tests in some magazines gave even better figures for the new car – a top speed as high as 80mph, not bad for a small car in 1936. Although the Midget had grown up quite a lot it still seemed

The engine compartment of a TA Midget with the 1292cc engine as fitted when new.

The dashboard layout was neat and practical, although the passenger had more idea of the speed of progress than the driver. The black coloured lever by the right side of the steering wheel operates the petrol reserve tap.

The Tickford version of the TA Midget is now highly prized. This car was fully restored by its current owner.

With the substantial hood in place the Tickford coupé provides saloon car levels of comfort.

With the Tickford hood fully down the TA is transformed into an open sports car.

The glass rear window on the Tickford gives a restricted rear view and makes the standard outside rear view mirror a necessary fitting.

An early TA with the narrow rear wings taking part in a pre-war trial.

to appeal to the same sort of customers and many part-exchanged their older models for the new car. The price of the T Series Midget was £222, the same as that charged for the PB, so this was in its favour and those deserting the ranks of six-cylinder MG owners to buy the Midget were actually purchasing a cheaper car, but of similar size and performance to their old one.

However, to further widen the appeal of the car, in 1938 a more luxurious model, on the same chassis and with the same mechanical specification, was announced. This was the Series T Tickford Drophead Coupe. Salmons and Sons Limited of Newport Pagnell, later to become part of Aston Martin, built special bodywork for a number of different makes of car. In the late 1930s MG offered, as standard production cars, versions of the VA, SA, WA and of the T Series Midget fitted with Tickford bodywork incorporating their versatile three-position folding soft top. This hood could be used either fully closed, with the front section opened, or completely stowed away. Allied to proper winding windows and higher-sided doors this coachwork was, perhaps, better suited to the vagaries of the British climate than the standard open cars. Of course, the bodywork was a bit heavier, and this affected performance, but nevertheless the new model was a practical alternative to the open two-seaters, and even to saloons from other manufacturers. Now the T Series Tickford coupé remains one of the most desirable of the pre-war MGs.

This view of a later TA with hood and side-screens in place shows the smaller petrol tank and wider wings.

Unlike the normal two-seater, the Tickford coupé was built as a rolling chassis at Abingdon and then driven to Newport Pagnell for the special coachwork to be fitted. For the journey the chassis had rudimentary bodywork that gave the delivery drivers little protection and one can imagine this was not a popular task in mid-winter. The Tickford coupés were available in a wider choice of colours than the standard cars and, in addition to the better weather protection, they were also fitted with separate bucket seats, fully carpeted interior, semaphore-style direction indicators, an ashtray and an interior light just above the glass rear window. The windscreen wiper motor was no longer fitted on the top of the windscreen frame, but was installed beneath the bonnet, and the dashboard was modified to fit the differently shaped bodywork.

The greater bulk of the lowered hood restricted rearward visibility a little, compared to the ordinary TA, but the higher doors reduced wind buffeting for the occupants, and when the soft top was raised the extra layers of material and wadding in the Tickford hood made the interior of the car much quieter. There is no doubt that the Tickford TA and the later TB version were extremely attractive small cars and it is just a shame that so few, just 252 TAs and 60 TBs, were built.

From May 1939 the T Series Midget benefited from the introduction of a new range of engines for the Morris 10. Originally designed as a 1100cc unit, a modified version of this engine with a capacity of 1250cc and twin carburettors found its way into the Midget, which was now called the TB. This engine was the legendary XPAG unit, which proved to be so strong and amenable to tuning and which after the war powered many sports/racing cars. In the TB it offered a much more suitable engine for a sports car. Gone were the oil-immersed clutch and white-metalled bearings of the TA and in came a thoroughly modern engine with shell bearings and an ability to thrive on hard driving. It is a pity that production of the TB was curtailed by world events after only a total of 379 cars had been built.

RECORD BREAKER EX135

The chassis of K3023 modified to offset single-seater form. With the car are Cecil Kimber, George Eyston, Reg Jackson and Nobby Marney.

The long story of EX135 began with a commission from Captain George Eyston to build a special K3 Magnette for both road racing and high-speed runs on banked tracks like Brooklands and Montlhéry. The modifications he specified were designed to cut the frontal area, and thus reduce drag, by placing the driving position as low as possible in the car. As had previously been done for EX127, the engine, transmission and differential housing were offset to allow the driver's seat to be placed between the prop-shaft and the offside chassis rail. To achieve this, the standard chassis side members were lengthened by five inches and the power train was set at a six-degree angle to the centreline of the car. Special light-alloy rear axle castings were produced to keep the differential mechanism as close as possible to the nearside rear wheel, the chassis side member being cranked at this point to provide more room. Extra strength was provided by boxing-in the side rails.

Braking was standard K3, although the front brakes could be taken off for record runs, and the springs and dampers provided a much stiffer ride than normal. The instrument panel was fitted to the rolling chassis by means of an open framework so as to remain in place when the body was removed. The reason for this becomes clear when we learn that in line with its intended dual function two completely different bodies were made for the car. The record attempt body was designed to be as aerodynamically efficient as they knew how, possessing smooth lines and with the cockpit almost totally enclosed. A cream and brown striped colour scheme made it very distinctive. At Abingdon, Reg Jackson and Nobby Marney, neither of them skilled panel-beaters, hastily built a road-racing body over a weekend and its resulting ungainly appearance led to it being named the coal scuttle. In this form

Mechanics with the three Eyston team K3s prior to the 1935 Mannin Beg Race. The lower build of EX135 is very evident in this picture.

the driver was not so tightly enclosed within the cockpit and had a much better field of vision.

The first competition entry for EX 135, dubbed the Magic Magnette, was in the JCC International Trophy Race at Brooklands in May 1934. For this event the car wore the streamlined body, but problems in practice meant that the car failed to make the starting line. Next on the calendar was the Mannin Beg Race on the Isle of Man and, as this was held on the street circuit in Douglas, the streamlined body was replaced with the one designed for such events. George broke the lap record for the circuit, and had he not been delayed by refuelling and plug trouble could have finished higher than third place.

The new car really came into its own on the banked track at Brooklands in the June 1934 British Empire Trophy Race. With the coal scuttle body still fitted, George Eyston lapped the track at an average speed of 80.01mph and took first place in this handicap event. The average speeds for unmodified K3s ranged between 71mph and 74mph. For the BRDC 500-mile Race at Brooklands in September he shared the car with Wal Handley but they failed to finish. In this race the outer circuit was in use so the car was fitted with the streamlined body and circulated easily at an average speed of 113mph. After George handed over to his co-driver a seized wheel bearing caused the car to skid off the track, fortunately without significant damage to the car or any injury to the driver.

As one of Britain's foremost record breakers, George was keen to make an attempt on the International 1100cc records with the modified K3. Reading between the lines, it seems that there was something of a difference of opinion between George and Abingdon at the time. George had a commercial interest in the Powerplus supercharger and had intended fitting one of these for the projected runs at Montlhéry. However, experiments with the rival Zoller supercharger seemed to indicate that with one of these installed the car would be capable of challenging the outright one-hour world speed record, which at the time stood at 134mph.

Despite the fact that the car belonged to George, instructions were given for the Zoller blower to be fitted just before the car went to Paris. The result was a fiasco. The engine misfired so much that the con-rods bent and eventually the supercharger itself expired in a cloud of smoke. With what must have been a measure of relief, George had the engine reassembled with new con-rods and installed a Powerplus supercharger. The K3 then ran faultlessly and established a string of new records, including 10 miles at 128.53mph and one hour at 120.88mph. That outing proved to be the one and only such attempt George was to make with the car and the following year it was sold to Donald Letts.

Donald was an amateur racing driver whose money came from the famous firm of diary manufacturers that bore his name. Bellevue Garage

Col. A.T. "Goldie" Gardner OBE, MC.

EX135 fitted with the record-breaking body is loaded into a van prior to the record attempt at Montlhéry in October 1934.

now prepared his car, as he and the Evans family were close friends. During 1935 and 1936 he drove the K3 at most of the major Brooklands meetings, with a small measure of success. The car was now becoming uncompetitive and the story of this particular K3 may well have ended there if it hadn't been for the intervention of another well-known British record breaker, A.T.H. "Goldie" Gardner.

For the 1934 500-mile Race at Brooklands, Gardner borrowed a K3 from the factory and shared the driving with Bentley racer, Dr. Benjafield. They managed to take third place overall, winning the 1100cc class. At the end of the season he bought an offset single-seater K3 Magnette Ron Horton had used for record attempts at both Brooklands and Montlhéry. For 1936 the car had further bodywork modifications carried out by Robin Jackson to improve streamlining. Gardner raced the car at Brooklands where at the August meeting he managed to win his event. He returned to the track later the same month for an attempt on the British National Class G records. First he did four flying laps of the Outer Circuit and recorded a fastest speed of 124.40mph, an 1100cc lap record that was to remain unbeaten when the track closed in 1939.

In 1937 Gardner went to an autobahn just constructed near Frankfurt-am-Main in Germany, having obtained permission to use this for attempts on the International Class G records. All went well and new International Class G records were set for the flying kilometre at 142.2mph and mile at 148.5mph. The party then moved to the banked track at Montlhéry to tackle the long-distance records. Here again, Gardner raised the records, this time for five, 10 and 50 kilometres, and five and 10 miles. The speeds recorded were around 130mph.

Never satisfied, Gardner returned to Frankfurt later in the year to take part in a record-breaking week arranged by a German motoring organisation. There he managed to raise the kilometre and mile records to 148.8mph and 148.7mph respectively. The five-kilometre and five-mile speeds were 143.6mph and 146.6mph. A misfire at over 6000rpm just stopped him recording his target speed, the magic 150mph.

Back in England, discussions with Cecil Kimber led to an approach to Lord Nuffield for permission for MG to officially support future attempts. It was obvious that the old car was pretty near its limit at speeds approaching 150mph, and the only solution was the construction of a purpose-built record car. With Nuffield's blessing, the small team at Abingdon under the direction of the brilliant Syd Enever tackled the task with their usual skill. Gardner had suggested using the engine from his old car and this was removed for rebuilding by Robin Jackson. For the chassis, it was decided that he would purchase the K3 that had been specially built for George Eyston.

The chassis was rebuilt at Abingdon and Reid

The Reid Railton-designed lightweight body being fitted to the chassis at the Abingdon factory. The body could be easily removed to carry out work on the car.

Railton, who had previously designed a record-breaker for John Cobb, was asked to design a special lightweight, streamlined body for the car. The engine developed by Robin Jackson for Gardner's previous car was tested at the MG factory and Syd Enever found that at high engine speeds water was escaping from the cylinder head gasket and spraying onto the plug leads. The solution was to fit a cylinder block without any water passages between it and the cylinder head. Fed by a Centric

ALBERT SYDNEY "SYD" ENEVER (1906-1993)

Justifiably, Syd Enever's name appears often in these pages. He was Chief Engineer at the MG Car Company from 1954 to 1971, but from the time he joined the company until his retirement at age 65 he played a huge role in the success of the marque. Leaving school at 14 he took a job as general dogsbody at the Queen Street showrooms of Morris Garages. After a probationary year he moved to the company's garage behind the Clarendon Hotel in Oxford and worked there until 1930, when he transferred to The MG Car Company in Abingdon.

Having an innate mechanical aptitude and an ability to learn from experience, his lack of a formal engineering and design training proved no drawback. At Abingdon he joined the experimental department, initially under Cecil Cousins and then Reg Jackson. His work on EX135 and the subsequent record breakers was crucial to the success they enjoyed and his was the guiding force behind the post-war MGA, MGB and Midget models. In 1938 he had been appointed as chief planning engineer and from 1946 ran the experimental department. In 1954 he was made chief engineer of The MG Car Company.

Syd Enever (right) is with John Thornley in this 1966 photograph.

After retirement he continued to be involved in the motor industry and one of his last jobs was working on the hardtop version of the Jensen-Healey.

Cecil Kimber, Lord Nuffield, Goldie Gardner and the man responsible for the body design, Reid Railton, outside the Abingdon factory in 1938 with the newly-built record car.

supercharger, the 1087cc engine produced 194bhp at 7000rpm. To reduce rolling resistance, special high-pressures tyre by Dunlop were fitted, these being carefully balanced to cope with the speeds envisaged. The completed car, although still referred to at Abingdon as EX135, was more usually referred to in press reports as the Gardner MG.

All this work had taken many months and it was November 1938 when they were finally ready to give the rejuvenated EX135 its first real test. A large convoy set off from Abingdon for the Frankfurt-am-Main autobahn. Initially they were thwarted by poor weather, but in the end managed to carry out runs in both directions and succeeded in raising the Class G flying-start records for the kilometre and mile to 186.5mph and 186.6mph respectively, faster than they had predicted. During the runs the final drive ratio proved to be too low and the engine speed had exceeded the proposed maximum. There was also evidence of possible trouble with the supercharger. Goldie Gardner decided to delay any further record attempts until the engine had been examined and the axle ratio changed. However, for his efforts in raising the record as high as he had done Gardner was given the Segrave Trophy, awarded annually for the most outstanding performance in the realm of transport.

Clearly the streamlined body was so efficient that the car could be capable of exceeding 200mph, provided the gearing was right and the engine reliable. The overhaul carried out at the MG factory included renewal of the brakes and examination of the engine and supercharger. The supercharger gearing was altered to increase the boost and the engine power was thus increased to 202bhp at 7000rpm.

At the end of May 1939 the team returned to Germany to try to raise the speeds to over 200mph. The high-speed runs were scheduled to take place on a new stretch of autobahn that had just been completed near Dessau. EX135 performed faultlessly during the runs and easily exceeded the 200mph target. The flying-start kilometre, mile and five kilometre records were taken at 203.5mph, 203.2mph and 197.5mph respectively. The team had taken a set of oversize pistons and a portable boring machine with them and once the first records were in the bag set about enlarging the bores in the cylinder block, whilst it was still in the car, and fitting larger pistons so as to take the engine to 1106cc, just over the minimum capacity for Class F. Gardner then made further runs over the same distances to raise the record speeds for that class to 204.3mph, 203.9mph, and 200.6mph before returning home.

MG were now in the record books in two classes and Gardner and Kimber decided to fit a smaller-capacity version of the engine, with the intention of returning to Germany in the autumn to try to break similar records in Class H, for cars with a capacity up to 750cc. A new cylinder block was cast and a short-throw crankshaft produced. The 746cc six-cylinder engine had a bore of 53mm and a stroke of 56mm. It was just about ready to be assembled, and the car returned to Abingdon from a publicity trip around the MG dealers, when war was declared and the whole lot had to be packed up and put into storage.

By 1945 Cecil Kimber had been killed in a freak railway accident; Gardner had lost a friend and the chief supporter of his record efforts. However, he was determined to carry on where he had been forced to stop in 1939, and went to the factory to see about getting the car into working order. EX 135 had been stored in an old clothing factory in West St. Helen's Street, Abingdon, for the duration of the war. Unfortunately, in 1944 there had been a severe fire in that building which destroyed much of the contents including the superchargers and the 1100cc engine for the record-breaker. Fortunately the car itself had survived.

Goldie Gardner decided to tackle the Class H records, using the surviving 750cc engine. The venue was to be the Brescia-Bergamo autostrada in Italy. To bring EX 135 back into running order he approached the suppliers he had used pre-war and was pleased to receive many offers of support, including one from Chris Shorrock, who immediately agreed to produce the necessary superchargers. Factory support was unofficial, but Syd Enever and "Jacko" Jackson used part of their annual holiday to accompany the party to Italy. Success eluded them. The road proved to be unsuitable for the high-speed runs, being both poorly surfaced and having a humped bridge that caused the car to leave the ground at speed. They returned home empty-handed.

The telegram sent by Gardner to John Thornley at Abingdon telling him of their success. The mobile telephone was still some way in the future.

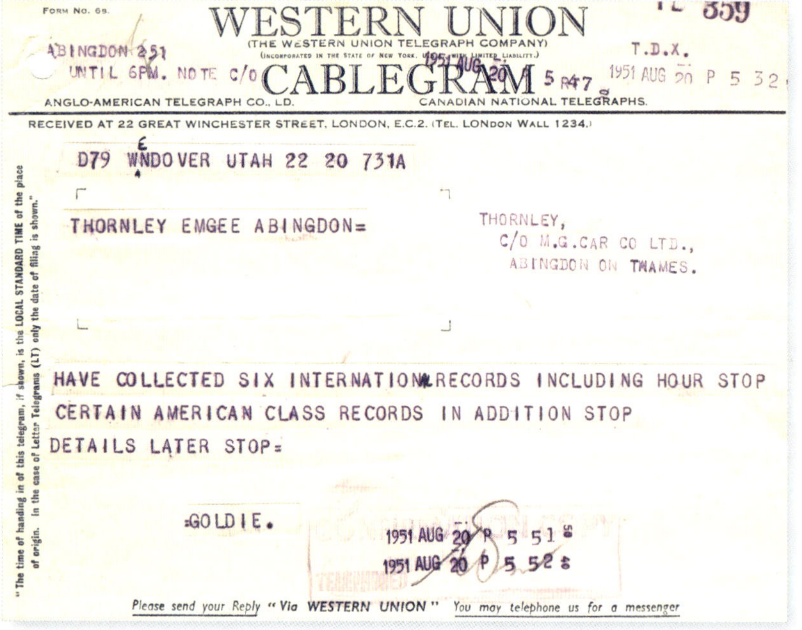

FORM No. 69.

WESTERN UNION
(THE WESTERN UNION TELEGRAPH COMPANY)
(INCORPORATED IN THE STATE OF NEW YORK. WITH LIMITED LIABILITY.)

CABLEGRAM

ANGLO-AMERICAN TELEGRAPH CO., LD. CANADIAN NATIONAL TELEGRAPHS.

RECEIVED AT 22 GREAT WINCHESTER STREET, LONDON, E.C.2. (TEL. LONDON WALL 1234.)

ABINGDON 251 UNTIL 6PM. NOTE C/O

T.D.X.

1951 AUG 20 P 5 32

D79 WNDOVER UTAH 22 20 731A

THORNLEY EMGEE ABINGDON=

THORNLEY, C/O M.G.CAR CO LTD., ABINGDON ON THAMES.

HAVE COLLECTED SIX INTERNATIONAL RECORDS INCLUDING HOUR STOP CERTAIN AMERICAN CLASS RECORDS IN ADDITION STOP DETAILS LATER STOP=

GOLDIE.

1951 AUG 20 P 5 51
1951 AUG 20 P 5 52

Please send your Reply "Via WESTERN UNION" You may telephone us for a messenger

"The time of handing in of this telegram, if shown, is the LOCAL STANDARD TIME of the place of origin. In the case of Letter Telegrams (LT) only the date of filing is shown."

The search was now on for a suitable alternative venue. Purely by chance, Gardner heard about a section of dual carriageway road built in Belgium in 1939 as part of an incomplete transcontinental highway. He went with Syd Enever and Jacko to take a look, and they found that it would be ideal for the purpose. Permission to use the road was forthcoming and a large party of friends, press and officials from the Nuffield Organisation made the short journey to Jabbeke, which was only about 50 miles from Ostend. The car ran faultlessly and new 750cc records were obtained for the flying-start kilometre, mile and five-kilometres distances at 159.098mph, 159.15mph, and 150.46mph respectively. In setting these times Gardner knew that he still had some power in reserve, and vowed to return to raise the speeds in the future.

Whilst in Belgium, the car had been tried with two pistons removed from the six-cylinder engine, these being replaced by ones with holes in the crowns. With the valve gear disabled for those two cylinders, and the engine capacity now effectively below 500cc, the car ran well enough to show that an attempt on the existing records for that class would be successful. In 1947 Gardner arranged for a 500cc engine to be built and tested at Harry Weslake's Surbiton workshop. This engine, which had revised manifolds and bob-weights replacing the removed pistons, was fitted to the car that Thomson and Taylor had prepared for the venture. The team returned to Belgium and made a number of runs. Although Gardner managed to set new records for the class at around 118mph these were far below the car's potential. Fuel feed problems caused misfiring and some damage to the supercharger, so it was decided to return home and make a fresh attempt the following year.

Having succeeded with EX135 in setting record-breaking speeds in four classes, in 1948 Gardner managed to persuade William Lyons of Jaguar to lend him an experimental 1970cc four-cylinder version of the OHC XK engine for an attempt on the under-2000cc class. Using this he raised the kilometre, mile and five-kilometre records to 170.6mph, 173.6mph and 170.5mph. During one of the runs a tyre failure stopped the average speed from being even higher. EX135 was now, uniquely, a record holder in no less than five classes.

The 500cc records having by then been regained by Piero Taruffi, in 1949 Gardner had a new crankshaft made for his six-cylinder engine. This would run with just three of the six cylinders in use, and provided an engine with a capacity of 497cc. It was built and tested at Abingdon, who this time were also involved with preparing the car. The venue was the highway in Belgium and by a substantial margin Gardner raised the 500cc kilometre, mile and five-kilometre records; the speeds attained were 154.9mph, 154.2mph, and 150.5mph.

With his sights set on success in yet another class, back at Abingdon a new block was used for the engine and cylinders 4 and 5 were fitted with liners of 57.25mm bore, with suitable pistons, reducing the capacity for the two-cylinder engine to 332cc. Remarkably, this unit produced over 50bhp on the test bed. The final drive ratio was lowered to help the small-capacity engine propel the heavy car, and the team took it on the now-familiar trek to Belgium. The runs went well and the Gardner-MG recorded the remarkable speeds of 120.394mph, 121.048mph, and 113.125mph for the kilometre, mile and five-kilometre distances. EX135 was now the record holder in six classes.

In 1951 the Festival of Britain exhibition was staged on the South Bank in London. This involved the construction of a dome and other purpose-built exhibition halls. The main exhibition area was to the west of Hungerford Railway Bridge, on the opposite side of the tracks to the Festival Hall. Here, in addition to the Dome of Discovery, there was a large Transport Pavilion where the motor industry had staged what amounted to an impressive motor show. The public viewed the various exhibits by walking up an inclined ramp and were able to see components and complete cars, prominence being given to the latest models from British industry. At the top of the ramp the sleek green-painted Gardner-MG was given pride of place. This presented certain difficulties for the prospects of a proposed 1951 record attempt as the exhibition opened for a six-month season on 4 May. The car could obviously not stay there for the whole period and had to be taken off display in June, being replaced by a Frazer-Nash.

The factory were now very keen to promote the record attempts and, with their large American market in mind, wanted an engine to be used that was closer to those in current production. Two TD engines were prepared, one a highly developed unit and one in a milder state of tune. This time, partly because of the extra publicity it would generate, EX 135 was taken to the Salt Lake at Utah in America. There the object was for Goldie Gardner to attempt to set new National and International records in Class F. The milder engine was installed first and with this Goldie took a series of distance records at speeds between 127.8mph for 50 kilometres and 139.3mph for 200 kilometres.

The more highly tuned engine was then fitted to ready the car for the high-speed attempts. Some runs at speeds exceeding 190mph were made, but

Colour showroom poster issued to dealerships to publicise the successes of the Gardner-MG.

these did not enter the record books as the timing equipment failed. By the time it was repaired heavy rain had flooded the salt and the team had to return home. All was not lost, however, as the speeds they had achieved for the distance records provide much-needed publicity. Goldie Gardner resolved to return the following year.

In the event, 1952 saw the final record attempts with EX135, which proved a most frustrating and difficult session for Gardner and his loyal team. They had decided to go for records in Class E, using a 2-litre Wolseley engine, and Class F with the blown XPAG TD engine. Failure by the supercharger manufacturers to supply the large-capacity blower for the Wolseley engine led to test bed disasters and compromises right from the outset. At Utah, the Wolseley engine was run first and the car managed to take a number of international and American national longer-distance records with a car that was not running as well as it could, and on salt that was less than perfect. Partly because of the slippery nature of the salt, Gardner spun the car and hit a marker post; this smashed the Perspex canopy and dealt him a severe blow on the head.

The TD engine was then fitted and further records at international and national level were taken. However, anticipated top speeds were not attained as a considerable amount of wheel slip was being encountered, again down to the state of the salt that year, and also to tyres unsuited to the conditions. With speeds no higher than seen in the 1939 attempt in that class, it was all a bit disappointing and a sad swansong for the venerable record car. However, there were still quite a number of American records to celebrate as a boost for TD sales.

Plans were well under way for another Belgium run in 1953 when Goldie Gardner became ill. One problem he had was occasional double vision, perhaps the bang on the head at Utah the previous year did not help, and his doctors advised him to give up driving a 200mph car. The record attempt was abandoned and John Thornley persuaded the Nuffield Organisation, or British Motor Corporation as it was by then, to stump up £2000 to buy EX135, plus the spares still held by Goldie Gardner. Glazed inspection panels were inserted in the bodywork, and the car has been at numerous exhibitions and on display in museums ever since.

The salt flat at Utah in 1952. With the car are John Crook, Syd Enever, Goldie Gardner, Reg Jackson and Reg Avenall.

THE 2-LITRE SA

This magnificent SA saloon is a very original example of an early car with manual opening vents in the bonnet sides.

The announcement of a new range of much larger MGs marked a radical departure from the type of vehicle being offered at the time by the MG Car Company. Cecil Kimber had made the decision to move into a different market as the Midgets, Magnas and Magnettes that were the mainstay of the company's production needed to be keenly priced to sell and thus produced only small profits. Remembering that in 1928 MG had moved to building a large and expensive six-cylinder car, the 18/80, it is not surprising that Kimber wished to return to serving a different clientele, whilst retaining the sports car performance and handling that had become the MG trademark.

As we have seen, alongside work on the all-independent suspension R-type racing car there were well advanced plans for a large, luxurious saloon also featuring independent suspension. This project was given the designation S-type and the experimental department code EX150. It was designed around a new chassis of 10ft 3in wheelbase and, to cope with the work involved, extra draughtsmen were recruited to produce the hundreds of detailed drawings needed. A prototype chassis was soon completed and Mulliners of Birmingham designed an elegant body that looked similar to the one fitted to the SA saloon when it eventually appeared. EX150 was listed in the paperwork as a 3½-litre all-independent car, but it is not clear which power unit would have been chosen. Had the axe not fallen on the Abingdon design facility, then a world-beating machine may have resulted from these efforts, although it would have probably been expensive to build and perhaps not as profitable for the company as the car that did finally emerge.

However, the project was cancelled and it fell to the Cowley design office, including personnel

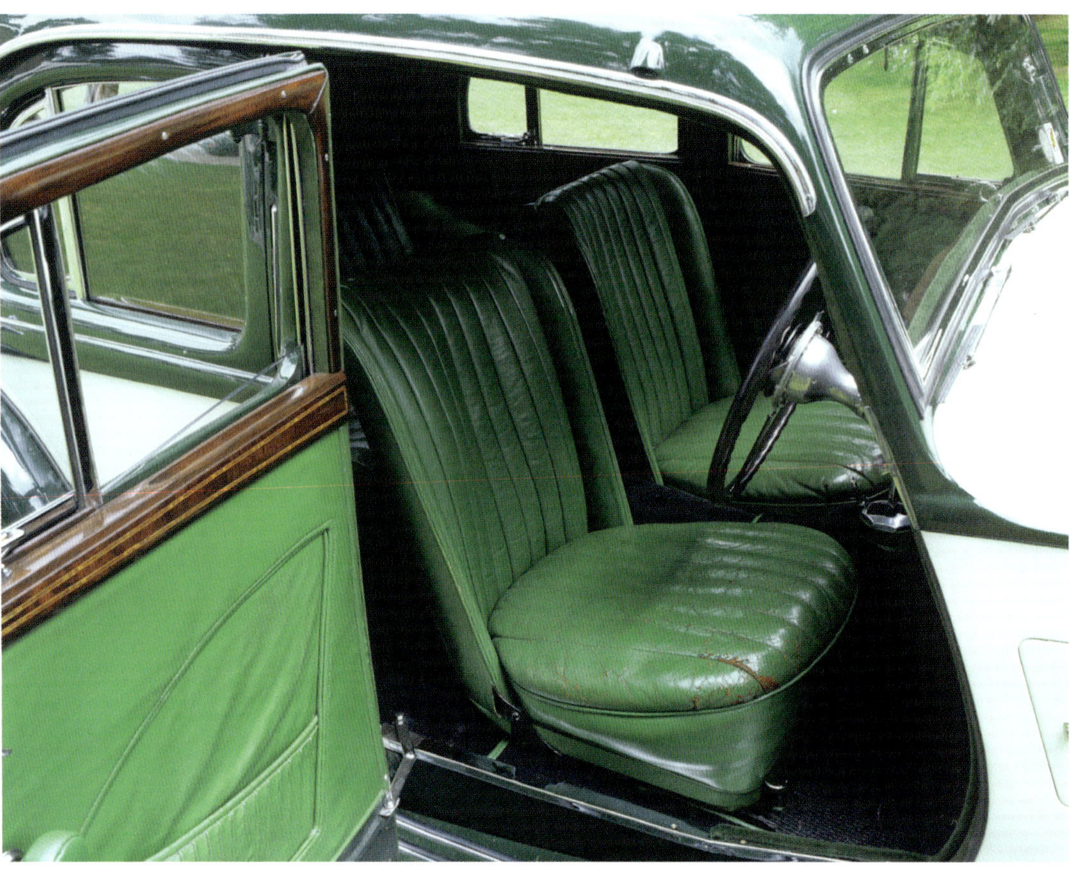

The interior of the SA saloon is very well trimmed and the seats are comfortable enough for the driver and passengers to enjoy making long trips in the car.

There is quite a lot of room in the boot for luggage on the SA; the car can be run with the boot lid open to increase available space.

transferred from Abingdon, to produce the large MG saloon. This now had to utilise components available from within the Nuffield Group, rather than ones specially made for MG.

August 1935 saw the announcement of revisions to the model range for the 1936 model year, but no completely new cars. The S-type development was continuing at Cowley, but now with a conventional chassis and suspension. However, the Mulliner-designed body chosen for EX150 was retained virtually unchanged, as were the track and wheelbase dimensions. The project was renamed the MG Two Litre, and Cowley had specified a Morris engine for the prototype. Like some of the earlier models, the factory designation SA-type did not start to be used in literature until the car was well into production.

The chassis for the new car was a substantial affair and in many respects departed considerably from previous MG practice. The fabricated side frames were boxed for stiffness. There was substantial bracing and, unusually for MG, the side members were taken above the rear axle to allow this greater vertical movement. Another departure was the adoption of hydraulic brakes in place of the cable-operated type so favoured by Cecil Kimber. There were lever-arm shock absorbers and built-in jacking and lubrication systems. Although the prototype had bolt-on wire wheels, the more fashionable and sporting centre-lock type replaced these before the car went into production. Drive was through a cork-faced clutch that ran in oil.

The engine fitted was completely different from the OHC units in preceding models. With six cylinders, it had been developed at Morris Engines Branch at Coventry and was based on the old-fashioned sidevalve units used by Morris for some years. This was the first overhead-valve version of the engine and was introduced at the same time for the Wolseley Super Six 16hp with a capacity for that car of 2062cc. It was initially intended that the SA should have the same size engine, hence calling it the MG Two Litre, but at a late stage it was enlarged to 2288cc. This may have been because prototypes on test had not performed as well as expected, or might have been in response to the launch at the same time of the SS Jaguar saloon with its 2½-litre 100bhp engine. For whatever reason, the new MG actually now had a larger and more powerful engine than its name advertised, an unusual occurrence in the motor industry.

The design and development team at Cowley seemed to be in a bit of a muddle at that time, reflected in the number of changes made to the mechanical specification of the SA, both before it finally appeared in the showrooms and once it was in production. The gearbox, for example, was originally intended to be a four-speed unit with synchromesh on the two higher ratios. The first illustrations printed of the new model appeared in

This restored later model of the Charlesworth tourer started life as a Lancashire Constabulary police car, one of many MGs used by that force.

THE M.G. TWO-LITRE TOURER
Four seater open model by Charlesworth
£375 (ex works)

A brochure drawing of an early tourer with straight tops to the front doors.

The SA tourer is a large and comfortable car.

The later tourers had cut-away tops to the front doors, fashionable at the time for cars with sporting pretensions.

that October 1935 press release and in these the gearbox was fitted with a long, cranked lever fitted directly above the selectors. By the time the car was in full production the synchromesh had gone and a shorter lever with a neat remote change mechanism selected the gears. Synchromesh on third and top was to reappear later. Likewise, we had that late increase in engine capacity, and this too was to be altered later when the bore was increased by 0.5mm, taking the engine to 2322cc. This was still just within the 18hp tax bracket.

The formal press announcement of the new car was in October 1935, to coincide with the London

Motor Show where the car was on display. However, it has to be said that this early proclamation of an important new model for the company was ill judged. Following the closure of the design office at Abingdon, new MG models could no longer be brought into production in the short time spans that were such a feature of the early 1930s. With the much larger and more bureaucratic regime at Cowley, delays were inevitable and design changes during the development period took longer to be incorporated into the production cars. The result was that a large number of customers who had ordered the new car soon after its announcement were very upset when they had to wait over six months for them to be delivered.

The MG Two Litre, or SA, was certainly quite different from the KN saloon it replaced. Not only did it have an overhead-valve engine of nearly twice the capacity, but also it was well over 16 feet long and weighed over one-and-a-half tons. However, with this bulk and weight came considerable comfort. In fact, the SA owed far more to the 18/80 models last produced five years earlier than to the high-spirited sporting machinery with which MG had made their name in the intervening years. Luxury was the keynote of the design. Generous space was provided for the four occupants, with deeply upholstered seats, arm rests and all manner of creature comforts to distract their attention from the relative lack of the pace and agility they may have expected from an MG.

A posed publicity picture of a later SA saloon with louvres in the bonnet side panels.

PRE-WAR MG MAGAZINES

The MG Car Company supported the publication of regular magazines that were sent to MG club members and available to dealers. The first magazine solely devoted to the marque was *The MG Magazine*. The first issue was dated May 1933 and thereafter appeared bi-monthly until March 1935. In the first magazine, under a picture of him seated in his Abingdon office, was printed a letter addressed to all MG owners from Cecil Kimber saying: "The editor has asked me to write a few words of welcome to you, that ever-growing body of enthusiasts, for whom this new magazine has been planned and produced. Through its pages we hope to interest you and keep you informed of all branches of motoring sport, of MG activities at home and abroad, and of factory developments and news. In short, our object is to provide a journal to knit together still closer the many friends the production of MG cars has created both for me, personally, and for those connected with their making, their sale and their use."

1935 brought many changes at Abingdon. The reorganisation mentioned elsewhere included ceasing production of *The MG Magazine*. To replace it the publishers of the short-lived *Brooklands Track and Air* launched a new monthly magazine called *The Sports Car* edited by F.L.M. Harris. Listed as the official journal of The MG Car Company and The MG Car Club, it was issued to members as a benefit of their annual subscription, with the first issue appearing in April 1935, thus taking over immediately from the previous publication.

Backed by the MG Car Company and a good selection of paid advertisements, *The Sports Car* attracted many of the best professional motoring journalists of the time and this shows in the quality of writing. It continued to be published until October 1939. That final issue had a more restricted circulation following the declaration of war the previous month and when trying to build a complete set is now the most difficult issue to find.

Compared to the immediately preceding MG models, the much larger SA saloon seemed to be aimed at a different market.

The spare wheel is concealed beneath a neat cover attached to the boot lid.

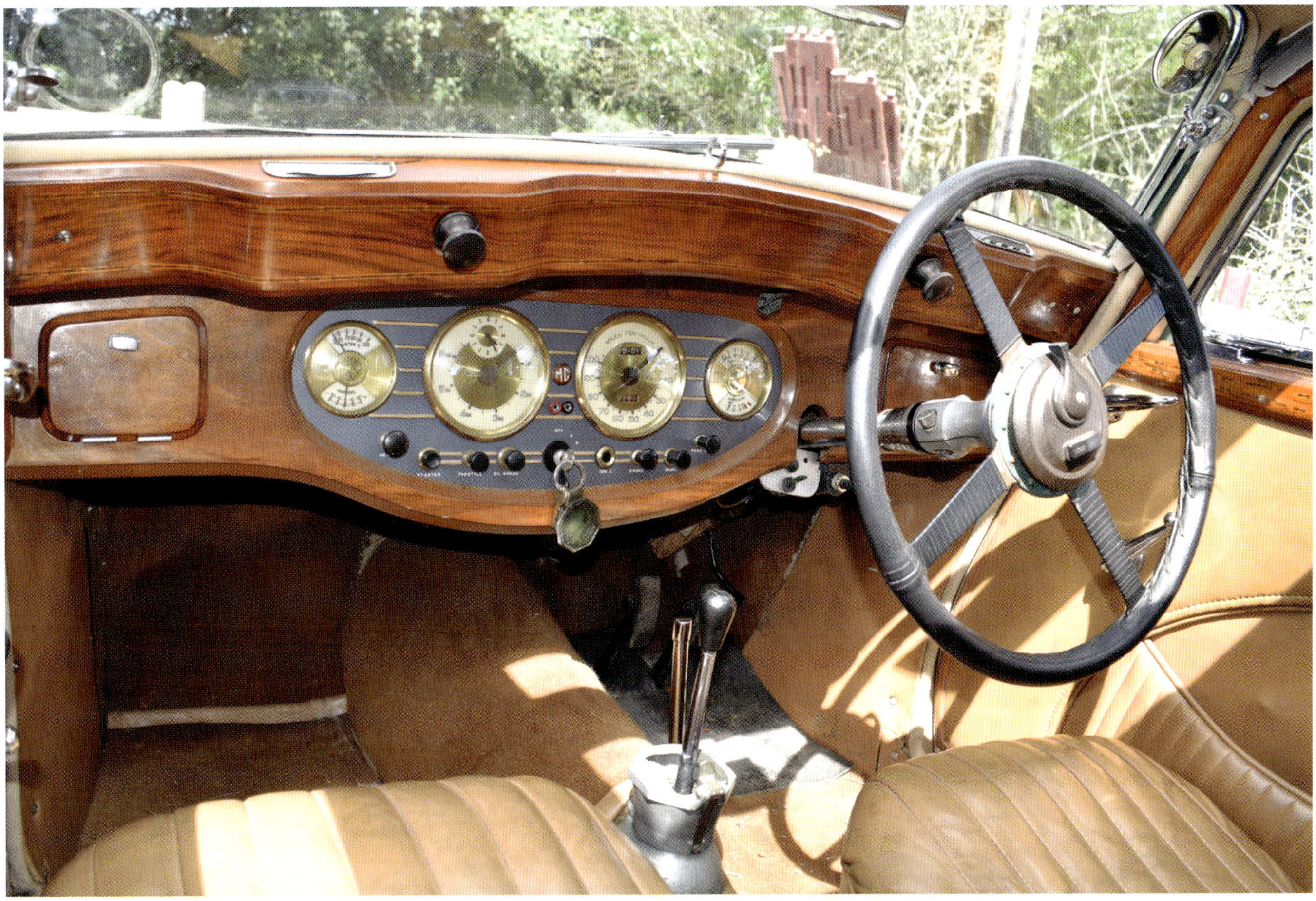

The driver is provided with a full range of instruments set in a polished wood dashboard.

The elegant Tickford version of the SA. (Photo Knudson Collection)

Side-opening bonnet panels provide easy access to the six-cylinder engine.

Below right: Brochure for the SA model.

On the main factory floor at Abingdon TA Midget and SA rolling chassis sit on adjacent assembly lines.

The reception the new car received was mixed. The types of owners who liked to use their MGs for production car trials and other sporting activities largely ignored the model. They either soldiered on with their OHC cars, or turned their attentions to the TA, which was itself a larger and more comfortable car than the previous Midgets had been. On the other hand, for long journeys, especially trips to Europe, the SA was a vast improvement over previous models. The chassis was indeed heavy but it was also strong, and the longer suspension travel gave a more comfortable ride.

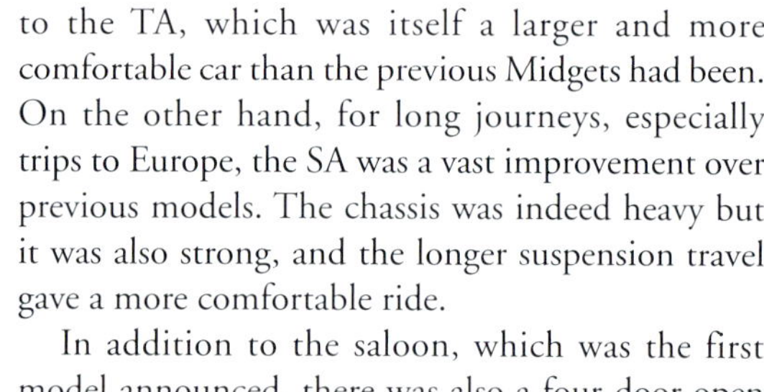

In addition to the saloon, which was the first model announced, there was also a four-door open tourer and a Tickford-bodied folding-head coupé. The latter is arguably one of the most elegant cars ever made and today justifiably is most sought by enthusiasts of these large MGs. The tourer body was by Charlesworth and the model was produced in relatively small numbers, just 90 cars in all. The earlier examples had straight-topped doors, giving a continuous straight line from radiator to the rear of the car, enhanced by an elegant moulding painted a contrasting colour. This design was first slightly modified at the rear and then, later, replaced by one that featured the then-fashionable cut-away tops to the front doors. A batch of the later tourers went to the Lancashire Constabulary. Overall SA production was 2738 cars; the majority were saloons, but there were nearly 700 Tickford coupés.

Drawing by Harold Connolly of the Tickford drophead coupé used as an insert in the lavish brochure for the SA model.

THE FACTORY TRIALS TEAMS

MG Car Club Rushmere Hill Climb held near Bridgnorth in 1934. Two of the Cream Cracker PAs, JB 3854 driven by Bastock and TJ 5000 by Toulmin, prior to their repainting in cream and brown. Note the stripes on the sides of the cars.

The connection of the MG marque with sporting trials began in the very early days, with a few Morris Garages customers for the 14/28 Super Sports models entering their cars in these events. There was also the enthusiasm of Cecil Kimber himself, who had won a first class award in the 1925 Land's End Trial at the wheel of the MG special we now know as Old Number One. These events were very popular at a time when other types of motoring events were rare and the sole mainland racing circuit was the banked Brooklands track. The 1929 Land's End Trial attracted over 30,000 spectators and a 228-car entry, of which 180 completed the 326-mile course. Fourteen MGs were entered including, in a sign of things to come, the first outing for four of the brand new M-type Midgets.

From then on MG owners in growing numbers participated in all the major trials. With successes in racing and record breaking, as well as in trials, the name MG came to mean sports car in the eyes of the public. Consequently, it seems, almost everyone buying a new M-type or J2 wanted to use it competitively. The MG Car Company were obviously well aware of the sales potential of trials successes and had from the outset given as much support to competitors as finance and Society of Motor Manufacturers rules would allow. However, by the mid-1930s this support became more overt, especially important since in 1935 MG had officially stopped their racing activities.

The factory Cream Cracker team cars made their first appearance wearing the cream and brown colour scheme for the 1935 Land's End Trial. Although this was the debut for the newly painted team of P-type Midgets, support for the cars by the factory had been evident well before this. Two of the members of the team, J. Maurice Toulmin and R.A. "Mac" Macdermid, had acquired their cars early in 1934 and the third team member, Jack A. Bastock, his in September that year. At first the cars remained in their original colours, two painted blue and

North West London Motor Club Team Trial 1934. The start at Hartland, North Devon. Toulmin in his PA wearing the cream and brown stripes leads the other two team cars.

one green, although later they also had brown and cream stripes along the sides of the bonnets. As they were still fitted with the heavy swept wings, and were thus overweight, they were not as successful as expected and the cars were all returned to the factory for comprehensive modification before competing in the Exeter Trial at the end of 1934.

Cycle wings replaced swept wings and the cars were fitted with lightweight aluminium bonnets, the lighter 8-inch brake gear and locked differentials, while much of the equipment, such as hoods, windscreens and side-screens, was discarded. Thus modified, the cars were more successful and took two first class awards and one second class award on the Exeter Trial. When they were returned to Abingdon to be prepared for the 1935 Land's End it was decided to call the team Cream Crackers and to repaint the cars cream with brown wings, front apron, scuttle and bonnet top.

Cream Cracker and Musketeer cars line up before a special test during the 1935 Abingdon to Abingdon Trial.

By the end of 1935 the factory had replaced the PAs with a team of three PBs, JB 7521, driven by Toulmin, JB 7524 for Ken Crawford and JB 7525 for J.E.S. Jones. The lessons had been well learned and the new cars, although similar in appearance to the earlier PAs, were more powerful, lighter and altogether more effective. In this form the cars enjoyed considerable success, which was exploited to the full in advertising to promote the sale of standard cars.

During 1936 the PB Midgets went out of production and were replaced by the pushrod T-series Midget and, to maximise publicity for the new model, the trials teams had to follow suit. A new Cream Cracker team of three TAs was formed for 1937 with ABL 960, ABL 962 and ABL 964 for Toulmin, Crawford and Jones respectively. Initially these cars were not as popular with the drivers but

eventually they were developed into very effective trials cars. For 1938, VA 1548cc engines were fitted to new TA Midgets, BBL 78, 79, 80 and 81, and later the capacity was increased to 1708cc by over-boring and fitting WA pistons.

In parallel with the efforts with the Cream Cracker cars, the company also supported the Musketeers team. Initially they ran three of the specially built NE Magnettes that had successfully competed in the 1934 Tourist Trophy. Driven by Lewis Welch, Freddy Kindell and Sam Nash, the NE Magnettes were very successful. Although finished in the same cream and brown colours as the Crackers the treatment was slightly different as the whole of the car's body was cream and only the wings, stays, front apron and the chosen name appeared in brown.

Following this success, three special cars based on an amalgam of various current components were built for the next Musketeer team of R.A. Macdermid, Jack Bastock and Alf Langley. These cars, JB 6865, JB 6866 and JB 6867, proved very fast and competitive. The original plan was for the cars to be an official works team, as distinct from the ostensibly private Crackers team. The nominated drivers were Lewis Welch, Athos; either Alex Hounslow or G.W.J.H. Wright, Porthos; and Sam Nash, Aramis. However, evidently it was later decided that the team drivers should not be so closely connected with the factory.

The cars were tested in the autumn of 1935 by

The 1935 MG Car Club Abingdon to Abingdon Trial. Bastock prepares to tackle the driving test in the Cream Cracker PA with the cream and brown livery.

A.G. Imhof's 1938 Cream Cracker TA with its spare wheel mounted in front of the radiator on the 1938 Abingdon Trial. He felt that being able to adjust weight balance by moving the wheel from back to front of the car gave him an advantage on certain tests.

The 1934 Tourist Trophy NE wearing the type of body it carried when it was used in the Musketeer trials team.

the competition department and entered in a few events. During this period the specification was being refined and arrangements for the 1936 season were considered. The selected private drivers, MacDermid, Bastock and Langley, were invited to comment on the cars and their recommendations taken into account. Lewis Welch, who lived in Oxford, was named as reserve driver for both the Musketeer and Cracker teams.

Like the other MG team, the Musketeers

TJ 5000 looks today much as it must have done when prepared at the factory for J. Maurice Toulmin to drive in the 1935 Land's End Trial. His son Jonathan now owns the PA, and the logo on the door celebrates the 80th anniversary of the establishment of the Cream Crackers Trial Team.

The sole surviving member of the L/N specials built for the Musketeer Trials Team. That the car survives with almost all of its original components is remarkable.

The cockpit of the L/N Musketeer.

All three of the 1935/36 Cream Cracker Team PBs survive and were reunited at the 2019 Triple-M Register Summer Gathering.

changed over to TAs for 1937, running ABL 961, ABL 963 and ABL 965 to the same specification as that used for the Cream Cracker cars. For the 1938 season BBL 82, BBL 83 and BBL 84 were replacements and BJB 412 was provided for the new team member, Dickie Green. However this series of team cars differed from the Cream Crackers as they were fitted with TA engines running with Laystall crankshafts and Marshall 110 superchargers. They were also painted red, rather than the previous scheme of cream and brown.

The outbreak of war in September 1939 brought all these activities to an end and for mainstream sports car manufacturers, like the MG Car Company, production car trials were never again to receive the prominence and support seen in the 1930s..

Unlike standard PBs, the Cream Cracker cars were fitted with lightweight cycle wings.

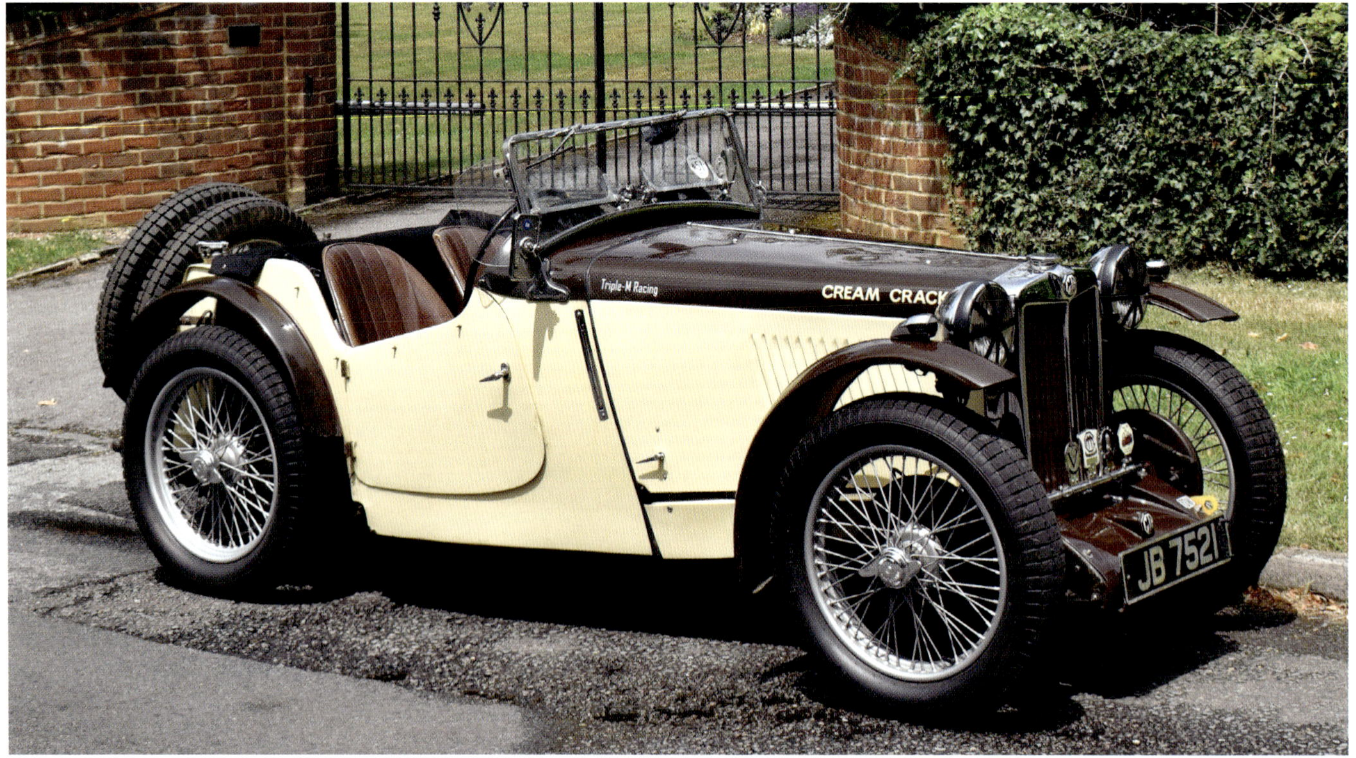

Twin spares were fitted in case of need and also to add as much weight as possible over the rear wheels.

This Cream Cracker TA was one of three prepared for the 1937 season to replace the PBs as that model was no longer current. The car was driven in events that year by Ken Crawford, with some success.

THE VA ONE-AND-A-HALF-LITRE

Saloon and tourer versions of the 1½-litre VA. Morris Bodies Branch made bodies for both these models.

Factory picture of an early VA chassis. Note that whilst at first glance it follows traditional MG practice for their mid-range tourers and saloons, major innovations were hydraulic brakes, under-slung rear axle and conventional shackles for the leaf springs. These features first appeared in the SA announced a year earlier.

In 1935 the SA was due to be launched, but this model was really built to cater for the sorts of customers unlikely to have purchased the previous MG saloons. The people the SA was aimed at were those who may also have considered an Alvis, one of the larger Wolseleys, the 14hp Rover, or maybe the 2½-litre SS Jaguar that was launched at around the same time. To cater for those wanting something a bit smaller, MG needed a mid-sized saloon to replace the last of the OHC six-cylinder cars, the N-type. That model was not built in saloon guise, apart from a handful of Airline Coupés, but the K1 saloon had continued in production with improved specification as the KN.

Although larger than the OHC MG four-seater tourers it replaced, the VA retained the elegant lines for which the marque was noted.

The car chosen to fill in the MG model range between the 1292cc TA Midget and the 2288cc SA saloon was the VA, called in MG literature at the time the One-and-a-Half-Litre. As this was still constructed on a traditional chassis frame there was

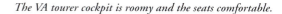

The VA tourer cockpit is roomy and the seats comfortable.

A contemporary publicity picture of a VA Tickford drophead coupé taken in the Cotswolds.

no problem about offering it in various guises, as a saloon, a tourer and as a drophead coupé. At a stroke they thought they had catered for those who had previously bought the four-seater NB, the Allingham 2/4 seater N-type and the KN saloon. Whether this was to be successful, only time would tell.

A sales brochure for the VA with the Tickford version on the cover.

The MG Car Company was entering a hotly contested class with the new model. Previously their cars may have been a bit fragile for the day-to-day rigours of providing family transportation, but they had what we might now term sex appeal. Like most sports cars, they certainly tended to be bought more with the heart than the head, something that Cecil Kimber would have been keen to see continue. However, under the new corporate management they were tasked with producing something closer to the mainstream saloon cars in the group, and this put them in direct competition with many other marques offering a similar product.

Take a look at what was on offer in the 1½-litre category at the 1935 Motor Show. There were a number of different Riley models, with four-cylinder engines of either 1087cc or 1496cc, which performed well, looked very attractive, and sold at prices that started well below £300. From within the Nuffield camp there were staid but solid Wolseley 12/48s and Morris 12s which shared the VA power unit but sold for a lot less. Although those were unlikely to appeal to an MG buyer, the new 1½-litre SS Jaguar certainly would. That model did very well and must have affected the sales of the

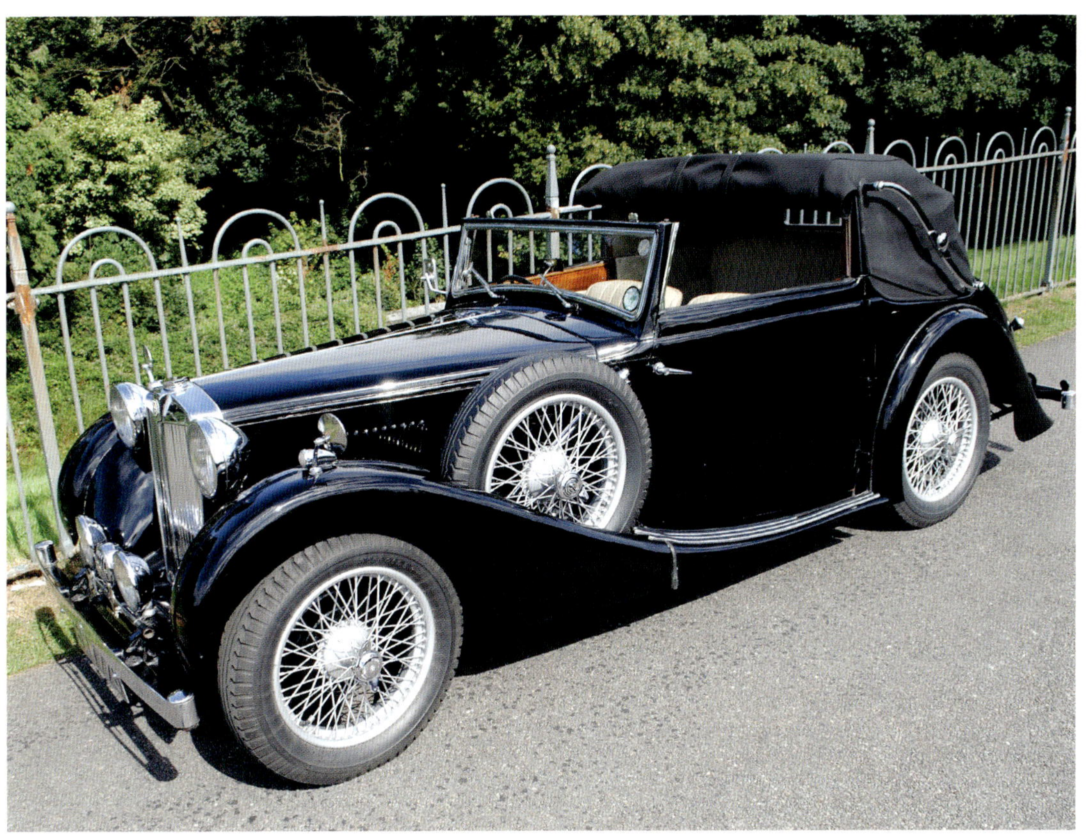

The Tickford three-position top with the section above the front seats rolled up.

The VA Tickford at just over 14 feet long is not overly large, but the designers managed to give it a handsome and imposing appearance.

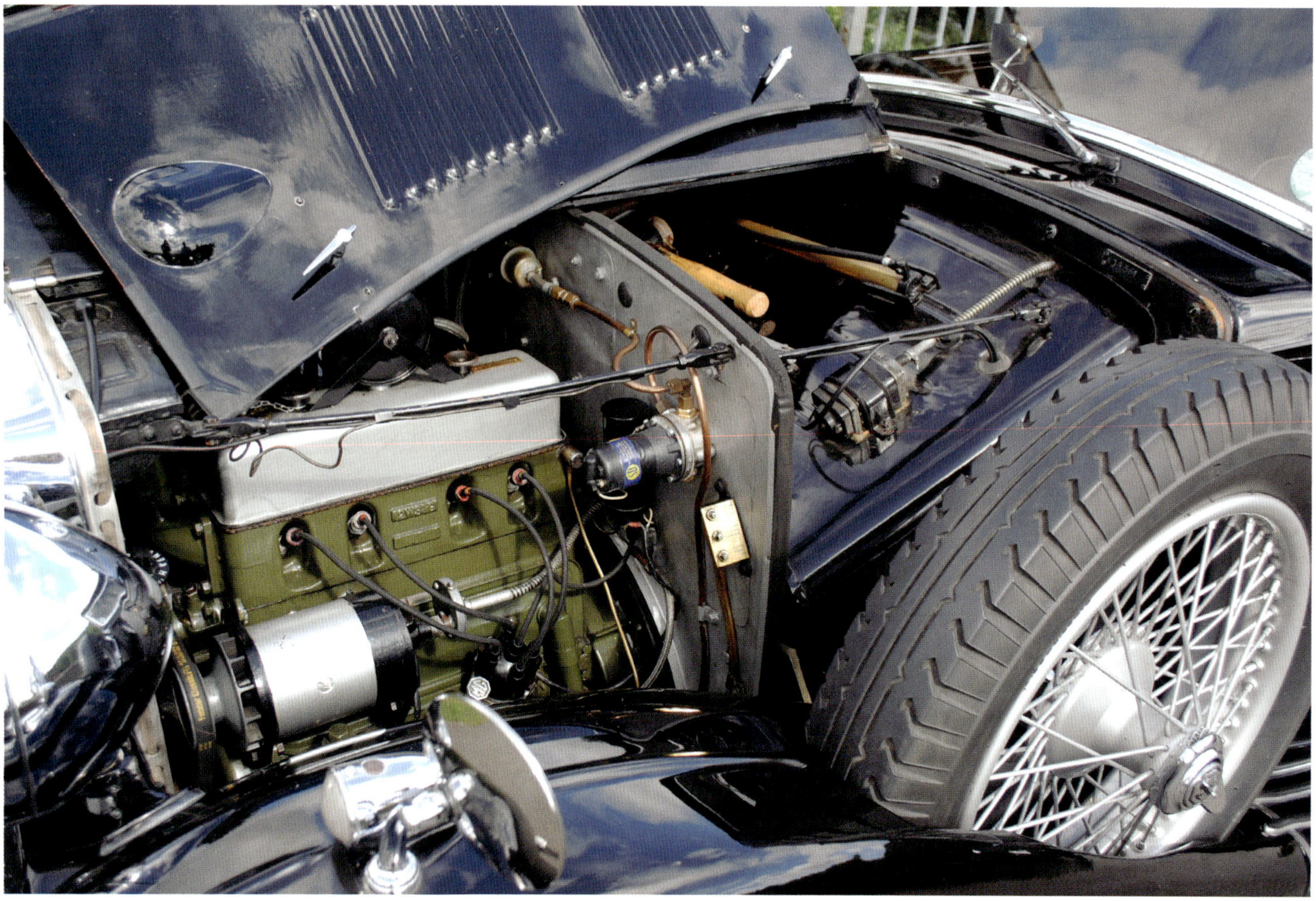

The 1548cc engine in the VA was developed from a Morris power unit. The grouped nipples on the bulkhead are for lubricating various points on the chassis.

The VA Tickford provides four comfortable leather-covered seats in its spacious cockpit.

A neat and attractive arrangement of instruments and controls is mounted in the wooden dashboard.

new MG. Triumph, Singer and Standard also built cars with 1½-litre engines, but few models had any special attraction.

The chassis frame of the VA, like that of the SA, was drawn up along traditional lines. Built with boxed side members that were carried over the rear axle, it had substantial tubular cross-members. Suspension was by leaf springs and there were hydraulic shock absorbers, adjustable at the rear, and the car had grouped-nipple central lubrication. A built-in jacking system was an optional extra. Much attention had been given to comfort for driver and passengers with soft springing for the beam axles.

The overhead-valve pushrod engine was really a four-cylinder version of the six-cylinder unit in the SA. Being of Morris manufacture, it owed nothing to the OHC six-cylinder MG engines in the previous models, but was a development of earlier Morris sidevalve units. With a capacity of 1549cc it produced just 55bhp against the 56bhp available from the 1271cc engine in the N-type, but the larger capacity did give the engine greater torque, which was certainly needed to propel what turned out to be a fairly heavy car.

Because the VA chassis had a wheelbase of nine feet and the SA 10ft 3in, it follows that there was going to be less room within the cabin for passengers. However, the overall design still provided adequate space for four to travel in some comfort, mainly at the expense of the flowing lines of the bigger car. The appearance of the VA was, nevertheless, one of its appealing features. Some observers have criticised the relatively small area of glass in the saloon and this, together with the lack of a side moulding, gives the model a slightly slab-sided appearance. The tourer and drophead coupé, on the other hand, attract few critics.

Despite being built ostensibly from the corporate parts bin, the MG VA could hardly be mistaken for anything other than an MG. Not only is there the handsome and imposing radiator shell, but also Kimber managed to squeeze octagons into almost every part of the car. There was an octagonal steering boss, octagonal top for the dipstick, etc., etc. There is no record of the extra cost involved,

CECIL KIMBER'S LETTERS TO SALESMEN

For the car companies, building a good and reliable vehicle with showroom appeal is but half the battle as it is still necessary to find someone to buy it. This is obviously vital now that factories can produce thousands of vehicles every day. However, even in the 1930s when the annual output of the MG factory at Abingdon could be easily surpassed at a modern car plant in a single shift, wooing customers was still a priority. Advertising and taking space at major motor shows was one way of reaching potential buyers, but far more important were the dealers.

Cecil Kimber was very good at promotion and under his guidance a lot of stylish sales material and attractive advertising was issued. By 1937, when the company was selling cars that were quite different in character from those produced earlier that decade, Kimber seems to have thought that he needed to provide the salesmen with more inside information from the factory. He did this by issuing a series of weekly newsletters, which fortunately survive.

The first newsletter is dated 19 February 1937 and was sent out to distributors with a covering letter signed by Kimber in his usual green ink, along with an application form so that a salesman could ask to receive his own weekly copy. The first paragraph read, "For some time past I have felt that we might considerably help your salesmen in their job by supplying them direct with little items of news of general interest that could form most useful subjects of conversation with prospective customers".

That newsletter began by saying that the previous week the Monte Carlo Rally had been staged and although there was no official factory participation Mr D.E. Harris, a private owner of a T-series Midget, had started the event from Stavanger. He had enjoyed some success, taking a trophy for best performance for a car from that starting point. Other news included details of an MG entered for the Le Mans race later that year and of success in a Scottish trial. News of more interest to those in the showroom was that producing the VA was well advanced.

Important events were covered in the newsletters and as 1937 was coronation year this merited a mention in a later issue, as did the shortage of steel supplies caused by a rush in Britain to rearm in response to the rise of fascism in Europe. In his letter dated 19 April, Kimber said that this was causing manufacturing shortages and that deliveries of the new VA models would consequently be delayed. By the time he wrote the 12 July newsletter Kimber must have been getting a bit fed up with the process as he said he was taking a summer break and that unless something very special cropped up would not be writing again until September.

The break in the newsletters lasted longer than predicted and it was on 5 November that a letter was sent to dealers saying that they were to restart, enclosing a card that was to be completed so that any staff changes could be recorded. The newsletters proper resumed with issues dated 8 and 19 February 1938 and followed the usual format. In the second letter, Kimber said that he was to take a trip to Germany to see the Berlin Motor Show. He was particularly keen to examine the independent front suspension systems now becoming commonplace in Europe

In March 1938 the final three newsletters were produced. One imagines that either pressure of work, or a poor response from those to whom they were addressed, hastened their demise. However, there appears to have been a later series of general newsletters from the publicity department, number six, dated June 1939, being the only one to survive.

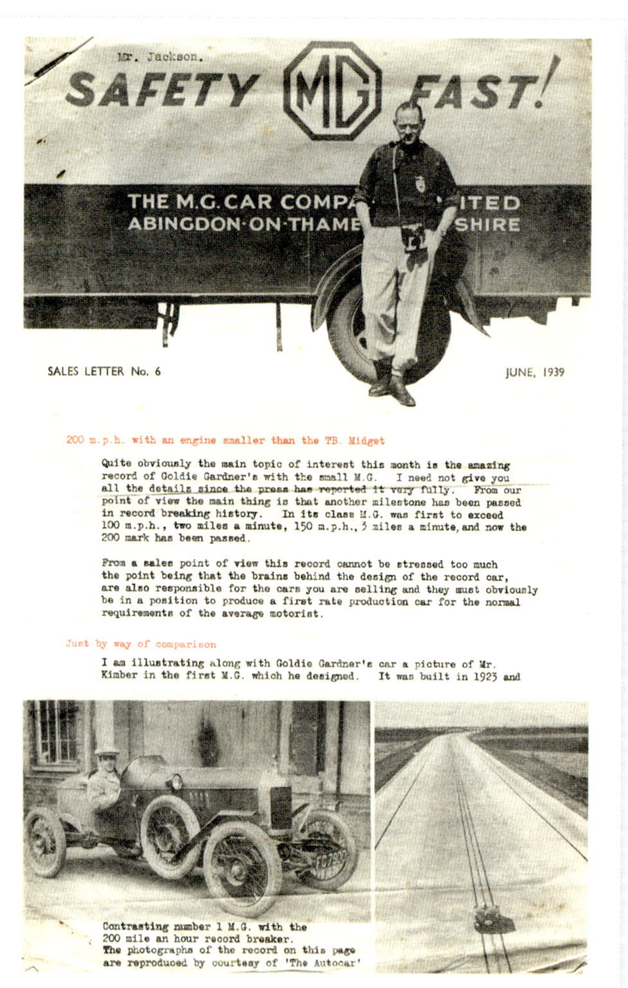
Mr. Jackson.

SAFETY MG FAST!

THE M.G. CAR COMPA... ...ITED
ABINGDON-ON-THAME... ...SHIRE

SALES LETTER No. 6

JUNE, 1939

200 m.p.h. with an engine smaller than the TB. Midget

Quite obviously the main topic of interest this month is the amazing record of Goldie Gardner's with the small M.G. I need not give you all the details since the press has reported it very fully. From our point of view the main thing is that another milestone has been passed in record breaking history. In its class M.G. was first to exceed 100 m.p.h., two miles a minute, 150 m.p.h., 3 miles a minute, and now the 200 mark has been passed.

From a sales point of view this record cannot be stressed too much the point being that the brains behind the design of the record car, are also responsible for the cars you are selling and they must obviously be in a position to produce a first rate production car for the normal requirements of the average motorist.

Just by way of comparison

I am illustrating along with Goldie Gardner's car a picture of Mr. Kimber in the first M.G. which he designed. It was built in 1923 and

Contrasting number 1 M.G. with the 200 mile an hour record breaker.
The photographs of the record on this page are reproduced by courtesy of 'The Autocar'

The final pre-war versions of the newsletters were issued by the publicity department and included some illustrations.

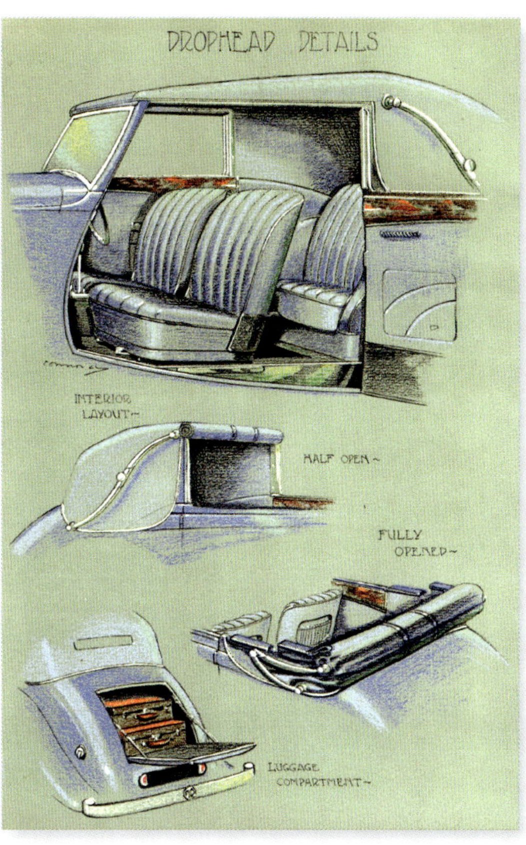

A detail from the attractive brochure illustrated by Harold Connolly.

but it must have accounted for a portion of the £325 asked for the saloon version.

There is every sign that MG production was in a bit of a mess during the first part of 1936. The SA had been announced at the London Motor Show the previous October and by the start of the year a backlog of 500 orders had accumulated. There had been a number of delays in actually getting the car into production, not all of them by any means the fault of the factory. However, £20,000 had been spent over the winter in reorganising and re-equipping the Abingdon assembly area so as to double the number of production lines to four. There was also a new cellulose spray plant capable of dealing with hundreds of cars a week, and a conveyor system to deliver wheels and tyres to the assembly line. Given the backlog of SA orders, and the launch of the TA Midget in June 1936, it is not surprising that the first announcement of the VA was delayed until the Olympia Motor Show in October 1936.

Bearing in mind that work on the model had really only started in earnest 12 months earlier, this would now seem to be quite a short gestation period, and it is only in light of their previous efforts that it seemed slow. However, the wait appears to have been worthwhile and there was a warm reception for the new car in the motoring press. As already mentioned, there were to be three versions of the new model, in addition to a rolling chassis for sale to outside coachbuilders. Unlike the SA, Morris Bodies Branch produced both the saloon and the tourer coachwork. The drophead coupé was still the work of Tickford of Newport Pagnell who had developed their particular bodywork to fit a number of different models and marques.

In the price lists the tourer was the cheapest version at £280. The VA open four-seater had just two doors, but both of these featured the popular cut-away top edges thought at the time to be essential for a sporting car. There was a well-fitted hood that stowed away into a recess at the rear of the body and the four side curtains had chromed surrounds to the plastic windows. Behind the rear seat was a barely adequate space for stowing luggage for touring holidays. This area also had to contain stowed side-screens, but there was no external access provided. The spare wheel was mounted on the back of the car.

The saloon was exceptionally well equipped for a car of its size and price. Leather upholstery, of course, plus a sliding sunroof, opening quarter-lights for rear-seat passengers and a windscreen that could be wound open for additional ventilation. There was a good choice of colour schemes on offer, with duo-tone cars having a contrasting colour for the wings and running boards. Unlike the SA, the body was painted just one colour as there was no convenient waist moulding to act as a dividing line between contrasting colours. A comprehensive tool kit was provided, which in the saloon was stowed in the boot lid; the tourer had a tool tray under the bonnet.

As with most new cars launched by MG at the London Motor Show, the salesmen were happy to take your order but only a handful of prototypes existed. Deliveries of new models traditionally started the following spring and production of the VA was fully underway by April 1937. The initial announcement in the motoring press, with full details of specification, models and prices, coincided with the show, but full road tests did not appear until 1937.

All the press reports emphasise the refinement of the car; this was particularly noticeable when it was compared to previous models. *Practical Motorist*, then a very popular magazine that sold in large numbers, tested a tourer. Their car reached a maximum of 90mph on a downhill slope, but this

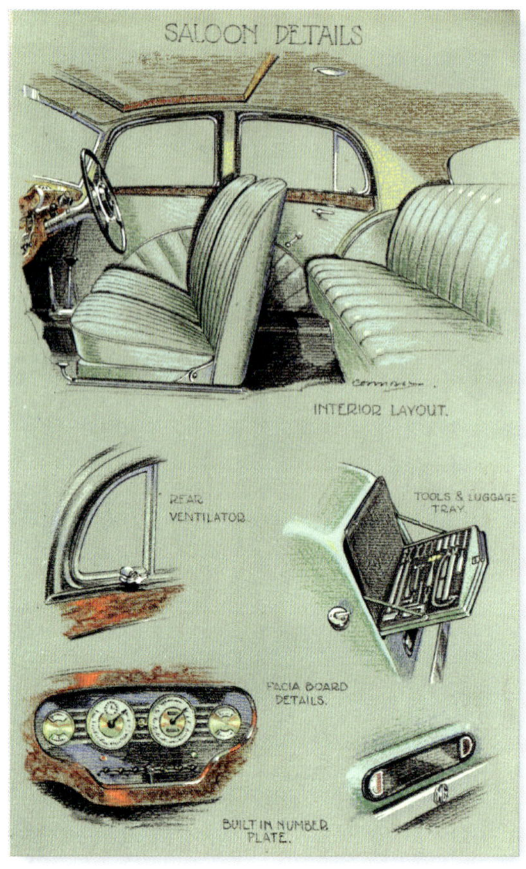

The artwork used in the early VA catalogues added to their appeal.

was probably recorded on the car's speedometer rather than on special test equipment. Their test was undertaken in poor weather and they particularly praised the hood and side-screens, saying they were almost watertight except in very heavy rain when water entered along the top edges of the side-screens.

The most expensive model in the range was the Tickford drophead at £335. These were attractive cars that are now seen as the best model to own, particularly in a country where the weather is not always good enough to travel hood down. Although the standard 12hp engine was thought the best for sale to customers, a few cars were fitted with a 14hp engine of 1707cc capacity. This unit had been developed for the TA trials cars and used the bore size and pistons that would eventually be those fitted to the 2.6-litre WA when this appeared at the end of 1938. These more powerful engines were specified for the VA tourers sold to police forces and one was fitted to a saloon that Kimber used himself.

In all over 2400 VAs were built. The last ones to be constructed left the factory during the early part of 1940 when they must have been assembled in whatever small areas were still devoted to car production. Although the model was a lot different from the mid-range MGs that preceded it, the 1½-litre MG won many new converts to the marque. Because the majority of owners were not as interested in using their cars for competition as those buying the two-seater sports cars, it did not matter to them that they were heavier and less agile than the OHC cars. What was far more important was their ability to provide up to four occupants with comfortable transport over long distances.

This picture taken at the end of the assembly line in 1938 clearly shows the difference between the VA on the left and the long-bonneted SA models alongside.

THE PRE-WAR MG POLICE CARS

One has to remember that in the early days of motoring, indeed right up until well after the end of the First World War, the average policeman was not motorised. Bicycles were the usual form of transport and few ordinary beat constables could drive, apart from those who had learned during military service. However, as early as 1904 there were a few cars in police hands, with the Metropolitan Police force taking the lead. However, these were usually solely for the use of chief constables or the more senior officers. In the 1920s it was not unusual for some higher-ranking policemen to use their own cars on official duties, and for those that were bought for the police by local watch committees to be registered in the name of the Chief Constable. Motorcycles were also used, often fitted with a sidecar, but they had their limitations.

The Metropolitan Police ran five M-type Midgets, one bought secondhand. The example here has a full-width windscreen and the spare wheel is mounted on the back of the tail rather than within the rear compartment. This must have provided a bit more room for any equipment carried.

The introduction of the Road Traffic Act in 1930 resulted in the formation of motor patrols, finance for which came from the money collected from road fund licences. There were annual grants that ranged from £60 for a motorcycle combination to £150 for a car of over 12hp, and with the treasury now footing the bill the incentive was there for every local force to modernise. It was from this point that the mechanisation of the police really began in earnest.

Some of the earliest MGs to be recorded as police cars were the 18/80 and the five M-types bought by the Metropolitan Police. Brighton Borough Police also ran an 18/80 and the Edinburgh force had two M-type Midgets. The M-type may seem an unusual choice as a police car, but the most likely reason for their purchase was their small-sized engine which, as the Home Office were keen to point out, was only 8hp and as such ranked as a motorcycle combination for grant purposes and was thus cheaper to finance.

Once the M-type had been replaced by the more powerful J2, more forces took an interest in the MG range. The Metropolitan Police were the earliest recorded purchasers of J2s, buying four of them in early 1933. Lancashire Constabulary took delivery of six black-painted J2s on 30th March 1933. It is well documented that many J2s suffered premature crankshaft failure and there was a special arrangement to supply reconditioned engines to the police at £20 a time. All cars were black with brown upholstery, and all seemed to suffer more than their fair share of problems in police hands. In 1935 one car was so poorly it had to be returned to Abingdon by train.

Buckingham Constabulary at Aylesbury ran two J2s and further north Leeds City Police bought the first of what would turn out to be quite a number of MGs. The East Riding of Yorkshire also acquired swept-wing J2s. They bought two cars painted black with green trim and wheels in a matching shade. In spite of all the difficulties with reliability encountered with the J2s, the cars were obviously popular enough for the police forces to consider using the replacement model, the P-type Midget. By this time the police were becoming increasingly involved with traffic duties of all sorts. A 1934 report noted that the cost of maintaining police cars now accounted for seven per cent of the budget and that there was a growing need for more traffic control measures, like speed traps.

A four-seater PA Midget used by Reading Borough Police.

A larger number of P-types were supplied to the police than of the earlier model. The MG Car Company was by then far more aware of the needs of the various police forces, even running one PA as a police demonstrator. An early PA buyer was the local Oxford City Police. A car was purchased in March 1934 and by May it was returned to the factory for an engine rebuild that included new pistons and con-rods, new cylinder head and valves, and a new radiator shell. In March 1934 Lancashire Constabulary purchased a batch of 10 PA Midgets, following this with a further eight cars a year later. All 18 were painted black with blue trim and silver wheels, The local dealer, Merigold Brothers of Preston, supplied all of these and in 1936 J. Edwards & Sons, Chester, supplied eight of the more powerful, PB models.

The City of Glasgow Police chose to buy eight

This four-seater NA Magnette was used as a patrol car by the Wolverhampton Police.

PAs for traffic duties. The cars were purchased through C.S. Grant, Glasgow. Five of the cars were blue with blue trim and the remainder appear to have been finished in a two-tone colour scheme, black and special blue with blue trim. PA Midgets were supplied in small numbers to other forces. Northumberland County Constabulary had two cars and Kent bought both PA and PB models for use in various areas of the county. Leeds City Police had seven PA and PB Midgets and Cheshire County Police had four PA Midgets, all built to a similar specification to those supplied to the nearby Lancashire force. Buckinghamshire Constabulary bought six PB Midgets, all but the first of which were prepared to police specification. Leicester City Police bought a pair of PA Midgets and a PB.

In addition to the Midgets, the six-cylinder cars were also used. Lancashire Constabulary ran eight L1 Magna four-seater tourers, having previously used a single F-type at Bootle. When the N-type Magnette was introduced as a replacement for the previous six-cylinder models, Lancashire Constabulary were again the prime users. Although they were available in open form with two-seater bodies, that force chose to use the four-seater version. Wiltshire Constabulary acquired three of the revised NB model, all two-seaters, and the police specification for these cars included staggered seats, 8-day clock, bigger silencer and different tail pipe, two push-pull

One of 16 TA Midgets supplied as a batch to Lancashire Constabulary.

The cockpit of the version of the TB Midget produced specially for police use. It had a glove box in the dashboard with a sliding writing tray beneath for the observer to use. The loudspeaker controls sit between the seats and a microphone was a standard fitting. Extra switches operated the illuminated police signs.

The 1½-litre VA tourers built specially for police use featured an engine with a larger bore to increase capacity to 1705cc. The cockpit had all the alterations required to make it better suited to patrol work.

switches, battery master switch, and modified hood canopy and tonneau cover. Wolverhampton Police ran a four-seater NA.

When the TA replaced the PB Midget, the MG Car Company still wanted the police business and made efforts to sell the new model to various forces. One TA appears to have been used as a police demonstrator. It was tested at Hendon and approved for police use provided cars were modified to comply with Home Office guidelines, black paint and blue upholstery, push-pull electrical switches, certified accurate speedometer, etc. Lancashire Constabulary were keen buyers, taking 62 examples between 1936 and 1938, and the other forces to use TAs included Yorkshire East Riding, West Sussex, Kent and Derbyshire.

Amongst the cars purchased with Home Office funds for the driving schools were some MG SA models. These were also to prove popular with the police as they were able to easily accommodate four large officers and had ample capacity for carrying equipment. Examples are known to have served with forces in Durham, Barrow in Furness, Northamptonshire and Kent, but there were probably many others. The most prolific buyer, once again, was the Lancashire Constabulary. They took at least 33 cars, quite a number of them four-seater tourers. The SA saloons known to have been at Hutton Hall were used for advanced driving tuition where their relatively high performance and good roadholding were an advantage. Chelmsford Driving School also had an SA. The Durham Constabulary purchased two SA saloons in 1938 and these were used on traffic patrol duties. They must have been satisfied with the cars as in 1939 they paid £400 to acquire one of the few 2.6-litre WA saloons.

The 1½-litre VA was also popular with a number of forces and MG built a special police version which, as well as having the usual items like uprated electrical equipment, extra switches, etc., also enjoyed a larger-capacity engine. Police forces known to have used the VA were Lancashire, West Riding of Yorkshire, Huddersfield Borough Police, Reading, Kent and East Sussex. In the late 1930s MGs, both Midgets and the larger cars were often used on the courtesy cop scheme where highly visible police cars stopped motorists following minor infringements of the law in order to point out the error of their ways. The idea was that they were

This surviving TA was originally supplied new to the Lancashire Constabulary in July 1937 and allocated to PC 807 Cecil Gratrix, who was to be its regular driver.

As with the majority of police MGs, the car was painted black with blue upholstery and was returned to this colour scheme when recently restored. In service, illuminated POLICE signs were fitted front and rear, but as the signs must be removed when it is driven on the road the car now has these plates.

usually just given a lecture rather than a ticket.

During the war there were obviously no new MGs available and many of the police MGs were used throughout the years of conflict and covered high mileages. When eventually sold, the shortage of new cars available to the general public meant that these often raised a lot more that they had cost new in the late 1930s.

THE WA 2.6-LITRE

Sales of the two-litre SA held up well in 1937 but did not match those of one of its rivals, the SS Jaguar 2½-litre. Like MG, SS Cars were relative newcomers to the field, having launched the first car to bear their name, the SS1 coupé, as recently as 1931. The Swallow Sidecar Company started off in Blackpool building motorcycle sidecars and then graduated to producing stylish coachwork for cars like the Austin Seven. With its exaggerated looks, when it first appeared many derided the SS1 as being more style than substance. However, even then the genius of William Lyons was to build cars that looked more expensive than they were, which gave them considerable showroom appeal.

The early SS1 had a Standard sidevalve engine of either 2 or 2.6 litres, and 70mph was just about possible with the smaller engine. In 1933, just like the contemporary MG models, individual wings were replaced by the more elegant and practical swept wings, while engine modifications saw the car capable of 75mph. Bearing in mind that the four-seater coupé cost just over £300, it looked good value in comparison to the 1100cc MG L1 Salonette at £345 or K1 saloon at £445. SS also introduced their version of the streamlined Airline coupé at just £340. Despite some shortcomings, all these cars sold well and certainly must have affected sales of those built by the MG Car Company.

A studio picture of the front of the WA used for exhibitions.

In 1935 SS introduced a new Jaguar saloon in 1½- and 2½-litre forms. These models were direct competitors to the MG VA and SA and looked even better value. In 1938 Jaguar made some improvements, introducing an overhead-valve engine for the 1½-litre model – the 2½ had had overhead valves from the outset, – and giving the larger-capacity model a longer wheelbase as well as the option of a 3½-litre power unit. Both models now had modern all-steel body construction. Bearing in mind that 3633 of the SS Jaguar 2.5-litre models were sold in 1936 and 1937 against just 2745 of the MG SA in the four years that model was on sale, one can judge the success of the relatively new marque. The strength of the Jaguar in the marketplace meant that MG really needed to make improvements to their models if they were to stay in touch.

The answer provided by Abingdon was another new model. The 2.6-litre WA was announced to the public in August 1938, a time when many were

A 1939 factory picture of a Tickford WA that remarkably has survived to provide the colour pictures seen in these page.

preoccupied with the likelihood of a war against fascism. The new model was the largest car ever to carry the MG badge and by the standard of the times was considered to be the height of luxury. Basically the design followed the pattern set by the SA, although the chassis was widened at the rear to allow them to fit a slightly altered body. The front axle came from the SA, but a wider rear axle was sourced from the Wolseley parts bin. Hydraulic dampers and brakes were fitted, with a tandem master cylinder giving separate circuits front and rear. It was to be the 1970s before split braking circuits were to become standard on all MGs. The WA had 14-inch diameter brake drums all round.

The engine of the WA was basically the same as the unit fitted to the SA, but with its capacity enlarged to 2561cc; the stroke remained the same at 102mm and the bore size was taken out to 73mm. The 2.6-litre engine produced around 100bhp, almost 20% more than the SA, and fell within the 20hp bracket for road tax. Running with a higher compression ratio the WA engine preferred a diet of alcohol-based fuels.

One feature of the car much emphasised in early publicity was the lubrication system. Oil pressurised by the pump passed through a copper-pipe coil

Publicity pictures used the sort of locations they thought would match the aspirations of prospective purchasers.

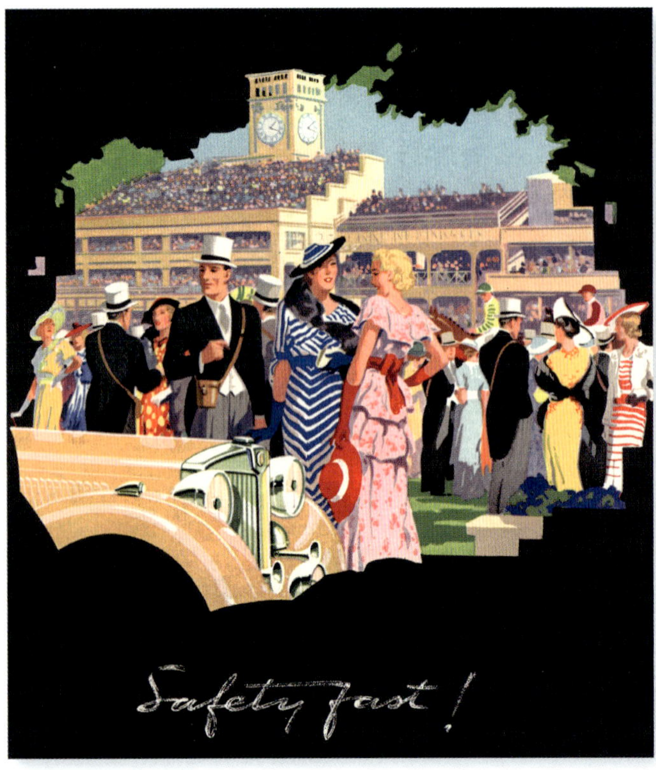

The Connolly drawings used in a lavish brochure produced for the WA model.

The WA saloon was a large vehicle and current owners would do well to avoid multi-storey car parks.

within a water gallery situated along the length of the cylinder head. Cold water fed directly from the radiator passed through the gallery, cooling the hot oil. Starting the car from cold, the thermostat in the cooling system prevented water circulation and the heat from the engine was thus able to quickly bring the oil to working temperature.

Externally, although the car was very like the earlier model, a number of important changes were made to distinguish the new car from the cheaper SA, which was to stay in production. The most noticeable features, and a sure-fire way to identify the model, were a new front bumper and radiator shell. The bumper dipped at the centre, rather than being straight, and in plan view the larger radiator shell had a pronounced V-shape. The front wings were altered in outline and also merged with the valances to improve their appearance. However, apart from a slight widening of the lower part of the body, the exterior design of the main cabin was unaltered. Although the same length overall, these subtle changes meant the WA looked even more imposing than the SA.

Interior comfort was not neglected. Like the earlier car, there were really comfortable, armchair-style front seats and those in the back had a generous amount of space, with appointments like cushions on which to rest heads and a central armrest for the leather-trimmed seat. The driver was presented with a revised facia layout that gave him a better view of the instruments. These were the same as previously used, but were now mounted higher up and had been given Cecil Kimber's favourite octagonal bezels. For ventilation there was a sunshine roof and swivelling quarter-lights, while the options list included an elaborate valve radio set. The boot of the WA was quite large and access was unobstructed because a side-mounted spare

The assembly area at Abingdon was re-equipped in 1936 to improve production capability. All the various MG models were assembled on adjacent lines.

wheel was standard. A pleasing and practical touch was the inclusion of a tool locker in the boot lid.

An interesting little note about the inclusion of a sliding roof in all MG saloons appeared in Cecil Kimber's letter to distributors dated 10 February 1938. He said that a recent survey had shown that abolishing the sunroof would be detrimental to sales. However, at the same time, it was found that fully 95% of owners used it seldom or never. The conclusion drawn was that buyers had been educated to expect such a feature on a luxury car, even though they never made use of it, and that MG would have to go on fitting them. This is something that persisted in the British car market until more recent years when air-conditioning replaced the sunroof as the must-have extra.

The new car looked good value at £442 for the saloon, £468 for the Tickford drophead coupé and £450 for the open four-seater, although the 3½-litre Jaguar was even more of a bargain. The motoring magazines did not seem to have been given WAs on which to carry out full road tests; maybe they were worried by possible comparisons with rival models. However, in December 1939, after war had been declared, H.S. Linfield of *The Autocar* did write a two-page article recounting his experiences with a saloon version.

In his feature, Linfield said that he sensed that with the WA MG had tried to produce a car of a type not previously made by the company. He compared the car directly with earlier six-cylinder models, both the current SA and the 18/80 from the early 1930s. His first impression was of how large the 2.6-litre MG appeared. Although only the track had increased when compared to the SA, the higher and longer bonnet gave the impression that the car was larger overall. Having pointed out that the WA power unit had a similar capacity to the one in the

Horsepower of the hay-eating variety was still supreme on farms in the late 1930s and the farm worker here seems singularly unimpressed by the far greater power possessed by the MG.

One of the advantages of the Tickford hood is that just the section over the front seats can be open and with the door windows raised provides relatively draught-free travel.

All WAs had the spare wheel mounted on the nearside front wing, leaving the boot clear to carry luggage.

Fold the hood down in fine weather and the car is transformed into a comfortable four-seater tourer.

Closed, the boot can accommodate a reasonable amount of luggage, but some can also be carried on the opened lid. The comprehensive tool kit is recessed into the lid.

The neat arrangement of instruments prominently features the MG octagonal surrounds.

For those relegated to sitting in the back there are large and comfortable seats.

The 2.6-litre power unit, with the double bulkhead fitted to stop fumes entering the cabin. The large air cleaners help silence the engine.

18/80, he went on to say how powerful it felt. MG had lowered the standard rear axle ratio for the WA, which must have improved acceleration.

Industry thinking on chassis and suspension design had undergone change during the 1930s and there had been a move from stiff springing and flexible chassis towards softer springs with a longer travel allied to a stiffer chassis. As MG retained solid axles, the ride was still compromised. However, the occupants were far better insulated from poor surfaces than had previously been the case and the change to hydraulic dampers was an improvement. The man from *The Autocar* was certainly impressed. Unfortunately, by the time of his report, cars were run on a diet of pool petrol, a sort of one-size-fits-all inferior product introduced as a wartime measure. This meant that he recorded no meaningful performance figures and merely confined his remarks to saying how well the car coped with cruising at 60-70mph without effort and how, with some restraint, he recorded 24mpg.

The model range of the WA was the same as the SA: saloon, drophead coupé and tourer. Each had its own character and appealed to different sections of the market. The open tourer was a rarity new as only nine were built. Like the SA, the bodies for these came from Charlesworth and it is interesting to record that all bar one of the tourers went to the Glasgow Police. The saloon was the most popular version by far and a total of 265 were made. The closed car was fully assembled at Abingdon, with the bodies coming from Morris Bodies Branch. Like the other MGs with Tickford coachwork, the coupés were built to running chassis stage at Abingdon and then fitted with rudimentary coachwork for the journey to Salmons and Sons at Newport Pagnell.

It is a pity that production of the 2.6-litre cars was curtailed by the outbreak of war in 1939. Certainly, the company would not have had the chance to sell enough to cover development costs but by the time the conflict ended the model was obviously not considered suitable for reintroduction. MG's return to saloon car building came with the much smaller and less costly Y-type, which had been developed in the late 1930s but was not put into production until 1947.

ABINGDON AT WAR

The declaration of war in September 1939 had an immediate effect on the British public. Draconian government legislation did not just force people to join the armed services and be killed in a war which they may, or may not, have supported, but it also controlled the amount of food they had to eat, allowed any number of petty bureaucrats to order their lives and requisition their property, and restricted civil liberties in a way that would these days cause riots on the streets and a storm of protest on social media. The effect of war on industry was equally dramatic. At the MG Car Company's Abingdon factory car production stopped almost immediately. The vehicles already in the pipeline were completed but records show that after war was declared only a few dozen cars were built and, for some reason, the actual build dates of these were never recorded in the ledgers. Government required that the car factories be turned over to essential war work, and this applied to all of the Nuffield Group establishments. Plans had been formulated a few years previously and component manufacturers such as SU Carburettors and Morris Radiators switched to making similar parts for military vehicles and aircraft. A specially constructed factory at Castle Bromwich built Spitfire fighter aircraft and others were already working on military contracts before the outbreak of hostilities.

In a manner familiar to anyone who has seen the way government officials attempt to run anything, plans for some factories, like MG at Abingdon, had not been properly thought out and once car production ceased there seemed little for them to do. Obviously the first job was to remove all the machinery, fixtures and fittings of sports car production. The assembly lines were easily cleared, but there were also hundreds of tons of spare parts for current and obsolete models to house, amongst them a large quantity of chassis frames. Luckily, Managing Director Cecil Kimber found a disused clothing factory situated in West St. Helen's Street in the heart of Abingdon. Although not ideal, being very neglected and subdivided into small offices and workshops, after some demolition work and strengthening and re-laying of floors this site provided suitable storage for the factory equipment and spare parts.

Moving all the parts and equipment was no small undertaking and in the absence of enough suitable vehicles the inventive men in the experimental department came up with a solution.

Constructed from odds and ends, this tractor and trailers unit was very useful transporting items between the factory and the storage facility in the centre of Abingdon.

Using any material to hand they constructed a short-wheelbase tractor unit powered by a 10hp engine. The power was transmitted to the rear wheels through a low-ratio rear axle, thus enabling the modest available output to tow an 8½-ton load. Three trailers were constructed, again from whatever was around, and these usefully carried everything the mile-and-a-half to the new stores.

By the end of 1939 the workforce had largely cleared the factory of parts and car assembly equipment. However, despite frequent approaches to those in charge of procuring military supplies, there was little to keep the workforce occupied. With the need to find something urgently, Cecil Kimber and George Propert, the works manager, spent a considerable amount of time touring the country trying to obtain contracts for war work of any type. This resulted in a wide variety of orders, from ammunition boxes to the degreasing and readying for use of stored Browning machine guns. There was also a contract to repair and put back into service light tracked vehicles.

Once the work started to arrive it became apparent that the factory lacked the necessary tools and machinery and urgently needed to re-equip at a time when demand for these items outstripped supply. Abingdon had been an assembler of cars, the vast majority of the components used being manufactured elsewhere. The relatively few machine tools they possessed were largely unsuitable for producing items to the tight tolerances necessary for military contracts. Larger press tools, lathes, milling machines and complicated jigs were urgently acquired, or built in-house, so that work could be carried out efficiently and quickly.

The initial orders received for shell racks, small bins and other similar items could easily be made using the existing facilities in the press shop, but over time the facilities were hugely expanded to meet demand. This department was utilised for the duration of the war producing short runs of items in urgent demand elsewhere in the works, and also for other companies. For the main factory the contract that Kimber had obtained to renovate light tanks involved vehicles suffering from wear and tear, rather than damage in battle. A system was evolved to deal with these that proved more efficient than the complete dismantling called for in the original Ministry specification. This led to the factory being awarded a contract to renovate much heavier tanks. A 20-ton gantry crane able to lift complete vehicles was fitted and, for the first time at Abingdon, a night shift was instituted. Kimber's tireless efforts by his own initiative to keep the factory running were for some reason not appreciated by his superiors, who eventually gave him the sack.

As well as carrying out tank repairs, the factory also assembled new tanks and commissioned lorries shipped over from the United States, some of this work actually being carried out at the docks. These vehicles arrived in packing cases made from a large amount of useful timber, and this provided the necessary material for the maintenance staff to construct a much-needed extension to the press shop. This department was in constant demand to produce small runs of components, but control on supplies of building materials by government made it difficult to construct extra space in a more conventional manner. Because of the skills and inventiveness of those in the factory, the press shop was able to tackle tasks that the larger and

Built utilising a damaged SA saloon, this pick-up truck had its own trailer and was used extensively to collect items from suppliers. It wears the regulation wartime headlamp cover and white painted wing edges.

less flexible facilities in other plants were unable to carry out. This included working to tight tolerances for aircraft parts, using aluminium alloys.

It was the contracts for aircraft parts and sub-assemblies that caused the most problems for the MG team. These had to be manufactured to an exacting standard and were rigorously checked by government-appointed inspectors working within Abingdon. Because of the limited manufacturing capacity there, the management team looked around the engineering industry to see if they could have the necessary tools and jigs built by sub-contractors. However, as everyone was working flat out on the war effort, they found little spare capacity anywhere and in the end had to make much of the necessary equipment, including a 15-foot-long main assembly jig. In spite of this, the complete bomber fuselage sections were built and tested at Abingdon before going to another factory for final assembly. Abingdon also manufactured parts for other aircraft and assembled aircraft engines from components made elsewhere.

The difficulties faced when taking on aircraft work cannot be underestimated. The nose section of the Albemarle fuselage built in the MG factory included all the flight controls and instrumentation and the structural frame had to be made so that it mated exactly to the other parts of the complete aircraft being built elsewhere. There were miles of wiring to be installed and tested, as well as runs of hydraulic pipes. A purpose made diagnostic device to test all the electrical circuits was designed and made in the works and this saved an enormous amount of time and effort.

A renovated Carden-Loyd light tank leaves the factory.

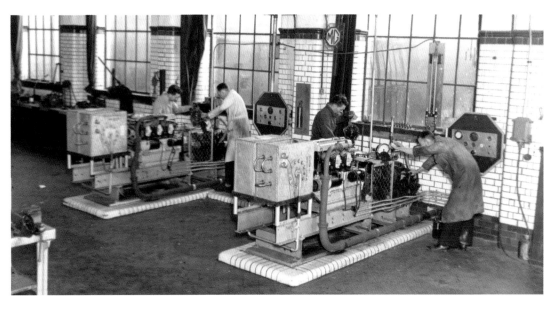

Tank engines were bench-tested in the engine house where once MG car engines were run. Note the octagonal panels on the wall.

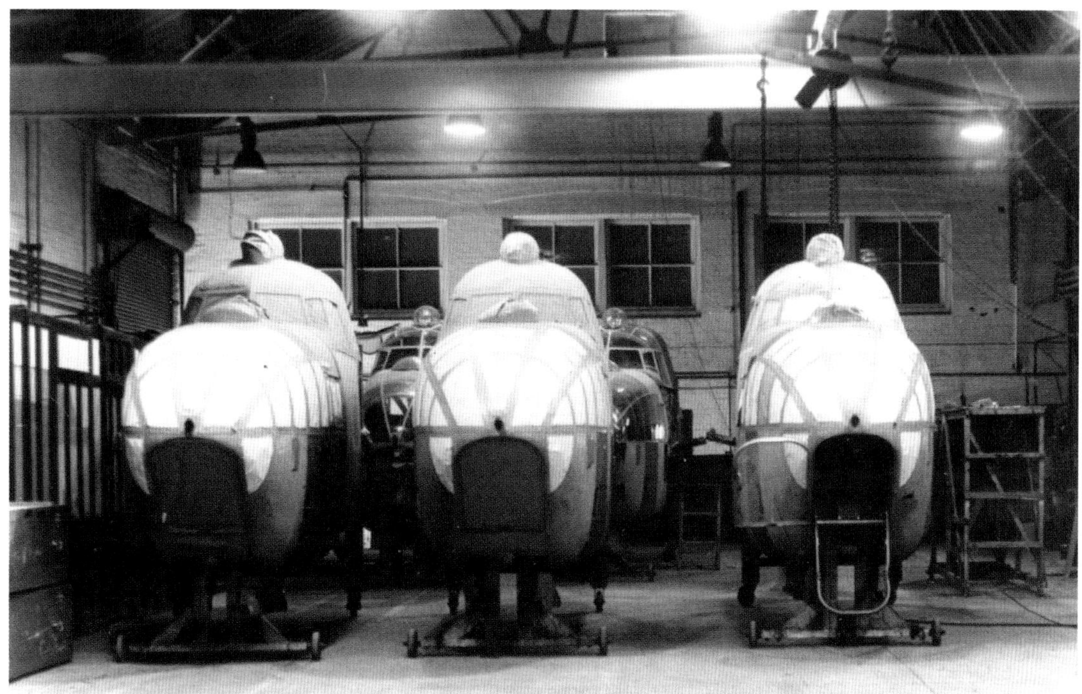

Completed Albemarle fuselage sections ready to be transported to another factory for uniting with the rest of the aircraft. Building these, and installing and testing all the instruments and controls, was an onerous task for a small car factory to tackle.

The accuracy of the large assembly jig was critical and allowance had to be made for variations occurring with changes in ambient temperature. Despite having much experience working at the cutting edge of car developments with projects like the R-type racing model, the technical demands of the tasks now undertaken was of a quite different order. It was, therefore, a great source of pride when the first completed assembly left the factory on a low-loader to be united with the rest of the aircraft. Later, so that those who had worked so hard could see the fruits of their labours, one of the completed machines gave a flying display for employees at the nearby airfield. Another demanding contract was for the leading edge assembly for the Tempest ll fighter. This called for the construction of a 40-foot-long jig, again built to tight tolerances.

Some idea of the disruption of everyday life caused by the war can be gained from the way the factory was manned during this time. A proportion of the pre-war workforce had not been called up to join the forces, but these men were too few in

A total of 103 Sherman tanks from the USA were taken to Abingdon for conversion work.

The drawing office in 1944. The war years saw many women working alongside men and doing the same jobs; when the men returned after the war most were dismissed.

number to manage the big contracts undertaken. With so many men now in uniform, the workforce had to be augmented by women recruited locally and from other parts of the country. They were mainly unskilled and had to learn to work to the high standard necessary for aircraft production. Employing a great many women brought problems that managers had previously not encountered with the regular male workers. They had to establish a training school and also deal with an accommodation shortage. Abingdon then was just a small market town of 8000 souls. During the war this rose to about 20,000 and room to house those recruited from other parts of the country was difficult to find. A bus service brought workers living in outlying villages to Abingdon, but some of the young women were housed in a hostel that was bought and equipped by the company. To make the place as comfortable and convenient as was possible, this building had its own canteen, laundry and ironing facilities and a sewing room.

Although the aircraft work was, perhaps, the most demanding, servicing, repairing, and later building tanks posed its own difficulties. Not the least of these was the sheer weight of the various components. We have already said that a huge gantry crane was constructed to lift and move the tanks whilst they were being worked on. However, they also had to be tested by staff previously more used to driving T-types and other MGs on nearby roads. The adjacent Berkshire Downs were an ideal proving ground, but there were some hazards in using them, including the possibility of turning a vehicle over on the steeper slopes, and some mishaps did occur. Towards the end of the war tanks capable of operating in shallow water were built and then tested in a special wading tank constructed in the factory grounds.

Despite all these difficulties, the small factory at Abingdon managed to deal with the disruption of their normal business in the same efficient manner as had previously made the MG marque into one of the best-known sporting cars in the world. During those difficult times they kept in touch with their customers by means of a series of advertisements in which they depicted service personnel driving tanks, flying fighter aircraft and sailing in fast motor boats under the slogan, "It reminds me of my MG". It was important that the MG name should not be forgotten if a healthy market for the cars was to be established when the fighting ended.

Once ultimate victory was in sight, thoughts must have once again returned to planning post-war car production. This really got under way after D-Day in June 1944, although at that time the factory was still working flat out on military contracts. After the end of the First World War the boom in car sales had caught out some manufacturers. Remembering this Lord Nuffield had applied pressure on his management team, under his deputy Sir Miles Thomas, to plan for the coming peace. Although work on new models in other parts of the Nuffield Group was started, for example by Alec Issigonis on the new Morris Minor, these were not to see the light of day immediately and it was to be largely unchanged 1939 models that were to be the first off the post-war production lines. For the MG Car Company the first post-war car was the TC Midget, of which a handful were built towards the end of 1945, ushering in a period of expansion at Abingdon.

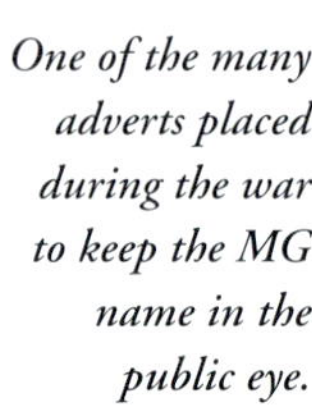

One of the many adverts placed during the war to keep the MG name in the public eye.

THE TC MIDGET

When peace returned in 1945 the small factory at Abingdon had been employed for the six years producing tanks, aircraft parts and many other vital products for the war effort. Members of the pre-war work force who had not been called up to join the forces had been augmented by women recruited from both the local area and from other parts of the country. These largely unskilled people had learned to work to the demanding standard necessary to assemble complex components and this ability would be of use when the factory returned to making cars now the military work had dried up.

When car production ceased after war broke out, the last few two-seaters produced had been TB Midgets. The basic design had been in production since 1936 and involved a chassis frame that followed the Abingdon practice, being of a flexible ladder type with the two main side rails set parallel and separated by tubular cross-members. The four half-elliptic leaf springs were pivoted at the front end and mounted into bronze trunnions at the rear, but when the car was being considered for re-introduction in 1945 it was decided to change to more conventional rubber bushed shackles to locate the springs. This alteration eliminated problems encountered when the sliding trunnions were insufficiently lubricated – particularly important now that many more cars were to be exported to countries where owners expected them to cover high mileages without much attention.

As with most MGs, the engines for the pre-war TA and TB had been based on units used in cars produced in other parts of the Nuffield Group. The TA engine had a long stroke to keep the horsepower rating to 10hp; important as the road tax at that time was based on the horsepower rating, and this was calculated not on the power output but on the cylinder bore. When the TB was introduced, the more up-to-date 1250cc 11hp XPAG unit was fitted, and in 1945 this engine was specified for the TC model with only minor modifications to the oil filter and with the addition of a timing chain tensioner to reduce noise from this area.

In a small corner of the Abingdon factory, otherwise given over to military work, was set aside for development of the post-war models.

The steel-panelled ash frame body fitted pre-war was retained for the TC, although widened by about four inches at the rear door pillar to give more elbowroom. This change produced one of the easiest ways to identify a TA or TB from a TC as the running boards were reduced in width and had only two tread strips as against the three fitted on the earlier cars. So there you have the latest from Abingdon in 1945. The chassis dated from 1931, the general body shape and styling from 1936 and the engine from 1938. Even before the war the MG Midget appeared old fashioned when compared with, for example, the 328 BMW with its aerodynamic bodywork, independent front suspension and flexible springing. However, in 1945 the choice of available new cars, especially sports cars, was very limited and it isn't surprising that enthusiasts queued up to put their name on the waiting list for a new MG.

In the drab early post-war years of rationing and shortages the majority of enthusiasts who saw the gleaming rows of new cars leaving the Abingdon factory could only look from afar as many would

The River Thames was a popular backdrop for MG publicity pictures. The number plate has been blanked out in this factory picture, probably because it was to be used in an overseas advertisement.

end up at the docks for transport to export markets. Shortages of raw materials in post-war Britain, and the desperate need for foreign exchange, led the newly elected Labour government of the time to impose restrictions on steel supplies. Manufacturers could only build cars if they could obtain supplies of steel, and priority was given to those producing at least three-quarters of their output for export. Actually a higher proportion of the TC production stayed in this country when compared to the

This picture of a TC chassis on the production line at Abingdon clearly shows the scuttle with separate boxes for the battery and tools.

A batch of TCs bound for Los Angeles in November 1947 were lined up in front of The Saracen's Head in Beaconsfield so that this picture could be taken for use in the Nuffield house magazine.

later TD, of which a higher percentage went for export. However, demand outstripped the numbers supplied to dealers and most cars went to people who had some sort of priority.

Once the military work ceased, the factory was stripped of all the jigs and fixtures installed to build the complicated weapons of war. The production lines were rebuilt and production of the TC started in earnest. The original work force, absent for the duration of the war when called up for military

A superbly restored late model TC finished in the correct shade of red with beige interior.

The secret of making a restored car look right lies in having smooth, continuous curves for the front wings and running boards. Some reproduction running boards are too straight, which makes achieving this almost impossible. Note too the way the join in the bonnet lines up with the lower edge of the scuttle.

The interior of a late model TC. Early cars had a veneered dashboard and a black finish on the instrument panel.

Finished in Brooklands Green, this restored TC has been fitted with deeper rims on the headlamps to accommodate sealed-beam headlamp units.

Beige trim was used for green-painted TCs, and this later car has a fabric-covered dashboard, an aftermarket Brooklands steering wheel and an additional dial to the right of the steering wheel.

Issued in January 1945, this advertisement for MG sports cars was intended to maintain interest in the marque against the time production could resume.

service, returned to take up their old jobs, releasing the majority of the female wartime workers.

According to factory records, in 1945 100 TC Midgets were built. These appear to have been laid down in batches and some sources give the total completed as only 81 cars. No matter which figure is correct, at least the factory was back in business and by December 1945 they had produced a full catalogue for the TC, advertising the car at a price of £375 ex-works plus purchase tax. The catalogue used much of the artwork from the pre-war TA and TB catalogues but the shortages of materials and the difficulties of production reduced the choice of colours for the new model to just one – Black. However, for the upholstery buyers had the choice of Vellum Beige, Shires Green or Regency Red. The hood and side-screens were made of tan cloth and the half tonneau of a black waterproof material. Although quite a number of cars produced in 1945 and 1946 seem to have had black hoods and side-screens instead, just how many is not recorded.

By June 1946 Regency Red and Shires Green had joined black as options for the paintwork. The interior of red cars was red and the green cars green but as previously buyers of black vehicles could

The TC was the last MG to use the traditional pre-war type of MG chassis with beam axles. To comply with modern regulations this car has additional flashing indicator lights and a second D-lamp alongside the rear number plate.

The 1250cc XPAG engine had twin carburettors and in standard tune produced 54bhp at 5500rpm.

chose any of the three options of interior colour. The price, however, had risen to £412 10s 0d plus tax. By comparison the last quoted price for the pre-war TB was £247 10s 0d in April 1940, when the last few cars produced were sold.

The factory lost no time in letting members of the press experience the new car and in October 1945 *The Autocar* tried one of them on a number of the more challenging of the hills used in production car trials. The magazine tester was very impressed with the car, which climbed all the hills he tried with great ease. He summarised the improvements over the previous model, making much of the wider cockpit and seats and the repositioning of the battery from behind the seats to a more convenient place under the bonnet. The modified spring mountings and new shock absorbers were felt to have improved comfort without sacrificing roadholding. He found that a cruising speed of 55/60mph was comfortable.

When *The Motor* subjected a TC to a full road test in 1947 their report also commented on the improvements and were impressed by the quality of the finish of the car. The leather interior and polished wooden dashboard with the full range of instruments, allied to the car's stability, comfort and performance, all for an all-inclusive price of £527 16s 8d, was thought excellent value and the cheapest true sports car on the market. Looked at today, a time of over 21 seconds to reach 60mph seems very slow, but when compared to the average small saloon car of the period this was real performance. It was only when the crop of more aerodynamic, post-war designed, sports cars arrived that the TC began to look really outclassed.

THE Y-TYPE ONE-AND-A-QUARTER-LITRE

An official factory picture of the YA in a suburban setting. The owners of houses like this were the target market for a car in this price range.

A restored Y-type chassis showing the rear side members running under the rear axle.

The first MG saloon to emerge from Abingdon after the war provided ample proof, if any were necessary, of the changed circumstances in Britain. The last saloon models produced pre-war by the MG Car Company were the VA, SA and WA models, the latter providing great comfort within its considerable bulk. Although an attractive small car, the One-and-a Quarter-Litre, or Y-type, can hardly be described as being in the same league as the large pre-war models. However, it did possess many of the virtues beloved by those who enjoyed the precise handling and roadholding of the MG sports models.

Pre-war most British sporting cars used a simple chassis that relied on a degree of flexibility to ensure that stiffly suspended beam axles maintained contact with the road. However, the introduction of cars with the body and chassis as a single unit meant that designers had to develop suspension systems that had greater compliance. Some manufacturers pre-war, especially on the continent, started to produce cars with more rigid chassis allied to softer springs and independent suspension, especially on the front wheels. The MG Car Company experimented along these lines in 1935 with the R-type before the project was abandoned.

There had been a move towards stiffer chassis and softer springing with the MG SA/VA/WA range where hydraulic shock absorbers controlled the longer suspension travel, but these models retained beam-axle front suspension. However, in 1938 work on a new MG saloon car was progressing alongside those of revised Morris models. At the Cowley Design Office Alec Issigonis and Jack Daniels had devised an independent front suspension layout for the Morris 10 that was rejected at the time being as too costly. The Morris Ten was to be the first of the cars from the Nuffield Group to have unit construction, while the first unit-construction model to be offered in Britain was a 10hp saloon built by American-owned Vauxhall Motors.

However, the prototype for the MG Ten saloon retained a separate chassis, but this was designed to be more rigid and to take the independent front suspension originally proposed for the Morris. Of course, the events that unfolded in 1939 scotched any thoughts of a new MG and it was to be eight years before the saloon made an appearance. The Y-type chassis comprised welded, closed box-section side rails and tubular cross members. At the back the side rails passed under the rear axle, which was suspended on leaf springs and had a Panhard rod to give lateral location. At the front a cross-member housed coil springs and provided a mounting for the rack and pinion steering. The shock absorber arms and the lower wishbones provided the upper and lower mounting points for the swivel pins. This front suspension was a neat and workmanlike arrangement that in modified form gave service right up to the end of MGB production. The body of the Y-type was closely based on the then current Morris Eight, but the addition of a longer bonnet, flowing front wings and the Abingdon radiator improved the appearance. A first for MG was the substitution of pressed steel wheels for the traditional, but hard to clean, wire variety.

So the car launched in early 1947 was the first post-war MG saloon, but it was in almost every respect still a product of 1930s thinking. Given the shortages of time, money, manpower and materials that were such a feature of post-war Britain, it is hardly surprising that it was impossible to contemplate designing and building an entirely new and up-to-date model. Customers would have to wait until the arrival of the Z-Magnette to have a really modern MG saloon in the showrooms. MG were not alone in bringing back into production 1939 models, and given that in much of Europe car plants were only just recovering from the effects of five years of war, Britain was able to sell at home and overseas every car it was able to build.

The new saloon was likely to appeal to a rather different customer than the TC Midget and at a total price of £671 13s 4d it looked relatively

This overhead publicity picture of a YA shows the standard sunroof.

The rear seats were comfortable and provided enough space for two adults. Note the cord for raising the blind to cover the rear window.

A restored YB painted in an attractive shade of red.

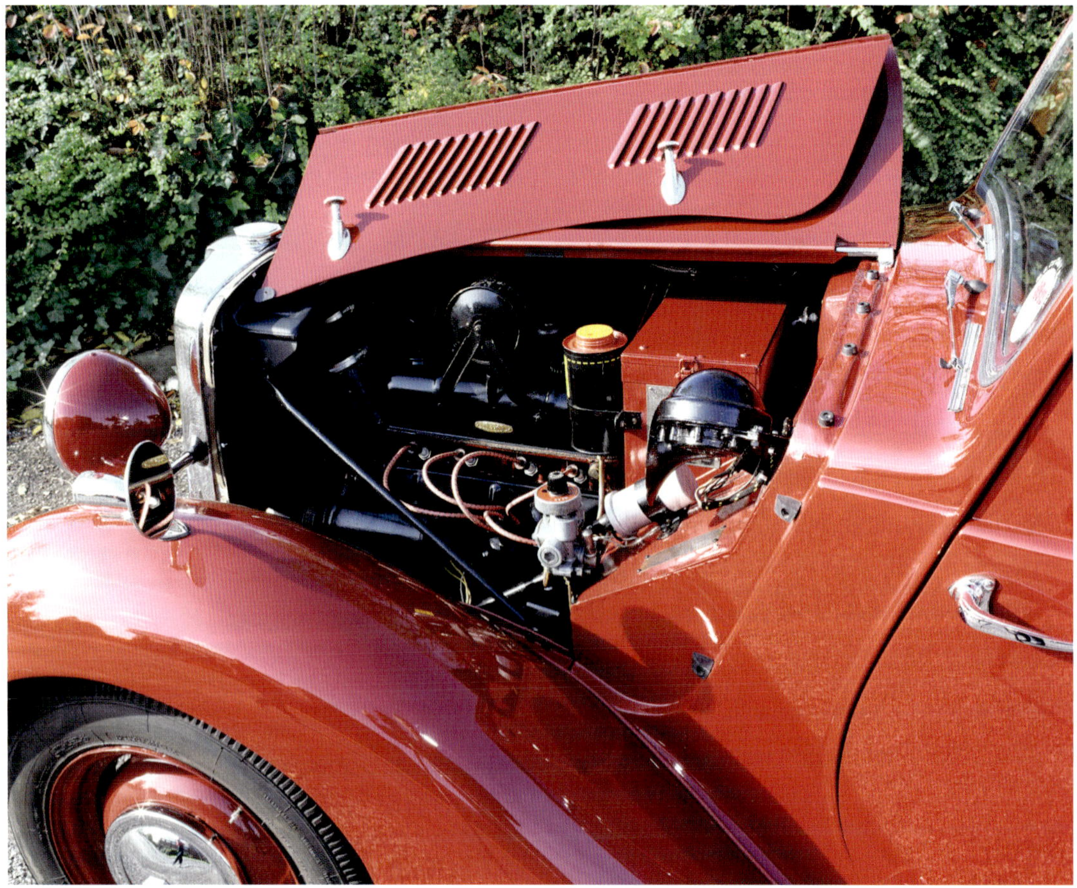

Lifting one of the two hinged top and side panels gives easy access to the XPAG engine.

expensive when compared to, say, an Austin Ten de luxe at £435 or Ford Prefect 10hp at £352. The contemporary Morris Eight four-door saloon complete with a sliding roof, with which the MG shared the basic body and therefore available cabin space, cost just £384 1s 8d. Still, with the MG one was buying a car that promised the comfort and performance of much larger vehicles.

With the war then over for two years, people were fed up with petrol rationing and, when in 1947 the government proposed abolishing even the basic ration for private motorists, there were protests in Central London and one million people signed a petition demanding its retention. However, the Labour government was keen to save spending dollars on imported oil and made the case that they would rather pay to bring in food. Imagine what it must have been like living with fuel saving restrictions that banned the use of lifts in commercial premises and any form of heating from April to October for factories, offices and even private houses.

Despite rationing and other privations, some people still managed to enjoy themselves. No doubt in a privileged position, John Dugdale of *The Autocar* borrowed a new Y-type for a continental trip and wrote of his experiences in the 15 August issue. Like others on the staff, he had nothing but praise for the car and managed on one of the days to cover over 400 miles. At that time there were

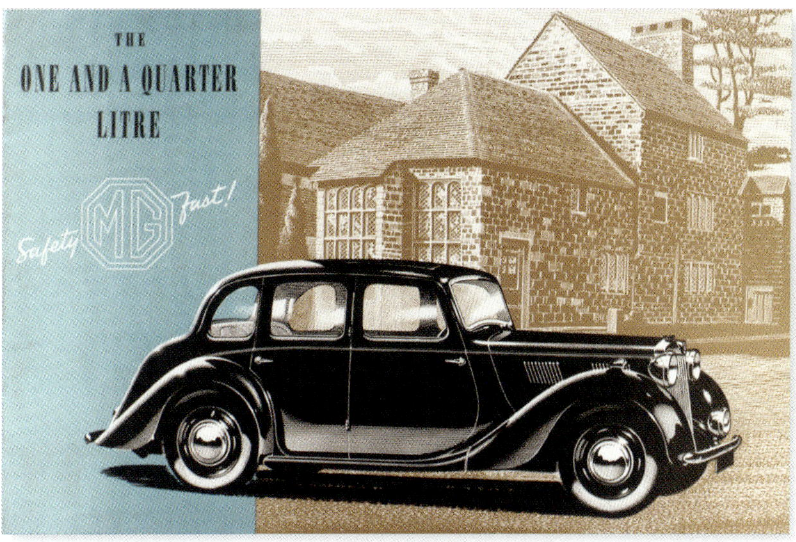

The brochure for the One-and-a-Quarter Litre saloon.

Attractive leather-trimmed seats are a feature of this small MG saloon.

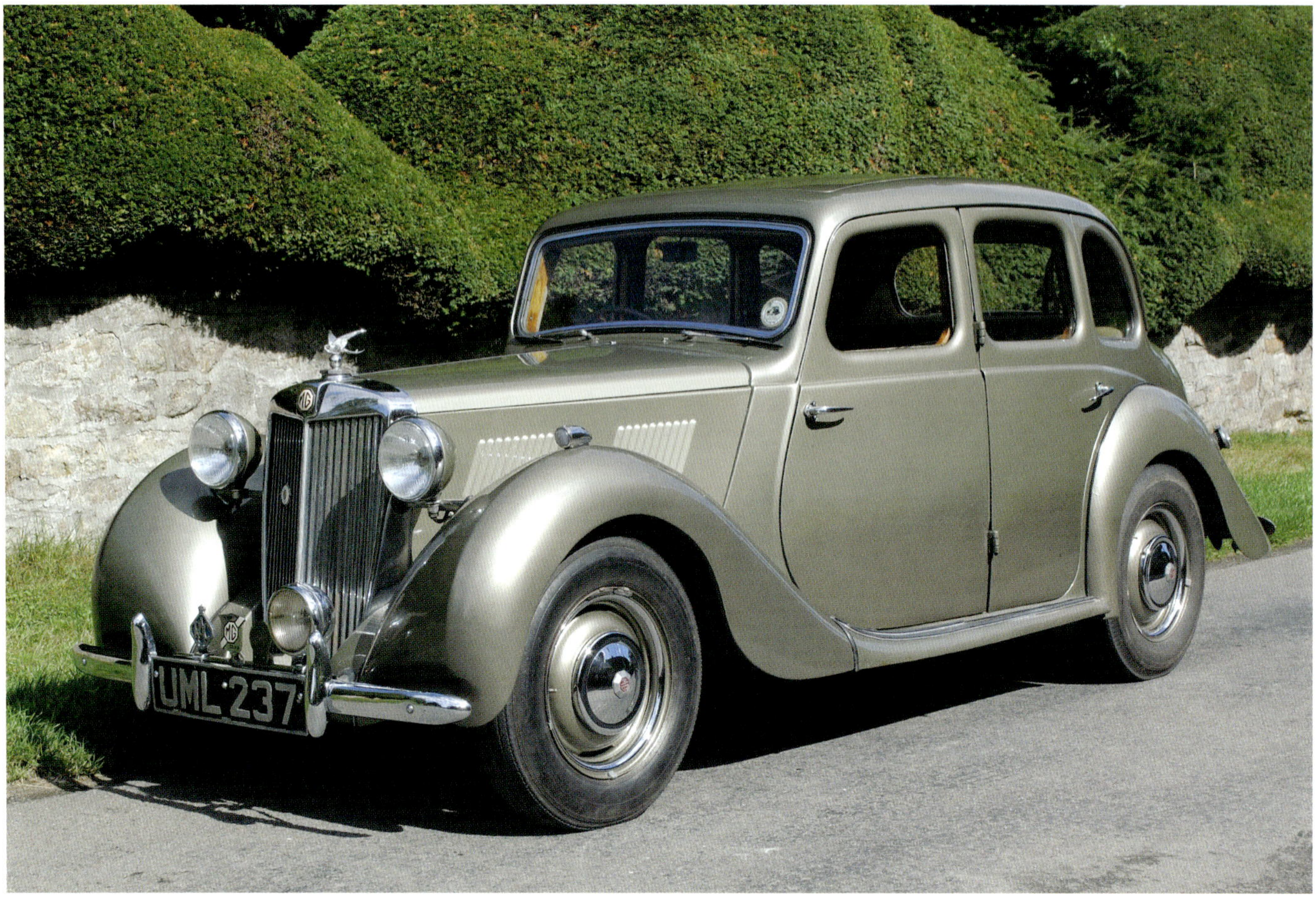

Although small by modern standards, the YB saloon comfortably seats four adults.

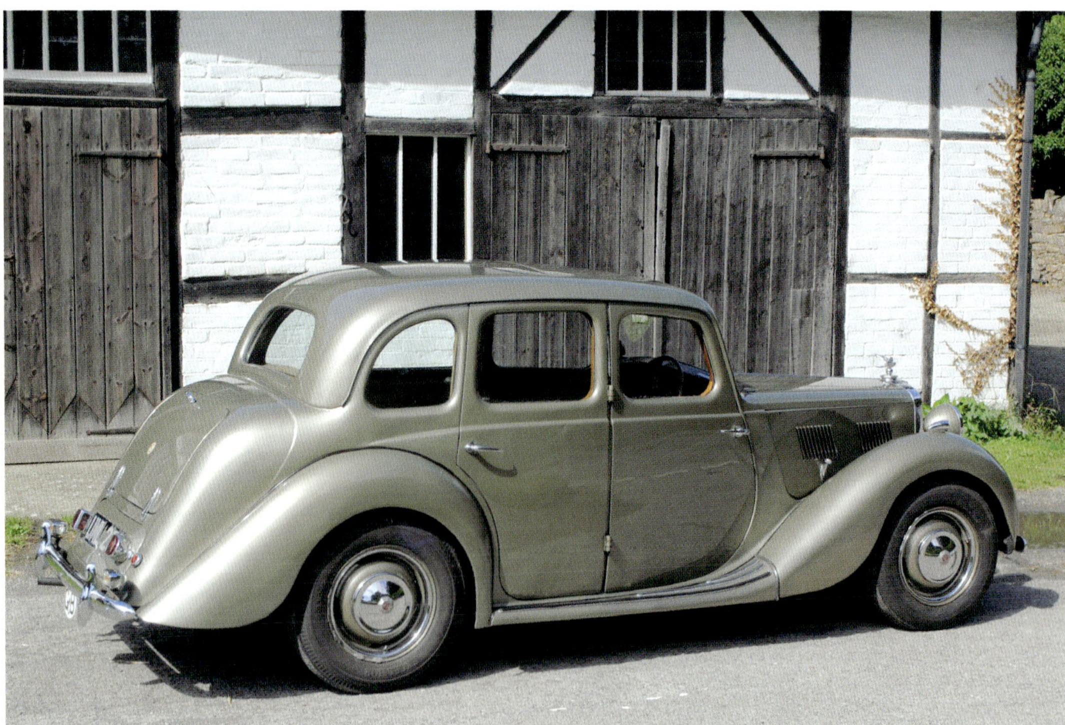

The styling of the Y-type was becoming dated even when the car was new, but this is part of its charm.

many restrictions placed on travellers, not the least of which was a limit on the amount of currency you could take out of the country. Petrol was also rationed in France and Italy, through both of which Dugdale proposed to travel. Coupons were available for tourists, but at a cost, and as supplies in Italy in particular were patchy he carried with him two large cans as a spare supply.

The MG performed faultlessly and only required that the radiator be topped up after strenuous runs in high temperatures. Much of the petrol he bought was of poor quality and resulted in the engine pinking. This did not seem to affect his average speeds and he records travelling 57 miles in an hour on an Italian autostrada near Milan. He found that the MG was not that fast, 75mph maximum on the speedometer, but that it was capable of covering the ground remarkably quickly because of the comfortable ride and superb steering. He recalled how in pre-war years he had raced a supercharged Magnette capable of 110 mph and how much better it would have been with the Y-type's steering and suspension.

Anyway, for what they are worth, here are the bare figures from the 1947 magazine tests. Maximum speed achieved was a shade over 70mph and the time to reach 60mph was around 28sec, on poor quality petrol. Reading the contemporary magazine reports it is apparent that the journalists liked the car enormously, feeling also that it was an entirely different breed of MG, one that was likely to appeal to more people than some of the pre-war saloon MGs based on sports car chassis.

Let us now take a closer look at the new saloon. Power came from a single-carburettor variant of the twin-carburettor XPAG engine used in the TC, and output was reduced from 54.4bhp to 46bhp. The saloon weighed over a ton but nevertheless the power to weight ratio at around 40bhp per ton laden was superior to that of the average British saloon car of the period. In addition to having a more up to date chassis design than its predecessors, the Y-type was the first MG saloon to feature an all-metal body, previous models having had wooden frames clad with steel or aluminium panels. Even by the standards of 1947, the overall styling was conservative.

Brochure for the Y-tourer.

A factory publicity overhead view of a LHD Y-tourer destined for export.

The hood and side-screens provide adequate weather protection.

For many the charm of the Y-type lay in the traditional appearance and attractive interior appointments. There were leather seat covers in a tasteful range of colours and a polished wood dashboard that displayed its MG heritage by the use of octagonal surrounds for standard circular instruments. Nice touches were a windscreen that could be wound open on hot days and, to avoid dazzle from the lights of following cars at night, a remotely operated blind for the small rear window. There were also twin sun visors and a central reading light, as well as a metal sliding sunroof. The cars were offered in an attractive range of exterior colour schemes, with some examples finished in two colours, usually the lighter colour for the body and a darker one for the wings.

By the end of 1951 the Y-type had been in production for over four years and the mechanical specification was inferior to that of the contemporary TD Midget. To remedy this a number of changes were made that markedly improved the 1952 model year cars. The alterations introduced for what was now the YB were extensive but not immediately apparent to the casual observer. The most substantial modifications were to the braking system and running gear. The YA Lockheed braking system using just one hydraulic cylinder for each front brake drum was replaced with a twin leading shoe system, and a new rear axle was installed. In common with most other cars of the period in the Nuffield Group, the YB benefited by being fitted with a hypoid back axle which was potentially much quieter in use. The wheels were at the same time changed from 16-inch to 15-inch diameter, and to improve the road holding the tyres increased in width from 5.00/5.25 to 5.50. A further improvement was the introduction of a front anti-roll bar and heavier duty rear shock absorbers. These mechanical changes forced a couple of body modifications. The smaller wheels took up rather less of the space under the rear wings so to improve the appearance of the car these were made slightly deeper, something that is quite apparent when viewed from the side of the car. The smaller wheels and wider tyres would not fit in the YA spare wheel stowage compartment so on the YB the compartment was made an inch taller.

Although the TC was selling well and the Y-type had a ready market, it was felt that there was also a demand for a four-seater open tourer, especially in overseas markets. The Swiss main dealers had already imported a few Y-types in rolling chassis form and local coachbuilders had fitted them with tourer bodywork. The results looked good and perhaps provided the inspiration for an Abingdon version.

Because the Y-type was built using a separate and quite rigid chassis frame it was practical to remove sections of the pressed steel bodywork, like the roof, without compromising too much the structural rigidity of the car. The design work for the open Y-type was carried out in the Cowley Drawing Office under the direction of Gerald Palmer. The main structure of the body comprised pressed steel sections, but the wide doors used a traditional ash framework panelled in steel, like the TC and earlier models. As the export market was the objective, the YT was made so that it could be assembled in either right-hand or left-hand drive configuration. To accommodate the steering column and pedals being

This YT, although RHD, actually spent most of its life in America where it acquired additional chrome strips on each side of the body.

The YT rear seat is very slightly narrower than the one in the saloon version as there are zipped pockets each side to house the stowed hood frame.

fitted on either side of the engine bay, the toolbox mounted on the scuttle was placed centrally, rather than offset, and the oil pump was modified for the same reason. Like the TC, the whole body was made by Morris Bodies Branch in Coventry and arrived at Abingdon fully painted and trimmed.

As the tourer used the wings and front and rear body sections from the saloon, the boot was virtually unchanged and provided adequate luggage capacity and the ability to carry additional suitcases on the lowered boot lid. The doors were cut away at the top, in the accepted sporting fashion, and the windscreen could be lowered if required. The interior trim was similar to that in the saloon, as was the available interior space, although rear seat passengers had their elbowroom slightly reduced by the pockets each side necessary to store the hood irons. The front passenger seat tipped up to ease access to the rear.

Although the standard saloon had to make do with a single carburettor version of the 1250cc XPAG engine, the open tourer was deemed to require something a bit more sporting and was fitted with a unit to TC specification, complete with twin carburettors and modified camshaft. Producing 54bhp, this was usefully more than the 46bhp available for the saloon. Another feature transferred from the sports car was the dashboard. Although not identical to the one used for the TC, essentially it looked the same, using a similar fabric-covered board with a large tachometer in front of the driver and matching speedometer placed ahead of the passenger. The minor dials and the switches were all contained in a TC-style central panel. This dashboard made more sense for an open car with sporting pretensions than the polished, walnut-veneered wooden one used in the saloons and could also be easily assembled with the instruments swapped over for left-hand drive versions.

The hood stowage was particularly neat. When lowered, the hood and frame stowed in a compartment that extended behind and round each side of the rear seat and could be concealed by zip-fastened flaps. The rear window in the erected hood could be lowered to provide additional ventilation. Apart from the more powerful engine, the mechanical specification remained unchanged, but the bodywork modifications reduced the overall weight by nearly 90lb, which helped to improve the performance. However, fewer than 900 T-tourers were made and all were to YA mechanical specification, most being exported.

The Y-tourer dashboard and instruments closely resembled those fitted to the TC.

BUILDING MGS IN THE LATE 1940S

In the early years of the motor industry a great many people decided that cashing in on the growing interest in motoring would be profitable. Almost none of those entrepreneurs moving over from bicycles or wagon making into the new field of automobiles built their own engines or other mechanical components. Whilst concentrating on assembling something that looked reasonably like a car and that worked well enough to sell they usually turned to companies like De Dion for power units and Rotax for lighting.

Of course, once the industry became established the successful manufacturers began to make more components in-house, although often by taking over established engineering works rather than expanding their own facilities. A major exponent of this was William Morris who, having suffered delivery problems early on, moved in the direction of owning as much as possible of the supply chain. As the MG Car Company fell within his empire it is not surprising that the majority of parts used to build MGs were made within the group and not at the Abingdon factory, which was merely an assembly plant.

Some of the rival manufacturers managed car production in a more organised manner than did the Nuffield Group, and later BMC. Ford, for example, established their new factory at Dagenham in 1931 with the object of concentrating the majority of manufacture on a single site. Constructed progressively over a number of years, Dagenham had its own power station, blast furnaces to produce steel, press shops to make the panels for the steel bodies and foundries to make castings for blocks, cylinder heads, gearbox casings, etc. There was a huge assembly area with all the necessary facilities for designing and making cars, paint shop, seat and trim manufacture and all this alongside good rail links and a dock for importing materials and exporting complete vehicles. It is hardly to be wondered at that the Ford operation was more profitable than the scattered companies run by William Morris.

Although Abingdon was always more of an assembly plant than a manufacturer, the chassis frames were completed in the press shop, and here the body mounting brackets are welded on to a Y-type chassis. After completion it would be painted black and stored until needed.

The chassis frame was brought to the line and clamped to a rig that allowed the worker to fit the front suspension and hydraulically compress the front springs, enabling him to fix the swivel pins to the shock absorber arms that act as a top link.

Rear axles were fitted with wheels before they were rolled over to the production line and attached to the chassis.

The build process for most MGs is best illustrated by a series of pictures taken in the late 1940s. The chassis frames were assembled in the Abingdon press shop and when completed they were painted with chassis black paint and stored until required. The work on a new car started with the chassis. The frame was brought to the line and clamped to a stand to allow the worker to fit the front suspension and hydraulically compress the front springs enough to be able fix the swivel pins to the shock absorber arms. The rear axle assembly, fitted with wheels, was rolled over to the line and bolted to the leaf springs. The chassis, with the brake pipes and some of the wiring in place, was lowered on to its wheels and the engine was installed. Once the radiator and steering gear were in place, the chassis was moved to a different part of the assembly line ready for the body to be fitted.

Completed bodies arrived in batches of four on open lorries, already painted, and awaited their turn to be hoisted to the first floor assembly area, or top deck. There they were mounted on trolleys and prepared for fitting to the chassis. During the war women had undertaken the majority of assembly jobs at Abingdon and some of these managed to find employment there when car production resumed, mainly working on trimming. With the Y-type there was a considerable amount of this sort of work to be done. Headlining, carpets, door trims, etc., had to be installed, and all of this had to be carried out in conjunction with fitting winding windows, an opening windscreen, wipers and wiper motor, dashboard and instruments as well as many other small components. Working on the top deck, close to the roof of the building, could be uncomfortable in hot weather and conditions were often cramped.

Once completed, the trimmed bodies were lowered down on to the rolling chassis. Here male workers completed most of the work. Now

The engine and gearbox were fitted as a unit to the rolling chassis.

The completed and painted bodies were delivered to Abingdon on flatbed articulated lorries.

Body shells were lifted to the top floor of the assembly building where they were mounted on trolleys so they could be rolled along this production line. Note the many female workers employed at the time.

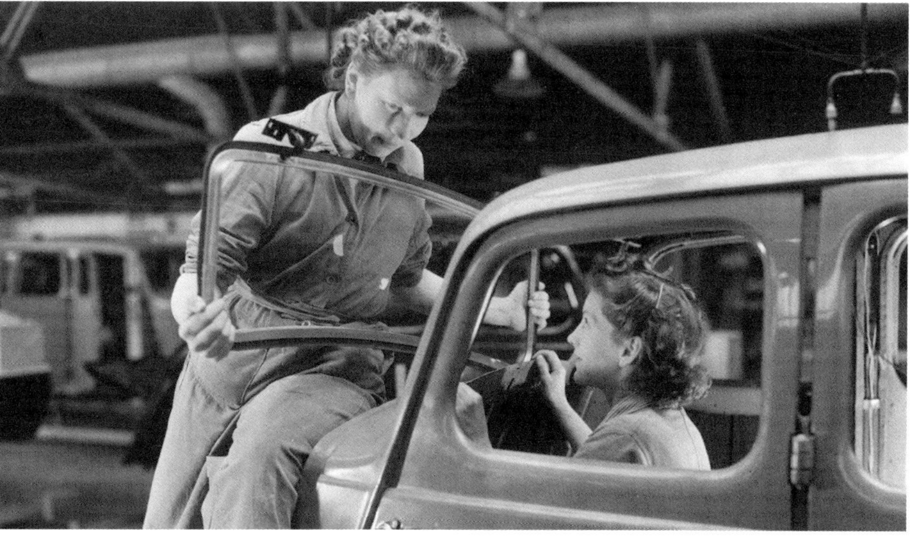

Two people were needed to fix the windscreen frame to the body; this was top hinged so it could be wound open in hot weather. For this reason the windscreen wiper spindles were fitted with knobs to stow the arms on the scuttle, below the windscreen frame.

Once the windscreen wiper mechanism was fixed in place the wooden dashboard with its attractive veneered finish could be installed.

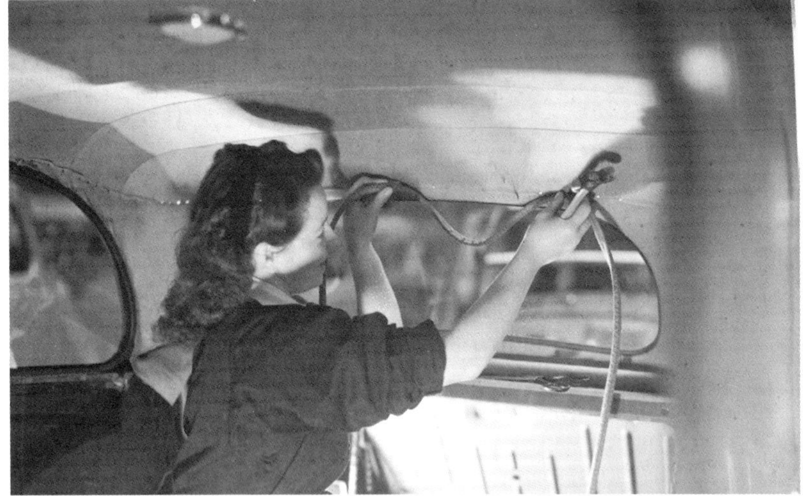

One of the trimmers installs the seal around the rear window.

As anyone who has ever attempted the task will testify, installing a headlining is not the easiest of jobs.

The lining panel for the door is installed. The interior of the Y-type was well finished and was one of the most appealing features of the model.

the wiring and controls were connected, bumpers fitted and the seats installed. The front and rear wings could then be attached. On the Y-type these could be either the same colour as the body, or in a darker shade, light green bodies with dark green wings being a popular colour combination. At the end of the line white-coated inspectors checked the cars over and they were given some petrol and started up.

The trimmed body shell is lowered from the top deck to be united with its rolling chassis. From then until it moves under its own power the car remains on the one production line.

Wings were fitted, which in the case of the Y-type could be either the same colour as the body or in a darker shade.

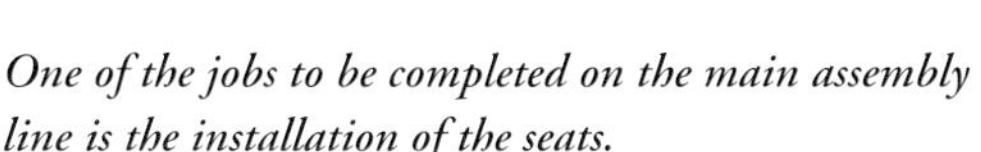

One of the jobs to be completed on the main assembly line is the installation of the seats.

Almost ready for final inspection and with the bonnet and headlights fitted, the wiring connected up, and petrol added to the tank, the car is then driven away for road test.

The final inspections over, the cars were road tested before being parked up to await collection by a delivery driver, or shipment to one of the many overseas markets.

An overhead view of the assembly area reveals that the Y-type and TC lines were adjacent, with storage bins for the new components placed between the two rows of cars.

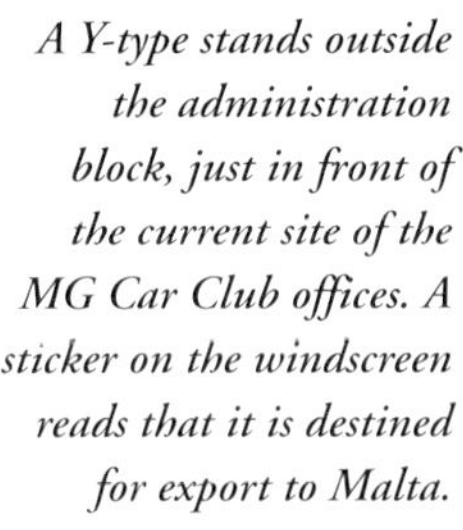

A Y-type stands outside the administration block, just in front of the current site of the MG Car Club offices. A sticker on the windscreen reads that it is destined for export to Malta.

JOHN THORNLEY

If any one person can be said to have contributed the most to the survival and expansion of the MG Car Company in the 1950s and 1960s, then this must be John Thornley. Without his drive, management skills, force of personality and sheer bloody-mindedness there were times when its future could have been rather different. John William Yates Thornley O.B.E. was born in 1909 in South London. His father was a businessman earning a modest income and his mother an independently wealthy and attractive woman who had interests elsewhere that led in 1914 to an expensive and well-publicised divorce case. Custody of John was given to his grandfather and sufficient money was set aside to cover his education. These difficulties in his childhood, plus being sent to boarding school at an early age, must have had their effect on his character and may have been instrumental in giving him the strength and tenacity he was to show when it came to pressing the case for the MG Car Company and for all those working at Abingdon.

John went to Ardingly, a respected public school in Sussex, and was visited there most weekends by his father. When John joined the Officer Training Corps at the school and learned to target shoot, he and his father would often go together to shoot at Bisley and elsewhere. Even at that early stage John showed some of the qualities he would later need as under his leadership the school shooting team enjoyed success in major competitions. Despite having the brain and ability to go to university, family finances meant that he was articled to the London accounting firm of Peat, Marwick, Mitchell & Co., and as part of his training he went to evening classes at the London School of Economics to read for a Bachelor of Commerce degree.

The course of his future, however, was set when in 1930 he reached the age of 21 and received the balance of the sum that had been set aside for his education. He was running a motorcycle and, having decided to invest his fortune in a car, visited a local dealer to trade it in. There he had the choice of a supercharged Triumph, an Aero Morgan or an MG Midget. Luckily he chose the MG. The M-type Midget had been launched at the 1928 London Motor Show, but the first production models only appeared in the spring of 1929. They were an immediate success and it isn't surprising that some of the young men driving them would be interested in starting a club for owners.

In September 1930 Roy Marsh wrote to *The Light Car* suggesting that MG owners might like to get together on the lines of other recently formed one-make clubs. The outcome was that a meeting was arranged and John left this with the task of approaching the MG Car Company at Abingdon to ask for permission to use the MG name and octagon badge for the club. This brought him for the first time into contact with Cecil Kimber, who was enthusiastic and commissioned artist, F. Gordon-Crosby to design the badge. The first public meeting was held at The Roebuck, near Stevenage, on 12 October 1930 and around 30 owners brought their MGs along. The club was well and truly established.

It is clear that although John was keen on

An official picture of John Thornley taken in the late 1940s.

In this 1930s picture of some of the Abingdon staff, we see in the back row, from left to right, MG Chief Designer, H.N. Charles, Jack Gardiner, Cecil Cousins, Bill Renwick and John Thornley. Seated in front are Dick Maynard, Ted Colegrove and George Tuck.

mathematics he was not happy with his position at the accountancy firm and that his interests lay elsewhere. His duties with the car club took him frequently to Abingdon and led to him to write to Cecil Kimber in January 1931 asking if the Company might have a position for him with the costing staff. He received a reply along the lines that he may be considered should a vacancy occur, but that none was available at the time. However, on Monday 3 November that year he left his position in London and joined the team at Abingdon.

Reading between the lines, it would seem that Kimber created a position for John because he wanted him, rather than actually needing another employee. On his first day he was told that he was to run the MG Car Club from Abingdon, but that this was not to be regarded as a full-time job and that in addition he was to help the service manager, John Temple, deal with customers. General Manager George Propert, however, set out his duties rather differently. His definition of the job was to assist the service manager and in any spare time run the Club. Initially the idea was that John was to spend some time in each department – purchasing, goods inwards, stores, progress, assembly, road testing, rectification, etc. – so that he would have a thorough knowledge of all aspects of the company. All did not go to plan as John quickly discovered that he could learn most about the cars in the test and rectification department and he spent the majority of his time there.

Two weeks into his initiation period John was told to report to the service department to have an intensive week of instruction under John Temple, who was to be moved to another department. So, at a very young age and with little experience, John Thornley was let loose on customers, some of whom were bound to have complaints about their cars that needed to be dealt with diplomatically. Luckily, he had the assistance of a couple of secretaries who were well able to compose suitable letters or answer telephone queries. A couple of new service managers were then appointed in quick succession, but neither proved suitable so at the age of 23 John

John's overseas contacts helped promote MG exports, and in this picture with John standing on the left of a Y-type with a Zagato body are Heinz Keller, the Swiss MG importer, and Marcel Fleury.

became the manager by default. Alan Hess took over John's responsibilities for the club.

As service manager under Cecil Kimber's regime, John had considerable freedom with regard to work under warranty. Like all cars at the time, the 1930s MG was by no means as durable and trouble free as we have now come to expect. Owners were used to very short intervals between lubrication services and even major work, like removing the cylinder head for cleaning and valve grinding, was needed fairly frequently. Nevertheless, surviving chassis files are full of letters replying to complaints from customers, not just about mechanical shortcomings, but also about paint flaking off panels, cracking door pillars and windscreens and leaking sunshine roofs. MGs were relatively cheap cars and the coachwork provided in the main by Carbodies of Coventry looked good, but was built down to a price. The balancing act John performed was to satisfy the customer without incurring too much expense.

One of the other responsibilities undertaken by John was to be in overall control of both the Cream Crackers and the later Three Musketeers teams, and it fell to him to negotiate the terms under which the MG would supply the cars to the drivers and to coordinate the entries in suitable events. The project could be seen as being a success and a good way of showing that the T-series cars, which from 1936 followed the popular OHC MGs, were also capable of being successful in motor sport. The administrative efforts must, however, have been an added burden to what was a busy department.

The outbreak of war in 1939 saw John called up, and having benefited from his OTC training at school he was ordered to report as a Captain in the R.A.O.C. to Chilwell, Nottingham, which was a camp responsible for supplying motor vehicles. He later went to Donington to take charge of the section dealing with radio and radar equipment. In 1943 he was transferred to the War Office with a rank of Lieutenant Colonel. There he was heavily involved with planning for D-day, including liaising with the Americans.

Having been dismissed from MG by Cecil Kimber when he had been called up in a gesture that gave him some severance pay, John had no guarantee of a job and when he was demobbed in October 1945 he needed to apply to Abingdon for work. He was re-employed as service manager and after 14 months was appointed service and sales manager. Initially, the service department was remote from the factory, which was still full of military work. However, the local council wanted

John was a very good communicator, able to get along with people from all walks of life. One of his duties when in charge of the Abingdon factory was to look after visiting VIPs and here he shows HRH Prince William of Gloucester one of the Mini-Coopers in the Competition Department.

this site in West St. Helens Street, which had been taken over by the Company at the start of the, war and MG exchanged it for additional land alongside their Marcham Road factory. John's department moved back to the main buildings.

It was from then on that John was to exert considerable influence of the future of MG. Exports were key to the survival of the company and through contacts he had made in Europe and with American importers he was first able to promote sales of the TC and Y-type, and then the later models. The merger of production facilities for Riley and MG cars at Abingdon brought Jack Tatlow from Riley as General Manager at Abingdon, a post that John had been led to believe would be his when Propert retired. However, he and Jack worked well together and John was kept busy with the introduction of the TD and consequent increase in sales. On top of his office duties, during this time he managed to write and have published the first edition of what has become the standard work on MG competition history, *Maintaining the Breed.*

John was appointed general manager at the end of 1952 and listed his objectives as being to maintain morale and car production at Abingdon, and to bring back there the responsibility for sports car design. He was also keen to build a quality MG saloon. To help in this task, he took on an ex-Wolseley man, Geoff Iley, who was to oversee production, leaving John to deal with design and development matters, competition efforts and communication with others in the BMC organisation.

With constant pressure from John, permission was given for work to start on a replacement

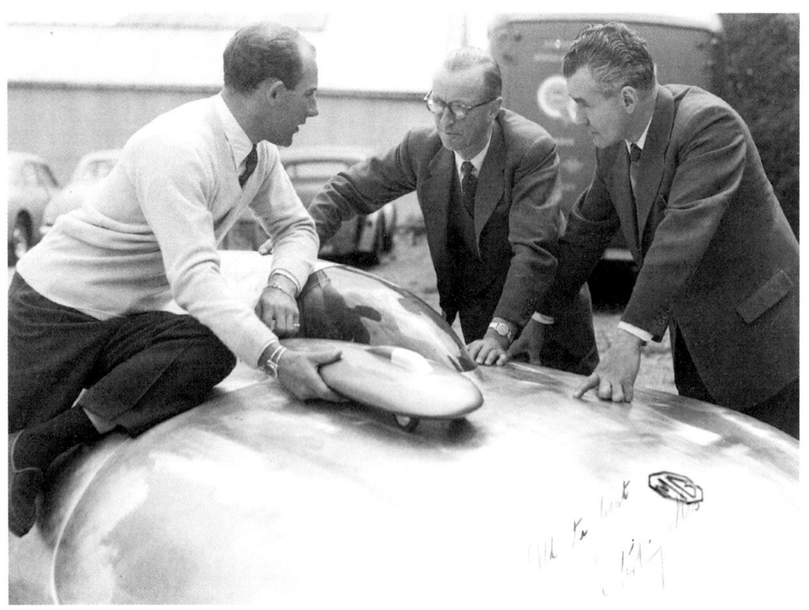

John was heavily involved in the record-breaking attempts. For the August 1957 runs at Utah, when five records at speeds of up to 245.64mph were set, the driver was Stirling Moss. With EX181 are Moss, John and designer Syd Enever.

sports car for the ageing T-series models within a revitalised research and development facility. The factory also had to cope with the replacement of the Y-type saloon with the Gerald Palmer designed Z-Magnette. It was in the promotion of motor sport and record breaking that John's influence in matters was crucial. Following the precedent set with the entrants in pre-war trials, some support from the factory had been given to a few MG competitors. The expenditure was unofficial, however, and had the hierarchy started asking questions then John could have been in the firing line.

Following the formation of the British Motor Corporation with the merger of the Austin Motor Company and the Nuffield Group, John Thornley had been lobbying for the establishment a more professional approach to motor sport entries. The BMC directors gave permission for the formation of a BMC Competitions Department and John appointed Marcus Chambers as head. This decision was to eventually lead to the remarkable successes enjoyed by the Abingdon-prepared MGAs, MGBs, Austin-Healey 100/6s and 3000s and, of course, the Minis. Work on what was to be the MGA went on apace during 1954 and one can see from surviving correspondence that the process involved a lot of work for John. There were many discussions and negotiations with suppliers over costs, and hundreds of day-to-day decisions to be made, but the result was a sports car that was at the time thoroughly up-to-date and proved to be a winner in the marketplace.

John pictured alongside an NE outside the Abingdon factory in the late 1960s.

Talk to anyone who worked for him during the time he was in charge at Abingdon and you will find that all held him in high regard. He always had the welfare of his workforce as a priority and tended to lead by example. Later in his time at the factory he became concerned that MG was the main employer in the town and feared for the future of the workers and the town should the factory close. This concern led to his involvement with local businessmen in promoting more sources of employment both before and after his retirement.

Most of the significant post-war MG achievements happened under John's leadership. Record breaking with EX135, EX179 and EX181 hit the headlines all over the world, production of sports cars at Abingdon, including from 1957 the Austin-Healey models, reached numbers undreamed of by those working there in the 1930s, and the MG name became so well known that it still exists long after most rival marques have disappeared from sight.

Having been suffering from ill health, when British Leyland took over BMC in 1968 John decided that it was time for him to bow out. He retired in July 1969 at the age of 60, but that was not the end of his involvement with the marque. He continued until his death in 1994 to play his part in MG Car Club affairs, and when the closure of the Abingdon factory was announced in 1979 it was to him that the American dealers turned for help in trying to reverse that decision. There followed a very well publicised campaign in which all those keen to save the marque became involved, but all to no avail.

SPECIAL MGs

The post-war survival of the MG marque depended heavily on exports. In particular, without the North American market taking British sports cars in large quantities the factory would not have survived until 1980. However, often forgotten is that quite a few MGs were sold abroad right from the early days of the marque, and that Cecil Kimber established good relations with importers in a number of countries, especially in Europe. Most prominent amongst the MG distributors was J.H. Keller, trading as Sportcar AG of Zurich, who in addition to selling a great many ordinary catalogued MGs was responsible for producing a number of very attractive cars based on rolling chassis purchased from Abingdon.

The Swiss government, both prior to 1939 and after peace was declared in 1945, imposed high import duties on complete cars, with lower duties levied on rolling chassis. The reason for this was to stimulate demand for the products of local coachbuilding companies, who were struggling to survive in an age when most cars were fully completed by the manufacturers and few buyers commissioned bespoke bodywork. However, there were some wealthy clients in Switzerland prepared to pay more for something out of the ordinary, and it was this market that Sportcar AG targeted with their non-standard MGs.

The story of Sportcar AG began when a young engineering student, B. Schuebeler, imported an M-type and with a friend tried to establish a company to sell MGs in Switzerland. They arranged to take advantage of an existing contract between the MG Car Company and a firm trading near the Italian border to import cars, and set up a showroom in Albisriederplatz in Zurich. However, the prevailing economic climate in the early 1930s meant that the enterprise was soon in financial difficulties, and to rescue the situation it was sold to Harald Romegialli. With sound financial backing, he was more successful and decided to take over the MG distribution contract for Zurich and, with his brother-in-law Heinz Keller as main shareholder, on 2 June 1933 formed Sportcar AG.

The Swiss government import regulations and duties severely restricted their activities and initially they were permitted to bring in only five complete cars a year. However, they could also take a number of chassis to be fitted with locally made bodies, and this led to them commissioning for sale some very unusual and attractive MGs. The owners set about trying to raise awareness of the company, initially by taking space at the Geneva Motor Show, but without a lot of success. However, advertisements in motoring magazines, and publicity achieved when Keller entered MGs in local competitive events, slowly brought the company the recognition it needed. They also managed to negotiate space in an established dealership premises in central Zurich where they could display their cars to best advantage.

This Swiss version of the P-type built by Hanni of Zurich retains the standard MG grille.

Another Swiss P-type, also by Hanni, was fitted with covers over the rear wheels and a modified grille.

In 1934, 1935 and 1936 a total of 51 cars were sold, quite a number with Swiss-built coachwork. The arrival of the SA and VA models provided them with more luxurious cars to appeal to local businessmen, and also chassis on which to have some very attractive models built. Heinz Keller had studied engineering and also went to Abingdon for training. Whilst there he established the close relationship with both Cecil Kimber and John Thornley that was to prove very important in the future.

Although the country was neutral, the war years meant petrol rationing saw private motoring virtually cease in Switzerland. In 1941 Sportcar AG effectively stopped its usual business and Keller took full control. He had to undertake military service for a set number of days a year, but kept on a few mechanics to work on maintaining military vehicles at their Zurich premises. Once it became obvious that the Allies would eventually regain control of Europe, Keller began preparing for peace, and through contacts at the British embassy in Switzerland had been in touch with the Nuffield Group, which included the MG Car Company. In 1945 he took the first direct Swissair flight to Croydon Airport and arranged to import some of the earliest cars produced by the group after the war. This was not easy and he and some of his employees had to meet the boat at Dieppe and drive the vehicles in convoy through France to Switzerland.

A boom in private motoring began when fuel rationing was first relaxed in 1946 and then cancelled altogether. Keller was in a position to take full advantage of this and soon found that his premises were too small to cope. He initially managed to find some extra space in a basement before taking the bold step of moving to Zurich's premier shopping street, Bahnhofstrasse, where he set up an imposing showroom to display MGs and other Nuffield products. The company name had by this time been changed to J.H. Keller AG. The company prospered and by the late 1950s were in new architect-designed premises.

The earliest recorded Swiss special MGs were based on P-type running gear and were built for Sportcar AG by Hanni Coachbuilders of Zurich, who are also known to have constructed bodies for chassis of other makes. A Swiss-produced MG brochure shows a two-seater roadster design with a long sweeping tail section. At least one P-type was fitted with coachwork of this type, but there was probably more than one example as there are pictures of a car with enclosed rear wheels and a different radiator grille. One source gives the designer of that car as Karl Bucher. The same body style was also available on the N-type chassis, but it is not known if any were built. Chassis NA0676 was imported by Heinz Keller, but remained unsold for a while. He then obtained a licence to bring in an Airline body and had the car completed by Hanni Coachbuilders, who fitted locally made wings.

Two N-type chassis were fitted with attractive cabriolet bodies in the Continental style by Fritz Ramseier of Worblaufen and sold through Sportcar AG. The obvious advantages of this type of bodywork over the factory two-seater N-type were the folding hood and proper side windows in the doors. Although it did not have the versatility of the three-position Tickford design later fitted

This was the first N-type built by Fritz Ramseier of Worblaufen for a customer of Sportscar AG. It was painted beige.

The second Worblaufen N-type was painted red, but remained unsold until 1937.

Another Swiss-bodied N-type, this time with cut-away doors and two-tone paintwork.

to the TA and SVW range, it did offer very good protection from the elements. Despite the attractive appearance, only one of the cars sold immediately and the other remained in the showroom until 1937 before finding a purchaser.

Having by 1936 sold quite a number of new cars, the company were able to have a larger import quota than had been the case when the venture started. However, with the arrival of the popular TA, SA and VA models, the practice of taking rolling chassis for local completion continued. These arrived complete with dashboard, radiator and shell, lights, spare wheel and, usually, the wings. The most elegant examples of the Swiss coachbuilders' art were the work of Reinbolt and Christe SA of Basle on the MG SA and WA chassis.

The large and impressive Reinbolt and Christe cabriolet based on the SA chassis.

A Reinbolt and Christe cabriolet on the WA chassis outside the premises of J.H. Keller.

Already in standard form large and impressive vehicles, this company fitted two-door cabriolet bodies, the styling of which made the cars appear even longer.

The first cars imported from the Nuffield Group by Heinz Keller after the war included a few TC Midgets. However, as soon as the Y-type was launched a number of complete cars and rolling chassis were brought into Switzerland. The open version of the Y-type had yet to be produced by the factory, and in 1948 a Mr. Emil Frey imported three chassis and arranged for Reinbolt and Christe to fit distinctive drophead coupé coachwork that was arguably much better-looking than the model later produced by Abingdon.

J.H. Keller AG commissioned a number of slightly different open versions of the Y-type. One had cut-away doors and a hood and side curtains that looked similar to those fitted to the contemporary TC, with the longer chassis providing an extended boot section that gave adequate space for carrying luggage for the two occupants. The four-seater model had full-height doors incorporating proper windows and the hood stowed away behind the rear seats.

The Reinbolt and Christe four-seater model based on the Y-type chassis.

When the TD replaced the TC in 1951 there was another possible candidate for an enhanced version for the Swiss market designed to appeal to a different type of customer than would be drawn to the ordinary two-seater. A small Swiss coachbuilder, Aigle, had been attracted to the work of Italian designers, especially that of Ghia of Turin, and wanted to build cars with similar styling to sell in Switzerland. Rather tongue-in-cheek he approached Ghia to ask if he could use their name and, rather surprisingly, they agreed to his giving the vehicles he produced Ghia-Aigle badges.

Italian designer Giovanni Michelotti was then employed on a freelance basis to come up with proposals for open and closed models using the TD rolling chassis as a basis. J.H. Keller AG as Nuffield agents would source the chassis and market the cars, which were first shown to the public at the 1952 Geneva Salon. They printed a four-page brochure in French and German for what they called the MG Cabriolet-Ghia, as they obviously thought that there would be a reasonable market for the car. Despite the more substantial coachwork, the data panel in the leaflet reveals that the chassis was to

A two-seater body, possibly the type used for the standard TC, fitted to the Swiss Y-type chassis.

standard TD Mark ll specification.

One of the major advantages over a standard TD was the provision of a generous luggage compartment and proper glass side windows. The rear treatment was neat and overall the car had reasonable proportions, given the limitations of the high seating position imposed by the TD chassis. There was no attempt to include room for a back seat. The usual TD instruments were neatly arranged on a new dashboard and the steering wheel was also an MG item. Handbrake, gear lever, pedals, etc., were unaltered. Despite being aimed at the European market, the cars were right-hand drive.

Although virtually all the MGs exported to North America were standard products, there was also a small market for special models. One entrepreneur keen to exploit this was Roger Barlow of International Motors Los Angeles. In 1948 he had plans for a small production run of bespoke versions of the Y-type for sale through his company. Early in 1948 he made a journey to Europe and visited both the MG factory and Italian coachbuilders. At Abingdon he discussed with

With Ghia-Aigle one of the major advantages over a standard TD was the provision of a generous luggage compartment and proper glass side windows. The rear treatment was neat and overall the car had reasonable proportions.

This view of the Ghia-Aigle coupé shows the neat tail treatment by Michelotti.

designer Syd Enever the modifications that were needed for the American market. These included lowering and lengthening the steering column, additional instruments, changing the inlet and exhaust manifolds as well as fitting a remote gear lever, like the TC, and a Shorrock supercharger.

The next step was to consult the designers and builders of the bodywork. The Italians had flair so after discussions it was anticipated that a range of open two-seaters and drophead two- and four-seater cars would be built by Zagato, Farina and Castagna, about 70 in all. The prices were fixed and delivery dates anticipated. But there, it would seem, the dream came to an end. Zagato of Milan did put a body onto a Y chassis but not the two-seater sports car that Roger Barlow envisaged. The car was a two-door four-seater coupé. The doors curved at the top, effectively giving extra interior light by way of roof windows. A cut-down MG radiator grille was retained, with a large Z badge on the bonnet. The headlights were modernised by incorporating them into the wings. The car was taken to the 1949 Salon at Lugano and shown to the motoring world. John Thornley was present and took an interest in the changes made to the Abingdon product.

An MG Cabriolet-Ghia sits alongside an ordinary TD on the J.H. Keller stand at the March 1953 Geneva Motor Show.

There was another, and more successful, attempt to import special-bodied MGs into America. The 1952 Turin Motor Show had initially been cancelled, but was reinstated following an energetic press campaign. Many of the exhibits came from the United States and Britain, but the undoubted stars of the show on the Nuffield products stand were a pair of MG TD chassis with coachwork to designs worked out by Bertone in collaboration with Franco Scaglione. There were two styles of body on offer, a coupé and a convertible, and both looked modern and elegant compared to the standard models ranged alongside.

Early on the opening day of the show, Bertone was surprised to be approached by an American who, when he discovered that they had constructed these special MGs, hugged him and said he wanted to buy the cars. Assuming that he only wanted the two on display he said he should speak to Franco Scaglione as they had originally intended to share the profits on the sale of the cars. However, Stanley Harold Arnolt II said that he was interested in buying not just the cars on show, but at least 100 of each type.

Fitting the more modern body to the standard MG TD rolling chassis transformed the appearance of the car.

The brochure for the open and closed versions of the Arnolt TD.

Arnolt had built up a company developing marine engines during the Second World War. After buying an MG TC, he went into the distribution of British cars for the American mid-west from his Chicago headquarters. Following the Turin show he shipped the two cars to the United States and showed them to the American public at the Elkhart Lake Road Races in September 1952. One of the main selling points for the American market was the ease with which the hood of the convertible was raised and the snug fit of the windows. He also claimed that owing to their steel and aluminium construction the cars weighed a mere 40lb extra for the coupé and 20lb for the roadster. The price for each model was $3585, half as much again as a standard TD, and deliveries were expected to start in January 1953.

Although MG did produce a higher-performance TD, the Mark II, only the engine with the larger-valve head designed for that model was incorporated in the chassis supplied to Bertone. It would appear these were delivered with the MG guarantee plate bolted to the toe-board support box and the dashboard instruments and switches packed separately. As the bodies were hand-made, and varied to quite a degree, each item of trim fitted

A major advantage of the Arnolt TD was the provision of a large lockable luggage compartment.

to each car had to be marked with the appropriate body number. A standard TD dash panel was used, but mounted upside down. Available options included Borrani wire wheels, radio and heater.

Constructing the body on the TD chassis was not a simple affair. Unlike the ash-framed standard body, which was bolted to outriggers, the Arnolt main steel body frames were permanently welded to the chassis, with the doors hinged directly onto the steel framing. Most of the body was covered with hand-formed steel, but the doors, bonnet and boot had aluminium cladding. On the rolling chassis most was left unaltered, the installation of the engine and radiator was standard and the bracing bars for the radiator and toe-boards were retained. The side panels of the engine compartment had louvres for ventilation and an entirely different scuttle was fabricated.

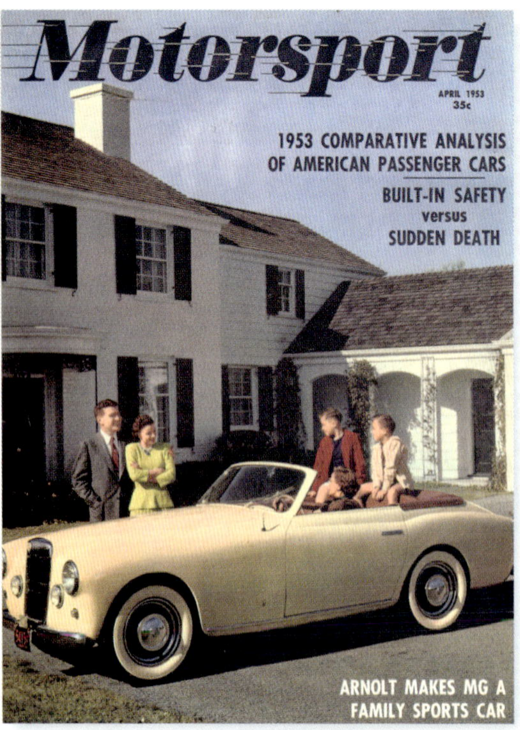

The smooth shape of both the coupé and roadster produced less drag than the ordinary TD with its separate wings and headlights. This helped offset the higher overall weight and gave them a respectable cruising speed. Nevertheless many of the survivors have been supercharged. One of the most appealing aspects of any Arnolt was the interior and the high standard of trim and equipment. There is also quite a lot of room in the cabin and luggage space is far more generous than with an ordinary TD. The boot lid was released by pulling a knob behind the front passenger seat and the rear-hinged bonnet also had a cable pull, this being placed under the dashboard.

In the event the 200 cars were never built. The TF was introduced and the market for that number of cars was just not there. The final production numbers have been variously quoted as 65 coupés and 35 convertibles or 67 coupés and 33 convertibles, not including the two prototypes.

THE TD MIDGET

As we have seen, the TC was merely a development of a 1930s design and followed then accepted practice in having stiff springing, beam axles and, to keep the wheels in contact with the road over bumps, an element of flexibility in the frame. This was fine on the track where a hard ride was the accepted trade-off for good roadholding and cornering, but was not so beneficial in everyday use. By 1938 work had been well advanced on a small MG saloon with independent front suspension and rack and pinion steering, and there is the possibility that this work would have been carried over to the sports model had not war intervened.

The main Cowley drawing office had done some planning for a replacement for the TC, but little progress had been made as the priority was to get new mainstream models, like the Issigonis-designed Morris Minor, into full production. By the late 1940s, at Abingdon there was now the situation where the family-oriented Y-type saloon enjoyed a much more advanced specification than the flagship sports car produced alongside. With little encouragement or direction from the main company, those within the factory set about rectifying this.

It must have been a busy time at Abingdon, as well as a worrying one. A short-lived export-only open version of the Y-type, the YT, was built in small numbers, but earned few friends. A new sports model being urgently needed, the small team at Abingdon cobbled up a prototype by the simple expedient of fitting a TC body on a shortened T-type chassis fitted with a twin-carburettor TC engine. Odd though it may have looked, it showed sufficient promise for the Cowley design office to work up drawings for a production version.

it's the new T.D. Midget!
Safety MG Fast!
Important "plus" features have made this new M.G. Midget the most talked-about sports car of the year. They include independent front wheel suspension for smoother riding; tougher, roomier body; disc wheels . . . new hydraulic brakes for greater control. Here is a car with all the liveliness and character of its famous predecessors—built in the true tradition of "safety fast."
TD 1950
£445.0.0 EX WORKS PLUS
£124.7.3 PURCHASE TAX.
THE MG CAR COMPANY LIMITED, SALES DIVISION, COWLEY, OXFORD
Overseas Business: Nuffield Exports Ltd., Oxford and 41 Piccadilly, London, W.1
London Showrooms : University Motors Ltd., 7 Hertford Street, W.1
A NUFFIELD PRODUCT

It is interesting at this stage to look at other sports cars available in the late 1940s and also at the trend in car design generally. Jaguar had introduced the XK120 at the 1948 London Motor Show, where its appearance and performance produced far more orders than could be fulfilled

using the methods employed for the first few cars, prompting a change in the way the bodies were built. Morgan had continued making the four-wheel 4/4 models introduced in the mid-1930s, but now with a 1300cc Standard engine. The company introduced the Plus 4 in 1950, which had the larger-capacity Standard Vanguard unit used later in the TR sports cars.

Higher up the price range there were sports saloons and some open models from the likes of Alvis, Alfa-Romeo, Allard, Aston Martin, Bristol, Healey, HRG, Lea-Francis, Singer, and Triumph with their heavy-looking Roadster. In truth, few of these sold in large numbers and would have had little effect on MG sales. As for styling, led from Detroit, there had been a move in the late 1930s to a rounded look to coachwork. The British motor industry followed the trend and cars designed post-war lost the separate wings and running boards so popular earlier. Although part of its appeal, the large wire wheels fitted to the TC were an anachronism as smaller wheels became normal and many MG owners replaced their 19-inch examples with 16-inch.

With the development of a new Midget came the opportunity to replace components no longer fitted to everyday Nuffield products, whilst at the same time modernising the car and making it more appealing in overseas markets. Although few claim that the TD was quite as elegant as some of its predecessors, especially those produced in the mid-1930s, the styling was pure 1940s British, similar to products of the same era from other manufacturers. There were none of the aerodynamic lines already seen on cars like the XK120 Jaguar and some of the Healeys.

The TD chassis, based closely on that used for the Y-type, was considerably stiffer than the TC frame. The independent front suspension with coil springs, hydraulic dampers and rack and pinion steering was a tremendous improvement. Unlike the Y-type, the rear side rails now curved over the top of the rear axle, increasing suspension travel. Although the main body frame was still made of ash, a pressed steel rear bulkhead replaced the wood and metal bar arrangement used for the earlier car. This provided a rigid mounting for the rear door pillars. Of course, a stronger chassis and slightly larger and more substantial bodywork increased overall weight by about 160lb.

One of the most striking differences between the TD and the earlier cars was the introduction of steel disc wheels in place of wires. The first few TDs had plain disc wheels of 15-inch diameter, like those fitted to the updated version of the YA saloon, the YB, For both practical and aesthetic

A publicity picture of an early TD showing the neat layout of the dashboard. The early cars did not have pierced wheels.

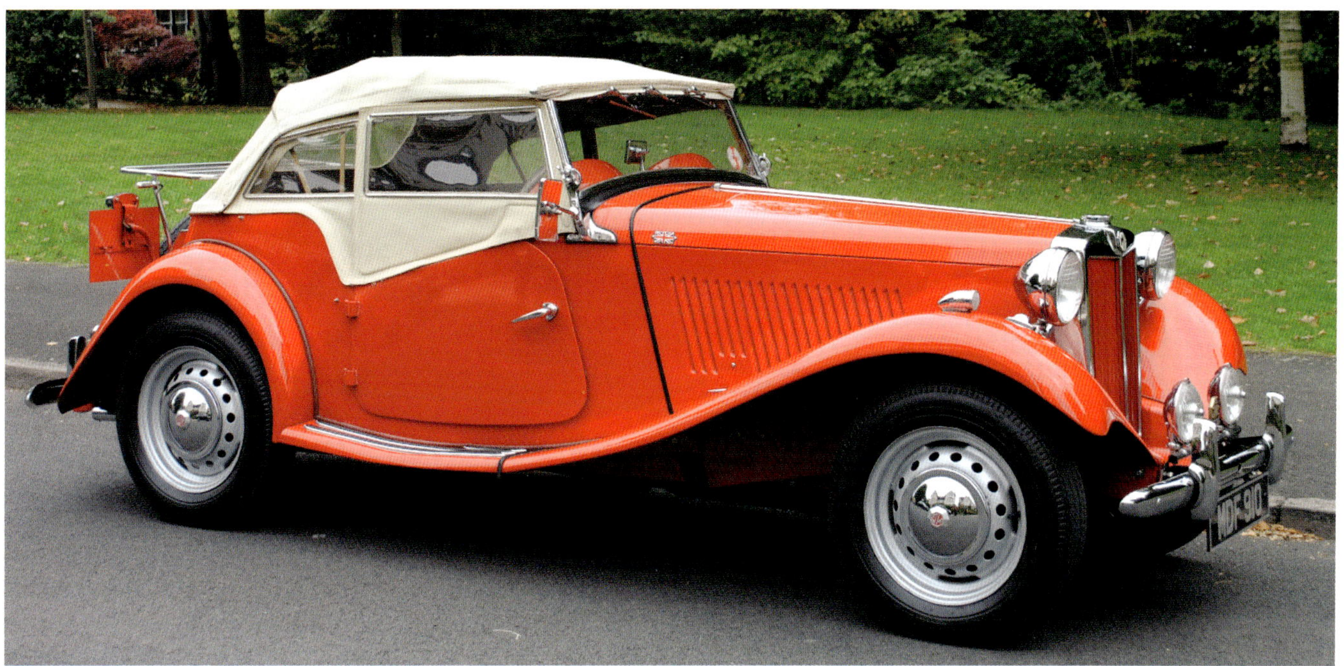

reasons, after about 250 cars had been built, wheels with cooling holes attractively arranged around the chromed hubcaps replaced these. Wire wheels were never an option for this model, although pressure from buyers saw these available as an extra on the replacement TF model.

Other improvements included a revised braking system with twin leading shoes for the front, 9-inch drums and a transmission tunnel-mounted fly-off hand brake lever. The twin-carburettor XPAG engine from the TC, producing 54bhp, was mated to a standard Nuffield four-speed gearbox.

A later TD with pierced wheels. The windscreen could be lowered for a sporty look, but travelling at any speed then became uncomfortable. The weather equipment supplied with the TD included four side-screens that when not in use could be stored in a locker under the rear shelf. As it was built towards the end of production, this car has triple windscreen wipers.

Standard TDs had twin 1¼-inch SU carburettors and a single electric fuel pump.

Given good weather, the TD is best enjoyed with the hood lowered.

The TD Mark II had twin fuel pumps, with larger carburettors and air cleaner.

As we said, the rack and pinion steering and front suspension were carried over from the Y-type and, for the first time, an MG sports car was to be built with left-hand drive for appropriate overseas markets. This had always affected sales in America, although many there celebrated the fact that their MG did not look like the average car on the streets.

Another concession to overseas buyers was the fitting of strong bumpers and over-riders. Towards the end of TC production a special export version was made for North America fitted with bumpers, while accessory vendors there did a trade fitting cars not so equipped with locally sourced alternatives. The deeper, wider front and rear wings, together with the substantial valance covering the rear of the chassis, gave the TD a far more solid appearance

This is one of the very early TDs with the plain disc wheels. Later cars left the factory with pierced wheels to aid brake drum cooling.

than its predecessor and one that has retained its appeal. Although not considered as attractive as the TF model that replaced it in 1954, its bench front seat and fairly generous cockpit make the TD the more comfortable of the two models for the taller driver. The layout of the dashboard, with the neat central panel and conveniently placed speedometer and tachometer, is also better than the arrangement that was adopted for its successor.

So the TD was technically more advanced than its predecessor but looked very similar, apart from the wheels. Endowed with a largely unchanged power unit propelling a heavier car, the TD was not any quicker in a straight line, and only kept pace by virtue of lower overall gearing. However, acceleration and top speed were not the whole

This superbly restored early TD correctly has the dashboard fabric covered to match the upholstery colour.

story. Smooth-surfaced race tracks apart, the better roadholding, steering and improved ride of the TD made it every bit as quick from A to B. All T-types suffer from being too low geared and the TD is very little worse in this respect. One would certainly not have rejected the TD purely on performance grounds.

Partly to counteract claims about poor performance, and also to homologate the changes for competition entries, the TD Mark II was introduced as a separate model. Larger valves, stronger valve springs, higher compression and larger carburettors increased power output from the 1250cc XPAG engine. Additional Andrex friction shock absorbers stiffened damping and twin fuel pumps increased the flow of petrol. Having a chassis number prefixed TD/c can identify the Mark II and later cars also gained Mark II badges each side of the bonnet. Of the nearly 30,000 TDs built, 1710 were Mark IIs.

It is interesting to see that some 28,007 cars were exported. The largest market was in North America, with the USA taking 20,007 and Canada 1146. In Europe sales to American servicemen saw Germany taking 1248 TDs, some of these being locally assembled using some German components. Relatively rare on the home market when new, many TDs have been re-imported in recent years to satisfy demand from enthusiasts.

XPAG-POWERED MG SPECIALS

At Silverstone in August 1955 the Parson MG exhibits stable cornering. The circuit then was a far cry from the highly developed motor sport venue we see today.

The period following the Second World War was an interesting one for amateur motor sport. There were many young men who had spent some years in the services, developing there both a taste for adventure and familiarity with the technology and materials developed during that period. Those keen on taking up the sport immediately peace returned had to contend with the restricted availability of both new cars and the petrol to run them. This meant that competitors had either to use and modify pre-war machinery, or build cars for themselves, utilising whatever components and materials they could obtain. This proved to be the age of the home-built special and a whole industry developed to serve those wanting either to construct a car for competition use or just make something that looked a bit more interesting than the pre-war Austin Seven or Ford Anglia on which the majority were based. At the top end of the market were the competition cars constructed largely from new components, and here it was often the XPAG engine from the MG TC/TD that provided the power.

Many future international racing drivers were serving their apprenticeship on the British club racing circuits in the late 1940s and early 1950s, often at the wheel of old or home-built cars. With the use of lightweight materials developed in the aircraft industry during the war, it is not surprising that progress was made in areas like chassis design. Many small companies were formed; some even went on later to build Grand Prix cars, others quietly disappeared from the scene. Construction of specials based on MG components was by no means confined to Britain. Particularly in America and Australia, both good markets for the products from Abingdon, amateur racing was popular and a great many MG specials were constructed, proving very successful on the track.

If one described every MG that had been modified in some way for use in competition as an MG special then the list would run to thousands. Restricting the definition to those cars where MG components form only a small part of the overall package reduces the list of possible candidates, but still many hundreds were built and we can mention here but a few of these. However, the one thing all the cars have in common is the use of the very successful XPAG power unit, first introduced when the TB Midget was announced in 1938.

The low build of the Parson MG is evident in this photograph.

One surviving MG special is the Parson MG. Stuart Young and his father, who owned the Fulham firm of Weldengrind Limited, built this special in 1955 and the name they gave it came from the pa and son involvement in its construction. Built around three-inch diameter main tubular longitudinal chassis rails, there are tubular cross-members fore and aft. The lightweight body is attached directly to the chassis and has a one-piece front wing/bonnet assembly hinged at the front. The sculptured shape of the body is reminiscent of other sports-racing cars of the period and betrays no evidence of the lack of experience in car design of its constructors. The panel work was possibly carried out by Peels of Kingston, who certainly built the body for the only other Parson constructed a year or so later with a Maserati engine.

The MG content of the car goes further than the power unit. The front suspension and steering came from a TF, but the cross-member was lightened and an anti-roll bar incorporated. At the rear a TF hypoid axle was used, but this was suspended on quarter-elliptic rear springs and located by radius arms fixed to brackets welded to the axle casing. The Morris Commercial brakes have Alfin drums. The engine is a 1466cc XPEG unit, as fitted to the TF 1500, and has 1¾ -inch SU carburettors.

The Dargue MG chassis under construction in 1951.

Amateur racing driver, Tom Dargue competed in hill climbs, speed trials and races before and after the war with some success. Witnessing the arrival on the scene of the MG-powered specials, he decided that he would like to race one himself. He was introduced to Harry Lester, who was constructing quite a number around MG components at the time, and with his assistance Tom embarked on building a car of similar construction. The chassis was again made from two large-diameter steel tubes, linked by tubular cross-members. The independent front suspension utilised Y-type components with a Cam Gears steering box. At the rear, the front ends of the leaf springs were mounted with bushes and at the rear in sliding trunnions, in pre-war MG style.

The car was fitted initially with a supercharged 1100cc engine, basic bodywork, disc wheels and cycle wings. Tom Dargue drove it in a number of events and Dick Jacobs also drove the car in the Goodwood Nine Hour Race. During the winter of 1953/54, it was rebuilt and fitted with an attractive all-enveloping aluminium body; the original one is now fitted to another MG special. MG had built

modified versions of the XPAG engine for a record attempt at Utah and a number of extra blocks were cast and made available to the racing fraternity. These had sufficient room to allow them to be bored out to 1500cc and lacked water passages between the block and head, these being replaced by an external pipe. One of them was fitted to the re-bodied Dargue.

Harry Lester will forever be associated with MG specials, but he started his racing career on two wheels, not four. The first MG he ran was a J2, which he crashed, and thereafter he concentrated on trials, hill-climbs and sprints. After the war he returned to the motor trade and resumed his motor sport activities. To enter the very first meeting at Gransden in 1946 he built a modified P-type with a pointed tail, outside exhaust, but swept front wings. He also built a special using a standard L-type chassis, entering this in the Brighton Speed Trials and at Goodwood.

The second body fitted to the Dargue MG survived intact and was refitted to the car when it was restored a few years ago.

The Dargue MG wearing its original body in a race at Silverstone in July 1953.

His success brought requests for similar cars from customers and possibly as many as a dozen were built. However, Harry really wanted to have a more modern car. He especially wanted independent front suspension, and the only way this could be achieved whilst keeping weight to a minimum was to build his own chassis. He set about designing one and during 1948 he evolved a

The elegant, streamlined shape of this Lester MG sets it apart from the earlier cars produced by Harry Lester.

tubular frame, fitting this with the front suspension from the Y-type saloon. The good design of this chassis made the car successful, Harry's expertise in tuning the XPAG engine giving him the edge over his rivals. He turned his own flywheels from solid steel, lightened the rockers and pushrods, and balanced the engines. Quite a number of these cars were built for customers.

Margaret and Richard Ashby were watching a race from the stands at Goodwood, passing comments to each other about the efforts of one of the drivers. The famous racing driver Raymond Mays, who was sitting just in front of them, turned round and said, "If you feel you could do better, why don't you have a go yourselves?" At the time they owned a Wolseley 6/80 saloon that they had brought home when they returned from a spell in Gibraltar. For racing, the engine was carefully tuned, a straight-through exhaust system was fitted, and the rear suspension was stiffened. The car was otherwise standard. Despite being a somewhat unpromising vehicle for motor racing, the Wolseley was driven for a season by both Richard and Margaret, with some success.

Having thoroughly been bitten by the racing bug it was time to buy something more potent. A part owner of the garage that prepared their Wolseley was a partner in Liss Engineering Company, who had moved to West Street, Havant, following a fire at their original premises. There were three partners in the firm: Bob Marshall, Peter Tompkins, and Fred. Of these Fred was the prime mover. He had been in the RAF, where he had learned to make fuel tanks for aircraft, and was a skilled aluminium welder. The tubular-framed chassis was built in the workshop, with some of the ideas for the design cribbed from the AC Ace.

The partners in Liss Engineering did not come to the job entirely without experience, having previously built another special. The acknowledgement of this is recorded in the chassis number on the frame of the car built for Captain and Mrs Ashby, which was stamped LECO 2. The second car was larger than the first and was to be based around the components and identity of a crashed MG. However, in the event, the only parts used were the engine, gearbox, wheel hubs and brake drums. Everything else – spring hangers, brake back-plates, etc. – was manufactured by Liss Engineering. The differential assembly for the independent rear suspension was by ENV. One alarming feature of the rear suspension design, however, was a tendency for the pivoting drive shafts to lock-up whilst cornering at the limit of suspension travel. This was later to cause a few unplanned excursions into the straw bales.

The first engine fitted to the LECO was of standard 1250cc capacity. This started to use oil and smoke badly after a hill climb at Brunton. They then decided to fit a new engine and an XPEG 1500cc unit that had been tuned by Francis Beart for use by Stirling Moss became available. The 1500cc engine easily replaced the old XPAG in the LECO, the only difference being that it had been

Margaret Ashby at the wheel of the LECO MG leading a race at Goodwood in 1957. As she once said "one minute before the engine blew up".

One would be hard pressed to identify the MG parentage of the elegant Peirce MG built in South Africa.

converted to use an oil cooler. This modification was to cause them some trouble when the pipes carrying oil to the front-mounted cooler fractured on a number of occasions.

Oil starvation following fracture of one of those oil cooler pipes was the cause of a retirement at Goodwood in August 1957 when Margaret was leading the race. Low oil pressure was quickly followed by a loud bang when a piston vacated the block, taking the oil pump with it. That turned out to be their last race with the LECO, which was towed back to the builders and subsequently sold.

In South Africa motor racing was a popular pastime and quite a number of racing cars were exported there once their competition career in Europe was over. These included machinery such as ERAs, Alfa Romeos and even an R-type MG. Here again, MG specials were popular, the most successful exponent being Harry Peirce of Johannesburg, who built a number of cars around MG T-type components. His earlier efforts utilised TC chassis frames with modified suspension and lighter bodywork. Later the cars moved further from their MG origins, whilst always being run as MG-Specials. A quick and forceful driver, as well as a gifted engineer, Peirce recorded victories against ostensibly far more powerful machinery, these results coming both from his undoubted skill at the wheel and from the good roadholding and light weight of the cars he built. There were quite a number of XPAG-powered specials running in South Africa, where they remained competitive long after the Climax cars had dominated grids in Europe

John Cooper was at the forefront of the post-war expansion of British motor sport that had been encouraged by the creation of a number of new racing circuits on a few of the many airfields built for the war effort. Lightweight cars powered by 500cc motorcycle engines gave many their first taste of the sport of motor racing and the Cooper 500s were amongst the earliest in the field. Some measure of the success of John Cooper's design

John Bolster tests the prototype Cooper-MG when it was still running around on trade plates.

The chassis and body frame of JOY 500. Note the transverse-leaf springs and independent suspension.

can be judged from the results obtained by the 18-year-old Stirling Moss in his first season. He entered 15 hill climbs and circuit races, won 11, placed third once, fourth twice and was unplaced only once. His skill played a part, but as other drivers of Cooper 500s also notched up many wins the car was obviously very competitive.

At the end of the 1948 season John Cooper assessed the results of his decision to build series production racing cars. Of the 16 circuit races his cars had entered they had won 14, so for 1949 the company offered an improved Mark ll 500cc car and also a 1000cc version with either H.R.D. or J.A.P. power unit. John also built a prototype sports model powered by a 1.5-litre Vauxhall engine.

The Cliff Davis/JOY 500 pairing was pretty well unbeatable in their class. In the 1952/53 seasons Davis won 23 races.

The chassis followed what had become Cooper practice, based on welded steel box-section main members joined by three cross-tubes, two of which extended outwards to support the body. Later Cooper used large-diameter tubes in place of the steel box members. The front and rear independent suspension was fixed to fabricated mountings welded to the frame and consisted of transverse leaf springs, wishbones and hydraulic dampers, based on the Fiat 500 system. The aluminium body was built on a structure formed from steel strips and there were cycle wings, those at the front turning with the wheels. This first sports Cooper was sold to Sir Bernard Docker and after it had been trimmed by Hoopers, who were by then part of the BSA group of which Docker was chairman, it was fitted with a Daimler-style grille and used by Lance Docker on the family estate near Poole.

Having made arrangements with John Thornley at Abingdon, for 1950 John Cooper constructed a second sports model, this time powered by the 1250cc XPAG engine and transmission. John Lucas of Barwell Engineering tuned the engine to produce 75bhp at 6200rpm and the first outing for the car was at Goodwood on 17 June 1950. As the engine was running badly in its first race the best Stirling Moss could manage was fifth place. However, later in the day, and with the engine in better health, John Cooper finished second in a five-lap handicap race.

Production of the Cooper sports models had to take second place to racing cars in the cramped premises the company occupied in Hollyfield Road, Surbiton. The solution was to sell them as a chassis, with or without bodywork, for the customer to complete elsewhere, and the majority of Cooper-MGs were built this way, incidentally saving a considerable sum in purchase tax. The XPAG engine was fitted to some of the chassis, others received different power units.

Because they were effectively sold as kit cars and no two are identical, identifying exactly which cars can rightly be described as Cooper-MGs can be difficult, especially when studying contemporary entry lists and race reports. The problem is further complicated because over the years components like the distinctive factory-style body, often found their way onto non-Cooper chassis.

One of the names made famous in the early post-war era that has survived into the 21st century is Lotus, linked, of course, to that of the founder, Colin Chapman. Colin studied structural engineering at London University and learned to fly in the University Air Squadron, joining the RAF in 1948 to do his National Service. He credited his subsequent interest in racing cars to reading motoring magazines in the mess. Finding that there were few opportunities to do much flying in the RAF, his thoughts turned to building a trials special in his spare time as being an affordable way into motor sport. His first car was based on the remains of an Austin Seven fabric saloon he found rotting away in a garden. During 36-hour passes from the RAF he towed the car home, stripped it down to the bare chassis and then set about trying to make it into a competitive trials car.

Since nobody he knew had any experience of building specials he had to think things out for himself. He started by boxing the chassis to strengthen and stiffen it, and then built a body frame from ash and, using aircraft principles, fitted a stressed double skin of plywood. Mounting twin spare wheels on the back of this strong body had the effect of increasing the weight on the rear axle, and thus traction. He altered the links that located the back axle to reduce over-steer, modified the brakes and increased the power output of the engine. The car proved moderately successful, gaining him a couple of class awards, and encouraged him to proceed with a Mark II version.

He was spending increasing amounts of his spare time on cars when fortuitously the RAF decided that, as they were not in a position to offer him a commission and, as he had already spent three years in the University Air Squadron, he could leave without completing his National Service. He was sorry to give up the chance to pilot service aircraft, but for the rest of his life continued to fly privately.

The second Lotus was also based on an Austin Seven frame, but this time with an 1172cc sidevalve Ford power unit. Incorporating all he had learned with the first car, the Mark II had a more streamlined nose with swivelling headlamps mounted behind a neat grille. Although it was built for trials, Chapman entered the car in the 1950 Eight Clubs meeting at Silverstone where he won the 1.5-litre sportscar race. When building the Mark III Lotus Colin decided that trials were not the best proving ground for his ideas and that he would concentrate on circuit racing. Having sold the Mark II car to finance a replacement, construction began over the 1950/51 winter months. He teamed up with brothers Michael and Nigel Allen with the intention to build three cars, one for each of them to race. The first car was constructed to conform to the 750cc formula and again used an Austin

Francis Dundas in Glasgow seated in NKC 195 prior to the 1953 Coronation Rally.

This Cooper-MG wore a glass-fibre body when first registered in 1955.

As if to prove that the Cooper-MGs were road-going sports cars, JER 547 appears with hood up ready to face any weather.

Seven chassis modified as previously. The secret of the considerable success enjoyed by the car was the effort made to improve the power output of the 750cc Austin engine.

By the end of 1951 Colin was fully committed to the idea of building racing cars and, with the help of £25 from Hazel Williams, his girlfriend who was later to become his wife, he and Michael Allen formed Lotus Engineering Limited. Another Austin Seven-based car, the Mark IV, was built for Mike Lawson to use in trials. He had previously purchased the Mark II, but now needed something a bit more competitive. That was the last car built by Lotus that used an Austin frame. The Mark V designation was kept for possible future use.

The first Lotus to use a chassis frame constructed from scratch was the Mark VI. Chapman was not keen on the then practice of using twin large-diameter tubes for the main chassis members, preferring a system of smaller tubes to form a space frame that also supported the body panels. The major mechanical components – engine, gearbox, suspension, etc. – were bolted directly to the space frame, and lightweight body skinning was riveted

Peter Gammon in UPE 9 during the support race prior to the 1954 British Grand Prix. Colin Chapman won the race and Peter came home in second place.

Lotus-MG NUF 100 at Prescott in 1954.

directly to the tubular framework. The Chapman trademark of making every component work for a living, whilst being as light as possible, was emerging. By then British Aluminium Company employed him on the development of light alloys for commercial vehicles and construction.

From the outset it was envisaged that the Mark VI would be sold both complete, and in component form for owners to build into a car suited to their needs. To this end the main components had to be easily available and cheap, so modified Ford front axle, brakes, rear axle, torque tube, radius arms, gearbox, wheels, etc. would be used. A range of engines could be fitted of capacities up to 1500cc. To demonstrate potential, the prototype, HML 6, was constructed with a tuned Ford Consul 1500cc unit. This caused a sensation at its first outing at an MG Car Club meeting at Silverstone. Unfortunately, before the first major race Nigel Allen was involved in an accident on the way to Boreham that wrote off the one-month-old car, but luckily the other driver was at fault and the insurance company money they received kept the company just about solvent.

Michael Allen resigned from his position as director of Lotus and Hazel took his place on the board. A batch of eight Mark VI models was built for customers, who fitted them with a variety of engines. One was given a supercharged MG J4 OHC unit to suit the 750cc racing class; others had Ford 1172cc, MG TC XPAG or Ford Consul engines. Colin then built the ninth chassis into a car to use himself. The company went on to build a considerable number of Mark VIs in kit form and their adverts at the time promised a top speed with engines in standard tune of 75mph for the Ford Ten, 99mph for the Consul and 104mph for the TC engine.

Colin employed directly or indirectly a talented team that included amongst many others Mike Costin in charge of engine and chassis maintenance and preparation, his brother, Frank who was an aircraft aerodynamicist who spent his spare time working for Lotus on streamlining. A school friend of Colin's, John Teychenne established the Progress Chassis Company, just round the corner from the Lotus works, and they built the space frame chassis.

The company expanded rapidly as orders for the Lotus VI poured in. Mark VI production ceased at the end of 1955. By that time some 110 cars had been sold and quite a number still survive. In the 1950s cars with separate wings were looking dated and in sports car racing all-enveloping bodies were becoming universal. Chapman, always the innovator, was certainly not likely to be satisfied with making and racing the Mark VI, or its immediate successor, the Lotus Seven, which went into production in 1957 for sale mainly in kit form for use both on the road and in club racing. With his eye on international competition where cycle wings were banned, Chapman began in 1953 to plan a car that would exploit to the full the benefits of light construction and a very aerodynamic body. The target was maximum weight of 1000lb and a top speed of 125mph with an engine output of 85bhp.

Mike Costin passed a model of a streamlined car made by Dave Kelsey of Progress Chassis to his brother, Frank for him to unofficially test in the de Havilland wind tunnel. It came back much modified by the attachment of lumps of Plasticine to improve the airflow. Colin then drew up a design for a proper space frame chassis and this was passed to a pair of stress engineers at de Havilland for some more out-of-hours work. The only drawback of the design was that access to the engine was so limited that to remove it from the frame the body had to be partly dismantled. Nevertheless, the prototype was built with the streamlined body made by Williams and Pritchard.

An MG TD engine that had been bored out to 1467cc and tuned to produce 85bhp at 6200rpm provided the power for the new car. The first outing was a race meeting at Oulton Park in April 1954 but Colin was forced to start the race from the back of the grid as he had missed his practice session after Mike Costin had damaged the Lotus on the way to the circuit trying to outrun a police car. In the race Colin managed to get up as far as fourth place before a failed head gasket meant retirement. Subsequent outings saw the Lotus-MG score a number of successes, including first place and the team prize in the 1500cc sports car race at the 1954 British Grand Prix.

The success of Colin's Mark VIII Lotus-MG meant that the company received a number of orders. However, competition use had revealed that welds on the very stiff space frame were failing and there was also the problem of access to the power unit. So for the batch of customer cars the company used modified Mark VI chassis fitted with the aerodynamic body shell. A car sold to John Coombs had the Connaught engine and another, with an MG XPAG unit, went to Nigel Allen. In all, seven Mark VIII cars were built.

The Mark IX Lotus used a reworked Mark VI chassis fitted with a Costin body by Williams and Pritchard of a slightly different shape from that used for the Mark VIII. The rear fins were shorter, but taller, and the nose and the area behind the front wheels were reshaped. The car was offered in various specifications, depending on the class in which the owner intended to compete. For the new 1100cc category a 1098cc Coventry-Climax unit mated to an MG TC gearbox was favoured, and for 1500cc events there was the tried and tested MG XPAG unit. John Bolster tested both versions and found that with almost identical power outputs, 81bhp for the Climax and 85bhp for the MG, top speeds were much the same at 128.6mph and 127.7mph respectively. The MG reached 60mph in 8.6secs and the Climax 7.7secs; different gear ratios were fitted as the MG unit produced maximum power at lower rpm. In all some 40 Mark IX cars were built.

Although now just a episode in the Lotus story, and eclipsed by later successes in Grand Prix and by the large number of road cars bearing their name, the Lotus-MGs did play an important part in establishing the company.

Colin Chapman in Mark VIII Lotus-MG SAR 5 at Goodwood in 1954.

THE TF MIDGET

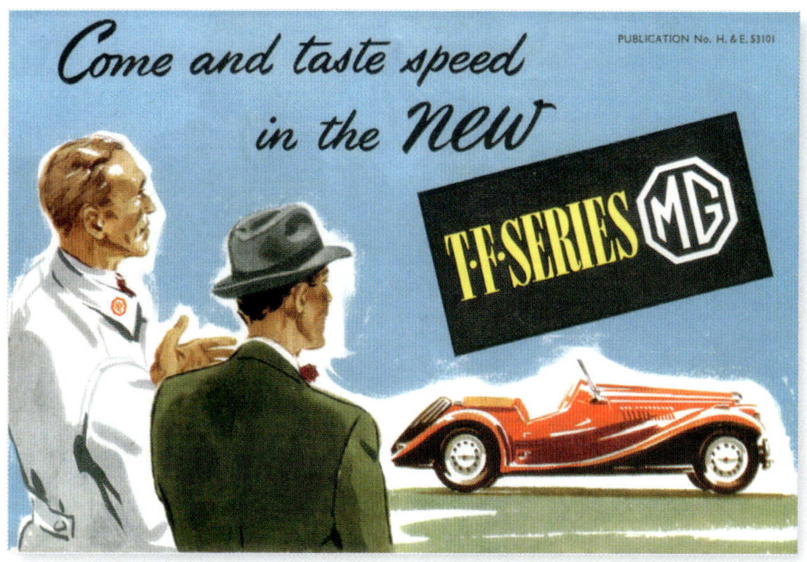

If there were prizes available for the MG design that has been most admired and copied, then the TF Midget made from 1953 to 1955 would very likely take first place. A unique blend of pre-war tradition with the more streamlined look that became fashionable in the late 1940s produced a timeless design that has ever since been admired and copied all over the world. With its immediate predecessor, the TD model launched in 1949, it has inspired the production of more replicas than any other car, aside from the legendary AC Cobra. Even now there is probably a kit car manufacturer somewhere churning out parts for their particular TF pastiche. In Britain the Naylor TF is probably the most plentiful, best engineered and most recognised replica.

Despite its undoubted appeal to later generations of sports car enthusiasts, at the time the TF was produced it was seen by many as out of date and just a face-lifted TD introduced to try to maintain sales whilst the British Motor Corporation came to grips with the fact that really what was needed was a completely new car. In 1953 there was no full design office at Abingdon, and this was not re-established until 1954 when the urgent need for an entirely updated car was realised by the BMC management. However, when the TD was redesigned to produce the TF all this was in the future and the powers-that-be would only sanction a facelift of the old model. The design office at Cowley carried this out. Gerald Palmer, who at the time had overall design responsibility for MG, Riley and Wolseley, did produce proposals for a new MG of unitary construction, but pressure of other work and shortage of money had prevented these going beyond the mock-up stage.

Liaising with Syd Enever at Abingdon, the brief given to the design team at Cowley was to improve the appearance of the car without spending too much money, and at the same time to deal with a few issues that were causing problems in service. One of these was the use of separate headlamps on the TD. These were costly and also were easily damaged and knocked out of alignment by careless owners when opening the bonnet. Another area where the old model was showing its age was the lack of a pressurised cooling system, particularly important in some export markets where hot weather was the norm. However, changing this meant modifying the header tank and filler cap.

One has to admit that despite the limited brief the design produced was aesthetically very successful. Basically it consisted of a revised body tub with a lower scuttle that blended well with a gently sloping bonnet with fixed side panels. New, beautifully sculptured front wings that incorporated the headlights, plus elegant running boards and chunky rear wings, produced a very attractive car.

Pat Moss drove a Competition Department TF 1500 into third place in the Ladies' Class in the 1955 RAC Rally.

A dummy radiator cap sat on a sloped radiator shell and the filler for the pressurised cooling system was placed under the left-hand bonnet top. This bonnet still featured a centre hinge, but now only the top panels lifted for routine maintenance. The side panels could be unscrewed for major work.

At the rear, the fuel tank was reshaped and lowered, while the rear wings had a curved leading edge to merge with the running boards. The strips on the running boards were chrome plated, rather than aluminium with rubber inserts, and were now longer and were carried up on to the front wings. The circular rear lights fitted to later TDs were unaltered for the TF, as were the front sidelights.

Inside the cockpit much was new. Gone was the bench seat familiar to generations of Midget owners from the first M-type to the last TD. In its place was a pair of leather-upholstered bucket seats, which, although very comfortable, did not have quite the range of adjustment of the earlier arrangement. Behind the seats the side-screen stowage had been changed. On the TD the four side-screens packed away vertically in an enclosed area at the rear but with the TF this compartment was moved so that they stowed flat in a box beneath the luggage platform. As with the previous models, a half-tonneau cover was supplied with the car to conceal the stowed hood and the luggage compartment, and this could be left in place with the side-screens fitted.

Both as a styling gimmick and to ease production of both left- and right-hand drive cars on the same production line, the instruments were now all grouped in the centre of the dashboard. These were set in chromed octagonal bezels with the rev counter placed nearest to the driver and the speedometer on the passenger side. In the centre a combined instrument took care of water temperature, oil pressure and ammeter. There was still no fuel gauge, just a flashing low-fuel warning light.

Either side of the instrument panel was a small open glove box. These, together with the door pockets fitted to all T-types, gave sufficient useful storage for oddments. When a radio was fitted the controls were placed in one of these glove boxes and

A few TFs found use as police cars, this one by Kent Constabulary.

Appearances in films enhanced the reputation of the TF, especially in America. Here one was used in the Doris Day/Rock Hudson film **Pillow Talk**.

The TF is a handsome car from any angle and looks particularly good finished in this original colour scheme of red with biscuit trim.

the valve amplifier was mounted under the dashboard. A modern wiper motor mounted on the scuttle replaced the unreliable and vulnerable unit mounted on the windscreen frame of the TD, and a pair of knobs inside the glove boxes was provided to park the blades clear of the screen.

However, the changes to the exterior and interior of the car couldn't disguise the fact that the chassis and other mechanical components were pure TD. The only improvements made for the new model were the standardisation of a higher state of tune for the engine, similar to that on the TD Mark II,

From the side the elegant lines of the car are evident. The side-screens stow in a compartment beneath the area behind the seats.

Although the XPEG power unit is a tight squeeze under the bonnet most service items are accessible.

The TF had comfortable bucket seats in place of the bench fitted to earlier T-series cars.

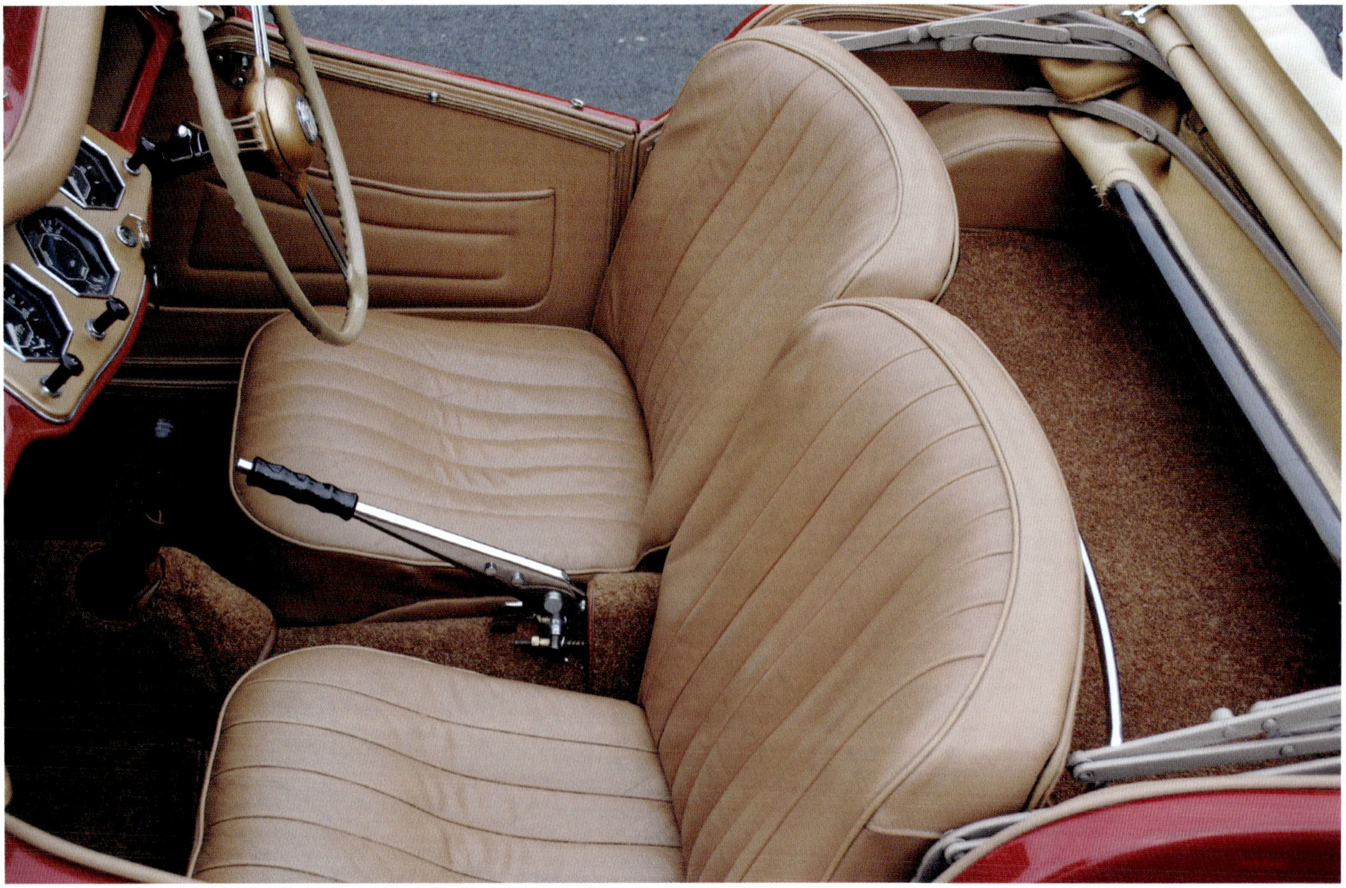

The central position for the instrument panel did not need moving for right-hand or left-hand drive options.

THE NAYLOR TF 1700

The Naylor TF was the brainchild of Alistair Naylor, whose company had set the standards for T-type restoration. The TF 1700 was sold as a completely new car that met all current safety requirements, and had undergone the same crash test procedure as any other new car. The basis of the Naylor was a re-created TF chassis, correct in every detail, but mated to modern suspension and running gear. A revised front cross-member carried co-axial coil spring/damper units, whilst at the rear coil spring/damper units carried the Ital axle, located by four parallel Panhard rods.

The body, wings, running boards, and bonnet all came from the original TF, but front-hinged doors had to be used. The TF-like bumpers incorporated the lenses for the flashing indicators. Interior trim was luxurious, with leather-covered seats, thick carpets, and a wood-veneered dashboard fitted with modern dials and rocker switches.

The TF 1700 drove like a slightly more powerful TF, and most road testers reported well on the car in magazine articles. However, there were insufficient orders for the £13,000 car to enable the company to survive and the patterns and rights to build the TF 1700 were acquired by Mahcon Group, who subsequently built a few cars, and even sold a few in kit form to be assembled using second-hand Marina components and cheaper, fibreglass wings.

Naylor TF 1700 on chrome wire wheels.

One colour option for the TF was Ivory and came with either red or green trim.

Green is a popular colour for TFs and goes particularly well with the beige leather interior.

and the adoption of the higher-ratio rear axle from that model. The engine amendments improved the power output by a modest 4bhp. In addition, because of the restricted space under the bonnet, a pair of pancake filters replaced the bulky TD oil bath air cleaner.

One important chassis change for those sports car buyers who lamented the lack of wire wheels on the TD was the adoption of them as an optional extra on the TF. In overseas markets in particular they were popular and, indeed, some kits of parts were sold to convert earlier TD Midgets to wire wheels. The new car sold in Britain at £550 plus £230 5s 10d purchase tax, which was £20 more than the TD but £35 less than the more highly tuned TD Mk II which it resembled mechanically.

The need to try to improve sales of the car, which was not really holding its own in competition with other marques, led to the development of the larger 1466cc engine introduced after some 6000 TF 1250s had been built. For some while a number of people had been enlarging the XPAG engine by over-boring. This process was not always successful as it reduced the wall thickness around the bores below acceptable limits. To enlarge the capacity without changing the cylinder bore centres, or the head stud positions, the factory produced a new block casting which eliminated the water jacket between cylinders 1 and 2, and 3 and 4, and reduced the size of the jacket between the two pairs of cylinders and at the front and rear of the block. The effect of raising the bore size from 66.5 to 72 mm was to increase the capacity from 1250cc to 1466cc. The cylinder head was unchanged so the increase in swept volume meant a corresponding increase in compression ratio to 8.3:1. The power went up by a useful 6bhp and the torque was also improved. To help market the new version of the TF the factory added "TF1500" badges to the sides of the bonnet.

THE ZA AND ZB MAGNETTES

A publicity picture for the ZA Magnette. This is not one of the first few cars as it has quarter-lights fitted to the front doors.

The 1950s were an exciting time in which to grow up. The young were just starting to be thought of as a race apart, with disapproving adults coining the term teenagers to describe a breed that was starting to enjoy music, clothes and affluence ever more alien to the experiences of their own youth. Without having been much affected by the dreary years of war, 1950s youngsters grew up in an optimistic age when the exploits of British industry, and the continuing existence of a worldwide network of colonies and dependent territories, gave them the feeling that, in spite of starting the decade still burdened by debt, Britain was one of the leading nations in the world. There was much talk of a new Elizabethan age and a feeling of optimism for the future hard to credit now. Of course, there was also much concern about nuclear weapons, and towards the end of the decade many of the young were involved in Ban the Bomb marches.

An obsession with speed and streamlining had an influence on car design and one effect of this was to produce cars during the 1950s with styling that has stood the test of time. Cars like the Jaguar 2.4 and 3.4, some of the Lancias, the AC Ace, the MGA, and, of course, the Z-Magnette. Even today, the simple, uncluttered lines of the ZA and ZB Magnettes look thoroughly modern. Although work on the design started in the early 1950s, they remain practical and stylish family classic cars.

Good though the Y-type saloon was, its 1930s styling meant that by the early 1950s it was starting to appear rather old-fashioned. The modern taste for all-enveloping bodywork had seen cars like the Morris Minor abandoning separate headlights and running boards. Furthermore, the small body on the Y-type meant that the interior was rather cramped, and the luggage locker was not able to carry a much luggage unless the fold-down lid was used to extend the capacity. As the only saloon car in the MG range it was obvious that its replacement would have to both look modern and provide the occupants with more room and comfort.

The early 1950s were a time of increasing affluence for the citizens of the developed world and there was certainly a demand for the sort

The early ZA Magnettes had a metal top for the dashboard, painted to resemble wood. The lower part of the dashboard was also a different shape from the one used on later cars.

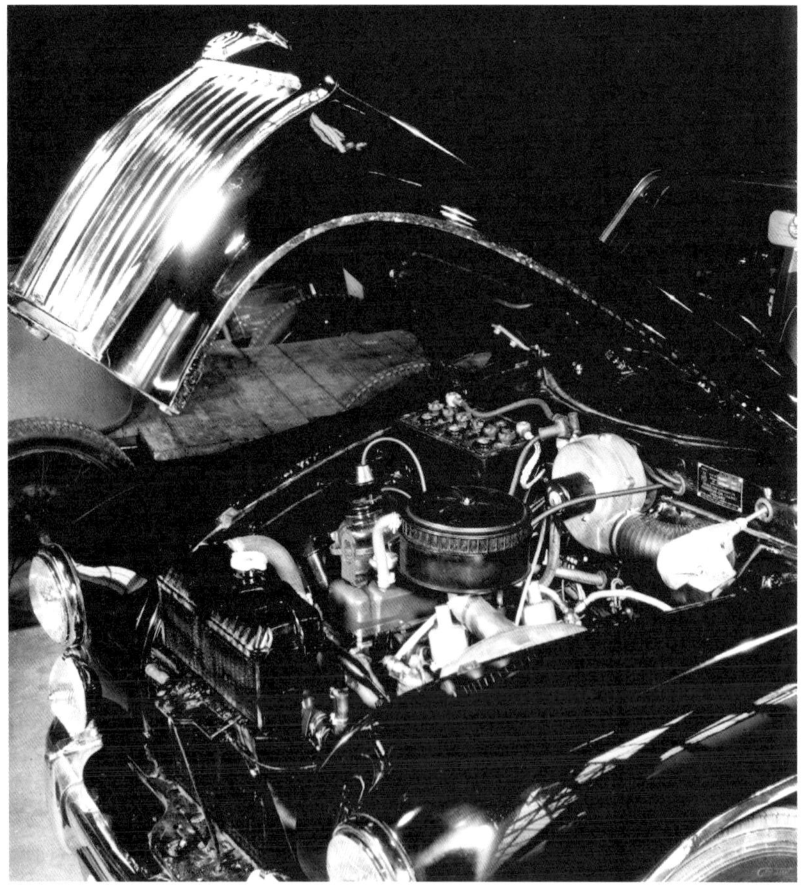

A factory picture of the engine compartment of an early ZA.

of sports saloon the MG name represented. The arms race, fuelled by the cold war between East and West, meant increasing spending on military hardware. In both America and Europe bulging order books and full employment saw the take-home pay of the average worker increasing sharply. Car ownership was high in America, and growing fast in Europe, and many buyers were looking for more than just the most basic transport. Many potential customers, indeed, for the products from Abingdon.

Prior to the 1952 merger with Austin that produced the British Motor Corporation, Gerald Palmer had been instructed to produce new designs for MG and Wolseley four-seater saloons and large six-seater saloons for the Riley and Wolseley model ranges. All of these cars were to use standard Nuffield engines, transmissions and many smaller components. He was granted a free hand as far as size and styling were concerned, but had to take into consideration the sort of car that would appeal to the potential buyers for each marque and model. Giving the task a lot of thought, it soon became obvious to Gerald that the solution lay in designing all the cars around just two basic body shells. The smaller of these would be used for the MG and small Wolseley, and a larger for the six-seater Wolseleys and Rileys. The use of different grilles and badges, together with minor exterior panel changes and different levels of trim, would identify one marque from the other. For example, Palmer proposed giving the MG small saloon a lower ride height, with some necessary changes to the sills and wings, in addition to a floor-mounted gear change, an MG octagon-inspired dashboard layout, and MG radiator grille.

The most urgent need within the group was for the smaller cars, and it was here that the small design team that assisted Gerald Palmer at Cowley concentrated their efforts. Gerald had always been keen on developing cars with long-travel, all-independent suspension as he saw that this was the way to go if they were to appeal to world markets. Unfortunately, the policy at Nuffield was to use existing components, which meant the retention of leaf springs at the rear. For the front wheels, however, he was able to opt for a development of the independent suspension already in use on the Y-type saloon.

It was decided at an early stage that the new saloon was to have an all-steel monocoque chassis/body unit. The Magnette body was developed and built by Pressed Steel and consisted of a number of sections that during manufacture were welded together on a jig. The floor incorporated a stressed prop-shaft tunnel and strong sill sections at either side. At the front, twin chassis extensions were welded to the front suspension cross-member and these also had the engine mounting brackets fitted to them. At the rear, the boot floor and inner wheel arches formed the basic structure. The main door and screen pillars, scuttle panels and roof added to the stiffness of the shell, the bolt-on doors, boot lid,

A catalogue picture of a ZA finished in the attractive Island Green paint.

The graceful air-smoothed lines of the Magnette enclose an interior which is truly planned for travel. The car seats four adults cradled between the wheelbase in quiet, relaxed comfort. The deep seats provide the full support which is the real secret of fatigue-free long trips. All doors are double sealed against draught and dust, and a heating and ventilating unit keeps the interior at an even temperature in every extreme of climate.
THE INTERIOR IS PLANNED FOR TRAVEL
Safety MG Fast!

A picture of the interior from the catalogue of a later ZA with the revised dashboard.

A cherished surviving example of the attractive ZA Magnette, which for many years had one owner.

bonnet and front wings being non-structural items.

With his proposals accepted by management, work proceeded on the MG and Wolseley variants of the saloon, which at that stage were to be mechanically similar. Both were planned to have the 1250cc engine already used in the YB, with the MG version probably enjoying the benefit of a higher state of tune. Here though the upheavals that came with the 1952 merger were to play a part. As one of the advantages of establishing the group was to have common mechanical components across the whole range of cars, a decision was taken at a late stage to replace the engine in the MG version with one of the new BMC units.

There were to be three new engines in the BMC range, a 950cc A-series, 1489cc B-series, and 2.6litre six-cylinder C-series. The B-series engine, destined for the Magnette and smaller Wolseley, was a development of an earlier four-cylinder Austin unit. With the cars almost ready to go into production, changing their design to accept the new BMC engines and transmissions would delay their launch. The course of action chosen was to go ahead with the programme to build the Wolseley 4/44, whilst delaying the release of the MG until it was ready to accept the bigger engine. The Wolseley 4/44 was revealed to the public at the 1952 London Motor

Bags of room for luggage!

The well-planned luggage locker effortlessly houses the whole family's holiday luggage. The upright spare wheel allows the extra depth to the compartment which gives this remarkable roominess. A trigger mechanism concealed inside the number-plate light opens the locker. The lid is counterbalanced by torsion bar hinges for easy lifting, and it stays open as required.

Safety MG Fast!

The size of the luggage compartment was a selling point emphasised in the brochure.

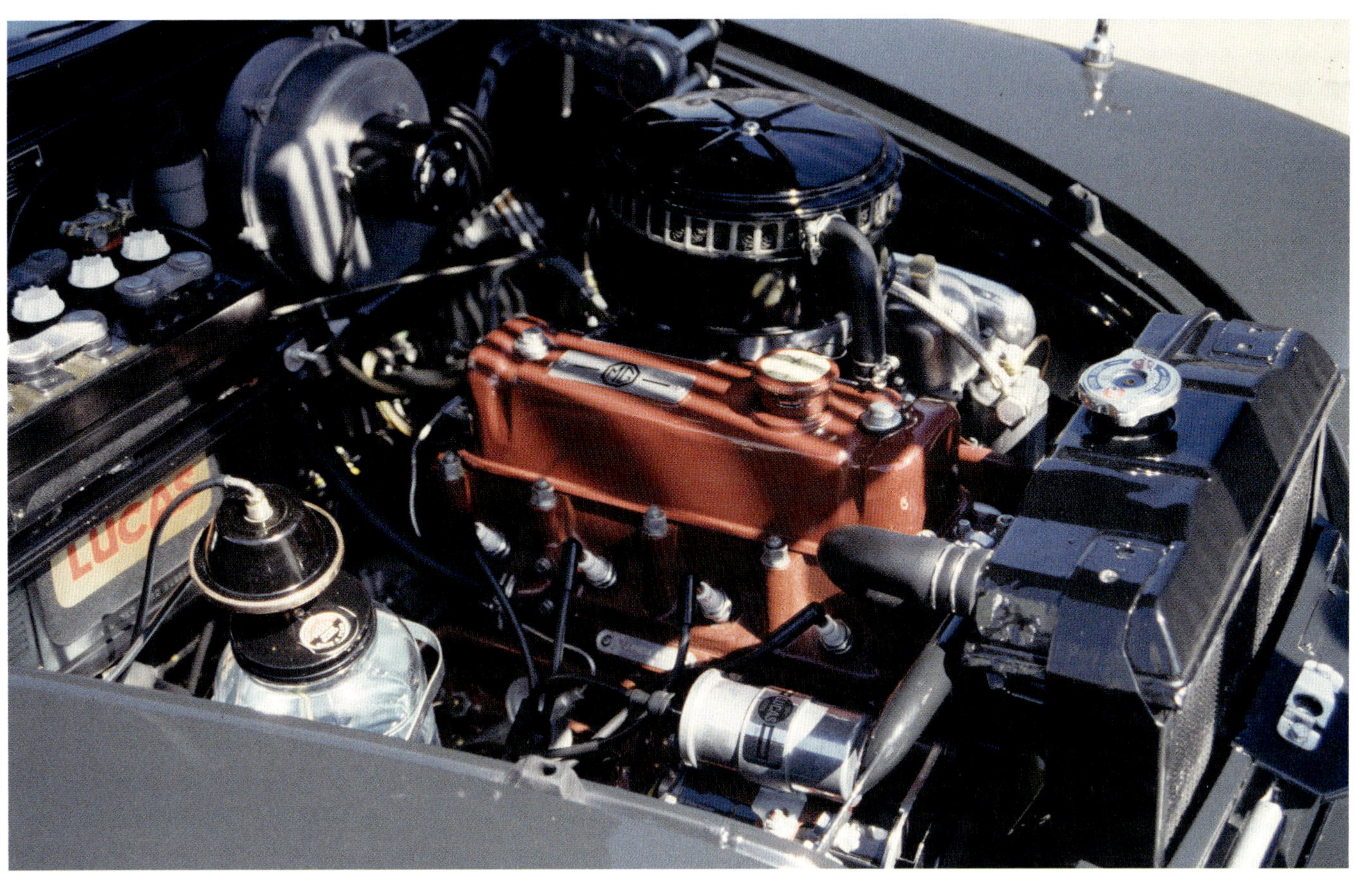

The engine bay of a restored early ZA Magnette. Service items are easily accessible.

Show, and the MG variant arrived a year later where it shared the MG stand with the TF Midget.

Developing any new model is not always a straightforward process and the ZA Magnette was no exception. To distinguish the sportier MG from the Wolseley, Palmer had decided to give it a lower ride height by fitting flatter rear springs. He proposed attaching the axle casing to these by means of rubber bushes, using a torque arm to resist axle twist under acceleration and braking. This system had to be abandoned when the testers driving one of the prototype cars experienced severe axle tramp under heavy braking, making the car almost unmanageable under these conditions.

With the cars almost ready to go into production, there was no time for further development work on this design of suspension and the only sensible solution was to revert to using convention U-bolts to attach the axle to the springs, and to remove the torque arm. The rear springs were given greater camber, which made the car sit a bit higher than Palmer had originally intended, but the axle tramp disappeared. The suspension was by coil spring and wishbones at the front, and half-elliptic leaf springs at the rear. As a departure from previous MG practice telescopic rather than lever arm dampers were fitted.

The B-series engine fitted to the ZA Magnettes produced 60bhp at 4600rpm, which was considered a reasonable output for the time but not really sufficient for a sporting saloon weighing 22cwt. Later, when the ZB was announced, the incorporation of engine modifications from car number 18101 saw this rise to 68bhp at 5200rpm. In comparison with the 60bhp available for the ZA, the Wolseley 4/44 had a power output of 46bhp at 4800rpm from its single-carburettor engine.

At the 1953 show visitors were able to see both the Magnette and the Wolseley 4/44, which still retained the 1250cc Nuffield engine. The Wolseley was designed to appeal to the middle-class family man and had a steering-column gear-change, a popular 1950s feature, with the advantage of allowing three people to sit together on the front seats. The Wolseley had leather trim, a wooden instrument panel with the light-faced dials centrally placed, and the traditional radiator grille with illuminated badge. Different wings and sills, and the taller radiator grille, made the car seem bulkier and less attractive than the MG on a nearby stand.

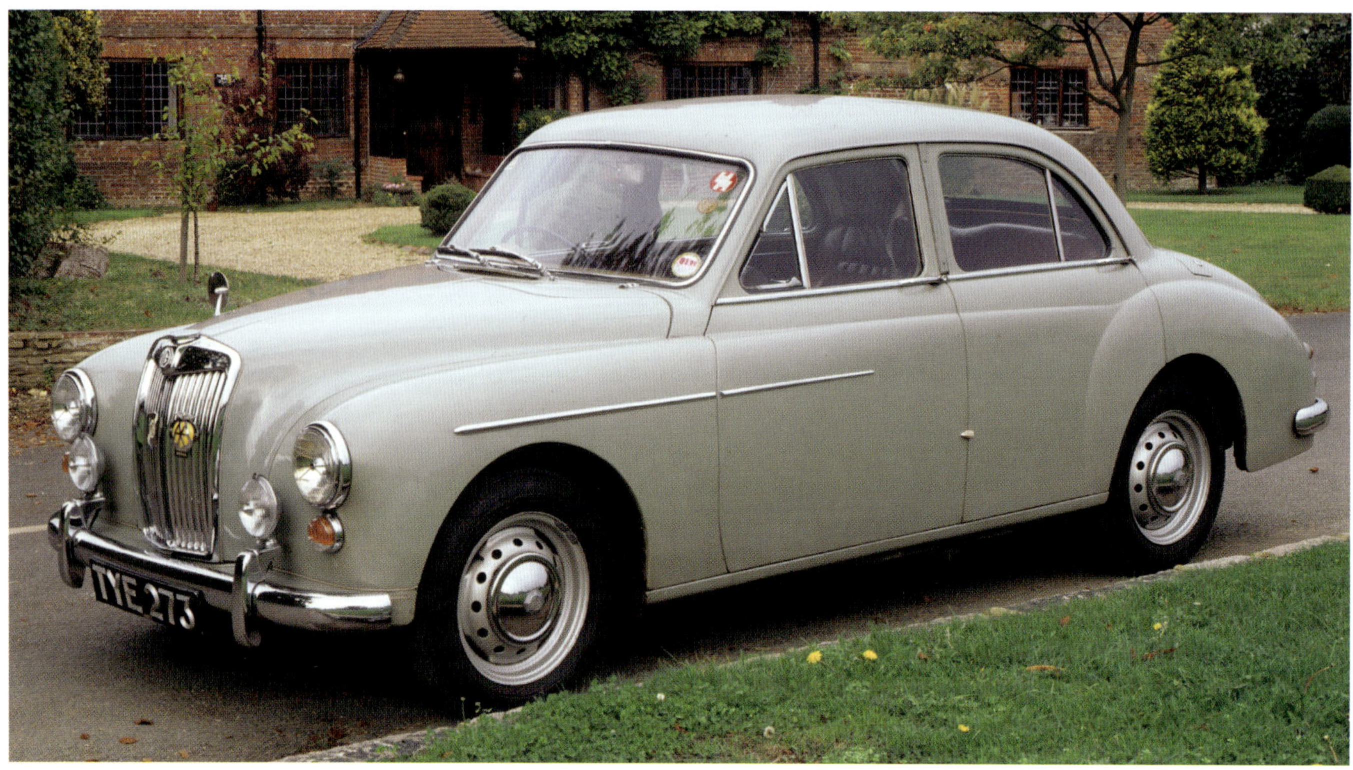

With the ZB, a straight side chrome strip replaced the one curving over the front wheel-arch on the ZA. This car is very original, having never been repainted.

Like the Wolseley, the seats on the Z-Magnette were trimmed in leather, but the MG was fitted with bucket-shaped seats in the front and had a central gear lever. The car was trimmed to a high standard and well equipped for the time. Unlike the MG open cars, it had a heater and de-mister as standard. There were wooden door trims and a wooden dashboard, which initially had a metal top panel that was convincingly painted to resemble real wood. Fuel, water temperature and oil pressure gauges, as well as an ammeter, flanked the half-octagonal shaped speedometer. The more sporting driver regretted the lack of a tachometer. A clock was mounted above the rear-view mirror. The passenger cabin was roomy and beneath the spring-balanced boot lid was ample space for luggage. A neat touch was the push-button release for the fuel filler cap and the provision for this to be locked by means of a thumbscrew from within the boot.

Adding to the showroom appeal of the new Magnette was a well-chosen range of colour schemes. Priced at £645, plus £269 17s 6d purchase tax, it must have represented good value for those buyers looking for a well-appointed, sporting car. Like the previous post-war MGs, the export market provided many sales, with the cars going to far-flung parts of the world. Their inherent strength of both body and mechanical components was an asset, although the electrical equipment, like fuel pumps, ignition system and instruments, was just as troublesome as on other British cars of the period.

At first, few full road tests appeared in the

A factory picture of the dashboard of the ZB and Varitone Magnettes.

The rear window seen here was fitted to the standard ZA and ZB models, but was enlarged on the Varitone version.

British motoring magazines as cars from the publicity department press fleet were not available for almost a year. Some journalists reported on experiences with privately owned cars, with John Bolster writing in *Autosport* of his own Magnette that it fully qualified as a high-performance car as it was able to cruise at over 70mph and had suspension that was beyond criticism. When press cars were available towards the end of 1954, *The Autocar* recorded a maximum speed of 81mph and *The Motor* 80.7mph. Both of their cars reached 60mph in about 23sec. The Wolseley 4/44 tested by magazines when it was introduced in late 1952 recorded a top speed of 73mph and took 29.9 seconds to reach 60mph.

Quite a number of last-minute specification changes were introduced while the first few cars were being assembled and delays were encountered at the factory caused by problems encountered when adapting the Abingdon assembly lines and building techniques to deal with the monocoque car. The first 250 cars off the line differed from those built later in that they lacked swivelling quarter-lights on the front windows, had slightly different grille slats and surround, and were fitted with a higher ratio final drive, 4.3:1 instead of the 4.875:1 fitted to subsequent cars to improve their acceleration. Interestingly, only the first 6500 cars built had the metal top to the dashboard. On these the wooden section was also a different shape, the lower part being recessed. Later cars featured real wood throughout.

There is little doubt that in styling terms the ZA Magnette was one of the most advanced British saloon cars on the market when it was launched at the Earls Court London Motor Show in 1953. In giving it a modern aerodynamic shape, Gerald Palmer had designed a car that has stood the test of time better than many of its contemporaries. Palmer had been aware that the standard B-series engine gave insufficient power for the cars to have rally-winning performance. He had drawn-up a design for a twin-cam cylinder head to boost power output and this was eventually developed by Morris Engines branch and used in the MGA Twin Cam, but never found its way into the Z-Magnette.

When the MGA arrived it also used the BMC B-series engine and to improve the output for the sports car the compression ratio was raised initially from 7.15:1 to 8.15:1 and then to 8.3:1. With a revised camshaft power was increased first to 68bhp and then to 72bhp with the 8.3:1 compression. The benefits from these changes worked their way into the Z-Magnette engine in 1956. This also had initially received the 7.15:1 ratio head and then one with a compression ratio of 8.3:1 and, with a

An attractive range of two-tone colour schemes was available on the Varitone model. The small badge on the front wing identifies this car as one of the rare Alexander-tuned versions.

different camshaft from that used on the MGA, power eventually increased to 68bhp. A full-flow filtration system was now fitted, necessitating an external oil pipe to return oil to the block. With more power at their disposal the engineers were able to give the car the 4.55:1 axle ratio and higher cruising speeds were possible without sacrificing acceleration. In the public announcement of these alterations the revised Magnette was now designated as the ZB, the first of the new models being car number 18577

In a manner typical of the sales efforts of the British Motor Corporation in the 1950s, little was done to give people the impression that the car had been improved. The sales brochures were retouched to show the alteration to the chrome trim on the front wings, the only external change made to the Magnette. Incidentally, the Wolseley sister to the Magnette, the 4/44, was revised mid 1956, gaining a single carburettor, 55bhp version of the B-series engine in place of the XPAG power unit. Now called the Wolseley 15/50, it also enjoyed the revised axle ratio and other mechanical refinements carried out to the Magnette.

Another model was added to the MG range when the ZB was announced, the ZB Varitone. This was mechanically identical to the standard cars, but the option of two-tone paint and large rear window changed its appearance considerably. The Varitone models were initially announced as such by the Press Office of BMC, who almost immediately issued instructions that the cars were henceforth to be called Duotone Magnettes. However, this did not find favour and Varitone appeared in all official literature. This confusion over nomenclature was compounded by the availability also of the cars in a single colour, which retained the chromed strips that ran down both sides of the car intended to separate the two paint colours. The shell of the Varitone was identical to that of the ordinary model; the story goes that the rear window was enlarged by hand rather than being formed on the press tools.

The ZB Magnettes were also available with a clutchless gear change. The Manumatic transmission was not an automatic in the accepted sense, merely a system for relieving the driver of the chore of using a clutch. Briefly, the mechanism was powered by vacuum from the inlet manifold, which opened and closed throttle servos and pressurised the hydraulically operated clutch. At idle the clutch was disengaged. When the throttle was opened and engine speed increased, bob weights within the clutch forced it into engagement and the car moved off. Gripping the gear knob activated a solenoid that allowed vacuum pressure to disengage the clutch and, once the gear change was accomplished, releasing the knob re-engaged the clutch. It was an over-complicated arrangement for the technology of the time and doubtless few Magnettes survive with the system intact.

The car certainly sold well. In the five years it was in production a total of 36,599 were built, with the numbers of ZA and ZB examples being roughly equal. Strangely, it seems that the inherent strength of the Magnette body shell led directly to many having an early and ignominious demise. For banger racing cars needed to be cheap, available and very strong. The Magnette in middle age certainly fulfilled these requirements and large numbers ended their days being battered into heaps of scrap in floodlit banger racing stadiums all over the country. Hardly the sort of use Gerald Palmer envisaged for his creation! Luckily sufficient enthusiasts retained their affection for the cars to ensure their survival.

The Z-Magnettes were comfortable well appointed cars.

The engine bay of the ZB Varitone with an Alexander-modified engine.

GERALD PALMER – A FORWARD-THINKING DESIGNER

In the modern world the influence of any one individual designer on the product is limited, with marketing men and focus groups often playing their part. In the motor industry in earlier years this was certainly not the case. Many individuals influenced the appearance of a product range, a prime examples being William Lyons of Jaguar and Issigonis at the British Motor Corporation. Now, although individuals are important, their efforts are diluted by committee decisions and outside influences. In the case of MG most of the cars built at Abingdon were produced as a result of the efforts of a very small team working under either H.N. Charles or later Syd Enever. However, during the period when overall responsibility for new models was under the control of Cowley there was one designer in particular who stood head and shoulders above the rest.

Gerald Palmer photographed in the late 1930s.

Gerald Palmer was born in 1911, the son of the district engineer of the Beira, Mashonaland and Rhodesia Railways, who was based in Umtali, Southern Rhodesia. Growing up in a country that was developing rapidly, he saw at first hand the benefits brought by major civil engineering projects at a time when almost all items that could not be locally produced had to be transported from the port of Beira by rail through difficult country. When his father was promoted to the post of district engineer the family moved to Bulawayo and it was there that they had their first car. However, Gerald spent some time in both Cape Town and in England and had experienced first-hand the effects of the increasing number of cars on the roads in more developed countries. This growing interest in cars, stimulated by subscriptions to all the current motoring magazines, was to determine the course of his life.

Gerald's first attempt at car design was this boat-tail body on a Ford Model T built by him whilst he was still at school.

The family purchased a Model T Ford, a vehicle with the stamina and suspension to cope with local conditions. When this was later replaced with a Fiat the young Gerald seized the chance to try out some of his ideas on car design and replaced the

Ford coachwork with a two-seater boat-tailed body based on one he had seen fitted to a locally owned Scripps Booth. The result was a rakish two-seater car that, although it inherited the high stance and other shortcomings from the Ford, did have a sporting appearance. It was a creditable first effort in car design.

Even late in life Gerald exhibited the self-reliance and strong will that one often saw in children born to people serving in what was then the British Empire. This may have come from travel giving them a wider view of the world or perhaps because during education they were often distanced from parents. In Gerald's case when it came to preparing for his future career he was determined not to follow the path his father would have selected for him. With career opportunities in Rhodesia being limited, and determined to enter the road transport industry, the choice was between South Africa and Britain and the latter provided the better prospects.

Aged just 16, he travelled by Union Castle liner to Southampton to stay with an aunt in North London. He joined the Institution of Mechanical Engineers and through them obtained an apprenticeship with Scammell, a firm of lorry builders based in nearby Watford. This turned out to be an inspired choice as there he came under the influence of the remarkable designer, Oliver North, and from him learned much that was to be of use later in his career.

Of more relevance to his later work on MGs, however, was a project Gerald became involved with in conjunction with a young graduate, Chalenor Barson. He asked Gerald to design a sports car for the wealthy Brooklands driver Joan Richmond, who unfortunately returned to Australia before the project was off the ground. Undaunted, the two young men formed the Deroy Car Company and set about constructing the car in a rented garage in Penge. Gerald carried on working at Scammell and Chalenor worked full-time building the prototype. This had attractive styling and some novel features, like the panel that covered the hood when it was lowered and also acted as a solid support for it when erected.

Inspired both by his experiences of poor road surfaces and the work of Oliver North, Gerald had used independent suspension, a Dubonnet type at the front and a system similar to the De Dion principle at the rear. In both cases a transverse leaf spring was employed. Unfortunately, although the car looked tremendous, Gerald had used a 1.5-litre Scammell engine that, although cheap, was woefully lacking in the power necessary for a sports car. Gerald unsuccessfully tried to interest a larger manufacturer in the design but nevertheless building the car did lead to his eventually working on MG designs.

Gerald was given an introduction to Cecil Kimber and took the Deroy to Abingdon when he went to meet him. Kimber was impressed with the car but as by then design work had been transferred to Cowley he was unable to offer him a job. However, he telephoned A.V. Oak, the Morris Motors Technical Director, and arranged for Gerald to have an interview with him. In due course this resulted

The Deroy two-seater was an attractive sports car that led directly to Gerald obtaining a job working on MG designs.

Gerald's proposed T-type MG replacement went as far as the production of full-sized mock-ups. Here we see the monocoque chassis structure fitted with "traditional" MG separate wings, a style thought to have appeal in the American market.

in him being offered the post of being in charge of MG work in the Cowley drawing office. His first task there was to develop an MG version of the new Morris Series-E saloon, but before this could go into production war broke out and the project was shelved, only to emerge in 1947 as the Y-type.

During the conflict Gerald was involved in much work furthering the war effort, not the least of which was devising a way to mass-produce equipment to provide vaporised ether as an anaesthetic in field operating theatres. He was also thinking hard about his future in the motor industry, and when he saw an advertisement calling for a chief designer he replied and discovered it had been placed by the Bradford firm, Jowett. Given the chance to have a free hand building a new saloon car for world markets, he left his job with the Nuffield Group and moved north.

The Javelin was a ground-breaking design much loved by many owners at the time. There were some shortcomings, but these were mainly as a result of the lack of resources at Jowett. Nevertheless, the Jowett Javelin did incorporate some advanced features at a time when the major manufacturers were still selling products little different from those they had produced pre-war. For Gerald it was a showcase of his talents and led directly to his being offered the chance to return to Cowley to take responsibility for designing future MG, Riley and Wolseley models, which resulted in the successful Z-Magnette.

Gerald's MG work went further than just his Z-Magnette, and part of his brief was to design replacements for the ageing T-series cars. Here he

The Jowett Javelin was a brave attempt by a small manufacturer to build a world-beating small saloon car. Its success can be measured by the number of satisfied owners who bought it new and the strong following amongst enthusiasts now for the model.

took an innovative approach to sports car design in advocating the use of a monocoque basic chassis/ body unit that would be clothed with bolt-on wings, bonnet, etc. This approach allowed for there to be two distinctly different versions of what was basically the same car. The idea was to produce an up-to-date looking version with Italianate styling for the European market and a more traditional MG to sell in America, where it was thought that the styling should reflect that of the current T-series that had sold so successfully.

Had the finance and design resources been available to proceed with the new MG sports car there is little doubt that it would have been technically in advance of the Abingdon-designed MGA that was eventually built. Lighter monocoque construction and possibly more advanced suspension design would have been plus points, but some work on the styling would have been needed if the new MG was to look anywhere near as good as the pretty MGA.

Important as Gerald's talent undoubtedly was at BMC, internal politics saw that his time there would be relatively short. Having seen the Wolseley 4/44 and MG Magnette successfully underway, Gerald should have been able to devote all his efforts on finishing the other new vehicles. Alec Issigonis, however, had left the company to work on a new car for Alvis and technical director Vic Oak retired. In consequence Gerald was made a local director of Morris Motors Limited and chief chassis and body engineer for BMC, and his role became more that of an administrator rather than a designer.

Leonard Lord, BMC Chairman, was keen to have Alec Issigonis back in the company but the stumbling block was that he would now have to answer to Gerald, who would have been in the senior position. In a move typical of the way the industry was run at the time, he asked for Gerald's resignation after an otherwise favourable road test of the new Wolseley 6/90 criticised a number of minor points. Lord took the view that this was Gerald's fault and asked him to leave, albeit with a generous settlement and a new Magnette. The rest is history. Issigonis returned to see his ideas take precedence at BMC and there is now little doubt that although his front-wheel-drive Mini, 1100, 1800 and Maxi models may have been technically advanced they did not prove very profitable. They were one of the reasons the company failed and was absorbed by Leyland/Triumph. Gerald was to spend the rest of his time in the motor industry working for General Motors at Luton.

The "modern" version of the proposed T-type MG replacement had streamlined bodywork in a style popular in the late 1940s and early 1950s. Undeniably less attractive than the MGA eventually produced, a tidied-up version of this car coming on the market in 1953 might well have succeeded in the showroom.

MG RALLYING IN THE EARLY 1950S

Motor sport in post-war Britain was badly curtailed by the shortage of new cars and the petrol to run them. The Blackpool Rally held in June 1947 was Britain's such first post-war event. The eligibility rules must have been fairly relaxed because the overall winner was Ken Wharton in a homemade special hybrid Austin/Ford that proved more than a match for any of the standard production cars entered. MGs did not feature in the results. The following month saw the JCC Eastbourne Rally with a number of MGs in the entry list, and four first class awards went to MG drivers.

September 1947 brought bad news for British motorists when the Labour government abolished the basic ration of petrol for pleasure motoring. This was bound to have an effect on motor sport, and one result was the cancellation of any plans to run an RAC rally that winter. This restriction was not accepted without protest, which included petitions to parliament and demonstrations. The absence of petrol for anyone other than essential users continued in 1948. However, this did not preclude the VSCC from organising an Easter sprint at Luton Hoo for vehicles that were supposed to be running on fuels other than petrol. As the programme listed all the usual suspects, including a number of OHC MGs, one can only assume they were all running on methanol. Magazines gave details of public transport for spectators but omitted to say how the cars themselves were to be legally driven to the event. After that meeting, the good news was announced that the huge protests against the restrictions had forced the government to reinstate, as from the 1st June, the basic ration for some motorists.

Betty Haig and Barbara Marshall with the Y-type they used in the 1950 Monte Carlo Rally.

In Britain, with some petrol now available, the JCC again ran their Eastbourne Rally. There were quite a number of MGs entered, both T-types and Y-type saloons. January 1949 brought the first post-war Monte Carlo Rally, and although there was a record entry of 230 cars, many from Britain, there were no MGs amongst them. It was not surprising that the factory were unwilling to enter MGs in rallies as they were fully employed trying to meet export targets. The pound was devalued from \$4.00 to \$2.80 in 1949, making British cars far cheaper and increasing the numbers sold abroad. To qualify for a steel allocation, more than 75% of total output had to be exported.

One driver to receive some factory support at that time was Betty Haig. Pre-war she had been a successful MG competitor in long-distance European rallies and in 1948 she was able to persuade John Thornley to let her jump the queue to buy a new TC Midget. In January 1949 she had been one of the drivers in a works-supported entry for the first post-war Monte Carlo Rally. The car was the then-new Morris Minor and the crew was placed second overall for the Ladies Cup. That success decided her to enter the TC in the Alpine Trial that year, with Barbara Marshall as navigator. With some factory assistance, the car was carefully prepared and the crew spent much time writing out

One of the final tests in the 1950 Daily Express *1000-mile Rally. Geoff Holt won the event outright.*

comprehensive route notes. By the finish they were seventh overall and won the class.

The following year the same team was entered for the Monte Carlo in a factory-prepared Y-type. The car had been fitted with a larger fuel tank and additional dampers, while the engine had a raised compression ratio to improve power output. The weather that year was atrocious and of 282 starters only five were un-penalised. The Y-type's rally ended when they crashed early in the event. Betty Haig's last MG rally drive was in a TD, when she took part in the 1951 Paris/St. Raphael event.

Another recipient of factory support was Len Shaw. He had been able to buy a Y-type saloon soon after they came out and for a couple of years entered it in club events, with some success. His international debut was in a Ford Pilot as co-driver to Ken Wharton in the 1949 Lisbon Rally, and their second place in that event did his driving career no harm. In 1950 he was able to buy the ex-Betty Haig Y-type from the factory to replace his own example, and in this car Len entered the 1950 *Daily Express* 1000-mile Rally. In the event he was placed third overall and his team, which included another Y-type and a TD, took the team award, class honours and the best open and closed car awards.

The following year the first post-war rally staged under the RAC banner was run and, unusually, the date chosen was early June, rather than during the winter. There was a large entry and MGs were well represented in the up to 1500cc class. Len Shaw had once again entered the Y-type, as had Gregor Grant, one of the winning team the previous year. Unfortunately a crash eliminated Gregor from the results, but Len managed third in class despite some overheating problems. First in class was the Y-type of J. Readings.

At Abingdon in the early 1950s they were starting to get more involved in competition and record-breaking activities, without actually having a proper competitions department; this was to come in 1954. After the many successes earned by Y-types in rallies, three cars were specially built at Abingdon and in 1953 these were entered as a team for the 1953 RAC Rally. The cars had engines to roughly TD Mark II specification, carefully prepared to produce about 66bhp at the rear wheels. The MGs carried consecutive registration numbers and one, two or three stripes on each front wing.

That year the RAC Rally was held in March and at the time became known as the rally of the tests as road sections merely joined together a number of venues where tests of skill or speed were conducted. These included ones at Silverstone, Castle Combe

Reg Holt in one of the three works entered Y-types undertaking one of the tests staged on the promenade at Hastings.

and Goodwood. All the drivers of the three MGs were old hands at this type of event and the car's speed and agility, in comparison to others in their class, also helped. Len did particularly well and his sixth place overall ranks high alongside other giant-killing MG exploits. The other cars in the team finished high in the results and the three cars took the first three places in their class and the overall team award.

The factory lent the drivers the three YBs for the 1953 Morecambe Rally. This was a well-attended event that attracted a lot of attention in the press, a point not lost on those responsible for MG publicity. Once again the three cars were victorious in gaining the team award, and additionally Len Shaw took the award for the best-placed closed car. The final event for the team of YBs was the 1953 *Daily Express* Rally organised by the MCC, who also ran the Land's End and other classic trials. Staged in November and attracting an entry of over 400 cars, high winds and heavy rain made many a competitor's life a misery. The MG Y-types again managed to scoop the team prize. With the establishment the following year of a proper competition department, lead by Marcus Chambers, there was obviously going to be a more high-profile effort by MG in future years.

The YB saloon then being out of production, any rallying in an MG saloon had to involve the new ZA Magnette, and it was decided that a team of three cars would be entered for some major events. The first of these was the 1955 Monte Carlo Rally. Three ZA Magnettes were prepared at Abingdon for the ordeal and delivered to the nominated drivers, Len Shaw and the brothers Reg and Geoff Holt. All the crews, three people per car, were amateurs who competed for the fun of it and who right from the outset did not always see eye to eye with their new boss. There were arguments about tyre choice and equipment to be carried; this led to the initial stages of the rally being difficult for the team as the cars proved to be a handful in the slippery conditions. However, once a few items of equipment had been discarded to reduce weight and tape binding around the rear springs had been removed, things got better.

In the style of the pre-war trials cars, the team of three Magnettes carried the names of the Three Musketeers, Aramis, Athos and Porthos. They also had the same type of identification stripes on the front wings as had the previous YB rally cars. Carrying a team of three, plus spares, tools, two spare wheels, extra petrol, etc., meant that the lack of power was a real problem and there was no way the team could challenge the faster opposition. Their only hope was to finish as well as they could and try for the team award. Unfortunately, weather conditions, and some errors, put them out of the running for an award, although all the cars did finish the event.

One of the tests staged on the promenade outside the railway station during the 1953 Morecambe Rally. The three Y-types took the team award.

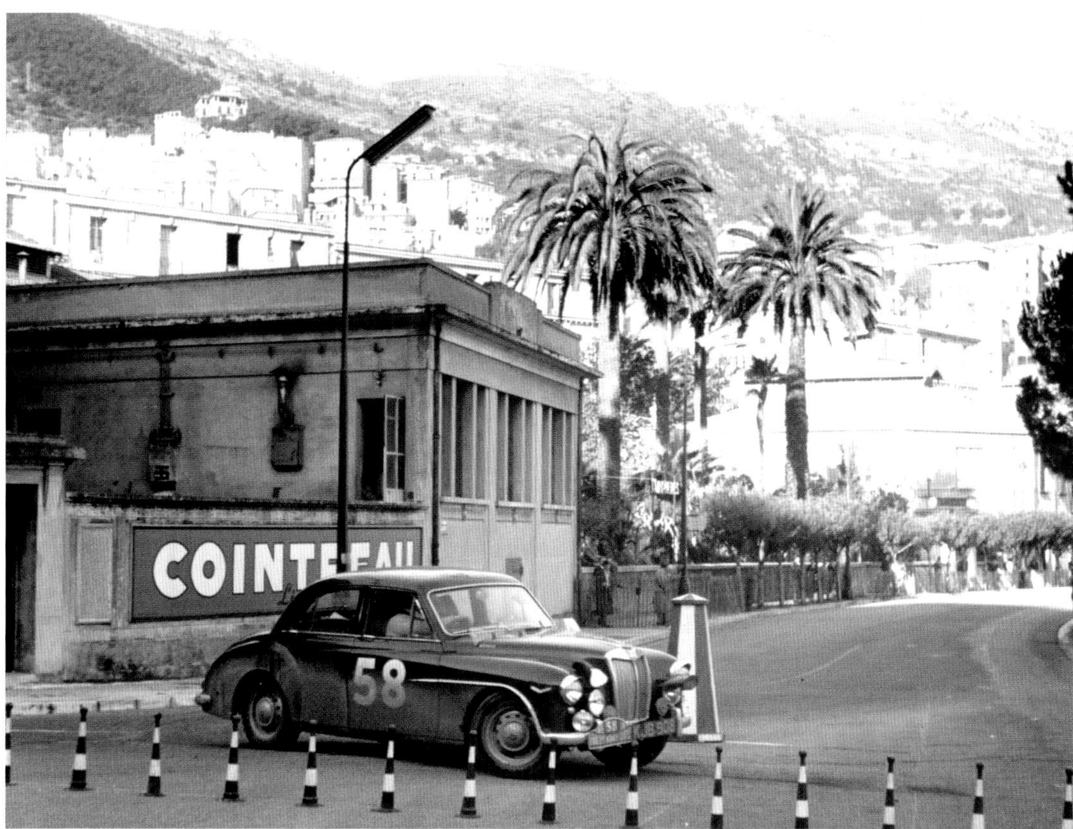

Reg Holt in one of three ZA Magnettes entered in the 1955 Monte Carlo Rally.

Despite their initial lack of success, the three Magnettes were entered for the 1955 RAC Rally. The BMC contingent was reinforced by the addition of three 2.6-litre Austin Westminster saloons and another MG, this time a TF 1500. The Austins possessed a better power to weight ratio than the Magnettes and were thus felt to have more chance of success; events were to prove this not to be so. Pat Moss, partnered by Pat Faichney, drove the TF in her debut for the BMC team.

The RAC Rally was getting tougher and the 1955 event proved difficult for most entrants, while ice and snow caused many crashes. Usually the road sections were timed but the weather that year made things so tight that many crews chose to cut out some parts altogether, thus incurring penalties for missing controls, rather than fall behind their overall time allowance. In all there were 240 cars entered and the 2000-mile rally route was confined to England and Wales, the emphasis being placed more on the special tests and careful navigation than on outright speed on the road sections. Hastings and Blackpool were used for driving tests and Oulton Park, Cadwell, Silverstone, Goodwood and Prescott staged speed tests. The organisers had been a bit ambitious in the way they had laid out and timed the event; icy roads led to delays and the cold caused problems with the time clocks. Only by some heroic last-minute efforts did they manage to declare satisfactory final results.

Pat Moss's MG TF had not undergone much in the way of serious rally preparation, but she

Scrutineering one of the works ZA Magnettes at Blackpool prior to the 1955 RAC Rally. The team did not feature in the results.

impressed all by her efforts. By Blackpool a quarter of the cars had retired and Pat Moss was placed second in the ladies section to the experienced team of Sheila Van Damm and Anne Hall. At the final Hastings test she headed the MG category but was only placed third amongst the ladies teams. The three Magnettes did not shine, but the car driven by Geoff. Holt did take first place in class three.

Despite their obvious shortcomings as rally cars, the Magnettes were given another outing when in May they were entered for the seventh Tulip Rally, an event of international stature that attracted most of the European factory-supported teams. Again there were three cars, one driven by Len Shaw, the second by Geoff Holt, and the third by Pat Moss. The MGs were in trouble even before the start when Pat Moss forgot she had to drive on the right and was involved in a collision that damaged the car. Although it was repaired and actually started the rally, it was later retired with bearing trouble.

Pat Moss and Pat Faichney entered a works-provided TF 1500 in the 1955 RAC Rally. Pat was placed third in the ladies' award in what was her first such event.

With starting points in London, Noordwijk, Paris, Brussels, Hamburg and Munich, competitors had between 360 and 530 miles to cover before the routes converged at Stuttgart. The rally offered a number of special stages, with the route for these and the road sections indicated in the instructions by the diagrams. The route worked southwards to Montélimar, and Monte Carlo Rally country, where the mountain passes weeded out a few of the competitors; most exacting were the tests taken on the downhill sections. After this the rally moved northwards, ending up at the famous 16.8-mile Nürburgring circuit, which was run in darkness. The following day came one of the most exciting parts of the rally when the speed test, consisting of 10 laps of the Zandvoort circuit, took place. Final overall winners were Tak and Niemöller in their Mercedes.

Len Shaw's car overheated when the radiator blind stuck in the closed position during a high-speed autobahn run. This problem says something about a lack of proper car preparation in the new department as the temperature gauge had failed in a previous rally and not been repaired. Overheating damaged the cylinder head and the one from the failed Pat Moss car was substituted. Although his car ran well for the rest of the event, and Len posted some fast times on the special tests, they were out of the final awards.

For 1956 Marcus decided to appoint John Gott as team captain. A senior policeman and already an extremely experienced rally driver, John was the ideal man for the job. Under his influence the team was to develop into a formidable force in international rallies. However, their first efforts in 1956 were not at all successful. The 12-car entry in the Monte Carlo Rally was rather more than they could easily manage and, to be honest, the quality of both cars and crews was not all it should have been. In addition to two MG Magnettes, there were six Austin Westminsters, three Riley Pathfinders and an Austin A50. Four cars crashed out of the rally and two retired with mechanical problems. One Magnette went out with dynamo failure and the other finished in 59th place overall, giving Nancy Mitchell third place amongst the ladies. For their vast expenditure of effort and money, BMC had just the ladies' prize to celebrate.

From an unpromising start, the Abingdon-based BMC Competitions Department was over the following years to amass an impressive array of successes.

GEORGE PHILLIPS

George Phillips was born in 1914 and in the late 1930s was a motorcycle despatch rider in Fleet Street. A larger-than-life character he was keen on beer and enjoying life, as were most in the newsprint industry at that time. His can-do, press-on nature meant that he was likely to succeed in any venture and his albeit fairly brief involvement as a factory-supported MG driver forms an important chapter in the sporting history of the marque. After the war he had become a professional photographer, preferring motor sport photography to taking pictures of society weddings, dances and other social events, and in 1950, with Gregor Grant and John Bolster, he was one of the founders of *Autosport* magazine. In that role he covered most of the major motor races at home and abroad and his personal collection of 60,000 negatives is now held in an American archive.

For British motor racing enthusiasts the annual 24-hour sports car race at Le Mans has always held considerable fascination, and a large number undertake the trip across the channel every year to enjoy the sights, sounds and atmosphere of this special event. After the war the most enthusiastic of amateur racing drivers to carry the MG flag at Le Mans was George Phillips. George's involvement with MG came when he was one of the lucky few able to buy a brand new TC from University Motors at a time when such cars were in short supply and great demand.

The TC proved initially to be too slow and to have poor steering. Fortunately George had signed a covenant not to sell the car for at least two years, usual at the time, so he decided instead to try to improve it, thus making it more suitable for the sort of competition use he had in mind. He had very limited knowledge and experience of the mechanics of motorcars, but proved to be a quick learner. He bought a grinder and used this to polish and match the inlet and exhaust ports. A trip to Abingdon brought little assistance as they said that to further tune the engine would invalidate the guarantee. Later, a more enlightened attitude would see them publish a special tuning booklet for the XPAG engine.

The lightweight steel tube framework for the body fitted to the TC chassis prior to being panelled with 20g aluminium sheet.

At Abingdon's suggestion, he partly covered the radiator and fitted richer needles to the carburettors. With these small improvements made, the car was entered for the 1947 Brighton Speed Trials, where George was placed second in his class. Thus encouraged and keen to make the car even more competitive, that winter he set about reducing the weight of his TC, this being easier than increasing engine power. The ash-framed body and the flowing wings account for a large part of the mass of the TC. George stripped his TC down to a running chassis and sold the body, wings and many other components. For replacements he turned to MG special builder Harry Lester, and asked him to supply a body for his TC.

During the transformation the car must have shed several hundredweight and, in addition, George had another go at the engine. This he stripped, polished and balanced. Larger valves and a higher compression ratio were also used. Thus lightened and given a power boost, the TC was ready for the 1948 racing season. Unfortunately,

The result of the transformation was a pretty sports/racing car that betrayed little of its MG TC origins. George and Barbara Phillips drove the car to Le Mans for the 1949 race.

there was a limited number of events and a surfeit of entries, and George was frustrated to find that he, as a comparative unknown, was refused a place on the grids. He came to an arrangement with the organisers of the Manx Cup Race, which was held on the Isle of Man prior to the British Empire Trophy Race, that he would travel over at his own expense to run in practice, so his competence could be judged. Having proved worthy of inclusion, he was awarded a place in the 2.5-litre category. Despite being outclassed by the larger-capacity machinery, he finished a creditable fourth overall, the first of the smaller-capacity cars.

Having proved himself, and his car, he joined the British Racing Drivers Club and competed in many events during the season, including the Ulster Trophy Handicap Race where he was again placed fourth. He also competed in a 12-hour race at Montlhéry, partnered by Oscar Moore, and finished fourth in class. The season ended with yet another run at Brighton, plus an entry in the first ever meeting at Goodwood, where in his race he was placed first in the 1500cc class.

The organisers decided to run the first post-war Le Mans race in June 1949 and George decided he would like to compete there with his TC. The regulations meant that he would need to modify his car to comply and he decided to have an entirely new body built. The work was entrusted to Ted Goodwin, who ran a one-man panel-beating firm in North London. Once again the car was stripped to the bare chassis and a framework consisting of both tubular and flat-section steel strips was constructed. Ted clad the body with 20-gauge aluminium sheeting, formed to fit the framework, and this resulted in a workmanlike little car. The engine was stripped, inspected, and new bearings, etc., fitted.

With co-driver Curly Dryden and a mechanic in the tender car, George and his wife Barbara drove to the circuit in the TC. Evening practice sessions proved the car capable of reliable running at competitive speeds for its class and showed that fuel consumption would allow four-hour stints between pit stops. In the race the car ran faultlessly for 20 of the 24 hours before being disqualified for what the race report in *The Autocar* said was "the mechanic going round the course to help the driver replace

As a result of the publicity earned by his Le Mans efforts, George was offered a works drive in the Production Car Race at Silverstone in 1949. The three-car team were placed second, third and fourth in the 1500cc class.

a faulty condenser". George recalled that they had already replaced the condenser and had sent the mechanic to try to pass a magneto to Dryden, but not to touch the car. He not only repaired the car but also cadged a lift in it back to the pits. They were rightly disqualified. The event for the MG team had not been without its dramas. One refuelling stop had seen spilt petrol ignited by a spark from the exhaust, the unflappable Phillips driving through the flames to rejoin the track, leaving the mechanic to extinguish the fire.

Despite his obvious disappointment over the result, George decided he would enter Le Mans again the following year. His 1949 entry had already led to recognition in the form of a race in a near-standard TC as one of the drivers of the team of three cars entered by John Thornley of the MG Car Company in the *Daily Express* Production Car Race on the Grand Prix circuit at Silverstone in August 1949. The other drivers were Dick Jacobs and Ted Lund and the MGs averaged around 70mph in the race, placing a creditable fifth, sixth and seventh overall.

As part of his preparation for the 1950 season, George Phillips built up another engine for the special and fitted it with hard-wearing chrome-plated cylinder liners. The team consisted of George and Barbara Phillips, co-driver Eric Winterbottom, and Denis Jones as mechanic. The car ran faultlessly, maintaining an average speed of 73mph over the 24 hours of the race. They were placed second in their class and classified as 18th overall.

Back home, George continued to compete in various types of events with his car and was again asked to drive one of the team MGs in the *Daily Express* Production Car Race at Silverstone in August. The TD had been announced at the end of 1949 and the factory had obviously entered a team of these new cars for the race. In standard form the cars would not have been as fast as the TCs had been the previous year, so the TDs were modified to what was to become Mark II specification. Additional shock absorbers, higher axle ratio, bigger valves, etc., were fitted, but nevertheless the lap times only just matched those of the unmodified TCs used the previous year. In the race, however, the drivers, Lund, Jacobs and Phillips, managed to take second, third and fourth places in class, beaten only by an HRG.

For the 1950 Le Mans the TC special needed some modification to meet regulations. Note the extensions on the leading edges of the front wings and the additional headlights. The lower units are long-range driving lamps that throw a very narrow beam.

Greater success for the TD team was to follow. The cars were entered for the Tourist Trophy Race held on the Dundrod circuit near Belfast and in a wet race performed well, taking the first three places in the 1500cc class. George Phillips had by now achieved a reputation as a fast, reliable driver and when he decided to take up the invitation to enter Le Mans again in 1951 the factory was keen to assist. The TC special was sold and it was decided that a modified and re-bodied car would be prepared for George on an unofficial basis.

A standard TD chassis was fitted with an all-enveloping body designed by Syd Enever. The engine was tuned and a higher ratio axle was fitted to give the car a competitive lap speed of over 80mph and

With the TC special at Le Mans in 1950 are Barbara Phillips, mechanic Denis Jones, co-driver Eric Winterbottom, and George Phillips.

For the 1950 Silverstone Production Touring Car Race the cars used were new TD Midgets modified to improve performance. Here George Phillips leads Ted Lund. The team took second, third and fourth places in class.

a top speed on the Mulsanne straight of 116mph. For the subsequent history of the marque, the most interesting thing about this special TD was its outward similarity to the later MGA.

The 1951 race itself was a disappointment for both George and the factory. In practice the car performed well, although the engine exhibited signs that it objected to the quality of the petrol supplied by the race organisers. The car lapped quicker than the TC special used the previous year, although George felt that the handling with the independent front suspension was not quite as good as his old car's. In the race, when Allen Rippon partnered him, the car attracted considerable attention, with its streamlined body looking unlike any previous MG. At first the car ran well and recorded creditable lap times. However, towards the end of his first stint at the wheel George had just reduced his lap

time to below six minutes when there were sounds of mechanical disaster from the engine compartment. He returned to the pits to find that a valve had dropped and holed a piston. His co-driver took the car out running on three cylinders, but their race was soon over.

There was some acrimony in both directions between Abingdon and George; he felt that the engine should have lasted as well as those he had rebuilt himself; they said he had pushed the car too hard. The charitable view is that the poor petrol in practice had something to do with it. The truth may be that the streamlined body allowed the engine to run at too high a speed for reliability.

The TD special built for the 1951 Le Mans. At the wheel is Alec Hounslow and behind the car, left to right, are Gerald Wiffan, Henry Stone, Syd Enever, who designed the body and oversaw the project, Wally Kinsey, who built the body, Reg Avenall, Johnny Crook and an unidentified Abingdon employee. Unfortunately the engine failed in the early stages of the event.

EX 175, THE MGA PROTOTYPE

EX175 in open form. It is very much a case of spot the changes between this and the showroom MGA. The bulge in the bonnet is there to clear the top of the XPEG power unit and the hand-made bumpers and over-riders have a different profile. However, few would notice these if you parked the car amongst a group of production MGAs – a tribute to the integrity of the original design.

The story of the development of the MGA really starts with that special built for George Phillips, when a standard TD chassis was fitted with a lighter and more aerodynamic body designed by Syd Enever. Its performance at Le Mans in 1951 was a disappointment, but the car attracted considerable attention and perhaps demonstrated the way ahead for a TD replacement that did not involve vastly altering the production methods that had served the marque for so long. There is no doubt that a Gerald Palmer proposal to build a new MG sports car using a unitary chassis/body was likely to produce a lighter and more modern design, but taking it through to production would have been more costly in terms of time and money, both of which were in short supply at that time.

The major drawback of the George Phillips car was the high seating position, which was dictated by placing the occupants above the main chassis side members. From both an aesthetic and practical standpoint Syd Enever felt this needed changing and he asked a young draughtsman, Roy Brocklehurst, to work on drawings for a new chassis where the side rails were moved outwards to sweep around the cockpit area so that the driver and passenger sat between rather than on them. At a speed that would now seem remarkable, two chassis frames were built by hand and one was fitted with a body, complete with full road equipment, lights, bumpers, windscreen, etc. The styling closely followed that of the Le Mans car and was strikingly like the production MGA that appeared some three years later. EX175, as this prototype was called, was shown to the BMC management, who rejected it out of hand, no doubt with the impending launch of the Austin-Healey very much in mind.

Record breaking had been one way MG had managed to promote the sporting credentials of the marque and as Goldie Gardner's venerable streamlined EX135 had been retired at the end of 1952 a replacement was needed. Initially EX175 was given various aerodynamic aids, fairings for the wheels, bubble cockpit cover, as well as a higher-ratio rear axle. Unfortunately these proved insufficient to turn what was designed as a road

EX175 in the Cowley studio. Here the hood and side curtains have been fitted and it appears that there is a clear panel in the canvas soft top.

car into an efficient record breaker and the scheme was abandoned. Starting again from scratch, Syd decided to use the second chassis as the basis of a new record breaker that would have a body shell closely following the one designed for EX135 by Reid Railton in the late 1930s.

The new car proved successful, and driven by George Eyston and Ken Miles at Bonneville in

Assembly of the early experimental chassis was very labour intensive. Here Cliff Bray works on one of them, which closely resembled the chassis used for the production MGA.

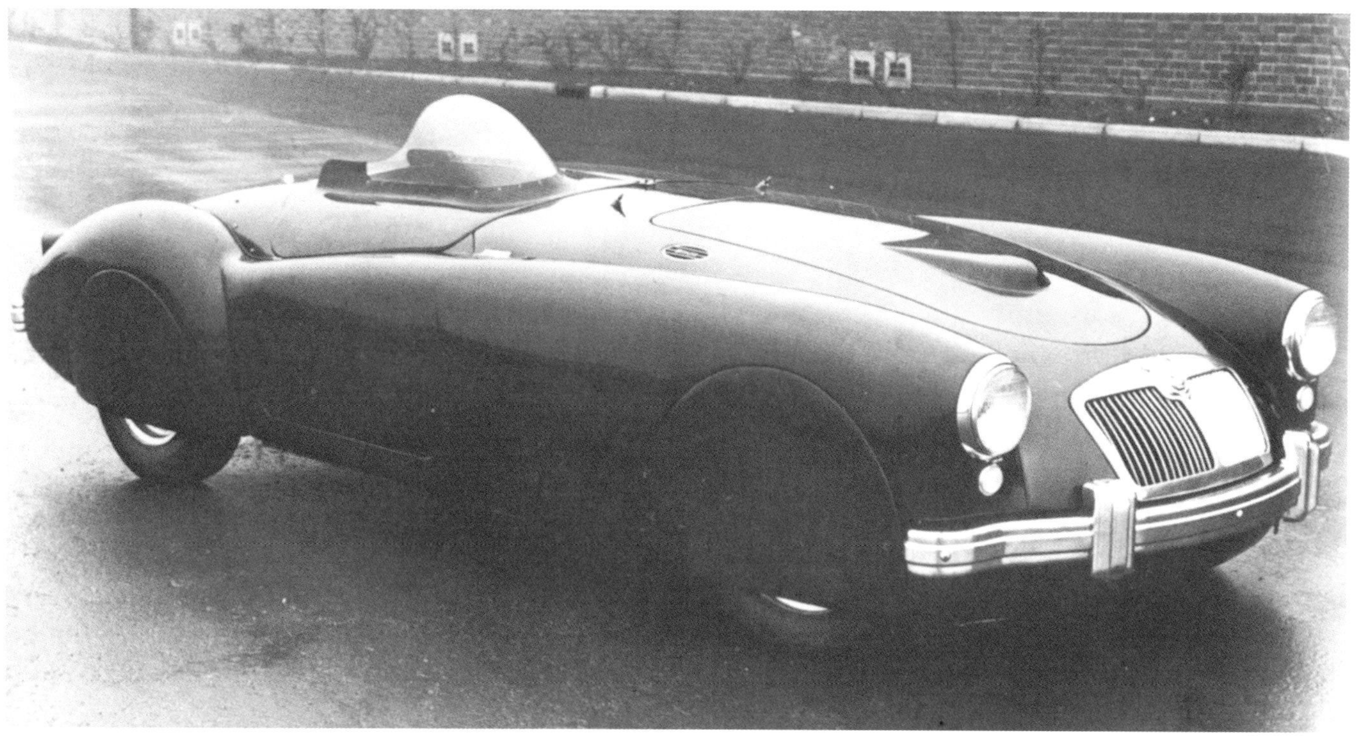

When they wanted a car with which to attempt new records using the T-series engine, at first they tried to streamline the EX175 prototype to equip it for the speeds envisaged. Only when it became apparent that a more radical solution was needed did EX179 emerge.

1954 it set a number of new records. The power unit was developed from the XPEG engine used in the TF 1500, and this success was used to promote sales of what was by then looking to be an outdated design. Back at Abingdon, however, thoughts had once again turned to building a completely new car. In a reversal of previous decisions, Abingdon were allowed to establish a full design and development department to get EX175 into production as the new MG sports model. The prototype had undergone a full evaluation by Cowley in May 1954 and a copy of their report to Syd Enever makes interesting reading.

In comparing EX175 (now designated HMO6 at Cowley) with the production MGA one has to remember that mechanically there were a number of significant differences between the prototype and the cars that appeared in the showrooms at the end of 1955. Firstly, the overall weight of EX175 was slightly less, probably because of the use of more aluminium panels. Secondly, the power train and rear axle came from the current T-type, so a TF1500 engine took the place of the BMC B-series unit eventually specified for the MGA. As they would have liked the car to appear in a good light, we can assume that the engine had been prepared to give better-than-average performance. The claimed output of a production TF1500 unit was 65bhp and that of the MGA 1500 68bhp. A graph accompanying the report gives the calculated maximum power of HMO6 as just over 70bhp at a top speed of nearly 100mph. Bearing in mind that this equates to power available at the wheels, rather than on a test bed, then one is pretty safe in assuming that the engine was not standard.

The report summarised the testing, which was carried out on Oxford's Northern by-pass near the Cowley base. Despite not being staged on a closed track, the test was thorough. Acceleration in each gear was recorded throughout the speed range in 20mph increments; figures for top gear, for example, are listed in stages from 10mph to 90mph. Selected at random to compare with similar figures for the production MGA carried out by magazines reveal that the prototype was in some cases a little bit quicker. Top gear time from 40mph to 60mph was 10.45sec with HMO6 and 13.1sec for the MGA. In both cases the car was run with two occupants and the hood and screens in place. However, the important dash from zero to 60mph took virtually the same time and top speeds were also very similar, 99.8mph for the XPEG-powered car and 97.8mph for the MGA. These results aside, the remarkable similarity between what was a one-off, hand-built prototype and the eventual production car is a tribute to the design team. The car looked a winner from the first and very little was altered between the initial idea and the final product.

MG AND LE MANS 1955

When Abingdon was eventually given permission to develop a replacement for the TD a very tight timetable had been set to get the car into production and in the event it proved optimistic. The intention was that the new cars be announced to the public around the time of the Le Mans race, and that it would be good publicity to have a team of three cars running in this prestigious event. As is often the case with new cars, difficulties with component suppliers and in setting up the production line caused delays and meant an autumn launch for the MGA. However, the company decided to proceed with the Le Mans entry, describing the cars as prototypes

Although the production MGA was not due for a few months, little secret had been made in the motoring press of its imminent arrival. *Autosport* in the 3 June 1955 issue fully described the Le Mans cars, saying that they were 1.5-litre prototypes from Abingdon designed for mass production. For the race the standard MGA chassis and suspension were used, although a higher rear axle ratio was necessary in view of the speeds attainable on the Mulsanne straight. The 3.7:1 ratio used gave 115mph at 5500 rpm in top gear. The bodywork looked standard but was made entirely from aluminium; the production cars had steel bodies with aluminium doors, bonnet and boot lid. The BMC 1.5-litre B-series engine came from the ZA Magnette, but was tuned to improve gas flow by fitting larger valves and extending the inlet tracts through the cylinder head to a balance pipe on the opposite side of the engine. This was said to give better results than the normal inlet manifold, but it may be significant that the system never reached production engines.

A completed lightweight body for one of the Le Mans cars fresh from the paint shop.

At the rear of the cars a 20-gallon fuel tank was used, double the fuel capacity of a road-going MGA, and the fuel filler protruded through the boot lid. To reduce wind resistance the full-width windscreen was not fitted, and to help shield the driver from the weather the cars had Perspex air deflectors, a metal cover over the passenger seat and a raised edge to the driver's side of the cockpit. An aluminium shield below the chassis helped smooth the airflow under the car.

The story of the 1955 Mercedes accident opposite the pits has been told so often that no further reference need be made here, save to say that the adverse publicity around the resultant death toll reduced the effectiveness of the efforts to promote the forthcoming new MG. Understandably, most popular papers were full of stories about the horrific accident and it was left to the motoring press to cover other aspects of the race. MG had secured two firm entries and one reserve in the race. They were pretty certain of having three cars running and thus took four MGA prototypes with them; one a practice car that could also served as a reserve in case of difficulties with any of the other cars. The drivers were Dick Jacobs, Joe Flynn, Johnny Lockett, Ken Miles, Ted Lund and Hans Waeffler. Marcus Chambers ran the team, with John and Joanne Thornley and Le Mans veteran Sammy Davis in attendance.

The Le Mans cars had been previously tested at Silverstone but conditions there were not the same as those encountered at the French circuit, which incorporated ordinary roads and where the Mulsanne straight saw cars running at maximum speed for a far longer period than on

One of the Le Mans cars was taken to Silverstone for a track test prior to the race.

the Northamptonshire circuit. As it happened, all the calculations of performance proved correct and maximum speeds approaching 120mph were recorded. The target of an overall average speed of around 80mph seemed achievable.

The race started well, all three MGs leaving the grid without any last-minute dramas. In the first couple of hours the MG drivers settled down to lap steadily well within their prescribed times. Ted Lund led in car 64, with Johnny Lockett in 41 just ahead of Dick Jacobs in 42. The big accident happened when the race was just over two hours old and the MGs were due to make their pit stops. About the same time the Dick Jacobs car was involved in an accident at White House corner, although the exact nature of this and the condition of the driver was not relayed to the anxious crew in the pits. At the end of their first stint at the wheel, the other two drivers came in for their routine pit stops and were relieved by Ken Miles and Hans Waeffler.

News of the fate of Dick Jacobs eventually filtered through the general confusion in the aftermath of the big accident and the team, including Dick's wife, learned that he had been injured and taken to hospital. His condition worsened over the next few days and in the end BMC flew a medical team to France and brought him home for treatment. Although he made a full recovery and was to continue to play a vital part in MGs competition efforts, he was never to race again.

The other two cars continued to circulate at steady speeds, Ken Miles posting the fastest lap at an average of 94mph and recording 117.39mph on the Mulsanne straight. In the early hours of Sunday morning Ted Lund had a minor accident at Arnage, denting a front wing against the tail of a Jaguar stranded in the sand. The damaged metal was soon straightened in the pits, but this caused a delay of six minutes, dropping the second car even further behind the Miles/Lockett MG.

Heavy rain arrived for the final hours of the race,

Ken Wharton at the wheel of the test Le Mans car at Silverstone.

The four EX 182 MGA prototypes prior to the 1955 Le Mans. One was taken as a spare practice car.

turning much of the area behind the pits into a quagmire and adding to the general air of gloom. For many, the excitement and sport had gone from the event and the Mercedes team had withdrawn as a mark of respect for the dead. The general desire amongst those still in the running was to get the job done so they could go home. A high point for the MG camp came when both cars had completed their minimum number of laps and looked set fair to finish the race. The Miles/Lockett car, in particular, was doing very well and holding 12th place ahead of more powerful machinery.

When the chequered flag fell at exactly 4pm, it was actually Ted Lund in 17th place who was first over the line. The other MG was still 12th and had it not been for the accident to Dick Jacobs's car, and the horrific Mercedes crash, this could have been a cause for real celebration of MG's return to front-line factory-supported racing. As it was, the cars themselves had stood up well and no significant flaws in the design had been exposed. This augured well for the production MGA when it finally arrived.

The three cars lined up in front of the pits prior to the start of the race.

The sad remains of the car in which Dick Jacobs crashed and was seriously injured.

THE MGA

The hood and side curtains used for the 1500 owed much to previous MG practice. Despite the provision of flashing indicators, there were flaps to allow the driver to make the hand signals stipulated at the time in the Highway Code.

It is interesting to recall just how dominant Britain used to be in the world sports car market during the 1950s and 1960s. Others built good sports cars, notably Italy and Germany, but at that time they produced nothing like the volumes coming from Aston Martin, Jaguar, Austin-Healey, Triumph and, of course, MG. The MG T-types had led the demand for sports cars in the best export market, the United States. These later faced competition from the Triumph TR range and the other BMC sports car, the Austin-Healey. Those with deeper pockets bought Jaguars and Aston Martins or, from Germany, the Porsche 356 and the Mercedes-Benz 190 and 300SL.

When the outdated T-type MGs were replaced late in 1955 by the MGA the new car had to be identified in the mind of the buying public as being modern, whilst drawing heavily on the sporting heritage of the earlier cars. Selecting a name for the model posed a bit of a problem as with the ZA saloon launched the previous year the MG Car Company had arrived at the end of the alphabet and had to cast around for an alternative model designation. The answer was to start over again and call the new car the MG Series MGA.

On the 22 September 1955 the new MG was announced to the public. *The Autocar* test team had already been let loose on a production car and their road test report made the point that the racing and record breaking activities of the MG Car Company had helped development of the cars, and that the differences between the Le Mans car they had driven earlier and the production car were small. The testers were impressed by near-100mph performance, which they thought commendable for a car with a full load on board. Interestingly the highest speed recorded, 99mph, was achieved with the hood and sides curtains in place and was some 3mph faster that reached by the same car fitted with the optional low racing screen and with a tonneau

The MGA 1500 rolling chassis. The car was assembled to this stage prior to having the body fitted. This gave the easiest access for the assembly line workers to all the mechanical components.

cover over the passenger side of the cockpit.

Public reaction to the new car was equally enthusiastic. Some, of course, bemoaned the scrapping of the familiar MG style but few of them would have passed up the opportunity of changing to one of the new cars had they been able to afford it. To enthusiasts the car had, indeed still has, almost universal appeal. The attractive cockpit layout features low-set, comfortable leather-covered seats and the large steering wheel is so placed as to make most drivers feel immediately at home. The short gear lever has a precise action that encourages frequent use and the haphazard arrangement of dials and switches on the painted dashboard soon becomes familiar. Even the dated dashboard-mounted horn button is easily reached from the steering wheel, as is the switch for the self-cancelling flashing indicators. Legroom is adequate for all but the tallest drivers and the high cockpit sides give weather protection not available on the earlier cars with cut-away tops to the doors. When the side curtains are removed the chrome-plated windscreen support bracket provides a useful grab handle for the passenger.

The attractive cockpit of an early MGA 1500. Note that the speedometer was calibrated in 20mph increments; these changed to 10mph when revised instruments were introduced.

To help sell the car the advertising department came up with the slogan "First of a new line, the completely new MG Series MGA" for the sales brochures and magazine advertisements placed in both the motoring magazines and in newspapers here and abroad. The lucky buyers in 1955 had a full range of attractive colours from which to choose and the MGA was available with wire wheels. These were almost invariably chosen for cars exported to America and white sidewall tyres could also be specified. There was quite a long list of extra equipment on offer, of which some was factory fitted and some installed by the dealer. Factory equipment included a lower ratio 4.55:1 back axle for competition work, adjustable telescopic steering column, heater or fresh air ventilator and heavy-duty Dunlop Road-Speed tyres.

The MGA quickly gained widespread acceptance and production increased from just over 1000 cars in the last few months of 1955 to over 13,000 in 1956 and more than 20,000 in 1957. In 1956 the factory listed as an optional extra a hard top, and this came with aluminium-framed side-screens that had sliding Perspex windows, which were not available for the soft-top car. In September 1956, one year after the first car appeared, a coupé version was announced. This very pretty car had an integral steel roof incorporating a wrap-around rear window and a larger and more curved windscreen. The doors were completely redesigned and featured winding side windows and swivelling quarter-lights. The doors were now lockable and had particularly neat exterior door handles that, when the door was closed, rested on rubbers set into the window frame. The designers couldn't bring themselves to spoil the good lines of the exterior of the MGA by adding conventional handles.

The interior of the coupé was more luxuriously trimmed. It had a Rexine covered dashboard and a neat map pocket in the passenger footwell. The roof had a headlining and the entire floor area, even the rear bulkhead and shelf, was carpeted. The motoring press welcomed the new body style and found that, in spite of a slight increase in weight of about 32lb, the top speed was higher. The MGA 1500 Coupé was a genuine 100mph car.

Competition from other sports cars was strong: in 1954 Triumph had introduced the TR2, which was faster than the Abingdon car and benefited from overdrive, but had less predictable handling and awful scuttle shake on poor surfaces. Nevertheless it was a tough car, very popular in overseas markets, and in 1957 Triumph increased the power of the engine and fitted disc brakes to the front wheels, a first for a lower-priced sports car. To compete, it was time for MG to make changes to the MGA.

Although the standard MGA 1500 was the main focus of attention, ever since its launch plans had been in the making for a higher-performance model. Prototypes of two different versions of twin overhead camshaft B-series engines had been tested, and successful record attempts at Utah in August 1957 with EX181 fitted with a very powerful DOHC 1500cc engine demonstrated potential. Following this, the MGA Twin Cam, with a 1600cc version of the engine, was announced as a production car in July 1958. The modifications for the new model were mostly mechanical and the body design appeared almost unchanged, although there were a number of not immediately apparent detail changes to the metalwork.

"Twin Cam" badges on the boot lid and alongside the scuttle vents plus standard centre-lock Dunlop steel wheels identified the performance model. These wheels hid the other main distinguishing feature of a Twin Cam, the replacement of the standard Lockheed drum brakes by the Dunlop all-disc set-up similar to that fitted at the time by Jaguar to their sports cars. The cockpit received a Rexine-covered dashboard, a different speedometer and tachometer, and there was also the option of more heavily padded competition seats. It is a popular misconception that all Twin Cams had these, whereas at first very few were so equipped. To add to the usual long list of extras offered for the standard cars, the Twin Cam also was available with an oil cooler and close-ratio gearbox, as well as the 4.55:1 rear axle ratio also available on the pushrod car.

Road tests of the Twin Cam published in the contemporary motoring magazines recorded a top speed of 115mph, which was quick in 1958 for a production sports car of such small capacity. With the engine producing 50% more power than the standard 1500 unit, acceleration to 70mph improved from 21.4 seconds to 12.3 seconds. However, in addition to the price increase of £180, the extra performance came at a cost, as testers

The phrase "First of a New Line" was used in advertisements to emphasise the fact that this was an MG for the modern age.

A superb original example of a late MGA 1500 roadster.

The cockpit of an MGA 1500 with the revised instrumentation found on later models. The leather seat covers are the original ones supplied when the car was new.

A restored MGA 1500 roadster. Wire wheels were a popular option when the cars were new.

found the car noisier than the standard car and with a greater thirst for oil.

Despite being better suited to those wanting a car for competition, many examples were sold to buyers who were just looking for something different, and these cars were often used for commuting in traffic without regard to the highly tuned nature of the power unit. Numerous engine failures resulted, and some cars were even given pushrod units under guarantee. Later modifications

The rear view of this MGA 1500 in Glacier Blue shows to good effect the attractive lines of the model.

Aside from the wheels and badges, there is nothing externally to indicate that this is the Twin Cam version of the MGA.

to the engine design, which should have been incorporated from the outset, improved matters, but not before the reputation of the Twin Cam had been sullied and the standing of MGs in general damaged. Small wonder then that the model was discontinued after a couple of years, although spare sets of Dunlop brakes and wheels were later used to produce the rare MGA de luxe models.

In 1959 the pushrod MGA received an update. The Twin Cam used a larger-capacity, 1588cc engine, achieved by increasing the bore from 73 to 75mm. This change was carried over to the pushrod car, raising the power by 7.5bhp and the torque by 12%. As the axle and gear ratios were unchanged this gave a welcome boost to the performance. *The Autocar* road test team recorded a 0-60 time of 14.2secs and rival *The Motor* 13.3secs. Both magazines recorded a top speed in excess of the magic 100mph.

By 1959 disc brakes were becoming generally available on sports cars. Triumph had them on the TR2 and the recently announced Sunbeam Alpine was also so equipped, as well as showing the way for future sports cars with its wind-up windows

This three-quarter rear view of the MGA 1500 coupé illustrates well its attractive appearance and the wrap-around rear window used for this popular model.

and comfortable cockpit. MG had to respond, and Lockheed front disc brakes became standard equipment on the new MGA 1600. Retaining drums for the rear wheels avoided having a more complicated arrangement for the handbrake.

Externally the 1600 differed little from the 1500 it replaced. Changes in legislation, outlawing the previous system of interrupting the brake light circuit to flash the rear lamps as turn indicators, forced the company to fit separate amber flashers at the rear and to provide an amber segment in the front side lights. At the back the existing style of brake/side lights were mounted on a plinth below the new amber flashers. The bodywork had "1600" badges on the boot lid and scuttle in the same positions as those occupied by the "Twin Cam" badges on the high-performance model.

Some new colour schemes were adopted and at the same time the side-screens were changed to incorporate sliding windows. These were similar to those already offered to buyers of the detachable hardtop, but were fabric-covered to match the hood rather than having polished aluminium frames. When the 1600 model was announced, the Twin Cam was still in production and the later cars received the external changes to colours, trim and lighting introduced on the pushrod cars. Incidentally, when the Twin Cam was introduced the bonnet had to be modified to clear the slightly bulkier engine and in due course all MGAs were

Aside from the Rexine covering to the panel, the Twin Cam dashboard was same as used for the MGA 1500 pushrod cars. However, the tachometer and speedometer were recalibrated. This car has the de luxe competition seats that were available as an extra on both the Twin Cam and later on the pushrod cars.

The impressive power unit in the Twin Cam is a tight fit and access to some components is far more difficult than on the standard cars.

fitted with this altered version.

The MGA Coupé launched in 1956 had proved popular and all the changes introduced for the 1600 roadster were also included in the coupé version. In addition the spare wheel was repositioned. On the 1500 it had been mounted as on the roadster with part of it protruding into the cabin. As a consequence there was little room to store anything much behind the seats. On the 1600 the wheel was stowed entirely within the boot and the shelf below the window was cut back far enough to allow a suitcase to be stowed there. This welcome change

The 1600 roadster featured here is fitted with the optional luggage rack, an essential piece of kit if serious touring was contemplated.

An MGA coupé finished in Dove Grey, a colour introduced with the 1600 model.

gave a little more room to store luggage but anyone contemplating serious touring usually fitted the optional luggage rack.

The improvements helped, and in 1959 over 23,000 MGAs were sold, the greatest number for any single year. In the following year there was a recession and the total sold fell to just below 17,000. At Abingdon, planning for an entirely new model was in the early stages, as cars like the Sunbeam Alpine were proving increasingly popular and Triumph were poised to introduce the much improved TR4 at the 1961 Motor Show.

The coupé version of the Twin Cam is a rarity, only 323 of the 2111 cars built leaving the factory in this form. Of those just 150 were for the home market.

Like a great many MGAs this 1600 Coupé has been fitted with a luggage rack to supplement the meagre space in the boot.

The writing was on the wall for the MGA and its days were obviously numbered. As a stopgap, whilst a completely new car was designed, in June 1961 Abingdon introduced the final version, the 1600 Mark II.

The most significant external changes were to the lights and grille. Light clusters from the BMC Mini were mounted on plinths on the rear panel, rather than as previously on the wings. Changes to the grille saw the vertical slats recessed at the bottom so that they were more upright, and "1600 Mk II" badges were now fitted. In the cockpit the

Cutting back the rear deck of the 1600 Coupé and placing the spare wheel entirely within the boot liberated room to carry a suitcase.

The 1600 Mark II was given a revised radiator grille in an effort to update the design. Some enthusiasts dislike this, although few would disagree that the more powerful engine and raised rear axle ratio introduced with this model were worthwhile changes.

The cabin of a 1600 Coupé. The pattern of the fluting on the leather seats in the closed cars differed from that used on the roadsters.

In many ways the Mark II MGA is the best model. Unlike other cars, the MGA did not put on weight or add ornamentation during the production run and the final version was faster and stopped better than the first cars off the line. Unfortunately, there were only 8719 built.

The engine bay of the 1600 Mark ll.

dashboard was fabric-covered, as on the Twin Cam, and the top of the scuttle was also given a Rexine cover to remove reflections in the windscreen on light-coloured cars. Although these were small changes, the cockpit looked much the better for them.

However, the most important changes were hidden from view. The engine capacity was increased from 1588cc to 1622cc and a substantial redesign gave wider main bearings and a stronger crankshaft. Pistons and con-rods were altered, as was the cylinder head. Much work was carried out reshaping the combustion chambers and the valve sizes were increased. The effect of those substantial changes was to raise the power output to 90bhp at 5500rpm, which compares favourably with the Twin Cam's output of 107bhp at the higher engine speed of 6500rpm. Later Twin Cams with lower compression had their power output reduced to 100bhp so the Mark II was potentially almost as fast in normal driving, where you used low-down torque rather than the ultimate power available at high engine speeds.

However, the adoption of a higher axle ratio of 4.1:1 for the Mark II meant that acceleration was not quite as quick as the extra power would suggest. In its favour, the higher ratio did give more relaxed cruising at motorway speeds and was certainly recommended for travelling long distances. The last MGA was in many ways the best of the bunch, and that is not true of many other cars where progressive changes dilute the purity of the original concept.

The 1600 Mark II Coupé is a pretty car and although for hot climates the ventilation is not up to modern standards it is quite at home in the average British summer.

The wrap-around rear window used for the MGA Coupé was a 1950s feature that gives the cockpit a light, airy feel.

MGAs AT SEBRING

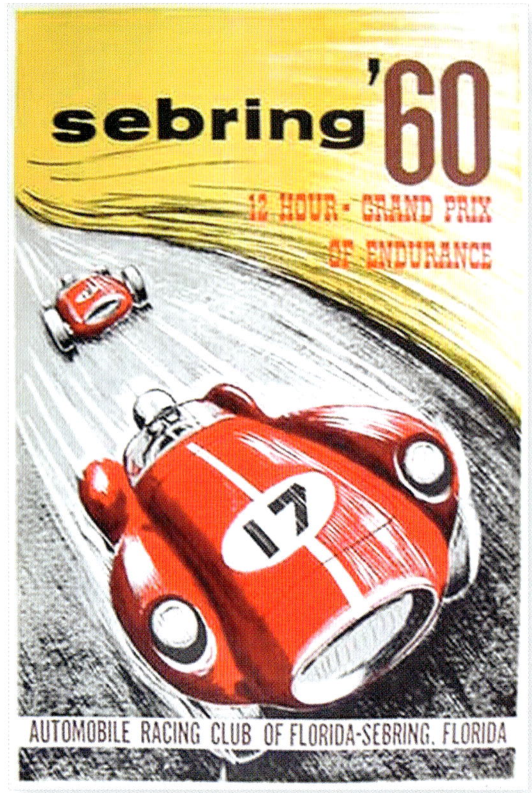

The MGA launched in 1955 proved to be a sales success in the important North American market. Of the total MGA production of 101,081 cars, 81,401 went to North America, nearly 81%. Accepting that the market was important, it is not surprising that the British Motor Corporation were keen to support any efforts to promote the MG marque in America. Record attempts were one route, the other was sports car racing. The growth of interest in road racing in post-war America was fuelled by the availability of sports cars like the MG, and without them the grids for many events in the 1950s would have been pretty thin. Racing circuits in America varied from ones that used public roads closed to ordinary traffic, to tracks specially constructed for the purpose. Some venues, like Watkins Glen, started out as a road race and in later years moved to a specially built circuit. Others, as in Britain, used airfield perimeter tracks. The most important of the latter for the MG story was Sebring.

Alec Ulmann, who had been the manager of the Briggs Cunningham team at Le Mans in 1950, wanted to run endurance races for production sports cars in America. He promoted the first Sebring Grand Prix of Endurance in December 1950 as the Sam Collier Memorial Race. This six-hour event started at 3pm and ended in the dark. Like Le Mans, tools and spares had to be carried in the cars and fuel, oil and tyres could only be obtained at the pits. Only the driver and one mechanic were permitted to work on each car.

That first race was deemed to have been a success and MGs figured well in both overall and class

After being built at Abingdon, the three cars for the 1960 race were taken to Silverstone for testing. Here with two of the MGAs are drivers Ted Lund and Colin Escott.

results. A second Sebring Endurance event was run in March 1952; it was the first long-distance race in America to gain F.I.A. approval. The endurance aspect was greater as cars now had to run for 12 gruelling hours on the bumpy track. The course had been lengthened to 5.2 miles by using a larger proportion of the existing runways and service roads on the airbase. Once again MGs acquitted themselves well. The MG special driven by David Ash and John Van Driel took fourth place overall, and TDs were placed second and third in class, gaining the team prize.

For competitors, Sebring at that time had a number of disadvantages. Firstly, the course was situated in a not particularly attractive part of South Florida and in an area where it could rain heavily. Secondly, it was laid out on wide expanses of concrete that may have seemed relatively flat to B17 bombers but proved very bumpy at racing speeds in tautly-sprung sports cars. Also, the course was marked out in part with oil drums or cones, and in poor visibility, for example in heavy rain or as darkness fell, drivers could become disorientated and miss braking points. On the credit side, however, was the sheer enthusiasm of the organisers and the excitement generated in the area by the recognition of Sebring as an international event.

Sebring was now established as a fixture in the sporting calendar, and 1953 saw the third meeting, with yet another good result for MGs. Although never able to challenge for outright honours when pitted against far faster machinery, MG participation was still important. The Cunningham of Fitch and Walters, with its large-capacity American engine, took first place overall. TDs were second, third and fourth in class. 1954 and 1955 saw the event continuing in a similar format but the T-series MGs were becoming increasingly outclassed. MG-powered specials were still competitive in the lower-capacity classes, but there was now little chance of standard models gaining much recognition.

Being aware of the importance on that side of the Atlantic of the Sebring race meeting, three North American MG importers each entered a standard MGA for the 1956 event. Down to run as a team, the cars were stripped, carefully prepared, and fitted with aero-screens and straight-through exhaust systems. The cars ran well and finished in fourth, fifth and sixth places in class. That year they were up against much faster Porsche 356s and could not have been expected to beat them.

The following year the same three BMC importers again sponsored the entry of a team of MGAs. They repeated the previous year's success by taking the team prize and, as a bonus, gaining first and second places in their class. However, the MGs were not the only cars sold in America by BMC. Austin-Healey was an important marque for the company and the competition effort with the then current model, the 100/6, was in the hands of the Donald Healey Motor Company of Warwick. Unfortunately, the experimental engines supplied for the three cars had a con-rod weakness and two of them failed to finish the race.

For the 1961 Sebring two MGA 1600 Coupés were prepared. One had a British crew, Peter Riley, in the front, and John Whitmore, right. Bobby Oltoff, left, went as reserve driver and mechanic.

In 1958 the higher-performance twin cam MGA had been announced but there were no officially supported MG entries for Sebring that year. For 1959 the Competition Department at Abingdon prepared three MGA Twin Cam coupés to run in the Florida race. Supported by a fourth practice car and a mass of spares, they were shipped to America through the United States MG concessionaires, the Hambro Corporation. The team of amateur drivers was under the control of Marcus Chambers, but all them had been chosen locally as had the mechanics, and they were allocated to drive the cars on the basis of the volume of sales achieved by the dealer in their area of the country. Seems strange, but one has to remember that a large measure of the finance for the venture was coming from the dealers and their motivation was local publicity, and thus more cars sold.

That year the weather played a large part in

the proceedings. A contemporary report said that the event was nearly rained off and, had the same conditions prevailed at any other American club race, everyone concerned would have packed up and gone home. Nevertheless, those who braved the elements witnessed an array of the world's finest racing sports cars. Ferrari sent a team of their new disc-braked 3-litre cars, Porsche a pair of the impressively fast RSK models and a Carrera coupé, in addition to the privately-entered Porsches, and Briggs Cunningham turned up with three of the exceedingly quick Lister-Jaguars.

The MG team had mixed fortunes. The MGA Twin Cams had problems in practice and engine revs had to be limited. In addition, temperatures in the closed cockpits were high and additional ventilation holes were needed. In the race these provided an efficient means of filling the cockpits with rainwater. The race started in sunshine but after about four hours the skies filled with dark clouds and the rain came down in earnest. Some parts of the track were hub-deep with water and one of the MGAs managed to tangle with the marker cones and returned to the pits with two of them jammed under the wheelarches. Competitors in the faster cars saw their laps times increase as they negotiated their way round the larger puddles and dodged displaced cones.

All the MGs made the finish and, whilst they were not as fast as promised by their advanced specification, put up a credible performance. The highest-placed was the car driven by Gus Ehrman and Ray Saidel, which took second place in the 1300cc to 1600cc class, while the Jim Parkinson/John Dalton car was third. The final MGA had some mechanical problem but struggled on to qualify as a finisher, albeit in 30th place overall.

1960 was the second year of participation by the Abingdon-based Competitions Department and, once again, it was three MGA Twin Cams that provided the MG element in the team. This time there were drivers from America and Canada for two of the cars, whilst experienced English racers Ted Lund and Colin Escott drove the third car. In the race the MGs did not fare well. The car with the British crew suffered valve gear problems and retired, whilst the other cars had repeated fractures of their brake pipes that lost them a considerable amount of time. This was attributed to the bumpy track, but it is also possible that the pipes themselves may have been at fault. The two MGAs running at the finish were placed third and fourth in class.

The following year Abingdon built two MGA 1600 coupés for the Florida race. Jim Parkinson and Jack Flaherty, the Americans who had driven the MGs in previous years, joined Peter Riley and Sir John Whitmore from England. South African Bob Olthoff went with them as reserve driver and mechanic. He was working at Abingdon at that time and had gained considerable experience racing his own twin cam MGA. The 1961 event proved to be a Ferrari benefit. The sports-racing Ferraris had been fitted with rear fins in an early effort to increase down-force and they took seven of the first 10 places overall. The MGA coupés ran in the Grand Touring category and were placed first and second in class. A good result that saw the MGs beat the Elvas and Sunbeam Alpines that were running in the same class.

1962 was the last year the factory-entered MGAs were to race at Sebring as in September that year the model was replaced by the MGB. Stuart Turner had taken over running the Competition Department in September 1961 and the major preoccupation was with rallying, where the Mini-Cooper enjoyed a run of competition successes. Nevertheless, time was found to prepare a team of three MGA 1600 coupés for the Sebring 12-hour race in March. Jim Parkinson and Jack Flaherty from America drove one car, joined that year in the other two cars by Sir John Whitmore and Bob Olthoff, Jack Sears and Andrew Hedges. The MGAs ran well and, whilst they did not win any awards, they finished in 16th, 17th and 20th places overall.

The 1962 team of MGA 1600 Mark II De Luxe Coupés at Sebring. This was the last time that an MGA team would run at this airfield circuit.

This historic MG is carrying the 1960 Sebring race number with red, white and blue flash on the front of the bonnet. The lamp on the top of the hardtop is for the pit crew to identify their car as it passes in the dark. Amazingly the car has remained almost exactly as it was in 1960.

Of course, cars raced without the weighty standard bumpers, but for night running they had extra spot lamps.

RECORD BREAKER EX181

Although in 1954 and 1956 EX179 had successfully established some new records at speeds up to 170mph, it was clear that it was at the limit of its potential and a new car was needed if higher speeds were to be achieved. To catch the headlines they would need to set a difficult target and an obvious one was 250mph or, failing that, to break the four-miles-a-minute barrier of 240mph. MGs chief designer, Syd Enever, calculated that to achieve this with EX179 would require power beyond the reach of any current MG engine, however highly tuned. A new approach was needed.

EX181 was revealed to the press for the first time at Abingdon in May 1957. As yet it was unpainted.

MG already held the 1500cc mile and kilometre records at speeds of over 200mph, set 18 years earlier with EX135, and it was surprising that in the intervening years nobody had mounted a challenge. To gain the maximum benefit from any publicity generated the power had to come from a currently available production unit, and with the MGA Twin Cam set for a future launch, the engine from that model was an obvious choice. It had been used for the 1956 runs with EX179 and had proved capable of sustained high speeds over distances up to 2000km. Given a car with less wind resistance there was every reason to hope they could achieve their target.

When calculating the power needed to achieve a given speed, Syd Enever was able to draw on the results already obtained with the previous record cars. Both EX135 and EX179 had proved to be equally efficient, and the data obtained from previous attempts showed that to propel either through the air at 250mph would require 350hp, more than could be expected to be reliably available from a supercharged 1500cc power unit. The solution would be a substantial reduction in drag, but this would require a far more radical approach than had so far been attempted by MG.

EX135 and EX179 had both been built using as a basis a modified production chassis. Although as much as possible had been done to reduce their frontal area and give them a light and aerodynamically efficient body, this was still a compromise. To build a really effective record-breaker they needed to start from first principles. In other words one first established the ideal size and shape of the car and then designed the machinery to fit, not forgetting to leave some room for the driver. Following wind tunnel experiments using models, a teardrop shape for the body seemed best, so long as it was designed to run as close as possible to the

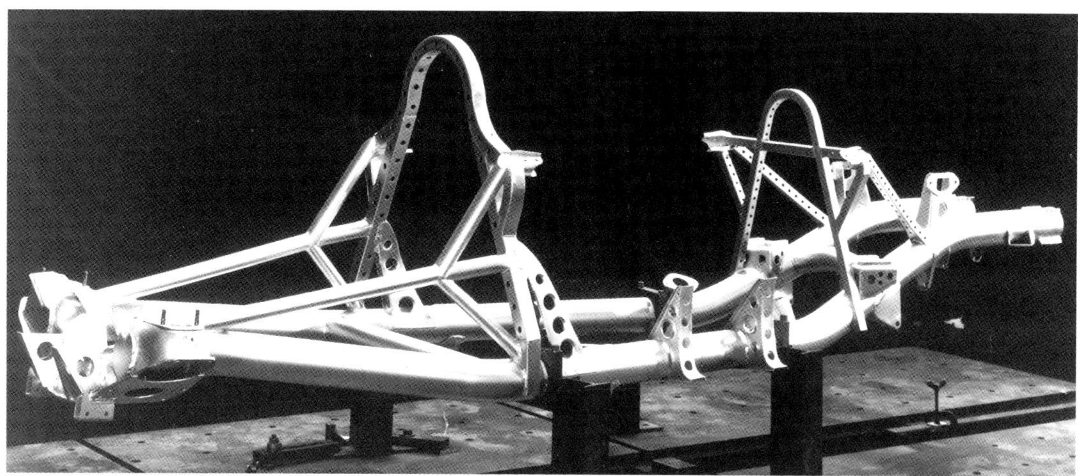

The specially designed chassis built for EX181. The tubular structure was very strong, tested to the full when the car was rolled with little damage some 20 years after it was built.

ground. Very little work had been done on making use of airflow beneath a car at that time. After the earlier runs with EX179 Reid Railton had written to George Eyston saying that for even higher speeds the down-force and lift generated needed to be ascertained in the wind tunnel. He said that the angle of attack of the body to the airflow could be adjusted by raising or lowering the front or rear, thus altering the pressure on front and rear wheels. Too little pressure on the front at high speeds could cause the driver to lose control as the car tried to become airborne.

On record cars tyres had always caused a problem, as they had to be capable of running at high speed and, in Utah, on the abrasive surface of the salt lake. Traditionally they had been made as large a diameter as possible, to reduce the speed of rotation. However, large wheels increased the frontal area of the car, and thus drag. For the new car Dunlop was confident they could produce a tyre for the standard 15-inch steel wheel capable of meeting the stringent requirements. It was now just a case of accommodating these within the vertical height of the teardrop body shape. Incidentally, these special tyres ran at a pressure of 60-65psi.

With EX181 the major departure from previous practice was to place the driver ahead of the engine and transmission. Using a hammock-shaped seat, set between the front wheels right at the nose of the car, meant the overall height could be kept to a minimum. MG used a purpose-built chassis and reduced the rear track to just under 31inches, 11inches less than the front, so as to have sufficient height to keep the rear wheels within the body, which tapered as it neared the tail.

The forward-opening front panel covered the driver snugly in the cockpit and incorporated an aircraft-style Perspex bubble to provide a small amount of forward vision. The cover was usually opened from outside, but internal release levers were provided for emergency use, although air pressure would have prevented it being opened if the car was moving at much more than walking pace.

The frontal area of EX181 was actually only 10% less than that of EX179, but its efficient shape reduced drag by 30%. Taking rolling resistance into account, this meant that it would require 20% less power to reach a given speed than the previous MG record cars. The chosen power unit was the twin overhead camshaft version of the 1500cc BMC B-series power unit, with development in the hands of Eddie Maher at Morris Motors Engines Branch at Coventry.

Chris Shorrock of Shorrock Superchargers had developed a new product for use with large diesel engines and calculated that this would produce

Stirling Moss tries the cockpit for size and suggests a few minor alterations.

The Shorrock supercharger used to provide 30psi of boost to the 1500cc twin-overhead-camshaft B-series engine was originally designed for a 10-litre diesel.

Stirling Moss with EX181 on the Utah salt flats.

30lb of boost at 7000rpm for a 1500cc power unit. Spur gears were added to the front of the crankshaft to provide drive, with alternative ratios available. A couple of engines were built to exacting standards using stronger cylinder blocks and heads, without water passages between these, along with stiffer crankshafts running in larger bearings and many other improvements. All major components were x-rayed to detect flaws. On test the primary and spare power units produced 290bhp and 300bhp respectively, both at 7300rpm.

The arrangements to transport the cars to Utah went smoothly and on Friday 16 August EX179, fitted with a supercharged A-series engine, ran on the circular course for six hours, setting six new international Class G records. That evening it made an additional run over the straight course and took the American national 1000cc record for the flying mile at 143.47mph. On Sunday Phil Hill gave EX181 its first runs. Initially the car, in the hands of Alec Hounslow, was given a tow start and warmed up. Hard plugs were then fitted and Hill took the driving seat with instructions to do a one-way run at 6500rpm. After this he reported poor ventilation in the cockpit so an additional slot was cut to allow in extra air. His second run in the opposite direction used 6600rpm, and although the speeds achieved were not publicised he had obviously broken the existing record of 204.3mph set by Goldie Gardner in 1939.

Unfortunately, before Stirling Moss was able to make the official runs in the car a storm broke out and the salt was flooded. However, the heat of the sun had dried things out sufficiently by the 23 August for him to make the attempt, although conditions were not quite as favourable as they might have been and the ultimate goal of 250mph was out of reach. The runs were not without incident as second gear had started to break up during accelerating for the first run and the second was done without using that ratio. The speeds achieved were nevertheless impressive and set a clutch of new international records, the highest of which was 245.64mph for the flying kilometre. The time allotted had now expired and the team returned home.

That was not the end for EX181. A fresh attempt to beat 250mph was made two years after the first and ultimately achieved its goal. Stirling Moss wasn't available so Phil Hill was the main driver. On 6 September 1959, this time with the engine bored out to 1506cc to take it into the next class, six new records were set at speeds of up to 254.91mph.

There was not a lot of space in the cockpit of EX181 and it was fortunate that Stirling Moss was not too tall.

Prior to going to America it was necessary to give the car a test run. The only space long enough was the runway at USAF Brize Norton.

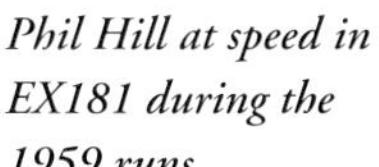

Phil Hill at speed in EX181 during the 1959 runs.

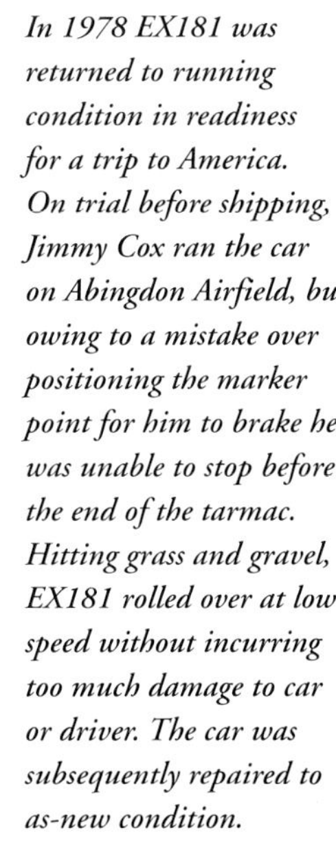

In 1978 EX181 was returned to running condition in readiness for a trip to America. On trial before shipping, Jimmy Cox ran the car on Abingdon Airfield, but owing to a mistake over positioning the marker point for him to brake he was unable to stop before the end of the tarmac. Hitting grass and gravel, EX181 rolled over at low speed without incurring too much damage to car or driver. The car was subsequently repaired to as-new condition.

MG MIDGET – THE REVIVAL OF A FAMOUS NAME

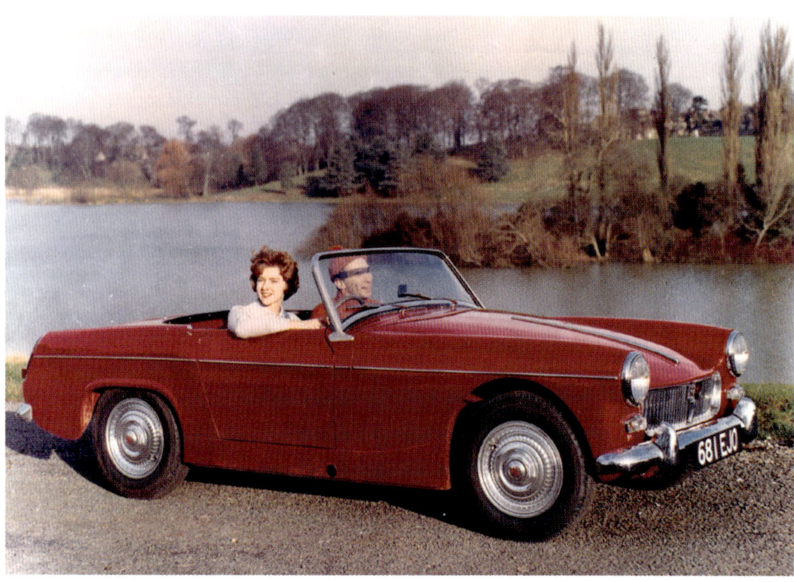

A period colour publicity picture of the Midget Mark I with Ace wheel covers.

Love them or hate them, lightweight small sports cars are at the heart of the MG story. The first was the Morris Minor based M-type Midget launched in 1928, and throughout the1930s and into the early 1950s this model was the best seller in the range. However, with the MGA the Midget designation was dropped; it had become less prominent in advertising the later T-series cars anyway.

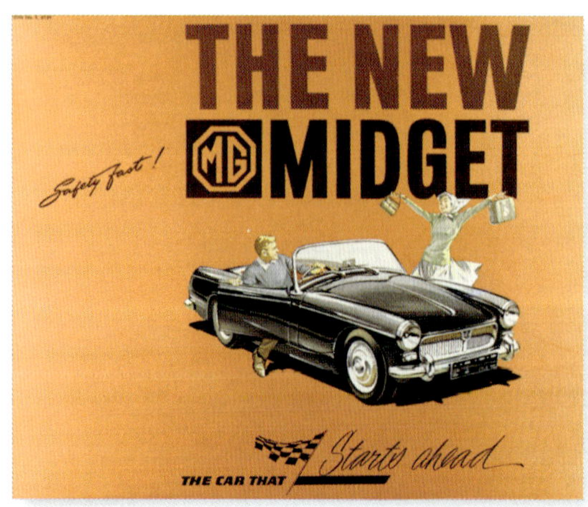

Early 948cc Midget catalogue.

In the late 1950s Britain car sales and public confidence was returning after the traumas of the 1956 Suez Crisis with its consequent petrol shortages. The effects of the crisis were still to be seen in the car showrooms, where many economy cars like the Meadows Frisky, Goggomobil, BMW 600, Isetta and Berkeley Sports were on offer. Mostly powered by motorcycle or scooter engines, these quirky devices were popular among those keen to have more weather protection than was offered by a motorcycle but as yet unable to afford a full-sized car.

At the more affluent end of the market, the sports car enthusiast had a wide choice of mainly British-built products. The Austin-Healey was by then assembled at Abingdon, but in many markets was a direct competitor to the MGA. BMC had now two sports car ranges in competition with each other, although neither the MGA nor the Austin-Healey 100/6 were exactly cheap. With this in mind, during a policy meeting in 1956 attended by Donald Healey and Leonard Lord, the idea of making a smaller and thus less expensive sports car was raised. In response, at their premises in Warwick, Healey started working on a design based around the engine, gearbox and front suspension components from the Austin A35 saloon. By January 1957 a prototype car was ready for assessment by the BMC management and, once approved, work proceeded rapidly to get the car into production.

The chassis and body for the new Austin-Healey Sprite were to be produced as a single unit, with the strength centred on a boxed scuttle structure, deep-section boxed sills and a rigid prop-shaft tunnel. The triumph of the basic chassis design was its light weight and rigidity, which gave the car good performance from engines of modest power output combined with a virtual absence of scuttle shake on bumpy roads.

The original brief for the new car had been to keep it as simple and cheap as possible, perhaps excessively so as some design compromises

Following the criticism levelled at the Mark I Sprite over poor access to the boot, it is not surprising that this publicity picture of the neat arrangement for the new Midget should be sent out to journalists with their press pack.

A view of the cockpit of an early 948cc Midget, complete with ivory-coloured steering wheel.

caused owners considerable inconvenience. The rear section had pleasing rounded lines, but no external access to the luggage compartment was provided. The front wings and bonnet were joined as a single rear-hinged unit which, when raised, gave excellent access to the engine and front suspension. The headlights were set in pods on top of the bonnet. The rear suspension used quarter-elliptic springs that gave the car a firm ride, allied to a small degree of rear-end steering as the axle deflected under weight transfer on corners. Morris Minor rack and pinion steering gear had been adopted, and the result was a car that delighted enthusiasts with its nimble handling and responsiveness to the steering wheel.

Because the Austin plant at Longbridge was in future destined to be fully employed building the Mini, and also because the assembly procedures at Abingdon were more suitable for the Sprite, it was decided that the cars would be built alongside the MGA and the Austin-Healey 100/6. The Development Department at MG were instrumental in preparing the car for production, which in turn meant that the Sprite inherited some Abingdon characteristics and could be said to have become virtually an MG in all but name.

On test, magazines recorded a top speed of just over 80mph and acceleration to 60mph in a tad under 21secs. This modest performance was sufficient to give the Sprite an advantage over the majority of 1950s saloon cars and the new model soon attracted a loyal following. However, there was some criticism of its appearance when the car was launched, and many complaints about the lack of external access to the luggage compartment. The heavy front section was also not universally popular and quite an industry developed producing replacement bonnet sections in fibreglass with the headlights faired into the wings in a more conventional manner. One advantage these had was the ability to mount them so that they opened forwards, which aided access to the engine and battery.

A number of tuning companies were supplying parts and services to those wanting rather more performance than was available from the standard product. Firms such as Powerplus and Alexander Auto and Marine were already established A-series engine tuners, and the Donald Healey Motor Company offered a number of engine and chassis modifications for their creation. The person most

This rear view illustrates clearly the single arm on the boot handle that was a feature of the early cars.

associated with performance Sprites was John Sprinzel, who in 1957 established Speedwell Performance Conversions and later branched out on his own to produce the Sebring Sprite.

The Mark I Sprite was a successful car that must have made quite good profits for BMC. However, the company felt that the lack of exterior access to the luggage compartment was deterring some buyers and that the styling of the front of the car could be improved. To update the design The Healey Motor Company were asked to prepare proposals for new front wings and a separate bonnet. Quite separately, Syd Enever at Abingdon was working on a re-designed tail with an opening boot lid. Luckily both parties met to compare their proposals so that the result would be harmonious.

Few changes were made to the basic structure of the body. The separate front wings and front panels were merely bolted in place and the separate bonnet hinged at the scuttle, using the same hinge points as were employed for the one-piece front section on the earlier car. The revised rear wings and rear decking were welded to the structure in place of the earlier panels and a separate the boot lid was incorporated into the rear deck. Behind the seats the top of the rear panel was cut away to provide more space within the cockpit. BMC adopted a corporate look based around designs by the Italian stylist Pininfarina, and the revised Sprite had small rear fins carrying the taillights, in the style of those already fitted to many cars in the Austin and Morris ranges. As with the Mark I, the new bodies were built by Pressed Steel, primed and painted at Cowley, and then transported to Abingdon for final assembly.

Although the chassis and running gear were identical to the earlier cars, the 948cc A-series engine received some improvements. The compression ratio was raised from 8.3:1 to 9.0:1, although engines with the lower compression were still available to suit some overseas markets. Larger inlet valves and double valve springs were fitted, along with larger twin SU carburettors. The crankshaft was strengthened and the camshaft changed to make best advantage of the larger valves and higher compression. Power output for the revised engine was raised by 4bhp to 46.5bhp. The gearbox received the previously optional close-ratio gears as standard equipment, which made second gear much better for overtaking, the maximum speed available in this ratio rising from 39mph to 48mph.

Although the chassis was unaltered and the stiff quarter-elliptic rear springs were retained, the ride was slightly softer as the greater weight of the revised body reduced the jolting on rough roads. Within the cockpit, the seats, dashboard and trim were little changed, although there were minor revisions to the switches and the rubber floor covering was of a different pattern. The area behind the seats was carpeted. The rails around the cockpit were of polished aluminium, although the section above the dashboard was covered with fabric to match the dashboard. The doors now had a fabric lining, instead of ribbed rubber, and removable aluminium-framed side-screens with a single sliding panel.

The Sprite Mark II, which carried the factory chassis code of H-AN6, was launched in May 1961 and was again greeted warmly by the motoring press. In spite of the increased weight, the more powerful engine and better gear ratios meant that the testers had little difficulty improving upon the performance figures they had recorded for the previous model. As with the Mark I, the car was offered both in basic form and with extras. The deluxe model had a tachometer, windscreen washers, fore-and-aft adjustment of the passenger's seat and full bumpers and over-riders, all for an extra £14. In practice such a large proportion of the cars sold were fitted with all these extras that the basic model was dropped from the price lists.

In spite of the Austin and Nuffield empires having being merged under the British Motor Corporation banner for nine years, in 1961 the dealer networks for sales of Austin-Healeys and MGs were still separated in most markets. The traditional MG dealers had been casting envious eyes at all the Sprites passing through Austin franchises, and it was decided by the BMC management that total sales would benefit from there being an MG version of the Mark II Sprite. Obviously nobody was likely to be fooled into seeing the new model as anything other than badge-engineered, but as the car was largely designed and built at Abingdon it was far more worthy of carrying the MG badge than were the Farina Magnettes built elsewhere and sold as MGs.

Details of the MG version appeared in the press a few weeks after the Austin-Healey launch. Much was made of the revival of the once-famous Midget name with some magazines proclaiming it as the first under 1-litre MG since 1936. The Midget's Mark designations were forever to run one behind those of the Sprite, but it was mechanically identical, with a number of minor external and trim

A beautifully restored 948cc GAN1 Midget fitted with a hard top. (Photo John Davies)

changes to distinguish the cars from one another.

MG owners were apparently felt to be the more affluent as the Midget, which was coded as G-AN1 by the factory, cost £669 15s 10d on the home market against the basic Sprite at £631 10s 10d. As we have said, most Sprites were built to include the extra equipment standardised for the Midget that would have reduced this price gap. For the extra money the buyer of the MG received different pattern seat trim covering more thickly padded seats, carpeting on part of the seat backs, covered cockpit side rails, different floor covering with felt lining, side-screens with two sliding panels instead of one, chrome side strips on the body, bonnet

Cockpit of a GAN1 Midget finished in the attractive colour scheme of Dove Grey with red trim. The carpets in this restored car are of better quality than those fitted when it left the factory. (Photo John Davies)

The 948cc A-series engine in the restored GAN1 Midget. Some improvements made on restoration include moving the fuel pump from above the rear axle to under the bonnet and fitting relays for the LED flashing direction indicators and hazard warning lights. There is also a battery cut-off switch. (Photo John Davies)

centre strip and, of course, the handsome MG radiator grille. The effect was to produce a car that looked a bit different.

The October 1962 Motor Show saw the 948cc Sprite/Midget engine enlarged to 1098cc, giving a welcome increase in power of 8.5bhp. The clutch was bigger by an inch and the gearbox gained much-improved baulk-ring synchromesh, which was being introduced across the BMC range. To answer criticisms made of the braking power, the front drum brakes were replaced by discs, producing a set-up that was to last until the end of Midget production in 1979. The cockpit trim was improved with padded rolls above and below

A restored 1098cc GAN2 Mark I Midget fitted with optional factory hardtop. (Photo John Davies)

Most items needing regular attention are easily accessible, but lifting the battery out can be a bit of a chore. (Photo John Davies)

the dashboard, padded door trims, full carpeting, and more deeply upholstered seats. The Sprite was given all the Midget cockpit refinements whilst retaining the simpler grille and lack of chrome side strips. The new cars were still called Mark I Midgets and Mark II Sprites, but the factory designation for the models changed to G-AN2 for the Midget and H-AN7 for the Sprite.

In December 1962 the pierced wheels carried forward from the earlier cars had given way to stronger unventilated wheels after a number of the earlier type had failed when used in competition. Wire wheels were now an option that was popular with many owners. Although Ace wheel discs

The appeal of the early Mark I Midget is its simplicity. A basic sports car that provided a great deal of enjoyment. (Photo John Davies)

Although the overall dimensions of the Midget place it firmly in the small car category, once you have negotiated the narrow door opening the cockpit is surprisingly roomy. Later cars with thicker seats and the door recesses filled with winding window gear are more cramped. The rear seat was an optional extra only useful for carrying passengers without legs. (Photo John Davies)

were still listed as being available few cars had them fitted and they are seldom seen on restored Midgets. Despite their popularity at the time and the numbers built, the Mark I Midgets in either 948cc or 1098cc guise are now very thin on the ground.

The introduction in 1959 of the Sunbeam Alpine, the TR4 in 1961 and the MGB in 1962 were making the more basic sports cars look outdated. Improvements were needed if the Midget and Sprite were to retain their share of the market, especially overseas. A more direct rival to the revised Sprite and Midget was the Triumph Spitfire, launched at the same 1962 Earls Court Motor Show as the MGB. The success that BMC had enjoyed with their small sports cars in both home and export markets had prompted the Triumph management to produce a contender built to the same formula. The Spitfire used the Triumph Herald chassis, which had independent suspension for the rear wheels as well as for the front. At a time when there was a move away from separate chassis frames for volume sports cars, the adoption of one for the Spitfire was unusual, but nevertheless the car looked thoroughly up-to-date with attractive, Michelotti-designed steel bodywork. Like the Herald the front wings and bonnet lifted up as a unit to give unrivalled access to the engine and front suspension.

1098cc Midget catalogue.

The new Spitfire sold well and it was time for the BMC engineers to come up with improvements for the Sprite and Midget. However, installing winding windows and a door locking mechanism into the small doors was a challenge and the solution the engineers hit upon was to keep the internal door handle with the lock at the rear edge of the door, rather than placing it more conventionally. This obviated the need to have a mechanism to link the

A superb example of a Mark II Midget finished in Riviera Blue.

A restored Mark II Midget. The seats on the earlier examples were the same as those used on the 1098cc Mark I.

door handle with the lock. The doors were made a little thicker at the top by changing their shape to incorporate a fold in the outer skin and a flat top section to accommodate the swivelling quarter lights and give space for the glass and seals.

Internally, the doors lost their useful map pockets and some much-needed elbowroom for driver and passenger, but gained proper door linings and a grab handle. Some effort was made to minimise the loss of elbowroom by incorporating a hollowed out section in the door lining – a feature dispensed with on later models. To replace the door pockets a small oddment shelf was provided above the passenger footwell.

The windscreen design was similar to that used for the MGB and incorporated a strut in the centre that doubled as a mounting for the rear-view mirror. The advantage of this arrangement was that the mirror could be positioned anywhere along the length of the rod to suit individual drivers, although most placed it towards the top of the windscreen. Because of the slightly larger glass area, the wiper

A late 1098cc Mark II Midget in British Racing Green.

blades were increased in length from eight to nine inches. The substantial windscreen top rail had lugs to locate the over-centre catches fitted to the hood. A new hood frame, but still fully detachable, was designed and the hood itself was stowed in the boot when not in use. There was a rigid front section fitted with two catches to mate with the screen, but this made the hood rather less easy to stow than those provided for the earlier cars. However, there is no doubt that the new model had greatly improved comfort for driver and passenger.

When the original Sprite chassis was designed, quarter-elliptic rear springs were chosen as these, with their single-point mountings, seemed to offer the advantages of simplicity and weight saving. However, there were disadvantages with the arrangement and for the latest model rear mountings were provided so that conventional springs could be used. These springs were considerably softer, giving a more comfortable ride, and the better axle location improved handling. Mechanically little changed. In the power unit the crankshaft was stiffened and the main bearing journal diameters were increased. Fitting the MG1100 cylinder head with larger inlet valves and improved gas flow raised output to 59bhp.

Detail from the Mark II brochure.

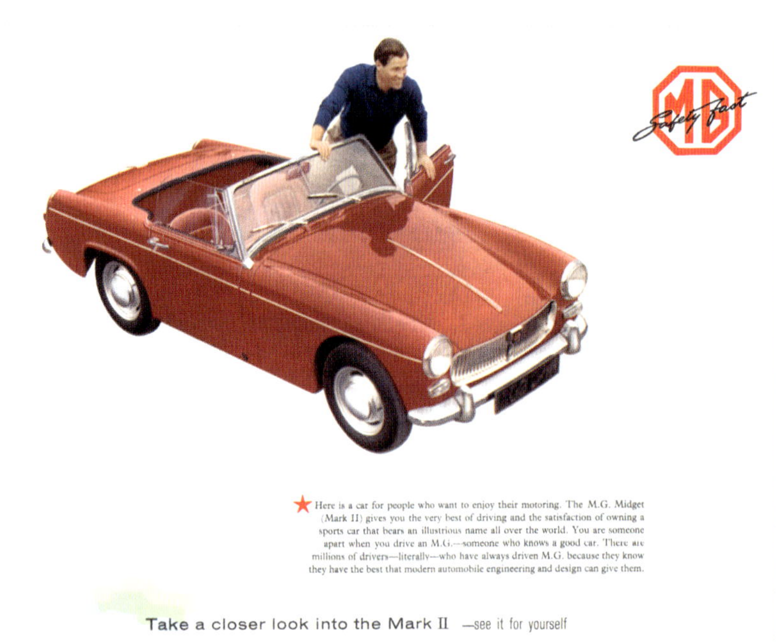

Safety fast
Here is a car for people who want to enjoy their motoring. The M.G. Midget (Mark II) gives you the very best of driving and the satisfaction of owning a sports car that bears an illustrious name all over the world. You are someone apart when you drive an M.G.—someone who knows a good car. There are millions of drivers—literally—who have always driven M.G. because they know they have the best that modern automobile engineering and design can give them.
Take a closer look into the Mark II —see it for yourself

Within the cockpit much had changed. The improved seats introduced in 1962 were retained but the dashboard was completely re-designed. The flat cloth-covered panel, with its randomly arranged set of instruments and controls, had given way to a black crackle-painted steel pressing. The speedometer and tachometer sat in angled housings conveniently placed on either side of the steering column. The fuel gauge and combined water temperature/oil pressure gauge flanked the centrally mounted ignition key/starter switch. At long last the manual switch on the dashboard for the flashing direction indicators had been replaced with a self-cancelling stalk on the steering column. A new steering wheel was similar in style to that used for the MGB.

In August 1965 the seat frames were changed to a pattern like those already in use on the MGB. These seats were a little more comfortable and more generously proportioned. In addition to an anti-roll bar and tonneau cover, extras also included

The 1969 model Midget lost the central chrome strip on the bonnet.

wire wheels, whitewall, heavy duty and Road Speed tyres, laminated windscreen, heater and, by October 1964, a headlamp flasher. One extra was a hard top made of double-skinned fibreglass that, unlike previously, was identical for both MG and Austin-Healey. This was attached to the car using the hood toggle catches at the front and the hood frame fixings at the rear.

The Mark II Midget and Mark III Sprite were to stay in production until late 1966. The success of the rival Triumph Spitfire must have hurt sales, especially in overseas markets like America. The Triumph was consistently outselling the Sprite and Midget, even taking into account combined sales, so there was obviously a need for further efforts to widen the appeal of the BMC product. The Midget and Sprite also faced a challenge from another direction. A new breed of high-performance sporting saloons was starting to emerge in the 1960s. Previously, anyone looking for a performance car automatically turned to one of the many sports cars on the market but now this was changing. Spearheading the change was a revolutionary small car from the same stable as the Midgets and Sprites, the Mini. Although never conceived as a sporting car, or even as a car with performance pretensions, the agility, roadholding and small size of the new model had endeared it to the keen driver. It is now part of motoring legend how John Cooper persuaded the BMC management that building a higher-performance version of their revolutionary small car would make business sense, and how the Mini and Mini-Cooper became the cars to have in the Swinging Sixties.

The growth in popularity of the Mini-Cooper, and of the rival Lotus Cortina, must have been partly at the expense of the traditional sports cars. Many people then, indeed many still do, like to own a car that is something of a wolf in sheep's clothing. There is also the added advantage that a modified saloon has the capacity to carry more than two people and can double as family transport. The competition versions of the Mini, the Cooper S, were available with 970cc, 1071cc and 1275cc engines.

October 1966 saw the announcement of the Mark III Midget and Mark IV Sprite, fitted with a version of the 1275cc engine first used in the performance Mini. This power unit differed in detail from the specialist engines built for the Cooper S, with the cylinder head having smaller valves and the compression ratio reduced from 9.5:1 to 8.8:1. The resulting power output was 65bhp, 11bhp less than the Cooper, but still an increase of 6bhp over the previous 1,098cc engine. Torque was up by 16%.

In addition to the larger engine there were a number of changes from the earlier model. The clutch, for example, was now a diaphragm-spring unit, which was both lighter to use and more powerful, and there were separate brake and clutch master cylinders; these would soon become a necessity in some markets with the introduction of dual-circuit brakes. Much more apparent, however, was the change made to the hood. A new frame had been designed which was permanently bolted to the rear door pillars. The rear deck of the body had been cut back and a raised lip around the edge

The revised bumpers and matt black grille introduced for the 1970 model year were retained for the later 1275cc cars.

of the compartment provided a fixing point for the permanently attached hood fabric. The front rail of the hood was now bolted to the hood frame and this, together with the hood fabric, folded down neatly into the space behind the seats. Once the hood cover was removed, it was a work of moments to clip the front frame to the windscreen, attach the side fasteners and raise the side windows.

The 1969 model year cars saw some alterations to specification. Fully reclining seats were fitted. Externally, the bonnet lost the central chrome strip. The takeover of BMC by Leyland had an effect on MG output, the first appearing on the 1970 model year cars. The Midget lost its chrome side strips and both models gained a chrome strip at the top edge of the sills, which were now painted satin black, with either Midget or Sprite in chrome lettering displayed along them. The radiator grilles for both cars were based on the cheaper-to-produce Sprite grille, which was now painted satin black with a chromed strip set about an inch in from the edge.

In place of the full-length rear bumper, a pair of

The neat overall appearance of the last of the A-series engine Midgets is evident in this overhead shot of a 1973 example.

thinner section bumpers flanked the number plate and at the front one of a lighter section was also used. Over-riders with rubber inserts were used front and rear. The rear light lenses were modified to give a larger lit area. The facelift for the cars was designed at Longbridge, not Abingdon, and the matt black image popular with car designers at the time was initially extended to include the windscreen surround and wiper arms, but luckily these changes were dropped after just a few hundred cars had been built.

To complement the styling changes, the Sprite and Midget were fitted with steel Rostyle wheels instead of the previous ventilated pattern with separate hubcaps. The option of wire wheels was still offered, and a large number of exported cars were so equipped. Bright colours for sports cars were popular at the time so it is not surprising that MG followed suit with a revised list of colours from which to choose. The next major revision was carried out at the end of 1971. The rear wheel arches were rounded off to match the style of the front wings. The result was a more attractive car and these models are now highly regarded.

A useful mechanical change was the adoption of a larger fuel tank, up from six to seven gallons, which improved the car's touring range. In the cockpit, the gear lever knob was made bigger and the dashboard gained rocker switches, which were considered to be safer in the event of an accident. Cars destined for overseas markets, and especially those for North America, received a large number of changes in keeping with local regulations. The dashboards of North American cars differed from those built for the UK market and emission controls meant that engine specifications also varied.

By 1974 the Midget had been in production for 13 years and each successive model had brought welcome changes and improvements. Despite their popularity in their home country, without access to the large American market it is doubtful that the Midget would have remained in production for such a long period and, if it were to continue to be made, then it would have to comply with the ever more stringent safety regulations being introduced there. One of the problems faced when working to meet the new regulations was finding out exactly what the legislators intended when they drew up the rules. Each country, and in America each state, had its own ideas on legislating for car safety. Pressure groups all over the world were trying to force governments to impose restrictions on car builders for a variety of reasons, and within every manufacturing country producers were lobbying to try to limit the effects that any proposed changes would have on their vehicles. As a result, there was a requirement to produce cars with variations to suit each market, a heavy workload for a comparatively small manufacturer like MG

Compared to other producers, the budget available to Abingdon for research and development was small, and any changes made to the basic design of the Midget necessarily had to apply to all cars made, rather than just to those built for one country. The position was eased slightly by a withdrawal from all but the UK and US markets for the bulk of MG production. To comply with the requirements of various clean air acts, for some years all cars built for the American market had been modified to reduce harmful emissions and the requirements were being progressively tightened year by year. As a result, even before the drastic changes introduced for the 1975 model year cars, the vehicles exported to that market differed from those sold elsewhere.

Legislation designed to protect the occupants from injury in the event of an accident had meant that from 1968 US-market MGs were fitted with rocker switches, padded dashboards and seat-mounted head restraints. Minor accident damage resulting from low speed collisions and careless parking was costing insurance companies a lot of money and legislators decided that it should be possible to design cars to be able to withstand these impacts without sustaining any damage at all. For the 1974 model year cars the regulations said that only minor damage should result from such impacts, and to comply the Midget was fitted with large energy-absorbing over-riders. However, for the following year the rules called for there to be absolutely no damage from 5mph collisions, even to items like side lamps, and this was a lot more difficult to achieve.

Faced with such a task, which was worsened by the need for the bumpers to meet a standard height requirement that meant raising the Midget by 1.5 inches, the engineers had to do a lot of work. The monocoque had to be considerably changed to take the additional loads imposed by the heavy rubber faced bumpers mounted front and rear on extensions to the chassis rails. The front units were bolted to box-section stiffeners welded to the main chassis structure and the front panel section was now welded in place, rather than bolted, and the front wings no longer incorporated the sidelight mountings. At the back the bumpers fitted to

One of the very last Midget 1500s built, photographed when it had covered very few miles.

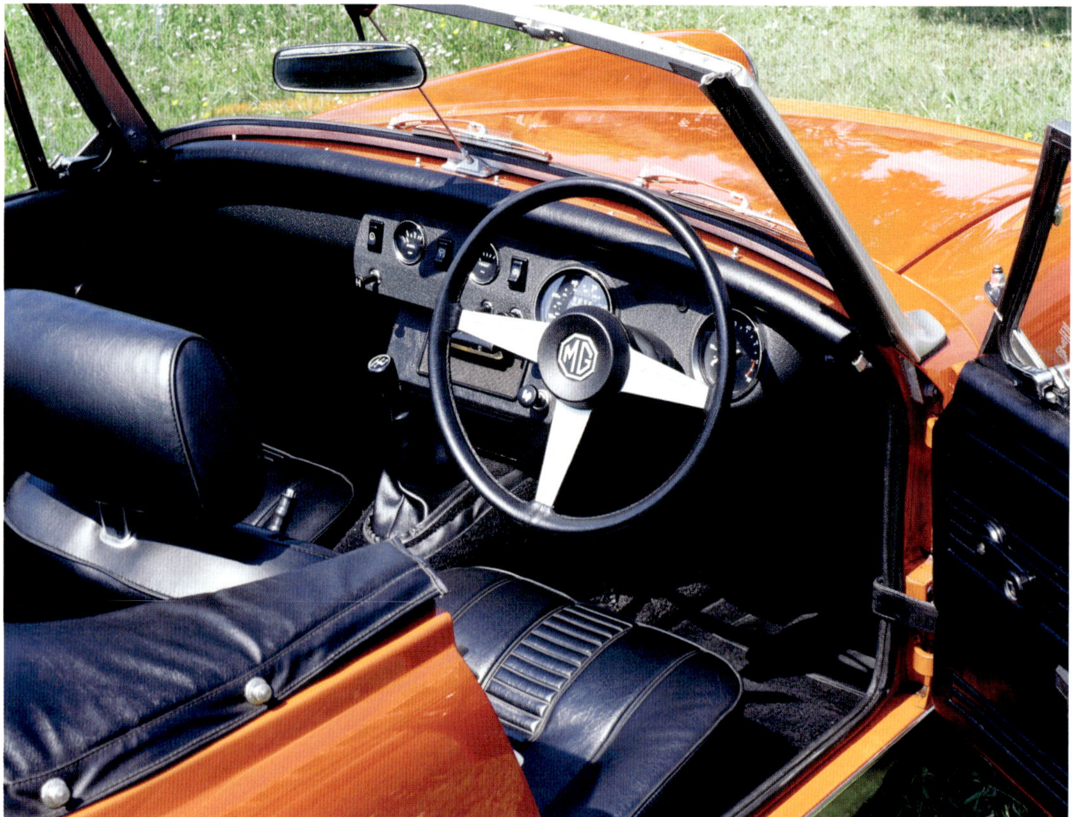

Although the cockpit of the 1500 was little changed from earlier models it was still attractive and one of the features that helped sell the car.

box-section beams welded to the boot floor and the rear panel was modified to accommodate these. The front cross-member was altered to increase the ride height and different springs were fitted front and rear. At the same time the rear wings lost the round wheel-arch used on the later 1275cc cars and reverted to the previous shape.

The chassis modifications and heavy bumpers increased the weight and to help offset this, and also to simplify the spares position for the company and their dealers, the A-series engine and gearbox fitted to all versions of the Sprite/Midget since it was first launched was replaced by the 1500cc engine and gearbox used by then in the Triumph Spitfire. From the driver's point of view it was the increase in ride height that had the worst effect. Both suspension mounting points and spring heights were changed, with the result that the cars rolled more when cornering, and the handling was less predictable

In the Triumph Spitfire 1500 an overdrive unit could be specified, which was a boon on motorways, but Midget drivers had to be content with a standard Marina-based, four-speed gearbox. Unfortunately, at first the 3.9:1 rear axle ratio used on the later 1275cc cars was retained, stressing the Midget 1500 engine at motorway cruising speeds. The Triumph engine had a mechanical fuel pump, like the early Sprites and Midgets, so the hard-to-reach rear-mounted electric pump was dropped, with few regrets.

Inside the cockpit little had changed. The gear lever knob for the all-synchromesh gearbox carried a revised gate pattern, and the accelerator pedal was modified, but the seats and trim were unaltered. Head restraints were still an extra on home-market cars. On the dashboard the choke and heater knobs swapped places, but the instruments were reassuringly familiar and the steering wheel was carried over from the earlier model. Sitting in the driver's seat the car seemed much like the previous Midgets. Out on the road, however, the story was different.

When given a full road test in June 1975 by the respected *Autocar* magazine, the outcome of the many changes made could be seen in the performance figures and in the comments made by the test team. The larger-capacity engine considerably improved the performance figures when measured against those recorded by the same magazine for the previous model. The top speed was up from 94mph to 101mph and the car accelerated from rest to 60mph in 12.3secs. The 1275cc model with the same overall gearing took 14.1secs to reach that speed.

Increasing the ride height and adding large and heavy bumpers to both ends of a small car were never going to do much for the handling and roadholding. In the test the handling limits of the Midget were fully explored and found to be inferior in all respects to the 1275cc model. They commented that the ride was still hard, but they reserved their greatest criticism for the cornering behaviour of the 1500. The steering was still felt to be quick and accurate but the car was far more sensitive and would break away should the throttle be closed suddenly mid-corner.

Midget 1500 brochure.

Although some greeted the revised Midget with alarm, it continued to sell at a similar rate to the superseded model. Now that the Austin-Healey name had been well and truly buried by the British Leyland management, all cars were sold as MGs alongside the rest of the BL range. In August 1977 a number of significant changes were made to the Midget 1500. The car was seriously under-geared for high speed and many engines suffered premature failure as a result. The introduction of a 3.7:1 ratio for the differential from chassis GAN6-200001 was an improvement welcomed by all, and along with this came a number of other changes. Most noticeable to the driver were the new instruments, which were now shared by the Spitfire and MGB. The oil pressure gauge was deleted and a low oil-pressure warning lamp substituted. The horn push was moved to the indicator stalk and the MG badge disappeared from the dashboard. The American market cars also had the revised gearing and instruments and, in addition, an MGB-style steering wheel. Further improvements were made in May 1978 when dual-circuit brakes, two-speed windscreen wipers, radio aerial, cigarette lighter and central console were fitted.

Minor improvements to specification did little to hide the fact that the poor old Midget was nearing the end of the line. In America the cars were still popular but it was necessary to gild the lily by offering specially equipped cars to promote sales. Many Midgets were locally fitted with chromed boot racks and wheel trims, plus decorative side stripes, to be sold as limited editions. Production of the Midget ceased in December 1979, after over 21 years of the Sprite/Midget model, and the last 500 home market cars were painted black, with either black or beige trim; most had a special plaque fitted to the dashboard.

THE ITALIAN SPRITE/MIDGET

Alongside the contemporary Mark I Sprite, one can hardly credit that the Innocenti 950 is almost identical under the skin, the only clues being the wheels and jacking points in the sills.

The BMC Austin-Healey Sprites and later MG Midgets were basic sports cars that sold well despite a distinct lack of creature comforts. This began to be remedied when the Mark III Sprite and Mark II Midget appeared, but just before this a more practical and attractive version of the original Mark I Sprite arrived in some overseas markets. The styling of this car, however, was far more in tune with modern Continental design than the average British sports car of the time – hardly surprising in view of its parentage.

The catalogue produced for the American market.

The Second World War devastated the Italian economy and left much of its industrial base in ruins. Recovery and rebuilding programmes saw a rapid improvement in the situation by the 1950s, but the average Italian worker was still less affluent than his British or American counterpart. To provide them with cheap and economical motorised transport, the innovative Italian designers came up with the idea of making stylish two-wheelers – motor scooters – and one of the leaders in this field was the Milan steel tubing and machine tool manufacturer, Ferdinando Innocenti, who produced the Lambretta.

By the late 1950s, as average wage rates climbed, many moved from motor scooters to four-wheeled transport. Here Fiat, the major indigenous car manufacturer, had established a near-monopoly with their attractive 500 and 600 ranges, which were available in a wide variety of practical body styles. Innocenti wanted access to the car market and had already established links with the British Motor Corporation through the supply of machine tools to Britain. In 1959 a deal saw the British company take a stake in the Italian firm and start to supply them with Farina-designed Austin A40s in kit form. These were assembled in Italy and carried the Innocenti badge. With this arrangement to manufacture the A40 under licence in place, the Italian company wanted to produce a small sports car which could also be sold in the lucrative American market and naturally looked to BMC for help.

Today, platform sharing is commonplace in the motor industry, but in the 1960s this was not so prevalent and the creation of an Italian/British sports Innocenti was therefore seen as innovative. The design of the car was in the hands of Ghia, who gave the job to a young American, Tom Tjaarda, and the body construction was undertaken by OSI. The A40 project had involved the supply from England of all the body panels, as well as the main mechanical components. For the sports car,

From the rear view the attractive shape of the rear wings is particularly pleasing.

however, only the pressings for the chassis, that is the floor pan, transmission, bulkhead panels, and the structural sills, as well as the inner wings, were supplied. They also took the front and rear suspension components, steering gear, wheels, rear axle, engine and gearbox, as well as the entire braking system.

Smart new outer panels hid what was basically a Mark I Sprite. Cleverly, unlike the redesigned British Mark II version that was also built as an MG, the Italian car was from the outset given winding side windows in the doors and an attractive windscreen frame with fixed quarter-lights. The hood they fitted was a masterpiece, being easy to erect, weatherproof and a far cry from the build-it-yourself contraption that lurked in the boot of the early Sprites and Midgets. The real genius of the Italian car is that by moving the front door pillars forward they managed to provide wider doors and a greater feeling of space within the cockpit. Unfortunately, the length of the steering column remained the same, placing the wheel closer to the driver than some would have wished. Also there was even less width in the cockpit to accommodate bulky occupants than in the early versions of the Sprite and Midget, where hollow doors provided some much-needed elbow room.

From the front, opinions vary as to the beauty of the large, Fiat-like grille that sits ahead of the front-hinged bonnet. From some angles it looks just right, from others it seems a bit overstated. One has to admire, however, the way the neat sidelights, and the headlamps, sit below the slightly protruding front edge of the bodywork. Also eye-catching are the rear wings, which were given slightly raised bulges just behind the rear edge of the doors. Accentuated by the chrome strips on the upper edges, the shape of the wings gives the car a hunched, purposeful appearance lacking from the British cars. The chromed side mouldings, too, add greatly to the overall appearance of the car, as do the beautifully made front and rear bumpers. The jacking points in the sills aside, the only external clue to the car's humble Sprite origins is the pierced, disc wheels. Shod with the skinny tyres that were standard equipment, to modern eyes they lack sufficient bulk to fill the wheel arches. The three-pronged Innocenti badges on the hubcaps are a neat touch.

The cockpit is well laid out, featuring a tidy instrument layout and a lockable glove box.

Erecting the hood does not spoil the appearance of this attractive Italian small sports car.

Lift the front-hinged bonnet and the familiar sight of an A-series engine greets you. All Innocenti 950s are fitted with the 948cc Sprite engine in Sprite Mark II tune and thus 1.25-inch carburettors and a 9:1 compression ratio. However, there are few similarities with the British cars when it comes to the ancillary components. Immediately obvious is the placing of the battery at one side of the engine compartment, where it is easily accessible. On the British cars this is hidden behind the heater in a situation difficult to reach beneath the rear-hinged bonnet. Ahead of the battery sits a fuse box with separate fuses for each of the 10 circuits in the special wiring loom. Like the distributor, pre-engaged starter, wiper motor, dynamo with tachometer drive, and the air cleaners, this is an Italian-made item, as are all the lights, fittings like door handles, and the dashboard instruments.

In the cockpit only the central tunnel and cover around the remote control for the gearbox displayed their Sprite origins. The dashboard was set further forward and on the earlier cars the instruments were placed in a separate curved binnacle. On later cars they were mounted on the face of the dashboard, below a crash roll. Useful on any open car is the lockable glove box. Luxury extended to the provision of an interior light built into the rear-view mirror, a combined key/starter switch, self-cancelling indicators, and a light under the bonnet. One had to open the lockable boot lid to reveal a petrol cap neatly inset into the edge of the boot aperture. This arrangement obviated the need for a lock on the filler cap, and also kept the rear panel clear of unnecessary adornment.

One of the later closed versions of the Innocenti Sprite.

The Innocenti sold in comparatively small numbers, and although the specification improved as changes were made to the donor vehicle – disc brakes and larger-capacity engines, for example – it never received the 1275cc unit; possibly the road taxation system in Italy had something to do with this. The 1098cc cars were sold as Innocenti S models, and for America were fitted with over-riders on the bumpers. *Road and Track* tested an example in 1964 and found that it was in many ways a very nice car. However, it cost around $800 more than the Mark III Sprite and, given that it had the same performance, they felt the car was just too expensive. By that time the Sprite had winding windows and the 1098cc engine. In Italy the Innocenti unfortunately earned the reputation of being not quick enough for a sports car. It also used to rust quite badly, even in that climate. The cars were built in small numbers until the late 1960s, with the final examples being fixed-head coupés. For all the open cars an attractive hard top had been available.

THE MAGNETTES MK III AND IV

The Magnette Mark III was an attractive car, combining Italian exterior styling with traditional British interior trim.

When the Magnette Mk III was launched in 1959 the booklet issued by the British Motor Corporation to the salesmen in the MG dealerships around the world listed the Sunbeam Rapier and Standard Ensign as its main rivals. The comparisons of performance figures, price and accommodation quoted placed the MG in a good position in the market, and the company obviously felt that they had produced a car that would sell well.

The competition from other British manufacturers at the time was not all that impressive and, with imports at a low level, the truth was that MG dealers were just as likely to lose sales to rivals selling similar cars BMC cars with Austin badges as to anyone else. The Fords on offer at the time that could possibly steal MG sales were beginning to look a little dated. The Mk II Zephyrs and Zodiacs had good performance and were cheaper to buy and run, but suffered from having a rather flashy image that was likely to deter some customers. Vauxhall were producing their well engineered but heavily stylised Victor, Velox and Cresta models, with acres of chrome and wrap-around windscreens, quite at odds with average British taste. Given the high price of such tasty imports as the Alfa-Romeo Giulietta and Borgward Isabella, there were few real rivals outside the offerings of BMC and Rootes with their two-door Sunbeam Rapier. Well-heeled customers could consider a Rover 80 or 100, or even perhaps a 2.4-litre Jaguar at £1445, but at a total price of a touch over £1000, the MG looked good value.

The prominent rear fins were inherited from a fashion popular on American cars produced in the second half of the 1950s.

Although the responsibility for styling new Austin and Morris models had nominally been in the hands of the respective designers at Cowley and Longbridge, company chairman Leonard Lord exerted a considerable influence over what was eventually produced. Partly in an effort to gain an a measure of independence from the in-house designers, as well as to give the cars a more fashionable look, at the instigation of deputy chairman George Harriman the company

Rear seat passengers have the benefit of a pull-down centre armrest.

commissioned Pinin Farina to act as styling consultant to BMC

The first car exhibiting his influence to emerge from the group was the Austin A40. The A30/A35 Austin was a dumpy little thing that performed well but it was hardly at the forefront of design. The A40, in contrast, looked neat, modern, and had the potential to be a world-beater, given the sort of finishing touches and marketing it really deserved. The two-box shape was way ahead of its time and, had the rear tailgate been made the one-piece lifting unit now so familiar on modern cars, it would have beaten cars like the Renault 16 and VW Golf to that lucrative market. As it was, the rear window was fixed on all but the Countryman version, confining access to the rear compartment to the drop-down boot lid. The pity was that the marketing men did not capitalise on the car's unique shape.

Having produced the design for the A40, Farina's efforts were then directed towards the mid-range models that were so important to the company's survival. He was given the brief to replace the Palmer-designed Wolseley 15/50 and Z-Magnette, the bulbous-looking Morris Oxford, the Austin A55, and to give the Riley buyers an alternative to the rather cramped 1.5 model. The car produced was roomy and modern in appearance, but unfortunately the underpinnings were based around the Austin A55 dimensions rather than on the Morris or Wolseley/MG. This meant that it had a short wheelbase, rather narrow track, and importantly was not fitted with the far superior

Press picture of a Magnette with two-tone paintwork.

The Magnette has comfortable seats and a good driving position. The handbrake is on the right-hand side of the driver's seat.

Chromium plate is much in evidence, with the MG grille an appealing feature.

The is ample room in the engine compartment for the 1500cc B-series engine, which in the Magnette has twin SU carburettors.

rack and pinion steering those cars enjoyed.

The first of the new models to be given publicity was the Wolseley 15/60. The new model incorporated those features thought to be of importance to the traditional Wolseley buyer: illuminated badge on the radiator grille, wooden finish for the dashboard and door trims, and leather upholstery. When the Wolseley was later subjected to a full road test, the vagueness of the steering, over-soft suspension and body roll on corners were commented upon.

The programme to use the same basic car in various guises saw the Austin A55 Cambridge arrive early in 1959. The use of a different grille and external chrome trim changed its appearance considerably. As befitted a lower-priced car, the standard model had a simple interior design with vinyl for the seat coverings, although leather was used in a deluxe version. As part of the muddled thinking that saw virtually the same car being built in two different factories – Austin at Longbridge and Morris at Cowley – there were other changes made to specification that must have increased overall costs. With hindsight, the money would have been much better spent on giving the cars the benefit of rack and pinion steering and an anti-roll bar, as well as sorting out spring rates and damper settings to improve chassis dynamics.

The other variations on the Farina theme made their appearance over the next few months. The Morris Oxford was of a similar specification to the Austin Cambridge. However, as befitted their sporting heritage, the Riley and MG saloons were given added refinements and more power. Of these it was the MG Magnette Mk III that was the first on the scene. It was not clear just how the Mk III title was devised; perhaps the ZA was the Mk l and ZB the Mk ll. The new Magnette was assembled alongside other Farina models, rather than at Abingdon. On the other hand it still carried an MG badge, and anyway the average buyer had probably never even heard of Abingdon.

By late 1959 the Austin Cambridge and Morris Oxford cost £805 and £815 respectively, whilst the MG Magnette was £1012 and Riley 4/68 £1028; a 25% price hike for the extra comfort and performance. Nevertheless, all the Farina models sold well in their early years, most buyers, as always, being more interested in appearance than roadholding. The motoring press were less impressed, however, although outright criticism was muted in an age when motor manufacturers punished magazines seen as too critical of their products by withholding advertising revenue.

With the later Mark III Magnettes and all Mark IVs, the two-tone colour scheme was revised.

Many who were already enthusiastic about the MG marque may well have moved from owning a two-seater sports car to an MG saloon when they had a family to consider. The previous ZA and ZB models, whilst not that rapid, were attractive cars that possessed good handling and many of the characteristics of a sports saloon. Moving over to their replacement the Mark III Magnette may have prompted some to regret the passing of the previous model. *The Autocar* carried out a full road test of the Mk III Magnette in April 1959 and found that performance was slightly down on the ZB they had tested a few years earlier, and that the steering and handling were markedly inferior. When driven as fast as possible round several sharp corners on a test circuit the car suffered from marked roll oversteer.

Sales brochure for the Mark III.

The MG grille enhances the appearance of the Farina Magnettes. The colour scheme now used on the car is not the one it had originally, but is close to one option, Snowberry White and Sandy Beige.

They also expressed surprise that the engine had not been developed to produce more power, rather than less, but generally praised the driving position and creature comforts provided.

The roadholding and steering were compromised by the insistence on basing the new range of cars on the floor pan of the Austin A55. Although a new front suspension assembly had been designed, retaining the narrow track and short wheelbase from the earlier car meant that the wheels were set too far in, and the rear overhang was excessive. In their June 1959 report, *The Motor* testers thought that increasing tyre pressures improved handling, and added that a front anti-roll bar would help. Their car managed an average top speed of 87.7mph and recorded 19.7secs for the dash to 60mph.

Export sales were still of prime importance to the company and the Farina-bodied cars sold well in some markets, notably Australasia and in the British colonies in Africa. There was also a lot of sales effort directed towards the American market, although there it would have been far better had the MG version been the only model sold. Attempts to interest Americans in the economy versions, like the Austin A55, were doomed once they had been dubbed as underpowered by the motoring press.

When the Magnette had been in production for about a year, the two-tone colour scheme was changed so that all the section of the body above the chrome strip on the waistline was painted the darker colour, not just the roof, boot and tops of the rear wings. Around 16,000 of the Mk III models were produced before a major redesign saw the introduction of the Mk IV in October 1961. The changes made were far more extensive than the largely unaltered external appearance would suggest. The revised Magnette was an improved car and many of the criticisms of the earlier model had received attention. However, in spite of this, sales were in decline as the competition improved and fewer Mk IVs were sold during six-and-a-half years of production than of the Mk III model during the 32 months that car was on sale.

To improve the roadholding and handling, the wheelbase was lengthened by moving back the mounting point for the axle on the rear springs by just over an inch. At the same time, the front suspension wishbone arms and outer steering rods were made longer, to widen the front track by about two inches, and the rear axle tubes and half-shafts lengthened by a similar amount. Wheel rim width was reduced from 4.5J to 4J, fitted as standard with 5.90-14 cross-ply tyres; Weathermaster heavy-duty tyres were optional equipment, as were those with white sidewalls. Anti-roll bars were now fitted front and rear, and to improve the ride modified dampers all round and rear springs of a different rating were used.

Under the bonnet, the 1489cc B-series engine was substituted by the 1622cc unit, which was also fitted at the same time to the other Farina models and to the MGA 1600 Mk ll. This unit produced slightly more power and torque. Because the longer track and wider wheelbase moved the rear wheels further away from the inner arches, these were given indentations that allowed more room for passengers in the rear seat. The seat base upholstery was changed to suit and it seems that, as a cost-cutting measure, the Riley rear seat back with straight top was adopted around this time.

When the single-carburettor Farina models received the larger-capacity engine the body shell was changed so as to reduce the height of the rear wings. At the same time, bumpers of a modified shape were fitted, the effect of these changes being to reduce the overall length of the car by about four inches. The body of the MG and Riley versions, however, retained the original rear wing line and bumpers, making it difficult for all but the cognoscenti to identify the Mk IV from the Mk III, which could not have helped sales.

Mark IV sales brochure.

The ZB Magnettes had been available fitted with a clutchless gear change. The Manumatic transmission was not a full automatic, merely a system for relieving the driver of the chore of

The rear seat in the Mark IV provided comfort for two adults. The terracotta leather seats are original.

The dashboard layout of the Mark IV Magnette.

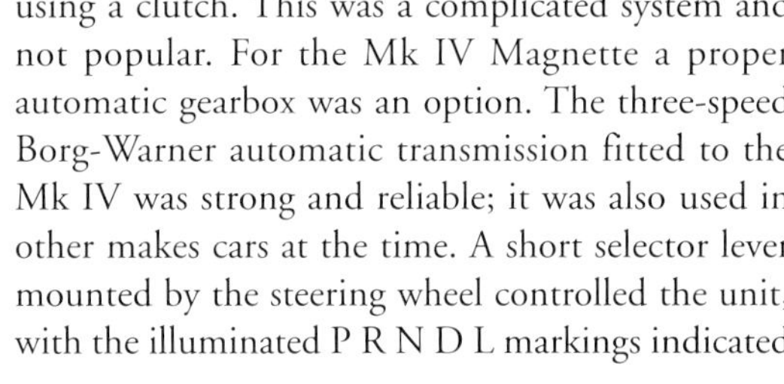

using a clutch. This was a complicated system and not popular. For the Mk IV Magnette a proper automatic gearbox was an option. The three-speed Borg-Warner automatic transmission fitted to the Mk IV was strong and reliable; it was also used in other makes cars at the time. A short selector lever mounted by the steering wheel controlled the unit, with the illuminated P R N D L markings indicated the gearbox status selected.

A feature of all the BMC Farina models was the generously sized boot.

Specifying an automatic added about £100 to the cost of the car and only a small proportion of MG owners were prepared to pay the extra. Quite a few Riley 4/72s, which was the sort of car often bought by retired people, did have automatic gearboxes and *The Motor* tested an example of this model in 1962. The magazine reported that it would reach 60mph in 20.6secs using fully automatic gear selection. If they manually selected the lower gears and held these to 6000rpm, the time was reduced to 19.3secs. Otherwise they found the car to have adequate performance, but still thought that gentle cornering best suited the handling characteristics.

When *The Autocar* tested a manual-transmission car in September 1962, they recorded the top speed of the revised model as 86mph, with the dash to 60mph taking 19.5secs, little different from the figure recorded by their rivals in the automatic Riley. The market for cars like the Magnette was far more competitive in the 1960s than it had been a few years earlier. 1962 saw the arrival of the Ford Cortina, which in GT form was a match in terms of performance, and a lot cheaper, whilst with the Lotus-Cortina, Ford had a model able to compete with MG in terms of sporting heritage, and able to run rings round the staid Magnette on road or track. Increasingly, the MG was being relegated to a small niche in the market.

DICK JACOBS

The MG story is as much about people as it is about the cars. From the time the first Morris Garages specials hit the road in 1923 to the closure of the Abingdon factory in 1980 it is those who designed, built, bought, sold and drove them that have influenced both the way the marque developed and its public profile. Time and again it was feedback from dealers, competitors and the buying public that influenced the MG story. Standing tall amongst these was Dick Jacobs, who was both a successful MG dealer and an enthusiastic competitor.

Dick's father had served in the army in the First World War, dealing with motor transport, and in 1919 he established a garage and haulage business at Mill Garage, South Woodford, Essex. Dick was therefore brought up with cars and aged 12 taught himself to drive. During his adolescence he read widely the tales of the racing exploits of drivers like Malcolm Campbell and the Bentley Boys, and he dreamed of driving at Le Mans, something he was to achieve many years later. However the course of his future was set when during his last term at school a young man locally took delivery of a British Racing Green MG J2. Dick immediately wanted one.

After he left school Dick was apprenticed to the repair depot of AEC, one of the largest commercial vehicle builders in the country. This involved a daily journey of some 10 miles each way, and after initially using a bicycle he graduated first to a series of elderly Austin Sevens and eventually to his dream car, a J2 Midget. The dream was short-lived as the first time he offered a lift to a girlfriend the crankshaft broke. In the late 1930s he spent much of his spare time attending motor races at Brooklands, Crystal Palace and Donington. The idea of racing himself was still very strong but events outside his control meant that this had to be postponed for a time. By 1939 he had graduated from the J2 to a TA and took this car with him to Devonport when he joined the Royal Navy in 1940.

In 1945 he bought a TB Midget, actually an ex-police car, and after his demobilisation attended as many motoring events as could be staged under the stringent rationing then in force. By that time Dick was running Mill Garage, and he had previously written in 1944 to the MG Car Company asking if he could take up an agency for the marque after the war. He reminded them of this and was appointed an official MG dealer. Over the 1946/7 winter he was able to obtain a TC Midget

Dick Jacobs's TC at the Brighton Speed Trials.

The MG special built by Dick based around a special chassis supplied from Abingdon with Y-type front suspension and a coil sprung rear axle.

for his own use. With his motor sport ambitions in mind he decided to fit a supercharger and to replace the standard 19-inch rear wheels with16-inch.

Despite only having the basic petrol ration, Dick managed by fair means or foul to cover some 11,000 miles in the TC during 1947 and to compete in a number of speed events and hill climbs, with modest success. The car performed well, although often placed in a higher class due to the supercharger. He found the brakes not up to the task of coping with the improved performance so these were replaced with those from a 1933 Wolseley Hornet Special, and for the 1948 season the heavy steel wings and running boards were removed and replaced with aluminium cycle wings. A lighter bonnet was also fitted as was a bigger supercharger and a lower rear axle ratio. However, a shortage of high-octane petrol proved a continuing problem.

In 1948 a major boost to British motor sport came with the opening in September of the Goodwood circuit. Dick entered the first event but had car problems in practice. In the race the next day, in order to get the car to run at all, he mixed some benzol with the stipulated pool petrol knowing that this would exclude him from the awards. Although the car was fast enough to finish further up the rankings, he deliberately slowed to end up in fourth place. He had raced in sprints and hill climbs during the season, but for the 1949 season he decided to build an MG special, rather than to further modify what was at the time a valuable TC.

A scruffy TA was the basis of the special, powered by an ex-army surplus Morris Ten engine, similar to the TC XPAG unit, with the bores sleeved down to 62mm to bring the capacity down to below the 1100cc class limit. An old Marshall supercharger was purchased and rebuilt. The 12-inch Wolseley brakes originally used on the TC were transferred and the engine mated to a TC gearbox. John Haesendonck then constructed a lightweight body that complied with international sports car regulations.

The first race with the special was at the International Easter Monday meeting at Goodwood. As the handicap event was for racing cars, after the drive to the track all the road

The MG Special constructed by John Haesendonck and entered by him and Dick Jacobs in the 1953 9-hour race at Goodwood in place of the then owner Tom Dargue, who is pictured here in the car.

In 1950 a team of three TD Mark IIs were entered in the production car race. Ted Lund drove car 18.

equipment was removed and the stripped MG performed very well. Dick for a while led the field until passed by Stirling Moss in his 998cc Cooper. However to finish second in the first race with the new car was pleasing. With the encouragement of a fellow MG special competitor, George Phillips, Dick entered the BRDC Manx Cup race held on the Isle of Man. In practice the car didn't run very well, but on advice from the Lodge Spark Plug competition manager a change of plugs and fuel improved matters. The car was obviously not quick enough to challenge for outright victory so Dick decided to limit the engine revs to 6000 and to try to finish the long race. At one time he was running in fifth place, but clutch slip towards the end meant seventh was the final result.

Entries in events at Silverstone and elsewhere followed and the efforts made by Dick and George Phillips had come to the notice of those at Abingdon, as a result of which the factory started to provide some assistance. The BRDC and the *Daily Express* were keen to promote a genuine production car race and, as recounted earlier, Dick and George tried to interest the MG Car Company in providing a team of standard cars. John Thornley was eventually persuaded to enter three TCs with Dick, George and Ted Lund as drivers. The 1949 race was held at Silverstone and the drivers were instructed to report to the factory on the Thursday before the race to collect the three cream-painted standard TCs, which they were drive in convoy to the circuit after a parade through Oxford, with three Rileys that were also entered by the factory.

After a fraught practice session in which the cars cornered badly on their standard wheels and tyres, Dick persuaded John Thornley to deviate from specification to the extent of binding the rear springs to stiffen them and fitting 16-inch rear wheels. In the race the cars ran well, finishing in fifth, sixth and seventh places and averaging nearly 70mph; not bad as the top speed of a standard TC was only around 75mph. This modest success persuaded John to

The Y-type coupé constructed by Dick Jacobs using a fibreglass body.

Le Mans 1955 with Dick Jacobs in the MGA prior to the crash.

provide the drivers with MGs to use in production car events for the 1950 season.

Dick decided to rebuild the special over the winter and obtained another Morris engine that was stripped completely, the flywheel lightened and the rods polished and balanced, along with the crankshaft. A larger-capacity sump and bigger radiator core were sourced to improve the cooling of both oil and water. Two sets of supercharger pulleys were obtained, one for sports car events where the car ran with wings, lights, etc., and one for racing car classes when the car ran in stripped form. The modified car performed well and was run in nine events, with some success, before being sold at the end of 1950 to Syd Greene.

Having sold his special, Dick began planning a new car for the 1951 season. The factory supplied him with a TD chassis fitted with Y-type front suspension and Syd Enever's version of the Fiat 1400 coil spring rear suspension. Dick had the chassis lightened by drilling holes all over it, and a local panel beater built a body from light tubing panelled with sheet aluminium. The engine was assembled using a standard XPAG block and a special short-throw crankshaft to give a capacity of 1088cc. Special pistons were used to give a compression ratio of 11:1. Dick enjoyed some outings with the car and in the International Ulster Trophy Races at Dundrod was placed third in a scratch race for cars up to 1300cc. Later, on return from a visit to the Isle of Man for the Manx Cup Race, where a seized blower had spoiled the chance of success, the car was sold.

During 1951 Dick used an ex-works TD he had purchased from Abingdon for a number of events, including the six-hour relay race staged at Silverstone by the 750 Motor Club. After this the TD was returned to standard Mark II specification and sold. After pulling a few strings Dick obtained a YB saloon to use in production saloon car events. It was entered at Silverstone just three weeks after Dick bought it and, apart from stronger valve springs and a larger jet in the carburettor, was completely standard. After a stirring race Dick came home in first place in class. 1953 saw Dick enter his

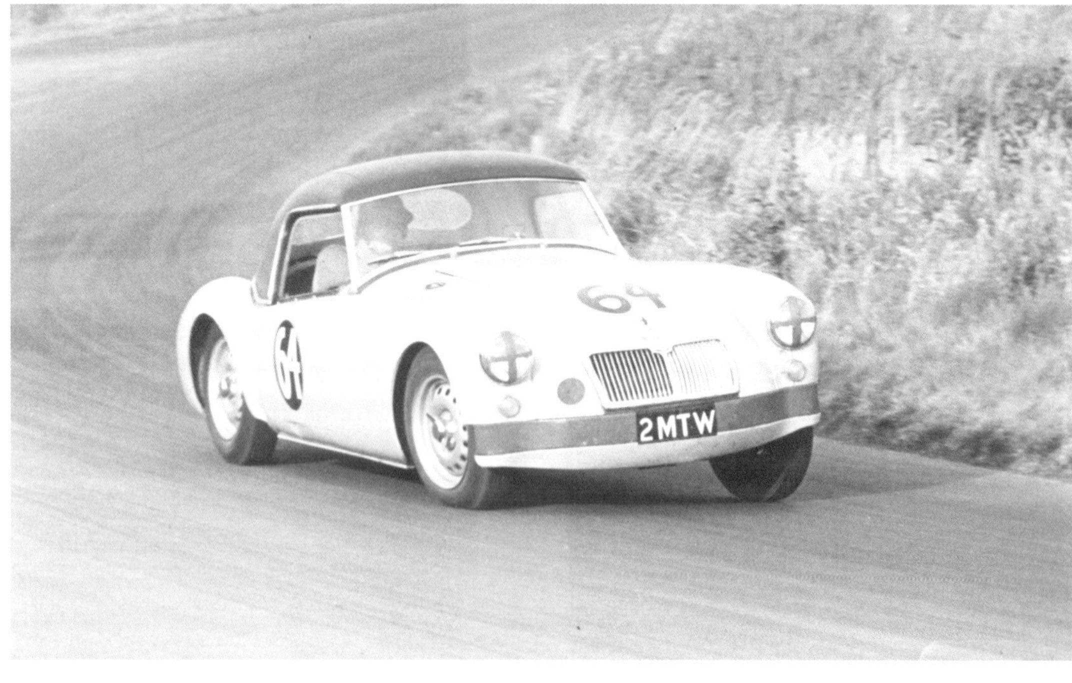

One of the two MGA Twin-Cam racers successfully run by the Dick Jacobs team.

YB saloon in the *Daily Express* touring car race and again win his class.

Dick's special-building career had moved on somewhat and now he was constructing cars for customers. Mill Garage had started advertising that they could supply fibreglass bodies produced by R.G.S. Automobile Components of Winkfield, Berkshire, fitted to MG chassis. Dick decided he would like to have another special to enter events in 1954, and through the good offices of John Thornley was offered the last Y-type rolling chassis. The car was completed using one of the R.G.S. Automobile Components coupé bodies and the engine capacity was increased to 1500cc. Braking was improved by fitting the larger-sized front drums from the Wolseley 6/80, and wire wheels from a TF made the car look more workmanlike. The car was completed and its first event was the BARC Goodwood Members' Meeting where it performed well. At the 1954 Whitsun Meeting at that circuit the car was placed second to Colin Chapman in the much lighter Lotus and Dick went on to score other successes in the car.

In 1955 John Thornley had told him not to arrange any commitments for June as he had other plans for him. These turned out to be a chance to race one of the MGA prototypes at Le Mans, the fulfilment of a long-held ambition. Unfortunately, as recounted elsewhere, Dick was involved in a serious accident and never raced again.

Wishing to remain involved with motor sport, Dick went on to manage the preparation and race entries of a great many MGs, including a Magnette and the MGA Twin Cam cars, 1 MTW and 2 MTW. He was also instrumental in the factory building the three Midget coupés that were so successful in the early 1960s. The Mill Garage business flourished, the premises being extended to include an office block and large parts department. However the axe fell in the late 1960s when plans were published revealing that the site would be needed to accommodate the M11 extension. The business closed at the end of 1974 and Dick died in 1988, two years before the Abingdon factory where he had spent so much time was closed.

Just four days after the model was announced to the public Dick Jacobs entered this car in The Motor *6-hour saloon car race at Brands Hatch. In the hands of Alan Foster and Andrew Hedges it was placed first in class.*

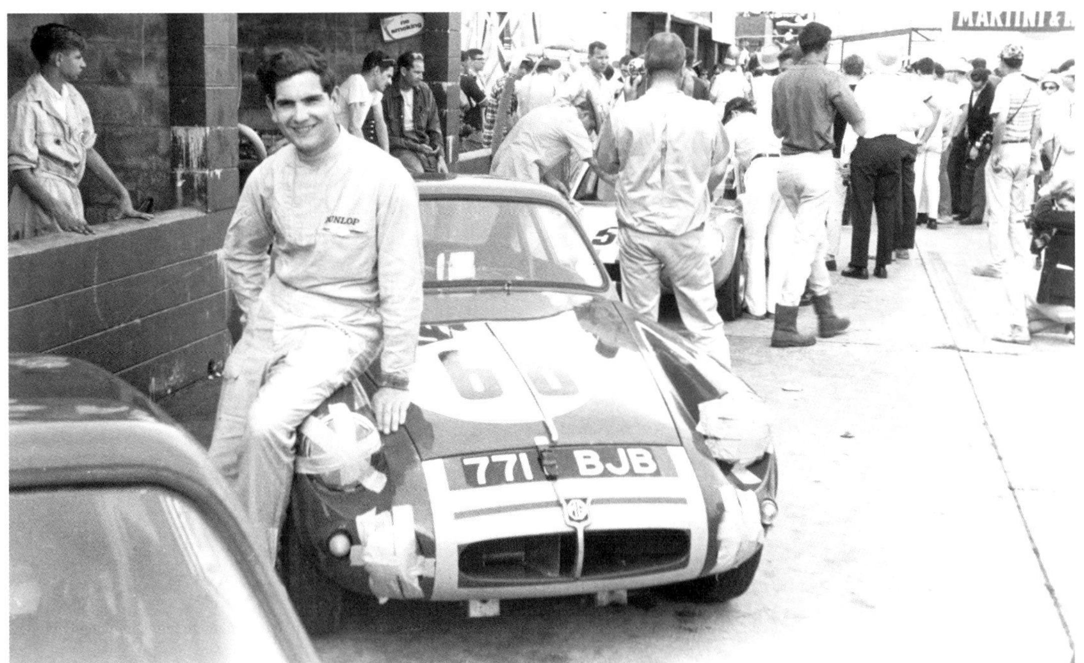

One of the two very successful Jacobs Midgets is seen here at Sebring in 1965, where Roger Mac and Andrew Hedges were placed first in class.

THE MGB

A publicity picture of an early MGB destined for the American market.

The majority of MGBs produced in the 1960s went for export.

Developing an entirely new car is a long process and work on the MGA replacement commenced as early as 1957. The Italian stylist, Frua, designed a new body for an MGA 1500 chassis he was given, and the result was sent to Abingdon for assessment. The car produced bore more than a passing resemblance to other Italian sports cars of the period, like the Maserati 3500GT, with an abundance of chrome trim and the wrap-around windscreen so popular on American cars at that time. Drawings were produced, and both hardtop and GT versions were considered, but the car was really both too heavy and too expensive to produce to be a real contender, and to avoid paying the government any import duty the sole prototype was destroyed.

There were a number of in-house proposals for replacement bodies for the existing chassis, but these equally suffered from similar weight and cost shortcomings. Eventually Syd Enever decided that the new car would have to be of monocoque design, in spite of the inevitable higher tooling costs. The project was now given a new experimental number, EX214, and work on the design started with a clean sheet of paper. Released from the constraints of using the old chassis, the wheelbase of the new car was to be shorter than that of the MGA by three inches but it was to retain the existing coil spring and wishbone independent front suspension, while at the rear he decided to try out a system using coil springs with trailing radius arms and a Panhard rod.

The initial designs for a new body on the old chassis had featured a rounded shape at the front influenced by the EX181 record car and the shape of the existing MGA. For the MGB the length of the bodywork ahead of the front wheels was reduced with the traditional slatted MG grille mounted vertically and the headlamps slightly inset into the front wings. This change both reduced the overall length of the car and improved its appearance.

Unfortunately, development and handling problems, plus the additional cost, forced the abandonment of the coil sprung rear suspension, and the traditional half-elliptic leaf springs and live axle were adopted for production. Actually finding sufficient money to meet the huge tooling costs of the body was causing Abingdon some difficulties. Pressed Steel was asked for an estimate but when this was received it proved to be rather more than the budget would meet. Fortunately the two companies worked out a deal that halved the initial tooling costs in exchange for a higher unit

This early MGB has the standard steel wheels with chrome-plated hubcaps. It covered over 300,000miles in the hands of its long-term owner.

price for each body. As the MGB was in production for rather longer than the five to six years originally envisaged, in the long run this must have proved more than profitable for Pressed Steel.

Although other power units were considered, once again cost restraints decreed that the MGA B-series engine in its modified 1622cc form was to power the new car. At a late stage the capacity was enlarged to 1789cc by increasing the bore size, which gave a quoted power output of around 95bhp and proved sufficient to make the MGB a genuine 100mph car. The gearbox was a standard British Motor Corporation unit, but available with the option of an overdrive that was particularly useful now that motorways were becoming common. For some years there had been a tendency for road wheel sizes to be reduced and the MGB was fitted with 14in rims in place of the 15in fitted to the MGA. Once again wire wheels were an option that was to prove popular, especially in overseas markets.

The most attractive feature was the cockpit. The unitary construction had enabled the designers to give the occupants a lot more room than was available in the MGA. There was sufficient leg and headroom for even the tallest although, in order to reduce drag, the windscreen height was set at the minimum allowed by United States regulations. This was retained throughout the life of the roadsters although the GT, when it arrived in 1965, was given a taller windscreen. Comfort was given a higher priority and no longer did the MG driver have to struggle to fit separate side screens in wet weather. The winding side windows and swivelling quarter-lights fitted to the doors brought the MGB into line with its competitors from Triumph and Sunbeam.

The MGB made its public debut at the 1962 London Motor Show at Earls Court. Motoring journalists and general public alike were quick to praise the new model. The wider cockpit, larger luggage capacity and improved comfort were much lauded, as was the excellent performance and safe roadholding. Particularly appreciated by owners with young children to accommodate was the space behind the front seats, and for a while a cushion for this rear shelf was an optional extra. The performance compared to the MGA was improved, the top speed recorded by *The Autocar* being 105mph, with the acceleration to 60mph taking just over 12secs. The car was an immediate sales success and the order books at Abingdon quickly filled.

With so many examples in everyday use and still

The cut-away display for the 1962 London Motor Show.

A restored early MGB with pull-type door handles.

such a familiar sight on our roads, it is a sobering thought that the MGB GT was launched as long ago as October 1965. What could not have been apparent at the time to the designers was just how popular the concept of a sporting holdall would become; a car as suited to a trip to the supermarket as it was at home in the car park at Brands Hatch or Silverstone. The announcement of the new model on the eve of the 1965 London Motor Show was covered but briefly by the major motoring magazines in amongst reports of other new cars, and it is only with hindsight that we see just how important the GT was to the success of the MGB.

Cars with lifting tailgates have become so universally popular that it is difficult to recall now that the concept had been hardly thought of when the MGB GT appeared on the scene. When it was designed it was not seen primarily as

This early roadster displays the attractive lines of the MGB with the hood erected.

the family runabout it was later to become. The inspiration was said to be the fastback shape of the Aston Martin DB Mk III, which in one form had a similar opening tailgate, but there is no doubt that the main reason behind producing the model was to widen the potential market for the MGB. There have always been people willing to sacrifice some of the space offered by an ordinary saloon for the appeal of a sporting car, but not attracted by open-air motoring. The closed version of the MGA introduced after the roadster had been around for a year or so was a steady seller, despite costing quite a bit more and having little more cockpit or luggage space than the open two-seater. The need for a fixed-roof version of the MGB was obvious.

Actually, as the MGB had a better hood than the MGA, as well as proper winding side windows, it proved more pleasant to use as a closed car and in June 1963 the position was further improved when a removable hard top was introduced as an optional extra. Despite this, one enterprising Brussels-based coachbuilder felt a demand still existed for a proper closed sports coupé based on the MGB. He designed his interpretation of an MG-based luxury grand tourer and exhibited the extensively modified car at the 1964 Brussels Motor Show. Such was the interest this attractive car created on the stand that he decided to go into series production, calling his creation the MG Berlinette.

Producing the first Coune Berlinette MGB had not been a five-minute process. Jacques Coune had been greatly influenced by Italian designers of the time and elements of their work can be seen in the coupé he created from a standard MGB roadster. The car cited as most influencing Coune's design

Wire wheels were an option on the MGB from the start of production. Whitewall tyres were specified on quite a number of export cars, but few for the home market.

The advantage the MGB had over the MGA was the size of the boot.

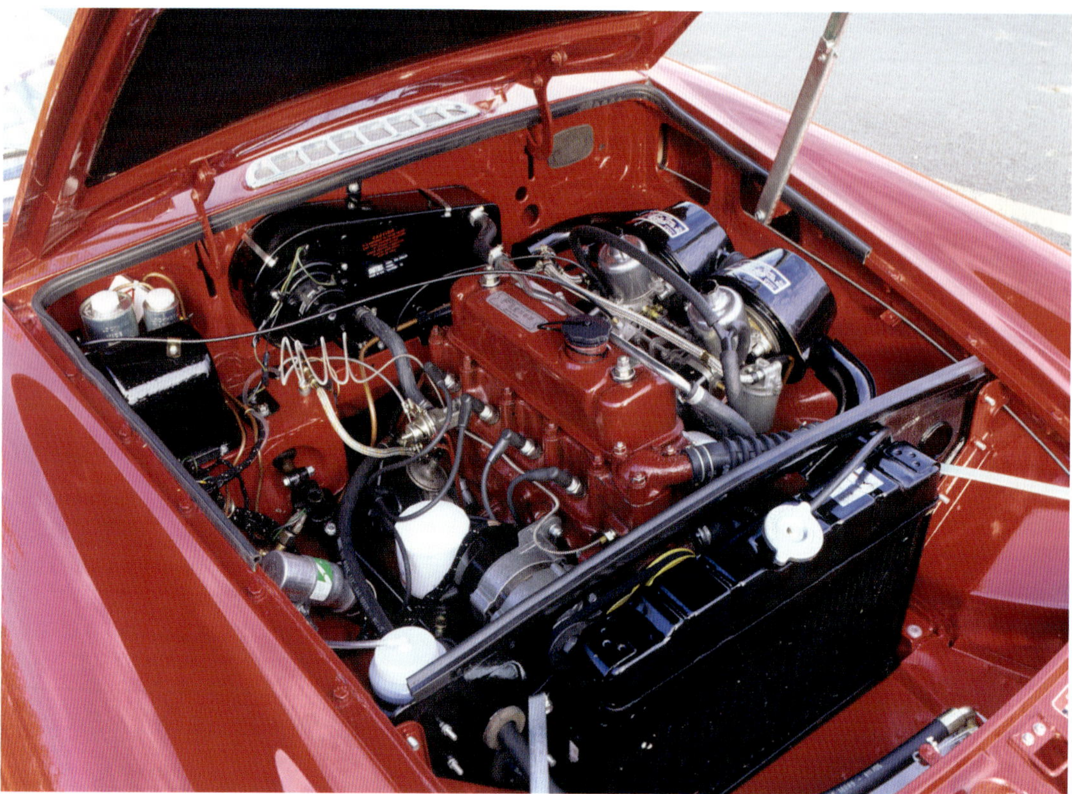

For routine maintenance the 1800cc B-series engine is very easily accessible.

was the Ferrari 275GTB. Although the main MGB chassis structure and mechanical components remained unchanged, the conversion process went far beyond merely attaching a few extra panels. The first task was to remove the windscreen, hood, interior trim, etc. With the car stripped, the major surgery began. At the front, the headlamps were removed and the nacelles cut back and re-profiled; a further alteration to the front wing was the addition of a small, protruding lip above the wheel. The chrome side strips were removed and the mounting holes filled. The front quarter-lights and door glasses were taken off as these were replaced as part of the conversion.

At the back of the car the wings, boot lid, plus the deck and rear panels, were cut away to leave just the inner wings, floor and chassis members. To strengthen the now weakened structure a three-sided box section was welded between the rear wheel arches and extra metal panels were fitted inside the final outer skin. On the prototype and first production cars the roof and screen pillars, rear wings and tail were hand-formed in metal and welded to the main structure. The remainder of the cars had a large fibreglass section bonded to the remains of the metal monocoque.

The result of all this effort was a distinctive car built and trimmed to a high standard that attracted a number of orders, the largest being one for 10 cars for delivery to the Dutch MG importer Molenaar. In all, there were some 56 cars built and the price of the conversion was about £480, plus duties, and this was in addition to the initial cost of an MGB roadster of around £850. One car was built with right-hand drive and first registered to Walter Oldfield, the managing director of Nuffield Press, but the story goes that this was built as a result of a meeting between Jacques Coune and Alec Issigonis. The roadster used was sent from the factory to Belgium, minus hood and the other parts that would not be needed. When completed it was delivered to Abingdon where it was driven by a number of the top management at BMC. There was a proposal to build examples under licence but this never came to anything and the company went ahead with their own design for a GT.

At Abingdon Syd Enever and his team had themselves been working on a closed version of the MGB and both Jim O'Neill and Jim Stimson had produced possible designs. However, marrying the rounded shape of the MGB roadster with a fixed roof that provided sufficient headroom was proving difficult and in the end Pininfarina was commissioned to take on the work of turning these

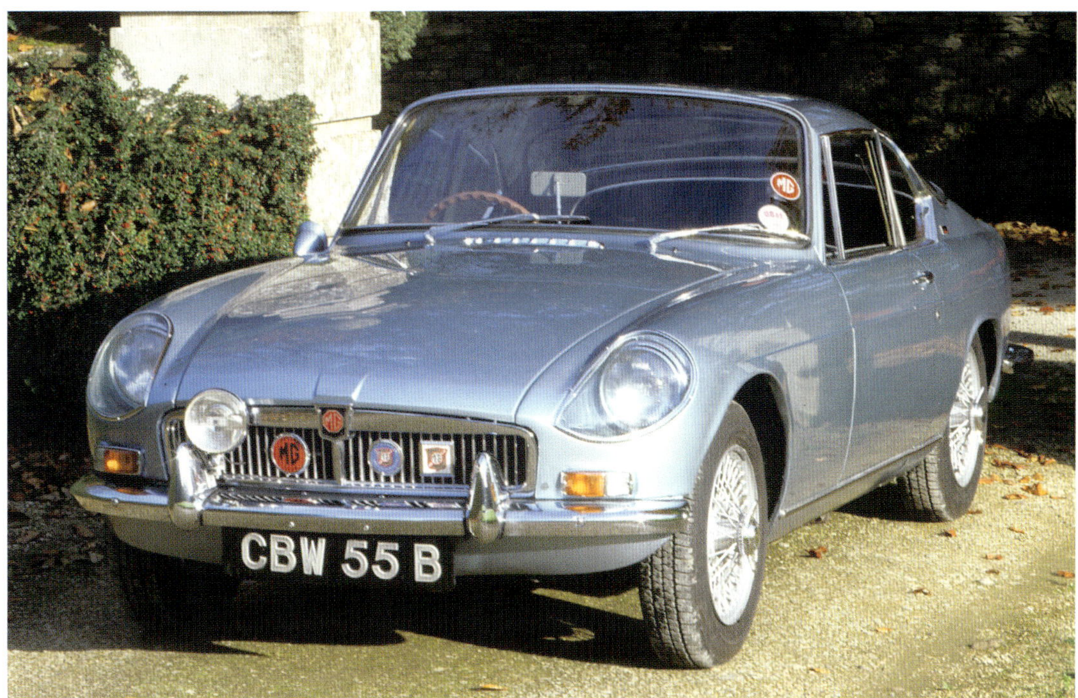

The new fixed roof and taller windscreen on the Jacques Coune car altered the appearance of the MGB considerably.

proposals into a cohesive design. They were also asked to build a prototype, and a roadster was sent to Italy for this purpose. When it was returned as a complete, running car, painted in the usual shade of light metallic green used for such prototypes, it met with immediate approval. The Abingdon team then had to set about the task of getting it into production.

The reason for the success of the GT's styling, and why it still looks good 40 years on, was its simplicity. Pininfarina made no unnecessary changes to the original MGB roadster but did alter the height of the windscreen, as on the open car the top rail was always too low. Despite adding a roof and rear section that was not as rounded as the rest of the car, the overall shape pleased the eye and made the car look larger and more imposing than the otherwise identical roadster. The higher windscreen certainly improved matters for taller drivers and the large glass area of the cabin gave

Jacques Coune built a single car with right-hand drive for assessment by BMC management.

The MGB GT was an immediate success with buyers, especially those who wanted a closed sports car for everyday use.

MGBs and Midgets were assembled at Abingdon on adjacent lines.

With the option of overdrive, the MGB GT was ideally suited for use on the rapidly expanding motorway network.

good visibility all round. To make the car attractive to the sports car driver with a young family, they fitted a rear seat and advertised the car as a two-plus-two. This caused some criticism from the motoring press who said that the leg and headroom were really insufficient to justify the term.

In spite of some adverse comments about the comfort of the seats, and of the ride, the press and the general public liked the car and before long the MGB GT was a regular sight on the roads. Many people bought them as second cars for use for the family shopping, and in the late 1960s they were almost as common in the suburbs on school runs as are now the ubiquitous SUVs. As a lot of us have found out over the years, the MGB GT is a very useful and adaptable car well capable of undertaking a wide variety of tasks. For a small sports car there is a generous amount of space for luggage, especially when the back of the rear seat is folded flat, and cars fitted with overdrive are easily capable of covering high mileages at motorway speeds. One could say that the MGB, and especially the GT, was the first MG designed with modern roads in mind, and publicity for the model made use of pictures of cars at speed on the M1 motorway.

The GT shared the mechanical specification of the roadster with the exception of the rear axle, which was changed for the quieter Salisbury unit, and the rear springs, which were uprated. A front anti-roll bar was also standardised. The extra weight of the closed car, about 150lb, reduced the performance slightly but the one tested by *Autocar* still managed to reach a maximum speed of 102mph and accelerate to 60mph in 13.6secs. This was good performance for an 1800cc car in 1965 and the road test team were also impressed by the engine's flexibility at lower revs. The basic cost then of a GT was £998 8s 9d and the overdrive option added an extra £60 8s 4d to the bill. In comparison the roadster was priced at £847 plus extras, so the additional cost of the GT version was comparatively modest.

The popularity of the GT increased the overall sales of the MGB to the extent that an additional production line was needed in 1966 when the annual output rose to record levels. That year 10,241 closed cars and 22,675 roadsters left Abingdon and if you compare that to the previous best MGA year, 1959, when a total of 23,319 were built, then one can see just how well the MGB in both forms was being received in world markets.

A publicity picture of an early MGB GT.

THE MG 1100/1300

Duo-tone colour schemes were all the rage in the late 1950s and early 1960s. The colours chosen for the MG 1100 in 1962 were particularly attractive and many buyers elected to pay the extra cost. The scheme here is Connaught Green over Old English White.

For the avid sports car enthusiast a visit to the 1962 Motor Show at Earls Court was well worthwhile as it was the chosen venue for the launch of a number of interesting new cars, including the Lotus Elan, Triumph Spitfire, the MGB and a revised Midget. Sharing the limelight on the stand with the new sports cars from Abingdon there was a revolutionary new MG. Traditionally the marque line-up had always included closed saloons and in post-war years the Y-type, the Gerald Palmer designed Z-Magnette, and the MG versions of the British Motor Corporation Farina mid-range family cars had filled this niche.

Alec Issigonis had been tempted back to the British Motor Corporation in the mid-1950s and given the brief to modernise their entire range of saloon cars. Although he had previously been responsible for the long-lived Morris Minor introduced in the late 1940s, this outwardly looked a fairly conventional vehicle and was not particularly space efficient, having a relatively small cabin for its overall length and a standard front engine/rear drive layout. The first entirely new car to emerge under his control was the Mini. Conceived in the petrol shortage that accompanied the Suez crisis, this was introduced in 1959 to a public that was at first singularly unimpressed by what they perceived as a utility vehicle and not a patch on their Austin A35s and Morris Minors. It took quite a time for the virtues of the compact overall size and superb roadholding of the Mini to make their mark in the showroom. Remember too, the word mini was new to the vocabulary and mini-skirts had yet to arrive on the scene.

In 1962, with Issigonis in the process of changing the British Motor Corporation model line-up, it was logical to assume models based on his philosophy of maximum space utilisation and advanced technical design would supplant the current range of cars. The vehicle intended to eventually replace the Austin A40 and Morris Minor was the Austin/Morris 1100. Again, like the Morris Mini-Minor and Austin Seven, this car had the A-series engine transversely mounted at the front and driving the front wheels through a gearbox and final drive that were integral with the power unit, sharing the same oil. However, the innovation for the 1100 was the adoption of interconnected Hydrolastic suspension which both helped smooth out the ride and dispensed with the need for separate dampers. The Mini at the time had rubber springing and telescopic dampers, but later it too had the Hydrolastic suspension for a while.

Developed by Dr Alex Moulton, whose other

Now almost universal for smaller cars, the two-box design of the 1100 was in stark contrast to, for example, the then current Farina Magnette with its prominent boot.

innovations included a well-known range of unconventional bicycles, the Hydrolastic suspension was a way to improve passenger comfort by reducing bounce, pitch and roll. To reduce pitch, a way had to be found to interconnect the front and rear suspension to share the effect of hitting a bump in the road more equally between both ends of the car. Thus, when the front wheel is raised by the shock of hitting a bump it lifts both the front and rear of the car, keeping it level and reducing pitch. When the back wheel reaches the same bump the shock will, in turn, be partly shared by the front wheel. The steel springs used front and rear in most cars could only be interconnected by a costly and heavy mechanical system. However, should a fluid be used as part of the suspension system, a hydraulic link between the front and rear springs was practical.

The Mini used rubber cones in place of steel springs, but for the new 1100 saloons, Moulton used fluid, actually a mixture of water, anti-corrosion liquid and alcohol as antifreeze, for the springing medium. Each wheel was connected to its own Hydrolastic unit, linked together in pairs, front to rear. A piston connected to the road wheel bore on a rubber diaphragm and a load on the wheel compressed the fluid. In an upper chamber, the fluid was contained at the top by a cylindrical block of rubber with a chamber in its centre and a pipe at the top, to interconnect with its twin unit, and by damper valves at the bottom. When stationary, the weight of the car was borne by the fluid pressing against the rubber spring. When that road wheel hit a bump, fluid was forced past damper valves and into the interconnecting pipe, thus pressurising the paired unit. As the rubber spring also offered a rising resistance as the load on it rose, the unit had the virtue of providing variable rate springing. The fluid working its way past the control valves also acted as a damper, obviating the need for separate units. As well as reducing pitch, the Hydrolastic system reduced roll as there was no interconnection side to side so the pair of units on the outside of a corner could not be compressed beyond a certain point. In the new mid-range 1,100cc saloons, the system worked well. The fitting of a rear anti-roll bar and anti-pitch bars, all contained within the rear sub-frame, also helped the ride. Comfort was greatly improved over more conventional systems and generally buyers liked the cars and magazine road tests were favourable.

At the time, the announcement of the MG saloon, and its appearance at the show, did not have a great impact on followers of the marque; they saw it merely as yet another badge-engineered version of a standard family saloon conceived to win sales from those wishing to own a car with an apparent sporting pedigree. The advantages, however, of a transverse engine layout, front-wheel drive with all its safety and roadholding benefits, and a revolutionary suspension system, meant that the new saloon was actually a very good car. To their credit, the designers sought to set the MG 1100 apart from the Morris/Austin models by endowing it with a twin-carburettor engine, two-tone paintwork at extra cost, a better standard of trim and the option of leather seat facings.

Like the Mini, the 1100 offered far more interior space than any other car in its class. Although at 147inches it was over two foot longer than the

To take the MG version up-market, it was given a wooden dashboard, but unfortunately a ribbon speedometer and no tachometer.

Pioneered in the Mini, in 1962 the transverse engine in the 1100 was still something of a novelty.

Graham Hill was employed by BMC to help publicise the new MG. At Silverstone he and his BRM were photographed with the new car. He also made a short film about the 1100 and appeared in some magazine advertisements.

Mini, it was still more compact than its rivals. For example, the VW Beetle was the same width but 14 inches longer, and the cabin and luggage space were cramped by comparison. The Triumph Herald, for all its modern styling and large glass area, offered its occupants far less legroom than the 1100 and was six inches longer overall. In cabin space the MG 1100 rivalled the Magnette Mk IV, although the larger car did posses greater luggage capacity to justify it being nearly 15 feet long.

Autocar provided a comparison between the power outputs of the Morris and MG engines. Twin carburettors, three-branch exhaust manifold and a higher compression ratio boosted peak power for the MG to 55bhp, a 14% increase over the Morris unit. Likewise, peak torque was raised slightly and this was maintained over a greater range of engine speed, making the MG 1100 more tractable. When they published a road test of the MG in December 1962 they recorded a top speed of 89mph and 18.4secs for the dash to 60mph. The Morris tested earlier that year reached 78mph and took 22.2secs to reach 60mph. Overall gearing was low, 14.9mph per 1000rpm, giving rise to concern about engine longevity in some subsequent road tests carried out by other magazines.

For the MG version the changes made to the monocoque body were few. The front panel and bonnet were a different shape so as to accommodate the MG grille; its traditional design being much like that already in use on the Magnette. Side chrome strips, a feature used on the Midget, Magnette and newly-announced MGB, further affiliated the car with the other models in the range. In the cabin the driver was presented with the obligatory veneered wooden dashboard, albeit one with a strip speedometer in place of the more usual circular dial, and there was no tachometer. Further instrumentation was confined to fuel level and water temperature gauges; the oil pressure gauge being replaced by low pressure and filter change warning lights.

For those used at that time to driving more conventional saloons, on first acquaintance it was the low floor and good glass area that had greatest impact. The seats were well padded and moulded carpets covered the floor. The transverse engine/gearbox unit was inherited from the Mini and with it came an upright position for the steering wheel. This took some getting used to, as did pedals offset towards the centre of the cabin.

When the MG 1100 was launched at the 1962 London Motor Show the price quoted for the four-door saloon was £590 plus £222 5s 3d purchase tax. By the time cars appeared in the showrooms in reasonable quantity reductions in tax saw the overall price fall to £713 9s 5d. The Morris 1100 was about £100 cheaper and provided adequate performance for the family motorists who were its customers. Nearly comparable performance, but less space and comfort, could also be found in the Ford Anglia 1200 at a mere £598 13s 9d, but then few of the sort of drivers who then bought MGs would have considered the Ford. However, despite its higher price tag, the MG 1100 sold in reasonable numbers

From the outset it had been intended that the

MG 1100 brochure.

From the side view, the two-door MG 1300 Mk II looks smaller than the four-door car. They are actually the same length.

MG 1100 would sell in overseas markets, with the United States taking a large proportion. Advertising there emphasised the virtues of the MG Sedan in comparison to that other popular imported saloon, the VW Beetle. It was the two-door variant of the MG 1100 that was chosen to spearhead the attack and, although the two-door car was initially also to be available on the home market, cars in that form did not actually go on sale here until 1968.

The landed cost of the MG was more than the VW. Also, it did not have the simplicity of an air-cooled engine or the high overall gearing that made the Beetle so suited to the American freeway, and their treatment of the cars. However, following stunts like a reliability and performance test organised by Hambro Distributors Inc. when four MG 1100s covered a total of 31,646 miles in seven days, initial sales were promising. Reliability problems, and a feeling amongst potential customers that the MG was too frail for American conditions, led to falling sales there which even the later introduction of both the four-door model, and a larger-capacity engine, failed to halt. Although the MG Sports Sedan was withdrawn from sale in America in 1967, that was not the end of the story. A two-door Austin America with 1275cc engine and automatic transmission was sold there for a while and some of the luxuriously-appointed Vanden Plas 1100s were imported and sold as the MG Princess 1100.

In the home market the 1100 range became one of the best-selling cars. There was little attempt to bolster its image by participation in competition, although a Dick Jacobs-entered car did score a class win in the Brands Hatch six-hour saloon car race just days after its announcement. An MG 1100 was entered in the 1962 RAC Rally, driven by David Seigle-Morris and the Reverend Rupert Jones, but failed to finish.

Having a few years earlier introduced the 1275cc A-series engine for the Mini-Cooper S; the Midget inherited a de-tuned version in 1966. In March 1967, and none too soon, the home-market MG 1100 received a single carburettor 1275cc power unit developing 58bhp at 5250rpm. This had started to be used in the US-bound cars some months earlier. The greater torque produced by the larger capacity allowed the engineers to give the car a more sensible 3.65:1 final drive ratio, producing a far less frenetic 17.1mph per 1000rpm. This meant that cruising at 60mph saw just over 3500rpm on the tachometer, while the 1100 engine had been spinning at over 4000rpm at the same road speed.

This car was called the MG 1275 and *Motor* published a road test in June 1967 that revealed a recorded top speed of 91.8mph and acceleration to 60mph at 17.3secs. This engine had given the car a new lease of life and the days of the original MG 1100 were numbered. The larger engine was introduced as an option, with the 1098cc model remaining in the price lists. However, in October 1967, in common with the rest of the models in the range, the MG 1100 and MG 1275 received a significant number of modifications and the larger capacity cars were now called MG 1300s. Externally the revised cars could be identified by the reduced size rear fins, side repeaters for the flashing indicators and pierced disc wheels. The cabin received different seats with an altered pattern for the seat covers, and leather upholstery was no

The MG 1100 was not available on the home market in two-door guise. However the 1300 Mark II was only sold here in that form.

longer an option. Reclining front seats could still be ordered, these having been introduced more than two years earlier. Cars destined for the home market were still only available in four-door form, but this model was destined for a very brief existence as in October 1968 the MG 1300 Mk II was launched.

With the car already having undergone a number of changes in the previous few months, the product planners must have looked again at the 1100/1300 range and decided to reposition the MG variant. In a complete reversal of previous policy, the MG 1300 Mk II was to be available solely in two-door form. They then obviously tried to give the car a more sporting image and in the process produced the most satisfying version. The car was then to remain virtually unchanged for the final three years of production.

Despite the MG 1100/1300 being of modest size, the boot was capable of carrying a reasonable amount of luggage. A pity that a hatchback version was not considered.

Under the bonnet a twin-carburettor 1275cc engine produced 70bhp at 6000rpm, with increased torque. The all-synchromesh four-speed gearbox had closer ratios that provided an impressive 75mph in third gear at the red line, just right for overtaking slower traffic. In the cabin the seats were covered in Ambla material and had a revised pleat pattern. The driver was faced with a set of proper sports car instruments with round dials, clear markings and, at last, a tachometer. The new steering wheel had a covered rim and pierced spokes – all very sporting.

In their road test published in the 17 October 1968 issue, *Autocar* said that the car was much more of an MG, although at £925 11s 8d they thought it expensive. The performance data for the car with the new engine is particularly revealing. The new gear ratios, as much as anything else, gave much improved acceleration times and top speed was higher, at 101mph not merely 9mph faster than the previous car but handsomely beating the two-seater MG Midget powered by basically the same engine.

So, here at last was the sporting saloon the MG 1100/1300 had always pretended to be. However, it was all a bit late, and one is left with the usual feeling about BMC products of that era. They were good cars, but let down by lack of development, poor planning, abysmal quality control and general ineptitude. If only they had listened more to what their customers and the motoring press were telling them. Still, that would not have been in the spirit of the game.

THE MGC

Much more than meets the eye

the new 6 cylinder MGC

SPORTS AND G.T.

Possibly the most controversial of the post-war products from Abingdon was the MGC. Disliked at launch by many of the journalists testing the cars, the MGC went on to gain many fans amongst those who actually paid out their own money to buy one. Currently, the surviving cars are much loved by most owners and many have had their cars a long time. While it is true that there were some inherent shortcomings in the cars as built, there were also many virtues. Development work carried out later by specialists and some owners has revealed just how good a well-sorted example can be.

First, how was the MGC conceived? The creation of the Austin-Healey marque in the early 1950s by BMC boss Leonard Lord was the start of the story. Initially the Austin-Healey 100 was assembled at Longbridge, but production moved to Abingdon in 1957 and remained there until the last example of the marque was built. When the design team there were considering a replacement for the MGA, the current version of the Healey, the 3000, was starting to look dated. Bearing in mind that Abingdon were then also assembling the Sprite, launched in 1958, to embark on a totally new big Austin-Healey in addition to designing the MGA replacement would stretch their resources and budget beyond breaking point. Someone then came up with the idea that a modified version of the MGA replacement, possible with a bigger engine, could be the next big Healey. As a bonus, perhaps an MG version could also sell alongside what was to become the MGB, but at a higher cost.

Longbridge development department were in overall charge of design and they allocated the experimental numbers ADO51 for the Austin-Healey version and ADO52 for the MG and initial plans for the six-cylinder version of the yet-unannounced MGB were incorporated into the programme of work required to launch that model. Few foresaw that it would take a further five years to get the six-cylinder car into production.

At that time there was a serious lack of direction of overall planning within the British Motor Corporation group and various projects to build new sports cars were being considered without any serious control being exercised. Acting without the help of the experienced sports car designers at Abingdon and Warwick, Longbridge were secretly spending vast sums on developing a high performance sports car based around the totally unsuitable 4-litre Rolls-Royce engine. This car was to have Hydrolastic suspension and was designed to be a Healey 3000 replacement. At a late stage, once a lot of money had been expended on development and tooling and after experts like Geoffrey Healey had seen and condemned the project, it was scrapped.

The other scheme using the MGB as a Healey 3000 replacement, with only minor badge changes to distinguish it from the MG version, found little favour with the Healey family and they pursued the

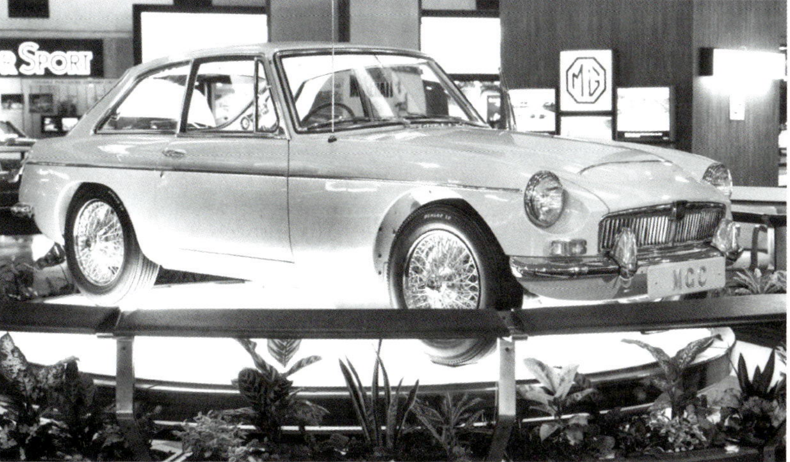

The new MGC GT was prominently displayed on the MG stand at the London Motor Show held at Earls Court in 1967.

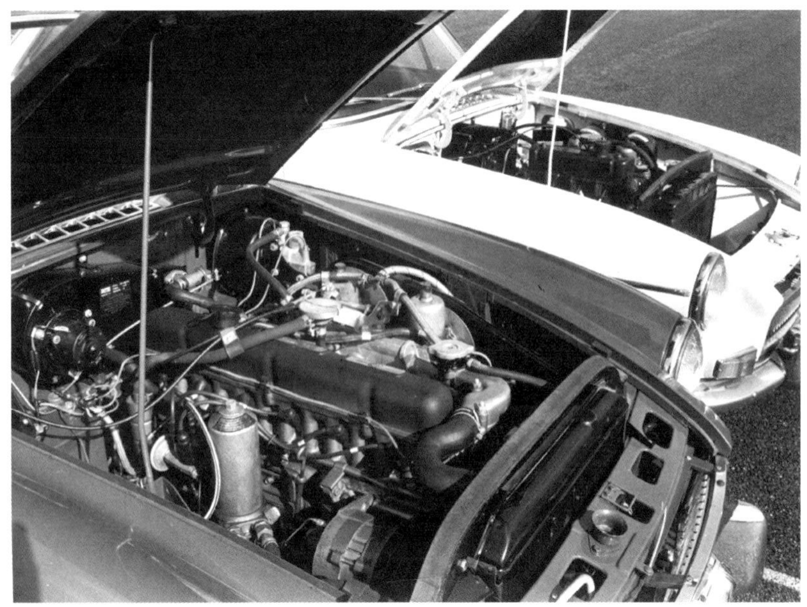

One of the publicity pictures issued when the MGC was launched clearly shows just how much more space the six-cylinder unit occupied when compared with the B-series engine in the contemporary MGB.

idea of updating the existing car by widening it and installing the same 4-litre Rolls-Royce power unit originally considered for the Longbridge project. In the end the BMC management vetoed this idea and Healey 3000 production ceased at Abingdon in 1967 without any replacement model in the offing.

Development problems with the new MGB in early 1962 meant that little work on the six-cylinder variant was carried out until the four-cylinder car was safely launched and in production. The first plan was to use a version of the 2,433cc Australian six-cylinder engine derived from the four-cylinder B-series unit already destined for use in the MGB, but this was later abandoned. The Abingdon engineers had failed to persuade the existing 3-litre Austin-Healey engine to fit under the low bonnet of the MGB and were casting around for another suitable power unit. Over at Longbridge, engineers were looking for a replacement for the large Austin/Wolseley saloon cars that used the same 3-litre engine fitted to the Healey 3000 and were asking the designers at Morris Engines at Coventry to produce an engine that was lighter, more powerful and less bulky than the old unit. Here at last might be the answer to Abingdon's problems. If the engine was to be lighter and smaller than the old 3000 unit it should be able to fit in the MGB as there was space in front of the radiator to accommodate the extra length.

However, despite the perceived space for a longer power unit, the problem was that the existing cross-member supporting the front suspension was in the way. It was obvious that a considerable amount of work on the body shell would be needed to persuade any longer engine to fit. In the event the changes made to the MGB structure for the new MGC were extensive, requiring what was virtually a brand new floor pan to accommodate the necessary revisions to the front suspension. To replace the substantial cross member that housed

An MGC GT set in a Continental scene was photographed prior to launch of the new model. The long-distance touring abilities of both the roadster and GT versions of the six-cylinder car were exploited in advertising material.

This picture shows clearly that disc wheels fitted as standard differed in design from the one-inch smaller ones specified for the MGB model. Although the majority of cars today have wire wheels, the disc version fitted with polished hubcaps looks very smart and is a lot easier to keep clean.

the coil springs and provided mounting points for the dampers, torsion bars were substituted for the coil springs and the floor pressings under the seats were revised to accommodate the rear mountings for these.

In place of the lever-arm dampers and wishbones used in the MGB, the MGC had two-piece upper and lower forged wishbones working with the torsion bars and telescopic dampers. A new cross-member, shaped to fit under the sump, provided the pivots for the wishbones as well as the mounting pads for the front of the engine. The torsion bars had splines at each end. The fronts were fitted into the rear of the lower wishbones, while the rear ends were anchored by adjustable pivots under the floor, beneath the front seats of the car. These adjustments for the torsion bars allow the ride height to be altered. At the rear, the conventional leaf springs and hydraulic dampers used on the MGB were retained, along with the Salisbury rear axle, which was fitted with higher ratio crown wheel and pinion. Externally, the only change made the bodywork was the fitting of an aluminium bonnet with bulges to give clearance for the radiator and the front carburettor. Abingdon engineers would have preferred the engine to fit beneath the bonnet without the need for these, but the new six-cylinder unit had turned out to be only slightly less bulky than the old engine and certainly larger, and heavier, than they would have wished. Actually the new engine was a disappointment as it was only two inches shorter, around twenty pounds lighter and produced 5bhp less than the Healey 3000 power unit, which had itself been developed from an engine designed some fifteen years earlier.

The failure of the engineers at Morris Engines at Coventry to come up with an engine that was more suited to use in a sports car has been given as the main reason why the MGC was not as successful as it could have been. The new engine was a strong unit with the potential to produce a good power output with considerable refinement. A lot of the problems encountered with the engine seem to stem from poor development before the engine

The MGC shared with the four-cylinder MGB an elegance of line that has seldom been bettered. A good example still turns heads so many years after the first cars appeared in the showrooms.

The MGC cockpit would be familiar to any MGB owner, although the revised chassis means that the floor beneath the seats is higher than on the four-cylinder model. This is the earlier version with seat covers featuring piping in a contrasting colour.

went into production.

Still, Abingdon had to make the best they could of an engine that was destined for use in the Austin 3-litre as well as the MGC. The front wheels of the MGC carried a small proportion of the extra weight of this engine, making this car slightly more front heavy than the MGB. However, the extra weight and the lower-geared steering fitted to counter this made the MGC feel less nimble than the four-cylinder car on winding roads, although it did add to high-speed stability. Because of the greater weight and power of the MGC, the engineers decided to fit larger diameter road wheels to the car, which also had the effect of making the car ride higher than the MGB. Unfortunately, the 15in diameter steel wheels, or optional wire wheels, were fitted with 165-15 Dunlop SP41 radial tyres, whereas wider wheels and tyres could have helped reduce the steering effort. With wider tyres the number of turns from lock to lock could have been maintained closer to the 2.9 taken by the MGB than the 3.5 of the standard MGC steering. Of recent years many cars have been converted to higher-geared racks which, in conjunction with 185 x 70 or 195 x 65 tyres, make a dramatic difference to the feel of the steering and the MGC then performs much more like the sports car it always should always have been.

Although the MGC body shell was extensively modified, and mechanically there were many important differences between it and the four-cylinder MGB, externally, apart from the letter C instead of B in the badge on the boot or tail

The engine bay of an early MGC. Note the water control fitted to the heater box and the closed circuit breathing system valve mounted above the inlet manifold.

One of the early prototype MGC GTs fitted with a different grille, possibly destined for use on an Austin-Healey version.

gate, there was only the bonnet and larger wheels to distinguish it from the cheaper car. Inside the trim was almost identical to the MGB and only re-calibrated instrument dials and slightly thicker rubber footwell mats identified that you were in the new car. The perceptive may also have noticed that the floor under the seats was raised on the MGC.

In October 1967 the major weekly motoring magazines carried full descriptions of the new model and pointed out the car weighed 345lbs more than the MGB and that 210lbs of this was due to the extra weight of the larger engine. The weight distribution changed only slightly from 54% front/46% rear to 54.8%/45.2%; hardly enough, one would have thought, to dramatically alter the handling. Both magazines included driving impressions in their descriptions but reserved most of their criticism for the full road tests they were to carry in later issues.

Performance figures in the road tests showed that the MGC was a fast car. Top speed for the *Motor* test car was 123.8mph and it reached 60mph in 10secs whilst *Autocar* recorded 121mph and the same time to 60mph. However it wasn't the bare figures the testers criticised as much as the way the car performed. They didn't like the heavy and unresponsive steering or the lack of low speed torque and the reluctance to rev exhibited by the engine. One tester writing in the *Autocar* commented "somewhere in the large BMC complex the latest example of a sports car from a famous factory that had produced many great cars in the past had lost the Abingdon touch". Testers compared the new model to the outgoing Healey 3000 and found it to be slower, more thirsty and less fun to drive, which must have given the sales staff at BMC cause for concern.

Given a high ratio top gear and the option of overdrive, the MGC was the ideal long distance touring car. In overdrive top gear the *Autocar* test team recorded a speed of 27mph per 1000 engine revolutions that meant that the engine was only turning over at about 3700 rpm at 100mph. Perhaps it was this high geared touring ability, more than anything else, that set the MGC apart from other MGs. It was the fastest production car

The engine bay of a 1969 model year MGC with the heater water valve moved to the cylinder head and the engine breather pipes feeding directly into revised carburettors. The rubber seal above the header tank is there to force all the incoming air through the radiator core, omitting this causes overheating.

This GT is finished in Old English White, rather than the brighter Glacier White finish given to the majority of white-painted MGCs.

The British Racing Green paintwork that was one of the standard colour options suits the styling of the MGC and is still a popular choice for restored cars.

MG built until the MGB GT V8 arrived in 1973 and was improved by the company when the 1969 model year cars appeared in late 1968.

Although the high gearing of the MGC gave relaxed high speed cruising it was one of the reasons why the road testers had remarked that the car didn't accelerate quite as quickly as they would have liked. When considering improvements to the car, MG development engineers completely re-thought the gearing and, except for the cars fitted with automatic transmission, it was decided for the 1969 model year to lower this so that a little more acceleration could be provided at the expense of slightly less relaxed high-speed cruising. The overall gearing in overdrive was still 24.1mph for every 1000 revs, giving a speed of nearly 100mph at 4000 revs.

With the mechanical changes introduced in late 1968 came changes to the seats and trim. The earlier MGCs featured leather seats and matching trim panels in black, blue or red with contrasting piping but for 1969 this was changed to plain black leather seat covers and trim panels, but the seats were fitted with reclining back rests. Externally the only change for the later cars was to the front wings, which had the gap between the side lamps and grille reduced by just over an inch.

The effect of these changes was to improve the later cars, but the sad thing is that the publicity department made virtually nothing of this. No cars were ever given to the motoring press to test, and the sales literature issued for the home market was never amended to show the improved seats and modified trim. The only mention made of the changes was a small over-printed note giving the revised gear ratios. At least for the American market the importers there did issue new coloured brochures illustrated by pictures of the 1969 model year MGCs. One has the feeling that the company had already given up on the cars and really didn't want to sell them.

It is a matter of history now that the MGC was quietly dropped from the price lists, and production at Abingdon stopped, after only 4542 roadsters

The ultimate expression of a fully developed MGC is this Sebring replica built in recent years by a well-known MGC specialist.

and 4457 GTs had been built. Sales had been falling behind production and there were stocks of unsold cars at the factory and at dealers so it was, perhaps, inevitable that the company would cut its losses, especially as the recent mergers had placed a Triumph-oriented management team in overall charge. By an odd quirk of fate, it was that stock of unsold cars at Abingdon that was to provide the basis of the most sought after version of the model - the University Motors Special.

In the autumn of 1967 the British Motor Corporation said that a series of Stage 1 tuning conversions, by Downton Engineering Works, were to be made available on their Austin-Morris front-wheel-drive cars, and that the full BMC guarantee would still apply. In July 1969, University Motors announced that they had been appointed as main agents by Downton Engineering Works, and that when customers wanted they would fit Downton conversions to any BMC models, and especially to MGs. Downton had established themselves as one of the foremost tuning firms dealing with BMC engines and they had been able to extract considerably more power from the poorly-developed 3-litre MGC engine by improving the gas flow in a modified cylinder head and by fitting special manifolds.

A number of these conversions had been sold both by University Motors and by Downton themselves before production of the MGC at Abingdon ceased. However, these cars can only be described as Downton modified. It is the later cars, built up by University Motors from the stock of unsold vehicles they purchased from the factory after production ceased, that were called University Motors Specials. University Motors marketed these unsold cars, mainly GTs, with the majority just being just treated to a special paint finish and their own badges. Often a different radiator grill with the original chrome surround, but horizontal alloy slats, was fitted. Some cars had interior re-trimming with at least one being modified to include two bigger rear seats that involved changes to the floor at the rear and moving the batteries from their position in front of the axle to the boot area. The suspension was also modified on some cars to improve handling. No two University Motors Specials were exactly alike, and at least one was fitted with rather ugly square headlights. Quite a number still survive and are cherished by their current owners, with those having the full Downton conversion being the most valuable.

The MGC has matured to become one of the most sought after of the post-war MGs. An example that has received engine and steering modifications is a delight to drive, and the distinctive sound produced by that large six-cylinder engine sets the car apart from the other models. Despite its early bad press and consequent poor reputation, this six-cylinder MG has matured into a car now desired by many enthusiasts and this is reflected in the premium asked for the better examples.

THE MGB WORKS COMPETITION CARS

As the MGB was not launched until September 1962, examples were not released to the Competition Department until later that year. Of course, the power unit and all major mechanical components were the same as, or similar to, those already very familiar from competition use in the MGA. The department was busy over the winter preparing for the Monte Carlo Rally in January, when no less than eight BMC cars were entered. These were an MG Midget, four Mini-Coopers, two MG 1100s and an Austin-Healey 3000. The first event pencilled in for the MGB was the Sebring 12-hour endurance race, for which cars would need to be prepared far enough in advance to allow time to ship them to Florida.

Given their workload at the time, it is not surprising that the effort to prepare two cars for Sebring in March 1963 was a little behind schedule. Once they were ready to be shipped to America for the race, however, they needed testing on a racetrack. Unfortunately, England in January 1963 was in the grip of the worst winter for many years and all the tracks were buried under a layer of frozen snow. Luckily, volunteers were found to carry out the running-in sessions on public roads around the local area, but the track work was a bit more difficult. Eventually the team were able to do some testing at Finmere Airfield, near Buckingham, where there were sufficient areas cleared of snow. However they did not run at a high enough speed on racing tyres to reveal a fatal flaw, something that eventually was destined to take both the cars out of the race.

7 DBL during the 1963 Le Mans, where after an early excursion into a sand trap it ran well, finishing first in class and 12th overall.

The two MGBs, 6 DBL and 7 DBL, received the usual thorough preparation for the meeting. Although reports say that the cars were near standard, a glance at the 11 pages of notes compiled for 6 DBL by the mechanic in charge reveals just how extensive were the changes made. For example, the engine block had a standard bore, but was fitted with stronger cam followers, special pistons, different camshaft and cam gears, and a distributor with a non-standard advance curve. The cylinder head was gas flowed and polished, and ran with a 9.5:1 compression ratio. The inlet and exhaust valves were standard size, but were made from a higher-grade material. The rocker assembly used steel pillars with spacers and special pushrods.

Although the suspension and body shell were assembled from standard MGB components, some important changes were made. There were competition shock absorbers, the rear being adjustable. Crash protection bars were incorporated and front and rear jacking points were fitted to allow the car to be raised easily to change wheels at pit stops. Finally, following usual competition practice, drain plugs and drain taps in the radiator, sump, gearbox, and rear axle were wire locked to prevent accidental loss.

For the race Jim Parkinson and Jack Flaherty drove 7 DBL and 6 DBL was crewed by Christabel Carlisle and American journalist, Denise McCluggage. This was to be one of the last major events for Christabel as she was to withdraw from racing following a serious accident at Silverstone just four months later. In spite of the careful preparation and testing, the one defect not revealed was oil surge in the standard sump when cornering. This caused the engines to be starved of oil for part of each lap, resulting inevitably in bearing failure and retirement for both cars. A baffled sump became standard on competition cars.

Competition Department prepared 8 DBL to enter in the 500km race at Spa for Alan Hutcheson to drive. In a field dominated by Porsche 356Bs, Lotus Elevens and Elites and Morgan Plus 4 Super Sports models, and won by a Ferrari 250 GTO, the lone MG had to retire with overheating. The next event was Le Mans. The sole MG entered in the 1963 race was 7 DBL and as there was still officially a company ban on racing, at least in Europe, it was nominally a private entry by one of the drivers, Alan Hutcheson. The other seat went to rally ace, Paddy Hopkirk, who was also highly regarded as a driver on the track.

For the race the pushrod BMC B-series engine had been bored to 1803 cc and fitted with a high-lift camshaft, single Weber carburettor, 10.4:1 compression, polished and gas-flowed cylinder head, and large-bore exhaust system. Equipped with a close-ratio gearbox and 3.3:1 gearing in the axle, top speed was around 130 mph and the team were confident of achieving qualifying lap times. A further modification was the addition of a longer nose section to aid air penetration at high speed. Once at the track, the team were relieved to find that their calculations were right. Limiting engine speed to 6500rpm allowed them to post a lap time of 4mins 50sec and to record 132mph through the speed trap on the Mulsanne straight. This was just good enough for them to qualify.

An estimated 340,000 spectators were at the track when the flag dropped for the 4pm start. It is interesting to see that BBC television were devoting a total of 90 minutes on the Saturday and 75 on the Sunday to live reports from the race, in addition to over one-and-a-half hours of radio coverage on the Light programme. How things have changed. Main interest centred on the cars capable of winning outright and it was the Ferrari/Cobra/Jaguar battles that gained most coverage. The lone MGB was matched against Porsches and Sunbeam Alpines in the two-litre GT category and received much support from British fans; many would have travelled to see the race in their own MGs.

In the heady excitement of his opening stint at the wheel, on the 12th lap Alan Hutcheson ran wide at Mulsanne and ended up in the sand trap. The MGB immediately bogged down and no amount of wheel spinning would break it free.

The additional fuel tank on 7 DBL was mounted in the boot with the filler pipe passing through the boot lid.

Alan spent the next 90 minutes frantically digging a pathway through the sand while keeping a watchful eye for any other cars that looked likely to join him. Eventually he managed to regain the track and from then on the MGB ran almost faultlessly for the remainder of the race.

Unfortunately, there was no way they would have been able to regain so much lost time and their 92mph average for the race was below expectations. The fastest lap was 104.14mph and the team had hoped to average close to 100mph. Luckily, their immediate competitors fared even worse and the MGB scored a creditable class win, finishing in 12th place overall. This was the year when Graham Hill drove the Rover-BRM gas turbine powered car, attracting much media attention and adding a quite different sound to the more familiar exhaust notes of the rest of the competitors.

In September the Le Mans MGB, 7 DBL was entered in the Tour de France Automobile with Andrew Hedges and Alan Hutcheson as crew. This event had been run on and off since 1899 and by 1963 was part rally and part race meeting, with competitors driving road sections between a number of race and hill climb venues. One of the attractions was the overnight stop at hotels with a good reputation for food and wine. The MGB drivers put in a spirited performance and by the third stage were lying in fourth place out of the 122 starters, behind two Ferrari GTOs and a 2-litre Porsche. Unfortunately this was as good as it got, as on the Col de Jau Andrew Hedges crashed the MGB and had to retire.

The first event in 1964 was the Monte Carlo

7 DBL on the 1964 Monte Carlo Rally. Crewed by Don and Erle Morley it came home in 17th place overall.

Rally in January when 7 DBL was prepared to rally specification and joined the BMC effort, along with Tommy Wisdom's MG 1100. In a stunning first outing in the model, the brothers Don and Erle Morley took the MGB to 17th place overall and won the GT category. In a year when a Mini-Cooper won the event outright and three other cars in the team collected awards, the MG effort received less publicity than might otherwise have been the case. Don and Erle Morley were out in the same car again for the Scottish Rally in June, but crashed and had to retire.

After the inauspicious debut of the MGBs at Sebring the previous year, for the 1964 12-hour endurance race three MGBs were entered. Regular drivers Jim Parkinson and Jack Flaherty raced one car. Of the other two, one was in the hands of Ed Leslie and John Dalton, and the Canadians Frank Morrell, Jim Adams and Merle Brennan drove the other. The Parkinson/Flaherty car retired after an oil seal failed, and the Leslie/Dalton car took third place in class and 17th overall. The Canadians were classed as finishers, in 22nd place overall.

The modest success enjoyed by the sole MGB in the 1963 Le Mans meant that for the following year there was to be an official BMC entry by the Competition Department. This was again an MGB with an extended nose section and the drivers were Andrew Hedges and Paddy Hopkirk, with Pat Vanson as reserve. The engine of BMO 541B was said to be to stage 5 and the car was in most respects similar to the 1963 entry. However, this time it ran with full interior trim, the object being to make it as close as possible to the showroom product.

There were no wild excursions into the sand to disturb things and, apart from one unscheduled stop to replace a slightly bucked wheel and some extra pit time to fit a replacement fuel filler cap, all went to schedule. The official responsible for fixing the seal had broken the original cap and the replacement was borrowed from the Sunbeam team. Unfortunately, there was to be no class victory as the opposition from Porsche and Alfa Romeo was far too strong for a near-standard road car. Their target was to be the first British entry to finish and this they achieved, taking the *Motor* trophy

BMO 541B prepared for the 1964 Le Mans Race. The smooth nose section was designed by Syd Enever to help the MGB attain high speeds on the Mulsanne Straight. To qualify for entry the car had to be capable of a fast enough lap time.

in the process. The average speed for the race was 99.945mph, just below the magic 100mph. There is little doubt that without the fuel filler delay the 100mph figure would have been achieved. Actually, to ensure a finish, the car was run below its full potential during the closing laps. One wonders if the team manager realised just how close they were to the magic figure.

The Spa-Sofia-Liège in 1964 was to be the last staged in its original form as the authorities in Germany and Austria were withdrawing permission for the cars to speed through their countries on public roads. 8 DBL had been retired from the team and with works support was entered privately by David Hiam and Rupert Jones. The official MGBs were BRX 853B driven by Pauline Mayman and Val Domleo, and BRX 854B in the hands of Julien Vernaeve. Unusually, all the MGBs retired with mechanical trouble, the two works crews suffering clutch and gearbox problems because of overheating caused by fitting full-length sump guards needed to negotiate safely the very poor roads encountered in Yugoslavia, while the third car had a damaged rear suspension. By way of consolation the Rauno Aaltonen/Tony Ambrose Healey won the event outright.

For the September 1964 Tour de France Automobile, BMO 541B, the Le Mans car, was prepared for the road and track sections encountered on this event. Mechanic Nobby Hall had to fit items like a Halda average speed calculator and a magnifier for map reading, accessories certainly not required at Le Mans. The rear axle gearing also required changing from the high ratio used on the fast Sarthe circuit to a lower ratio, with 4.55:1 being suggested on the build sheet. The sole MGB joined four Mini-Coopers in the factory effort for the start of the event at Lille. Despite meticulous preparation, the highly competitive pairing of Andrew Hedges and John Sprinzel did not manage to finish the event. A head gasket failed and the service team could not make a repair, so the car was retired.

For the RAC Rally in November the main effort centred on four Mini-Coopers, all of which retired. There were Austin-Healey 3000s for Don and Erle Morley and for Timo Makinen, the latter finishing the rally in second place. Two MGBs were entered, but both failed to finish. BRX 854B, driven by John Fitzpatrick, was involved in an accident and had to retire, while Pauline Mayman and Val Domleo in BRX 853B retired after the clutch once again caused trouble.

The first two seasons of racing and rallying the MGB brought modest success, and the 1964/65 winter saw most of the activity in the Competition Department centred around preparing the six Mini-Coopers and two Austin 1800s for the Monte Carlo Rally. There were no MG entries, but the team nevertheless had much to celebrate when Timo Makinen and Paul Easter won the event outright in their Morris Mini-Cooper S. The Swedish Rally in the following month saw all four Mini-Coopers retire with transmission failure, thought to be a lubrication issue in the extreme cold. In motor sport you win some, you lose some.

Paddy Hopkirk and Andrew Hedges standing in front of their pit at Le Mans in 1964 with BMO 541B.

The first outing for the MGBs was a trip to Florida for the Sebring 12-hour endurance race. Sebring is situated in a part of Florida where the main activity is growing citrus fruit. The heavy rain that often falls there must help the farmers, but is less than welcome when racing for 12 hours on a flat and exposed airfield. In 1965 the weather on race day played an important part in events; indeed it seems to have been exceptional, even for that part of the country.

The BMC Competition Department made a major effort that year and fielded no less than four MGs. In addition, the Donald Healey Motor Company at Warwick prepared two Austin-Healey Sprites and an Austin-Healey 3000 to run under the BMC banner. Two of the MGs were the pretty Midget coupés built in 1962 for Dick Jacobs. These were now back at Abingdon and were fitted with 1139cc engines for Sebring. The British drivers, Andrew Hedges and Roger Mac, had one car and Chuck Tannlund and John Wagstaff the other.

BMO 541B and DRX 256C prior to the 1965 Sebring Twelve-hour Race.

Merle Brennan and Frank Morrell were down to drive MGB BMO 541B, and Brad Picard and Al Pease the other MGB, DRX 256C. The North American importers in part sponsored the venture so it was not surprising that all the MGB drivers were American or Canadian amateurs.

The race started in blazing hot sunshine. The air temperature was over 90 degrees and track temperature closer to 130, so drivers of the closed cars, like the MGs, were bathed in perspiration as they battled round the bumpy track. One of the Midgets dropped out early in the race with engine trouble, hardly surprising as it had been used as the practice car and had already covered a great many racing miles. Other than an unscheduled stop to change a buckled wheel on one of the MGBs, the rest of the cars were running well.

After around four-and-a-half hours of racing the brilliant sunshine gave way to heavy storm clouds and within minutes the heavens opened. A huge volume of water fell in a short space of time and large sections of the track, as well as the pits area, were awash. So bad were conditions that wipers were unable to cope and drivers were opening doors to look round the side of the windscreen to get some idea of where to find the race track.

For some reason the race was not stopped and there were minor accidents as the drivers struggled to navigate round the worse of the puddles. In some cases mechanics and track officials waded out into the larger pools of water to point out the shallower areas to drivers. Pits stops became a farce. Spare wheels floated away before they could be fitted, mechanics trying to work under cars almost needed diving gear, and lap charts and time keeping became ever more difficult as people struggled to identify cars in the downpour.

However, the rain eventually stopped and both the track and the pits area started to dry out. The closed cars had fared better than those without a roof, and none of the BMC team dropped out during the rain. At the end of the race the remaining Midget, driven by Hedges and Mac, took first place in the 1300cc GT class, and MGB BMO 541B was second in the 2-litre prototype class. The Austin-Healey Sprites managed first and second in class, and the 3000 was first in the 3-litre GT class. With the second MGB finishing the race, although well down the field after losing time with an electrical problem, it was a good result for the boys from BMC.

In April the first rally of the year featuring an MGB was as part of a three-car BMC effort in the Tulip. BRX 854B was driven by Ken Tubman and Stefanoff, but did not feature in the results. However, Timo Makinen and Paul Easter won their class in a Mini, as did Don and Erle Morley in an Austin-Healey. In May the factory prepared an 8 DBL for Tony Fall and Liz Crellin to drive in the Welsh Rally and they finished the event in 34th place. Another smaller event with factory participation was the Nordrhein-Westfalen Rally in July where BRX 853B, in the hands of Andrew Hedges, was 11th overall and third in the GT category.

In May 8 DBL was again in action when it was prepared for John Rhodes to partner Warwick Banks

John Rhodes and Warwick Banks driving 8 DBL took first place in the Guards 1000-mile Race for production sports cars at Brands Hatch.

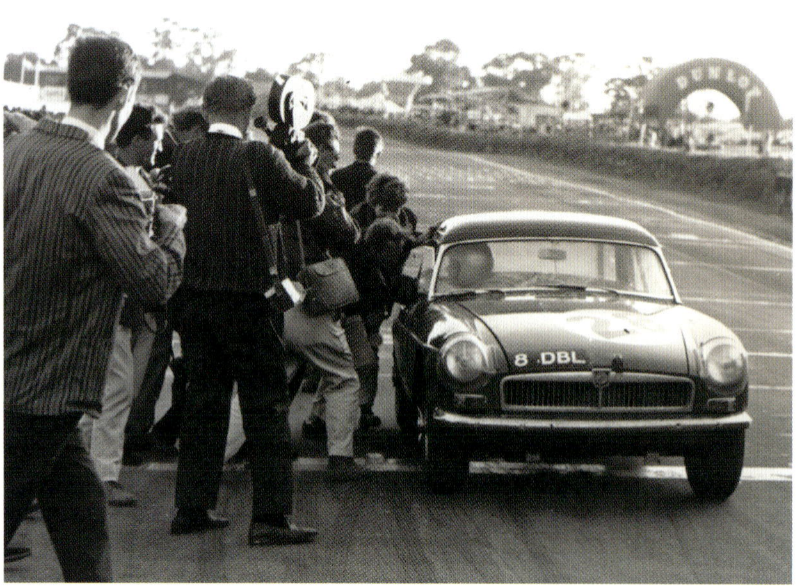

in the Guards 1000 Race for production sports cars at Brands Hatch. In a field that contained many Jaguar E-types, Triumphs, MGBs, Midgets and Lotus Elans, consistent driving during the long race and quick work by the mechanics during stops in the crowded pits saw the works MGB lead the field home to take first place overall.

Having had two good results from two starts with MGBs in previous Le Mans races, it was decided that DRX 255C would run in 1965 in an effort to score a hat trick of finishes. The new car was prepared to similar specification as previously, and there is little doubt that it was probably closer to its road-going cousins than any other car in the race. Apart from engine tuning and different gear ratios, only the extended nose and some lightweight panels distinguished DRX 255C from any other MGB. The team of Andrew Hedges and Paddy Hopkirk were again to share the driving.

MG Chief Designer Syd Enever at work on the nose of the 1965 Le Mans MGB.

That was the year when Ford decided that they were going to win at Le Mans in the GT 40, and failed miserably when all their cars failed to finish. It was also the last year that a near-standard production MG sports car was to run in a race that was becoming ever more geared towards providing entries solely for out-and-out racing machinery. The MGB maintained its unblemished Le Mans record by running for 24 hours at near maximum speed with only one failed component, a light bulb. The car achieved the best post-war placing for the marque, finishing in 11th place, and was second in class. They also took the *Motor* trophy for the highest-placed British entry.

In July BMC Hambro, Ridgefield New Jersey

Despite having seen a lot of competition use, BRX 854B is a rare survivor which retains its original body and aluminium panels and looks much as it did when built in 1964.

BRX 854B is finished in the standard colour scheme used by the Competition Department for almost all the MGBs they entered in events.

entered a works MGB in the Bridgehampton 500km race for production sports cars. Paddy Hopkirk made the trip to America for the event and was rewarded with fourth place overall and second place in the GT category.

In 1966 the Monte Carlo Rally was both a fiasco and a triumph for the BMC team. The Mini-Coopers made a clean sweep of the leader board and took the first three places. This was rather more than the organisers could stand, and they disqualified the Mini-Coopers along with some other British competitors on a technicality. Needless to say, this ensured far more British media coverage than if they had been declared winners. The sole MG was MGB GRX 307D for Tony Fall and Ron Crellin, which unfortunately retired after an oil cooler pipe burst.

The hard top now fitted to BRX 854B is a replacement; in 1965 the original was damaged beyond repair.

For the now annual trip to Sebring, in 1966 it was decided to try to contest two classes with the MGBs. This was achieved by producing a special, 2009cc engine for 8 DBL, the car to be driven by Paddy Hopkirk and Andrew Hedges, a formidable pairing. The other MGB, HBL 129D, was running with its engine tuned to stage 6 in the factory tuning book. This car was in the hands of Peter Manton, Roger Mac and Emmett Brown. The larger-capacity engine in the roadster used a special block and head, the latter machined to accept the larger valves from the Healey 3000. It produced 138bhp and was the most powerful MGB engine the team had fielded thus far.

In the race the prototype MGB in the hands of Paddy Hopkirk suffered an early failure of a rocker arm. This was changed in just 17 minutes and the car was off in hard pursuit of the class leaders. Having passed all the opposition, and then seen them fall by the wayside, it was a bitter disappointment when, after more than 10 hours of the 12-hour race had been run, a con-rod came through the side of the block. By way of consolation, the other MGB won its class.

The Targa Florio in Sicily was one of the most demanding events in the calendar. Staged over 10 laps of a circuit comprising 45 miles of winding and often poorly surfaced mountain roads, it was said to have no less than 700 corners per lap. Despite hours of practice, only drivers with an intimate local knowledge could hope to learn every twist and turn of the circuit. In 1965 one of the Midget coupés in the hands of Paddy Hopkirk and

Andrew Hedges had come home in second place in class and a creditable 11th position overall. For 1966 the BMC team decided to enter two MGBs and an Austin-Healey coupé. MGB JBL 491D was to be driven by John Handley and GRX 307D by Timo Makinen and John Rhodes.

Unusually for Sicily, the day prior to the race it rained torrents, washing mud on to the road surface and turning part of the circuit into what was described as looking like a farm track. Dawn the morning of the race saw the sun appear, although there were still some threatening clouds over the mountains. The cars were flagged off at intervals, the track being just too tight for a massed start. The roads had been closed for some hours in order that the owners of donkey carts, bicycles and other local vehicles could be dissuaded from getting in the way. At first it stayed dry, but when the race had been underway for a while down came the rain, making things especially difficult for the faster cars. The road was becoming ever more slippery and there were a number of crashes. The MGBs, however, pressed on, rain being nothing strange for the British, and by the time the winner passed the finish line and the remaining cars were flagged off Timo Makinen was in ninth place overall and first in class, with the other MGB second in class. This was a good result in a difficult event.

In July GRX 307D went to Italy for Andrew Hedges and Robin Widdows to enter the Mugello race. This again was an event staged on public roads and took place in the mountains north of Florence. The circuit, 40 miles long, was in essence a very much shorter version of the defunct Mille Miglia and even used the Futa Pass. Longer races on public roads suited the MGB and the car came home in 11th place overall and third in the GT category.

The 84-hour long Marathon de la Route in August saw GRX 307D out again, this time with Andrew Hedges sharing driving with Julien Vernaeve. Joining them in BRX 855B were Roger Enever, son of MG designer Syd Enever, and Alec Poole. The circuit used that year was the old 28km long Nürburgring, with all its twists, turns and hazards, and this provided a stiff test of both car and drivers. Another difficulty was that the regulations called for the average speed over the final 12 hours to match that set in the first 12, difficult if your car was ailing. The field encompassed a wide variety of cars, from a Ferrari to a team of DAFs, with the main competition for the MGBs coming from Lotus Cortinas and Alfa Romeos. At the end it was the Hedges/ Vernaeve MGB that took first place, having covered 8876km. The second MGB retired when a half-shaft broke.

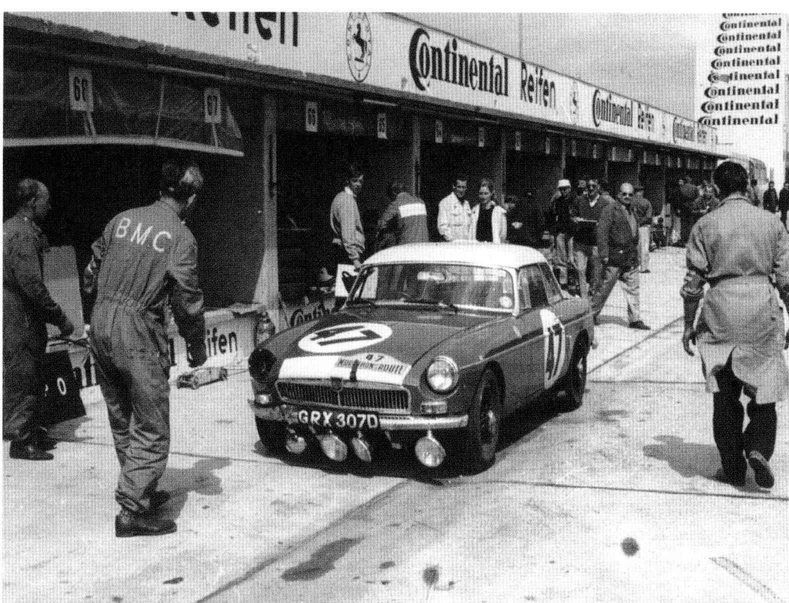

Having sustained some damage, GRX 307D enters the pits during the 84-hour Marathon de la Route.

The team returned to the Nürburgring the following month for the ADAC 1000km Race with JBL 491D, again with Andrew Hedges and Julien Vernaeve driving. This time luck did not go their way: a hose broke, overheating caused gasket failure, and they had to retire. However, better luck favoured these drivers on an outing later the same month when with GRX 307D they entered the 1000km race at Spa. The field included examples of most of the fast sports/racing machinery of that era. The MGB's reliability and the skill of the drivers saw it come home in 12th place overall and first in GT2 class, beating a great many potentially much quicker cars.

The final race of 1966 for the MGBs was held at the Paris Montlhéry track in October. The same cars and drivers as had turned out for the August Marathon de la Route once again made the trip to Europe. This time both MGBs finished the race and, in a field that included a lot of very quick cars, were well placed in 12th and 13th overall and second and third in class. The Enever/Poole car led the pair home.

In 1967 the team returned to Sebring with two MGBs, a roadster, GRX 307D and a GT, LBL 591E. The roadster was running as a Group III car in the 1300 to 2000cc Grand Touring class, fitted with an 1824cc engine. Although the GT had standard bodywork, the only major modification to it being an enlarged fuel tank and racing filler cap, it had not been homologated as a production car in time for the race and had to run in the prototype category. To make it eligible for the 2000 to 3000cc class, the engine was bored out to 2004cc.

The roadster, driven by Timo Makinen and John Rhodes, put up a faultless performance and was placed second in class. The MGB GT, in the hands of Paddy Hopkirk and Andrew Hedges, was first in class and 11th overall. The only problem for the MGs was a refuelling rig that fed more air than petrol into the tank during refuelling, and an unscheduled stop by Paddy Hopkirk to replace buckled wheels and a bent steering arm after an off-course excursion to miss a spinning car.

With the MGBs no longer the main focus of attention in the Competition Department, 1967 saw far fewer entries than in previous years. However, two MGBs went to Sicily in May for the Targa Florio, this time staged under clear skies and blazing sun. The lightweight MG GTS, MBL 546E was brand new and had been built to eventually take the 3-litre MGC power unit. However, for this race it was fitted with a 2004cc four-cylinder engine and was piloted by the strong driver pairing of Paddy Hopkirk and Timo Makinen. The second car, MBL 547E, was a fairly standard roadster, apart from the usual competition modifications, and was driven by Andrew Hedges and Alec Poole. In the race, brake problems delayed the GTS for a while, but afterwards it ran well and finished third in class. Andrew Hedges, on the other hand, had the bad luck to clip a marker stone, spin off the road and hit a tree. His race was over. Incidentally the surviving build sheet for MBL 547E bears the appended note "scrapped", so that is one competition MGB that hasn't survived.

The MGB GT, LBL 591E, being prepared for the 1967 Sebring Race. Drivers Paddy Hopkirk and Andrew Hedges took the car to first place in class and 11th overall.

The last MGs built by the Competitions Department were the special MGS GTs, one of which had run in the Targa Florio. The story of the development of these cars started in the mid-1960s when it was known that a six-cylinder version of the MGB, the MGC, was going to be built. The decision was taken to build specialised prototypes that looked like the proposed MGC whilst being much lighter than the production cars. To gain sufficient strength to cope with the projected power available from a tuned 3-litre engine, the cars were to be GTs, but constructed with alloy panels to reduce weight. The floor pans and chassis structure were made from steel, but the upper parts of the body, the wings, roof, doors, bonnet, tailgate, etc., were aluminium. The front and rear wheel arches were widened to give clearance over larger section wheels and tyres. The basic suspension was similar to that used on production MGCs. Rear springs of a different rating were fitted, plus dampers with adjustable settings. An anti-roll bar and axle radius arms also helped control the handling of the rear of the car. Girling disc brakes were fitted all round and the car had Minilite wheels with centre-lock fixings.

In 1968 for the Sebring race MBL 546E ran as a prototype MGC fitted with a modified six-cylinder engine and transmission. Drivers Paddy Hopkirk and Andrew Hedges had a relatively trouble-free run, finishing in 10th place overall and third in the Prototype category. They also won their class and had the distinction of being the highest ever placed BMC car at Sebring. The other MG entered, LBL 591E, the MGB GT used the previous year, was driven by Garry Rodrigues, Richard McDaniel and Bill Brack to a lowly fifth in class.

The final event we shall cover is the 1968 Targa Florio. MGB GT LBL 591E was entered with Paddy Hopkirk and Andrew Hedges as drivers. The race was notable because of a remarkable drive by Vic Elford in his Porsche 907. He lost time on the opening lap with tyre trouble and started the second lap some 15 minutes behind the leaders. Rejoining the fray he passed car after car on the twisting circuit before handing over to his co-driver for three laps. Taking over for the final section of the race, he managed to regain the lead and stayed ahead of the field until the flag fell. Of the MG entries, the MGB GT ran faultlessly, winning the sports car category and finishing in 12th place overall.

THE MGB GT V8

The MGB GT V8 was launched on 15 August 1973 at just at about the most difficult time to sell a 3.5-litre high-performance car. In October that year Egypt and Syria attacked Israel and this resulted in the five-week Yom Kippur War. The Arab producers stopped oil supplies to the West, with consequent shortages and huge price rises that were to frighten people off buying cars that might use more fuel. Actually the fuel economy of the V8 MGB was very good, but most people act more on feelings than on facts and the common perception of such cars was that they were bound to use more fuel than those with engines of a smaller capacity.

Sports cars, by definition, should possess sufficient performance and handling advantages over the current crop of family saloons to justify the higher prices and increased insurance cost borne by

Fitting the 3.5-litre Rover power unit in the MGB engine bay was a triumph of packaging and because the V8 engine had an aluminium block it did not upset the overall balance of the car.

their owners. When the MGB replaced the popular MGA in 1962, for a total price of £930 buyers had a 108mph top speed and acceleration to 60mph in 12.1secs. This compared well with 80mph and 19.8secs for the contemporary £700 Ford Cortina 1500, or the 88mph maximum speed and 17.6secs for the dash to 60mph provided by the £837 Triumph Vitesse. However, by 1972 things had changed and in the intervening decade Ford had introduced the Capri, which gave stylish 4-seater motoring at modest cost. Engines from 1300cc to 3-litre could be specified, with the higher-powered models giving sporting performance.

The price of the MGB with overdrive had risen to over £1400, but the performance had remained much the same. The most powerful Capri was more expensive than the MGB; it cost £1700 but did have a 120mph top speed and reached 60mph in 8.6secs. The 1600GT version of the Capri cost about the same as an MGB and had a similar top speed, but reached 60mph in just over 11secs. Saloon cars were becoming quicker and the MGB was fast becoming outclassed.

The company had been well aware of the need to give the sports car buyer more performance and the MGC had been their first move in this direction. However, that car was not as successful as the makers had hoped and the idea of having a more powerful MGB seemed to have been shelved. Individual owners had always been able to improve the performance of the B-series engine, either by working from the advice given in the factory tuning booklets or by approaching one of the independent tuning companies, like Downton or Speedwell.

However, few customers were likely to arrange for their cars to be tuned to improve performance – the attitude of most insurance companies to converted cars saw to that – and it was really up to the company to produce something suitable to satisfy the demand. The main difficulty Abingdon faced was the usual one of getting sufficient funds to improve the car. The management of British Leyland did not want to invest large sums to develop an MG that would directly compete with other cars produced within the organisation. The Abingdon engineers had examined various options that involved fitting different engines, but most of these needed considerable re-engineering of the car and this was ruled out on cost grounds. One engine that would have fitted, the lightweight Buick-derived V8 fitted to the Rover P6 saloons and Range-Rover, was initially disregarded because it was in short supply; or at least that was what those at Abingdon were told. However, it was this engine that was eventually to be used to build one of the best cars ever to emerge from the factory.

A Costello-converted MGB GT with a fibreglass bonnet incorporating a bulge to clear the carburettors.

The impetus behind the eventual adoption of the Rover V8 for use in the MGB was the efforts of an independent engineer whose name will forever be linked to his creation. Ken Costello had established himself as a person who could make Mini saloons go faster round the track than almost anyone else. However, he did not confine himself to working on these cars and one experiment was fitting an Oldsmobile V8 engine in an open MGB roadster. The result was so successful that he started building similar cars for customers. The small-block aluminium V8 engines were ideally suited to use in British sports cars. The Sunbeam Tiger had been an official factory effort by Rootes, who used a Ford engine and gearbox to transform the performance of their pretty but sedate Sunbeam Alpine. Only the sale of the company to Chrysler, a competitor of Ford, stopped them selling in larger numbers.

Ken Costello had turned to the British-built Rover version of the Buick V8 for his MGB conversions, using the engine in its standard 150bhp form mated to the MGB gearbox via a larger 9.5in diameter clutch. He retained the standard MGB rear axle but fitted MGC gears that gave an overall ratio of 3.07:1. The engine was too tall to fit under the standard MGB bonnet as the carburettors sat above the central V of the engine, so Costello designed a fibreglass one that incorporated an ugly bulge to clear them. He also fitted a black aluminium grille and special V8 Costello badges to distinguish his cars from the 4-cylinder models. Suspension, brakes and steering were unmodified, but harder pads were used to cope with braking from higher speeds.

Overall, the car actually weighed slightly less than an ordinary MGB so that handling was not adversely affected and all the extra power could

The engine bay of a Costello V8 with the standard carburettor arrangement that came with the Rover power units he used.

be used in enhancing performance. The effect of fitting an engine of similar weight but with twice the capacity can be judged from the road test figures recorded by *Autocar* magazine. Their car reached 60mph in 7.8secs and was timed at a maximum speed of 128mph. With engine torque increased by over 80%, the Costello V8 was an exceptionally easy car to drive fast, performance being available from low engine speeds in any gear. The only real drawback was the cost. A completely converted new car cost £975 more than a standard MGB or MGB GT, and was more expensive than other cars of similar performance.

In spite of having very limited development facilities, Ken Costello had built a good, well-engineered road car. Journalists found few faults with those they drove and most of their complaints owed more to equipment shortcomings in the original MGB than to any problems with the Costello conversions. In spite of the relatively high price of the cars, quite a number were built using new engines supplied direct from British Leyland, who must have been well aware of what he was doing with the units they sold him. In the end the company must have decided that there was a small market here that they could exploit themselves, and the Abingdon engineers were authorised to develop their own car using the Rover engine.

Given their head, the factory engineers had a prototype V8 MGB running in a few weeks and after a short period of development this was passed to go into production. The MG eventually built used the Range-Rover version of the aluminium V8 engine, which had a lower compression ratio and produced 137bhp at 5000rpm. The idea of having an unnecessary bonnet bulge obviously offended the factory development team, who worked out a neat alternative inlet arrangement that placed the carburettors at the back of the engine and kept the whole installation low enough to fit beneath a standard bonnet. The distinctive V8 air cleaners incorporated neat bi-metal valves that allowed warm air from around the exhaust manifolds to be drawn into the engine when it was cold, and cool air when the engine warmed up.

Some sheet-metal modifications to the inner wings were required to enable the bulkier V8 engine to fit in the standard engine bay. Although Costello deemed that when the V8 engine was installed little needed changing on his cars, the MG engineers decided to modify the gearbox, suspension and brakes of their V8. The gearbox was mated to a different clutch and bell-housing, with a modified clutch withdrawal bearing, and was altered to restrict overdrive solely to top gear after testing had revealed that the greater engine torque could cause difficulties with overdrive on third gear. Stiffer springs of similar specification to those used on police MGBs were fitted, and the brakes were uprated by using thicker front discs and

Damask Red was one of the standard paint colours available for the V8. Unlike the situation now, you did not have to pay extra to have you car in any colour other than white.

The closed versions of the MGB, be they four-, six- or eight- cylinder models, are attractive and practical cars.

different front brake callipers. Dunlop D4 wheels shod with wider, 175-section tyres were specified. These increased the rolling radius of the wheels slightly and raised the ride height a small amount. The wheels had alloy centres fitted to steel rims and were immensely strong, something wire wheels never were, which is why they did not join the V8 options list.

The motoring press praised the performance of the V8, but commented adversely on the lack of any interior or exterior changes to the car to justify its far higher price tag. Once again here was the criticism that had haunted the MGC five years earlier. It seemed that although the company assumed that it was really extra performance that buyers craved, journalists on the other hand felt that the provision of additional performance alone was insufficient to justify the extra prices charged for higher-performance models. They apparently felt that buyers would like everyone to see that the faster cars were also brighter, bolder and more comfortable than their slower rivals. Perhaps here was one of the greatest shortcomings of the MG philosophy laid bare. The Leyland marketing men thought that the MG enthusiast was willing to trade additional comfort for more performance whilst the journalists and the customers felt otherwise.

The truth was that, given the chance, MG would have been happy to incorporate more changes in the cars to justify the higher cost, or to reduce the price premium, but these decisions were out of their control. Leyland seemed happy to overcharge for the outwardly unchanged V8 models and to suffer poor sales in consequence. As some justification for the higher price, the MGB GT V8 did have tinted windows, a heated rear window and overdrive as standard; these were extras on the 4-cylinder cars. At launch the car cost £2293.96, the current price for the ordinary GT equipped with overdrive and tinted windows being £1627.71, so the premium charged for the V8 engine was over £600, an increase of no less than 40%.

Pricing the car the way they did, the company could have hardly been surprised to find that the motoring magazines compared it to other cars in the same price bracket and found it wanting. *Autocar* pointed out that the 3-litre Ford Capri with similar performance cost just £1824 and that the much-acclaimed Datsun 240Z was priced at only a couple of hundred pounds more than the MG. There were no complaints about the performance the big engine gave the car. In spite of its modest state of tune, top speed was 124mph and 60mph was reached in just 8.6secs.

The attractive steel/aluminium composite wheels fitted to the V8 look attractive, but once corroded are difficult and costly to restore.

The main sources of complaint were the heavy steering, poor ride, high wind noise, and the lack of some of the appointments they felt a GT car costing over £2000 really should have enjoyed. The dated dashboard was particularly disliked. Apart from the high price, one of the main reasons why the basic shortcomings of the MGB GT design were so obvious was because the engine was so quiet and refined. At the high speeds that the V8 was capable of maintaining hour after hour, the excessive wind noise from the frameless side windows became far more apparent. At higher speeds in the ordinary GT the sounds produced by the hard-working engine tended to cancel out the extra wind noise. Had the car they used been a roadster rather than a GT, the conclusions of the test team may well have differed. However, as the company had decided not to build roadster versions of the V8, this was not an option.

In truth, given the sort of development money available, there was little that could have been done about the wind noise. The GT had been developed originally from an open car and to save cost at that time the door windows were little changed. If the car had been designed from the outset as a saloon then the doors would have probably have had fixed frames around the windows, which would have eased the task of reducing air leakage around them. The complaints about inferior ride and flawed handling were also a feature of the basic design. It seems that the engineers were not able to carry out any major modifications, changes being limited to changing springs, etc. Stiffer rear springs had been

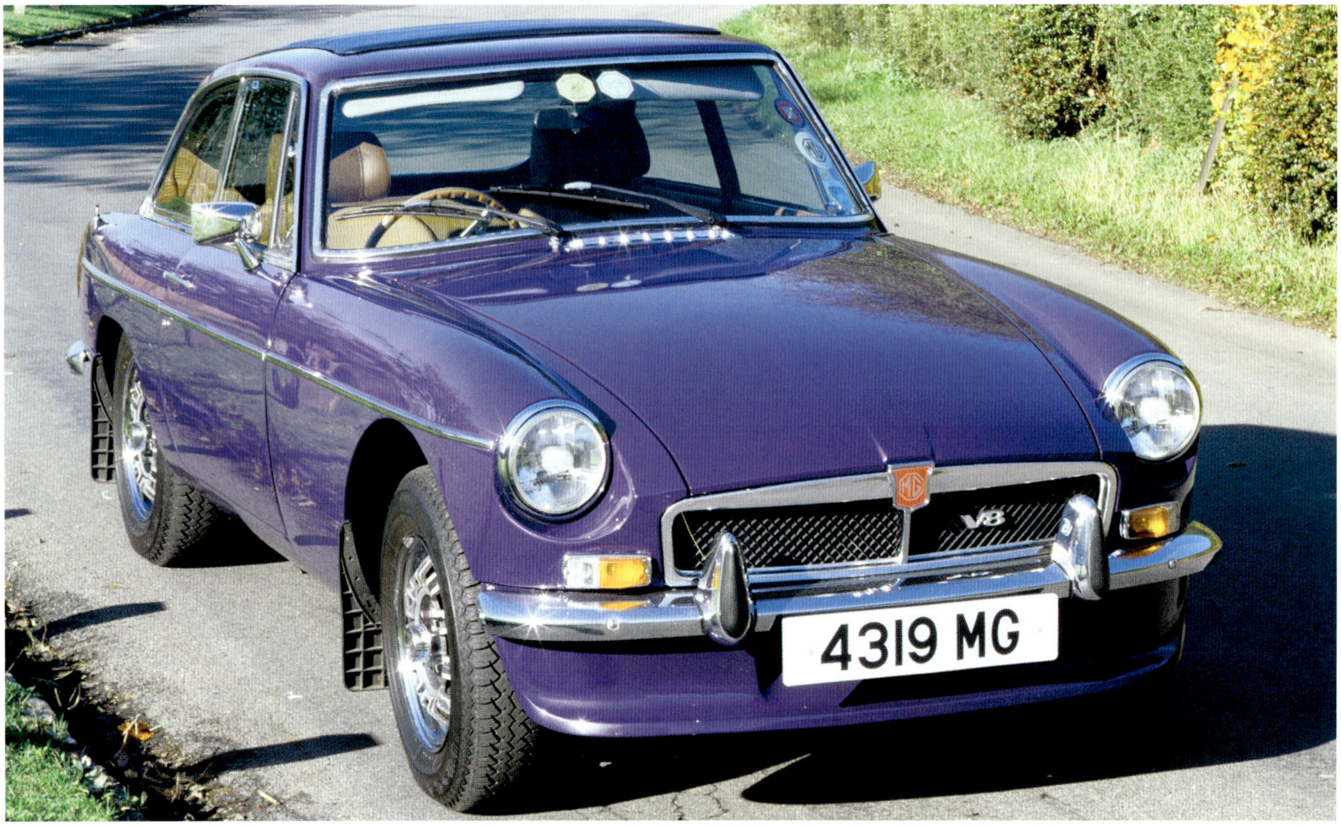

One of the colours available on the V8 was Aconite, a colour seldom seen on restored cars but shown well here on this totally original example.

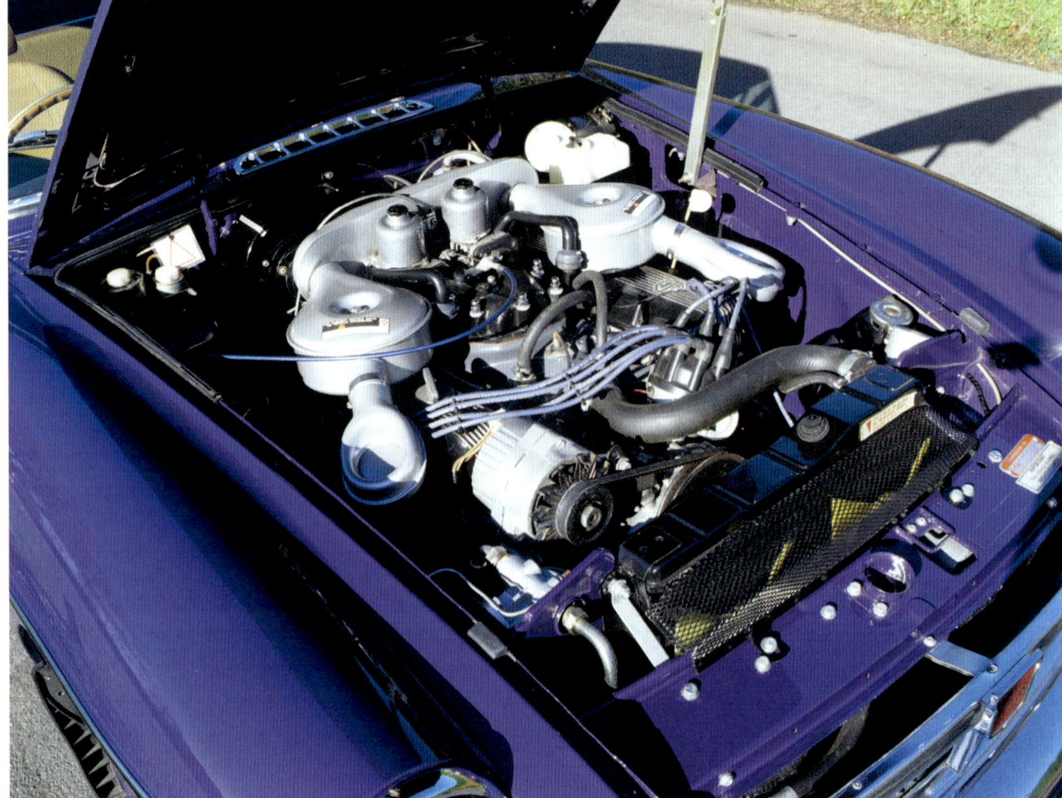

The engine bay of an unrestored car.

fitted to help control the axle tramp on acceleration produced by large doses of torque from the V8 engine. The stronger rear springs and wider-section tyres raised the ride height a little and, to compensate, stiffer front springs were used as well. The effect of these changes was to make the ride harder, and to introduce some instability if power was cut mid-corner. Neither of these characteristics enhanced the appeal of the car.

So that was the bad news in 1973, but what about the V8 today? Strange as it may seem, some of the things that testers complained of then seen less important now. Modern cars are all quiet, with well suppressed wind noise and high cruising speeds, and one hardly expects an aging sports car to match them in refinement. In fact, it is that very lack of modern refinement that is part of the appeal of older cars and anyone who buys one looking for the sort of motoring they get from their ordinary saloon will be disappointed. Actually, one of the nicest things about driving an MGB GT V8 is the way the ready access to ample power transforms the car. Driven gently, the torque of the engine makes it very easy to live with. On smooth roads the lack of suspension refinement is no handicap and you are always aware that dropping down a gear and flooring the throttle will, without really trying, dispose of many other cars on the road.

Mere acceleration figures do not convey the full measure of the performance available. There are many sporting versions of modern cars which on paper appear much quicker than the V8 but which, on the road, require high engine revs and a lot of effort to beat the MG, which seems to be capable of gaining speed quickly without drama. The ride deteriorates badly on the sort of badly maintained side roads now so common. Here is where the age of the design shows up most and the answer seems to be not to try too hard, just wind down the windows and enjoy the distinctive sounds emanating from the V8 engine as they are reflected from walls and hedges.

For many, the only real disadvantage of the MGB GT V8 is that it was only built in GT form. However, given the ready availability of V8 engines, and of new body shells specifically made to construct V8-powered roadsters, it isn't surprising that there are now quite a number of very effective open V8-powered MGBs around.

A factory publicity picture of a later MGB GT V8 fitted with energy-absorbing bumpers.

The steel and alloy wheels used as standard on the MGB GT V8 were chosen because they are stronger than wire wheels.

THE MGB: LATER YEARS

The first major alteration to the MGB roadsters and GTs came in December 1967 when a whole raft of changes were made that were extensive enough to justify giving the cars the designation Mark II. Some of these were prompted by altered regulations for cars sold in the United States to be introduced from 1968, and the first impact of these on the MGB came with the adoption of the 18GF power unit for that market. This engine was fitted with a pump to inject air into the exhaust valve ports and also had positive crankcase ventilation. Another feature of the USA market cars was the replacement of the pressed metal dashboard with an ugly padded one, while the switches for the lights, etc., were now of the rocker type and the steering column was collapsible. However, the glove box was no longer fitted. Quoted engine power was reduced with a consequent reduction in top speed. Acceleration was not badly affected as the gearbox had better ratios and engine torque was slightly improved. One characteristic of air injection for reducing pollution was the slow response to closing the throttle: one American magazine reported that it took nine seconds for the engine to return to idle if the throttle was closed at 3000rpm.

The revamp of the MGB in the Leyland era included replacing the traditional MG grille with this cheaper and less elegant arrangement.

Cars for the home and other markets were given the 18GD engine and all cars received a new gearbox with synchromesh on all gears. This unit was bigger than the one replaced and required a wider tunnel. The prop shaft and rear axle were also modified. A revised type of overdrive unit was fitted to those cars where this was specified as an extra. Another option introduced into the price list was a three-speed automatic gearbox. This was a departure for MG with their two-seater sports cars. The automatic version sold in relatively small numbers. However, on test the motoring reporters were surprised to find that performance did not suffer as much as one would have thought; the maximum speed at 104mph was very little different from that recorded with the manual car. The automatic option was dropped in 1973.

Along with most other British cars at that time, the MGB electrical system was converted to negative earth and an alternator replaced the dynamo; this change required a new control box. Two-speed wipers were now specified and flush-fitting internal door handles and modified quarter-light clips were part of the safety-related introductions. As the revised cars were introduced at a time when the company was in deep trouble and undergoing many structural changes it is not surprising that little effort was made to publicise them.

The problems in the British motor industry during the 1960s had a serious impact on the small Abingdon plant and eventually meant the scrapping of plans for a replacement for the MGB. The solution then seen by the government favoured fewer but larger car companies, and Jaguar was one of the first to expand when they bought the ailing Daimler concern, using both the production facilities and the name to enlarge the range of models they offered. This failed to ensure the company's independence and in 1966 they merged with the British Motor Corporation under the title of British Motor Holdings. This too was short-lived and, at the prompting of the Labour government, the Leyland Group, which by now had control of MG's rivals, Triumph, was merged in early 1968 with British Motor Holdings as British Leyland Motor Corporation.

Despite all of the problems, the MGB continued to sell well, especially in America. The introduction of the six-cylinder MGC in late 1967 obviously affected the numbers of four-cylinder cars purchased but as the new model was more expensive and received a bad press most buyers still opted for the MGB. Annual production figures for the GT dropped from over 11,000 in 1967 to 8352 in 1968, but recovered to 12,000 in 1969. However, roadster sales in 1968 were over 2000 higher than the previous year so overall the numbers of MGBs built altered little.

The non-USA 1969 model year cars assembled from November 1968 were fitted with the 18GG power unit with altered crankcase breathing. As with the MGC, other changes included the adoption of a new design of seat fitted with black leather covers without contrasting piping and a revised position for the front sidelights. The alternator now had a built-in control box and at last the heater became a standard fitting. Although produced for less than a year this version has proved popular with modern enthusiasts, who see it as the last of the models to be built with the attractive MG grille and leather trim.

The first substantial changes to the MGB under British Leyland were to appear on the 1970 model

The American market 1968 model year cars had to comply with more stringent safety regulations and were fitted with this padded facia.

Picture used in a catalogue of the period.

The recessed grille was almost universally disliked and was replaced by a more traditional arrangement, though without the vertical bars.

year cars launched at the 1969 London Motor Show. This was a facelift designed at Longbridge in an effort to both modernise the appearance of the ageing design and to reduce costs. The traditional slatted MG radiator grille was replaced by a matt black-painted, recessed one, but in a cheapskate move the bonnet pressing still retained the central bulge on the front edge above where the MG badge had originally been placed. Steel Rostyle wheels replaced the standard type, saving the cost of a set of hubcaps. The option of wire wheels was still offered and these went on a high proportion of exported cars. The traditional leather seat covers were replaced by the cheaper option of Ambla, a knit-backed expanded vinyl. All models carried British Leyland badges on the front wings.

A press picture of an early MGB GT with impact-absorbing bumpers.

In spite of the changes not being universally popular, the motoring magazines carried favourable road test reports of the revised models. Motor magazine tested an open MGB towards the end of 1969 and recorded an acceleration time from 0-60mph of 11secs, an improvement over the earlier model, and a top speed of 105mph. It was particularly pleased that it found the car less outclassed by more modern designs than it had expected, but it did criticise some of the controls and equipment.

In May 1971 the company announced that production of the MGB had reached 250,000, making it Britain's biggest-selling sports car with over 200,000 exported worldwide. The factory continued to make small changes and in October 1972 the controversial MGB recessed grille was changed to something closer to the original design. The surround returned to its original shape and the badge was relocated to again line up with the

Just one Golden Jubilee roadster was built, and was shipped to America to be offered as a competition prize.

An official picture of the Golden Jubilee MGB GT.

bulge on the front of the bonnet. The central area of the grille was filled with a matt black injection-moulded mesh. The specification of both open and closed versions was improved, with the GTs gaining brushed nylon seat panels and heated rear windows.

The next change to the roadster and GT radically altered their appearance and finally eliminated any claim to being performance cars. As with the Midget, the change was due to revised safety regulations in the USA. For the 1974 model year cars the regulations specified that only minor damage should result from low-speed impacts, and the MGB was thus fitted with large energy-absorbing bumper over-riders to meet these requirements. However, for the following model year cars the legislation called for no damage from 5mph collisions, not even to a sidelight lens, and this was a lot more difficult to achieve.

This task was made more difficult by the need for the bumpers to meet a standard height requirement, which meant raising the MGB ride height by 1.5in, so the engineers had to do a lot of work. The body shell had to be considerably strengthened to take the additional loads. Large and heavy bumpers were mounted front and rear on extensions to the chassis rails, and the front units had the flashing indicator lamps recessed within them. In an attempt to blend the bumpers into the overall design they were shaped to align with the existing bonnet and wings. The modifications increased weight and reduced performance at a time when many ordinary saloons were getting ever quicker, but from the driver's point of view it was the increase in ride height that had the worst effect. Both suspension mounting points and spring heights were changed to give the required 1.5in increase in ride height, with the result that the cars rolled more when cornering and the handling was less predictable. The situation was much improved with the introduction of a rear anti-roll bar, and a revised front bar, in August 1976.

1975 was chosen as the year to celebrate the MG Golden Jubilee and it was decided that a special version of the MGB GT would be built. Changes made for the short production run of 750 cars were few but significant enough for the car to look different from the standard GT. The cars finished in Racing Green and the chrome waistline strips were also painted the same colour to avoid a clash with the applied gold side stripes incorporating the jubilee logo. The other badges on these and all the rest of the MGs built that year were gold and black rather than silver. Instead of the standard steel or optional wire wheels, the special GTs had V8 alloy/steel wheels, but painted in gold and black to complement the dark green paintwork.

To improve the specification, all the Golden Anniversary cars were fitted with carpets in place of rubber mats, head rests, tinted glass and overdrive gearboxes. All of these were later to become standard items on the GT. In addition to the external badges there was a dashboard plaque that was supplied to the dealer for him to engrave with the car's limited edition number and the owner's name. Although there were originally to be 750 cars, an extra one had to be built to replace a car

A restored example of a Golden Jubilee GT.

damaged whilst making an advertisement, while in addition one roadster was finished with the same side stripes and wheels to celebrate the millionth car from the Abingdon works. This car was offered as a prize for a rally in the United States and still exists in an MG collection. One MGB GT V8 was also finished in the Jubilee colour scheme, as was a Midget, which was offered as the prize in a local raffle.

August 1976 saw handling improvements for the MGB introduced as part of a package of changes designed to address some long-standing criticisms. There were the improved anti-roll bars, an electric cooling fan with the radiator mounted further forward in a position previously adopted for the V8, lower-geared steering rack and halogen headlamps. Inside the car there were striped seat covers, head rests, a new fascia, glove box and central console, changes to switch gear and steering wheel, and a number of other detail modifications along with the addition of previously extra items as standard. This certainly improved the cars but could not disguise the fact that they were now too heavy, too slow and generally outclassed by the modern hot hatchbacks that were starting to appear. A road test of the new version of the GT appeared in 1977: it quoted the maximum speed as 99mph and 0-60mph from rest at 14secs.

In 1977, to celebrate the Queen's Silver Jubilee, a one-off special MGB GT was built. This was finished in the standard shade of Pageant Blue, but had special silver side stripes incorporating the official jubilee logo. A so-called limited edition MGB roadster was introduced as a sales tool at the New York International Motor Show in April 1979. All these were finished in black with either black or tan seats. Unlike the home market cars of the time, those destined for America were never fitted with the fabric-covered seats with striped pattern, but retained the style used prior to the introduction of the 1977 model year vehicles. Promotions were nothing new, but in 1979 MG sales in the USA were flagging, partly due to the high value at that time of the pound against the dollar.

Initially it was planned that 5000 of these not-very-limited cars would be made, but ultimately 6682 were produced. For the remainder of 1979 they were exported to all states, but in 1980 more stringent regulations in California saw MG exports there cease, with MGs only sold in the remaining

A sole MGB GT was built to celebrate the 1977 Silver Jubilee of Queen Elizabeth II and was offered as a prize in a local raffle.

The Silver Jubilee logo on the unique MGB GT.

parts of North America. The cars carried a price tag premium of $600 over the standard model and for the extra cash the buyers would have expected additional equipment. All the cars had as standard the optional alloy wheels, made by GKN and similar to those fitted to Triumph Stags. They were painted dark metallic grey with polished rims and edges to the spokes. Overdrive was available at extra cost. Additionally, the cars were given silver side stripes that incorporated the union jack, a three-spoke steering wheel with polished spokes and leather-covered rim, a front air dam and a tonneau cover. The stripes, spoiler and luggage rack, when offered, were sourced and installed in America and many cars had other extras in the price, such as special floor mats, stereo radio, etc. Some even had air-conditioning fitted by the dealer. *Road & Track* tested one of these LE roadsters, but with just 67bhp available from the American-specification engine they found the performance poor.

Towards the end of production quite a few MGBs were produced to sell as Limited Editions in America. All were black, but detail specification varied as some local dealers fitted them with extras to boost sales.

The Abingdon factory ceased production in late 1980 and the task of selling the final Abingdon-built cars centred around persuading people to grab a piece of British motoring heritage whilst stocks lasted. One advertisement run in a number of magazines in the spring of 1981 concentrated on the possibility of a future vast increase in value of the final MGs. They pointed out that had you bought a new J2 for £200 in 1932, it would have risen in value to around £6000 by 1981. Some

The engines of the American MGBs towards the end of production had complicated emission control equipment and a single carburettor. Power output was far lower than cars built for other markets.

Why a brand new MGB is already a valuable collector's item.

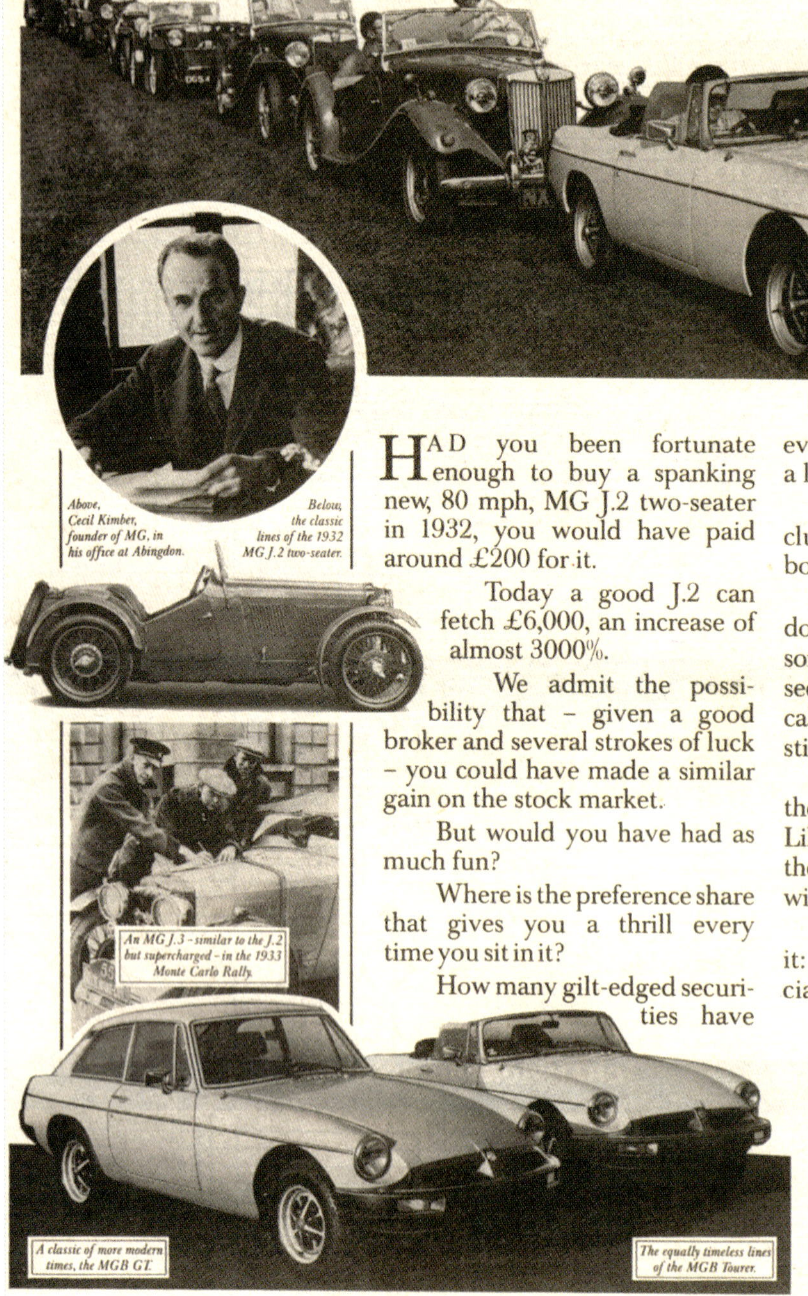

Above, Cecil Kimber, founder of MG, in his office at Abingdon.
Below, the classic lines of the 1932 MG J.2 two-seater.
An MG J.3 – similar to the J.2 but supercharged – in the 1933 Monte Carlo Rally.
A classic of more modern times, the MGB GT.
The equally timeless lines of the MGB Tourer.
HAD you been fortunate enough to buy a spanking new, 80 mph, MG J.2 two-seater in 1932, you would have paid around £200 for it.
Today a good J.2 can fetch £6,000, an increase of almost 3000%.
We admit the possibility that – given a good broker and several strokes of luck – you could have made a similar gain on the stock market.
But would you have had as much fun?
Where is the preference share that gives you a thrill every time you sit in it?
How many gilt-edged securities have ever turned the head of a man (or a lady) in the street?
Which property bonds include the sensations of foot-to-the-boards and wind-in-the-hair?
You take the point. But where does this leave you? What if by some mischance, you failed to secure a 1932 MG J.2? Remain calm; if you act quickly, you can still buy a new MGB.
Sadly, when they are sold there will be no more new MGB's. Like the J.2, a B is the epitome of the British sports car – and always will be.
Make no mistake about it: some early models are appreciating in value even as you read.
Buy one of the last made, either an MGB Tourer or an MGB GT and in a few years you could be driving around in a fortune.
To find out where the remaining MGB's are for sale contact your local BL showroom or telephone 021-779 2296.

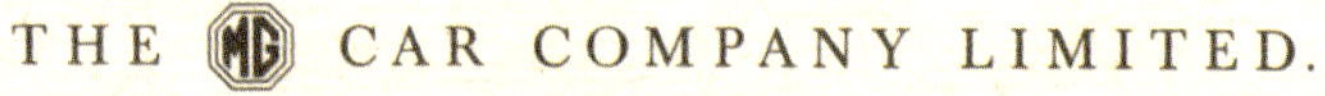

THE MG CAR COMPANY LIMITED.

Advertisement for the last MGBs.

One of the final MGBs built, this Limited Edition roadster was not first registered until some years after it had been built.

people did buy one of the last MGBs as investments and these have been trickling out into the market ever since. Some cars were not even first registered until the late 1990s, and there may even be the odd unused example still out there. One way of trying to give a product instant status as a collectors' item is to produce a limited edition, and this was the route chosen by British Leyland to boost sales of the final MGBs. A batch of 420 roadsters and 580 GTs were finished in a special colour scheme

All the final Limited Edition roadsters were painted this colour. Some had wire wheels and some alloys.

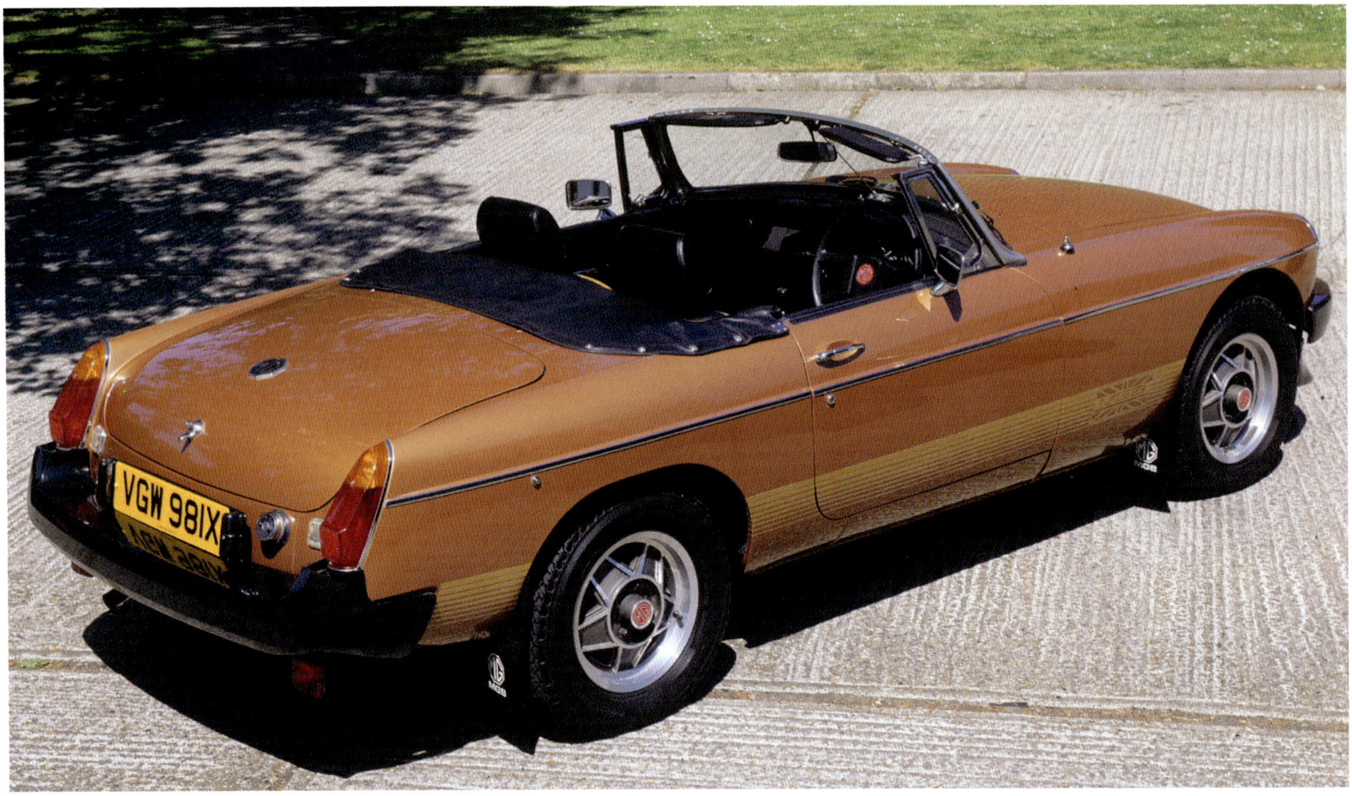

Despite the bigger bumpers, the final MGBs were still attractive cars.

The engine bay of the Limited Edition GT. This was the same as all the later home market MGBs.

The cockpit of an LE roadster showing the striped brown and orange seat covers. The GT seats had grey stripes.

featuring distinctive side striping like that used on the American-market MGBs. They were also given some extra equipment as standard. Billed as the last MGBs produced, they were not actually the final cars down the line, this distinction going to some normal-specification examples.

Mechanically the Limited Edition cars were identical to the rest of the home-market MGBs, but the GTs were all painted Pewter Metallic, with silver side stripes, and the roadsters were Bronze Metallic with gold coloured side stripes. Neither paint colour had been used previously in MGB production. As with all final home market MGBs, the 1000 Limited Edition cars had striped brushed nylon seat covers, two-tone grey for the GTs and orange/brown for the roadsters.

A press release on 26 January 1981 announced that the Limited Edition models were to go on sale at selected dealers from Wednesday 28 January. All the cars had front spoilers and all the GTs, plus 212 of the tourers, had alloy wheels and 185/70 tyres. The remaining 208 tourers had painted wire wheels.

The GT version of the Limited Edition showing the useful lifting tailgate.

Crash testing in the 1970s to comply with the then current regulations was carried out on land at the back of the Abingdon factory.

CAR ASSEMBLY IN THE 1970S

Bare Midget shells and completed MGB bodies were loaded from transporters on to the top deck of the assembly building. There they were placed on wheeled trolleys.

In summer, working on the upper assembly area could be a hot business.

Because all the MGs built at Abingdon were assembled on non-automated lines, anyone familiar with the process in the 1940s, described earlier, would see that little had changed by the time the factory closed. Yes, a great many more cars were being built, and the number of lines had increased, but essentially things carried on much as before. The series of pictures seen here were taken on visits to the factory in its final years and during these one appreciated the good spirit amongst those working under what were, at times, difficult conditions.

The assembly process differed slightly between the MGB and the Midget. The former arrived fully painted, trimmed, and on roadsters the hood fitted, while the Midgets came as bare painted shells. The bodies came on transporters, loaded on to the upper floor of the assembly building and placed on wheeled trolleys. In cramped conditions that could be cold in winter and hot in summer, the assembly process started with the installation of wiring, piping and all of the many smaller components. When ready, the bodies were wheeled over to an area where they could be lifted off the trolleys and lowered down to the main assembly line. Here the rest of the build progressed until cars could be driven away.

In separate areas of the factory site there were facilities where mechanical or electrical defects discovered during testing were rectified and damaged paintwork could be repaired. After protective wax had been applied, the completed MGBs and Midgets were driven to the compounds behind the factory to await transport to dealers. Those destined for export were moved to the station yard in the town for a journey by rail to Southampton Docks.

In 1977 British Leyland sold a total of 64,052 MG and Triumph sports cars to the United States, the highest total achieved since 1945. However, just a couple of years later it was announced that all small sports car production would cease and that the factories building them would close. One of the

On the top deck the bodyshells were fitted with fuel and brake pipes, the wiring loom, dashboards and pedals, plus all the hundreds of other necessary small components.

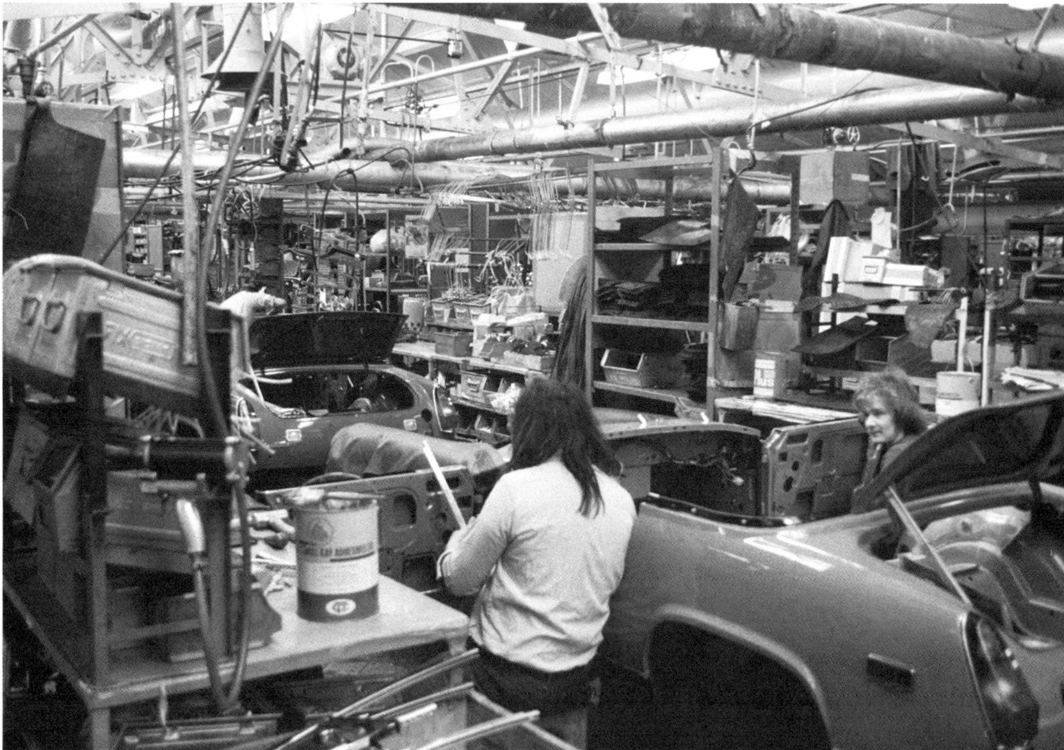

Space was very limited after storage was provided for all the components needed by the workers on the line.

reasons given was that the cars were unprofitable, especially because of the high value of the pound and the need to keep prices in America very low to help shift outdated models. Another reason was the insistence by the company that the Triumph TR7, at first only available as a closed car, was to be the main focus of sales effort.

It was a strange quirk of fate that the September

Completed bodies were lowered down to the main assembly line.

With engines and other mechanical components fitted, the cars near completion.

1979 announcement of the closure of the Abingdon plant should come almost exactly 50 years after the MG Car Company had moved there, and a day after a week-long celebration of the occasion by the town and by the factory. Once the closure of Abingdon became known, all the MG car clubs united to form a Save MG campaign. There was a serious proposal for Aston Martin to take over making a

The end of the line, where cars are started for the first time and driven away for testing.

The area set aside for rectification of mechanical defects.

revised version of the MGB and a prototype was built. However, this scheme was stillborn when neither the finances nor the permission to use the MG name were forthcoming. There were parades through Central London, petitions to Parliament and a huge reawakening of interest in the marque, with a consequent boost to club membership. All these efforts fell on deaf ears and the factory closed

Final inspection of paintwork was carried out under fluorescent lights.

The building where damaged paintwork was repaired.

after the last cars left the line in October 1980.

After all the last MGBs had left the factory, the majority of them Limited Editions to be marketed the following year, it was time for the auctioneers to move in and catalogue the fixtures and fittings. The sale was held at the factory between 18 and 24 March 1981 and there were over 2600 lots in all. Items included everything from forklift trucks, weighing machines, compressors, racking, four-post lifts and spaying equipment to the contents of the carpenter's shop and the kitchens. Walking around the almost deserted factory to examine the various lots was both interesting and sad. It was hard to imagine that one would never again be able to witness the bustle and noise of nearly 1000 employees building a constant stream of brightly painted Midgets and MGBs. Truly the end of an era.

The revised MGB that it was proposed Aston Martin would build. Note the taller windscreen.

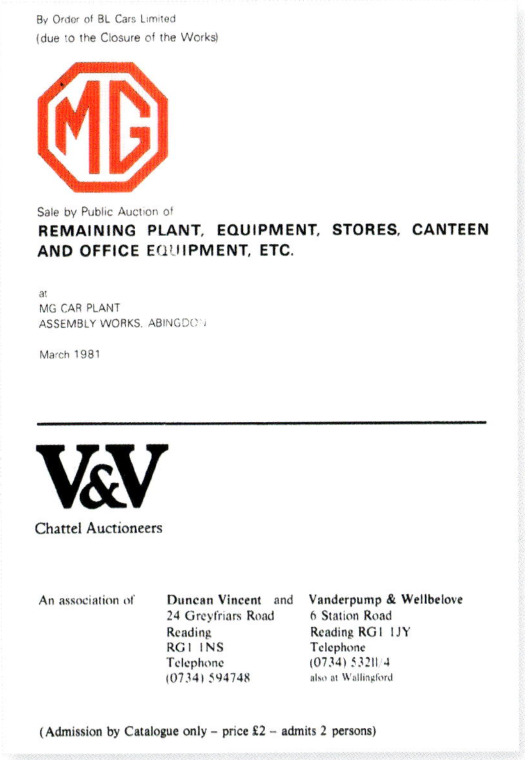

By Order of BL Cars Limited
(due to the Closure of the Works)

Sale by Public Auction of
REMAINING PLANT, EQUIPMENT, STORES, CANTEEN AND OFFICE EQUIPMENT, ETC.

at
MG CAR PLANT
ASSEMBLY WORKS, ABINGDON

March 1981

Chattel Auctioneers

An association of	Duncan Vincent and	Vanderpump & Wellbelove
	24 Greyfriars Road	6 Station Road
	Reading	Reading RG1 1JY
	RG1 1NS	Telephone
	Telephone	(0734) 53211/4
	(0734) 594748	also at Wallingford

(Admission by Catalogue only – price £2 – admits 2 persons)

The sale catalogue for the contents of the Abingdon factory.

The factory building is put up for sale.

INDEX

D

E

N

O

P

Q

R

S